G   U

TUNISIA

Travel Publications

Note to readers

To understand how the guide is organised, turn to the table of contents on page 6.

Just one point here about the practical information. The chapter entitled "Practical Information" gives general information to help you prepare your trip and get along once there. In the section "Exploring Tunisia", after each description of a town or site there is a practical section (eg page 144 "Making the most of Tunis") giving all the information about the place in question: access, useful addresses, accommodation, eating out, other things to do, shopping, etc.

The tour itineraries described and shown on the maps give ideas for excursions off the beaten track; ■ indicates possible overnight halts.

Hotels and restaurants are classed by price category (in US dollars) to help you plan your budget. However, we are obliged to point out that living costs vary constantly and opening hours may change, so that prices and practical information may have changed since publication.

Michelin Travel Publications
Published in 2000

◄N·E·⊙·S►

N ew – In the NEOS guides emphasis is placed on the discovery and enjoyment of a new destination through meeting the people, tasting the food and absorbing the exotic atmosphere. In addition to recommendations on which sights to see, we give details on the most suitable places to stay and eat, on what to look out for in traditional markets and where to go in search of the hidden character of the region, its crafts and its dancing rhythms. For those keen to explore places on foot, we provide guidelines and useful addresses in order to help organise walks to suit all tastes.

E xpert – The NEOS guides are written by people who have travelled in the country and researched the sites before recommending them by the allocation of stars. Accommodation and restaurants are similarly recommended by a 🏨 on the grounds of quality and value for money. Cartographers have drawn easy-to-use maps with clearly marked itineraries, as well as detailed plans of towns, archeological sites and large museums.

⊙ pen to all cultures, the NEOS guides provide an insight into the daily lives of the local people. In a world that is becoming ever more accessible, it is vital that religious practices, regional etiquette, traditional customs and languages be understood and respected by all travellers. Equipped with this knowledge, visitors can seek to share and enjoy with confidence the best of the local cuisine, musical harmonies and the skills involved in the production of arts and crafts.

S ensitive to the atmosphere and heritage of a foreign land, the NEOS guides encourage travellers to see, hear, smell and feel a country, through words and images. Take inspiration from the enthusiasm of our experienced travel writers and make this a journey full of discovery and enchantment.

Setting the scene 10

Meeting the People 48

Exploring Tunisia   116

TUNISIA

Official name: Republic of Tunisia
Area: 163 610sqkm
Population: 9 500 000
Capital: Tunis
Currency: Tunisian dinar (TD)

Setting the scene

The Great Erg,
or the desert
of your dreams

A LAND OF CONTRASTS

Three hours by air from London, Tunisia covers an area of 163 610sqkm (a little less than three-quarters the size of England, Scotland and Wales combined), with a great range of landscapes: the dunes of the Sahara and flourishing oases, *chotts, sebkhet* and other salt lakes, plains and mountains worthy of the American West, forests of oak trees and the rich grasslands of Khroumiria. The traveller should bear in mind that Tunisia is a small country (750km from north to south, and on average 150km from east to west), and that all these marvels are easy to reach, within a radius of 300km if you use Mahdia as your starting point (*see map, inside the front cover*).

On the frontier between Europe and the Sahara

Tunisia is like a notch cut into the map of Africa. Its tip reaches down into the Sahara between its two far larger neighbours, Algeria to the west and Libya to the southeast. The country is bordered to the north and the east by its 1 300km long coastline and some of its most charming landscape places it firmly within the Mediterranean world – vast plantations of olive trees extend over acres of the steppe-like Sahel, a transition zone between the world of the Mediterranean and the desert landscape to the south. The relief of the country is like its inhabitants, gentle and moderate. In the north, the final outposts of the Atlas Mountains and the Tell foothills sink down into the Mediterranean, while most of the south consists of plains and plateaux, with the exception of the small chain of the Dahar hills. The average altitude is 700m, and 65% of the land lies at less than 350m above sea level. The climate, however, is not so kind everywhere.

Typically mediterranean in the north and along the coastline, it is semi-arid in the interior and truly arid in the furthest south. When the annual rainfall is less than 100mm, the desert and its own life-forms take over; this applies to the whole of southwestern Tunisia.

Four Great Regions

Relief and rainfall create a **north/south contrast**, between the landscape on either side of the **Grande Dorsale** – Tunisia's hilly backbone – and three great natural regions: the north, the plains and the Saharan south. In addition there is the Sahel, its distinct identity owing as much to history as to geography.

The North

Rising to 1 544m at Jebel Chambi, the limestone heights of the Grande Dorsale trap rain-bearing clouds in northernmost Tunisia. This gives **Khroumiria** and the **Moghods** massif the benefits of a damp Mediterranean climate, with the Aïn Draham region recording up to 1 500mm of rain each year. Uniquely in Tunisia, the area specialises in cattle-rearing and dairy-farming, and the landscape is unusual in these latitudes: green pasture-land, stands of cork and evergreen oak trees, mossy undergrowth with arbutus and myrtle and sparkling springs. The Khroumiria massif is nearly 1 000m high, and people travel great distances to see the snow falling. Despite the eucaplyptus and oleanders in the wadi bottoms, this region is often compared to hill regions familiar to European visitors – the Vosges, perhaps, or the wooded hills of Normandy.

The green hills of Khroumiria

C. Vaisse/HOA QUI

A little further south, total rainfall is between 600 and 1 000mm each year, with more rain falling on the Gulf of Tunis, the Mejerda plain and the Cap Bon peninsula – the maritime regions – than on the High Tell inland. The main tree species seen on the heights of the **High Tell** is the Aleppo pine, while kermes oaks grow more widely in the **Cap Bon** area. This peninsula, which enjoys the combination of a very mild climate and high sunshine, is the major source of the classic trio of Mediterranean crops (vines, olives, wheat) and also of citrus fruit and market-garden produce. The **Mejerda Plain** has two major features which make it Tunisia's prime cereal-growing region – its clay soils and plentiful water supply; Mejerda is the only wadi in the country to have a reliable flow of water. The Mejerda valley, once known as the main source of wheat for Rome, now cultivates sugar-beet and forage crops for livestock, the result of several river dam projects.

The Plains

On the far side of the Grande Dorsale, two factors determine the pattern of vegetation: rainfall of less than 400mm per year, and mainly sandy soils. . This is the region of the plains, vast horizons dotted with esparto grass and sagebrush, where flocks of sheep roam in search of the occasional hardy grasses. South of a line between Kasserine and Sfax, aridity increases and rain-dependent growth becomes impossible except for occasional local sites in some wadis.

The **high plains** occupy the westernmost area of central Tunisia. Access is across gradually rising and shelving land, reaching heights of between 300 and 800m. In a few places esparto grass, which is used as a raw material for the paper

13

industry, gives way to trees. One feature of the **lower plains** region, extending eastwards as far as the Mediterranean, is that rainfall is dispersed here. The occasional watercourse does not flow to the sea but loses itself in depressions, forming frequent marshy and salty areas, or *sebkhet*. In irrigated areas, this semi-arid region is characterised by pockets of cereal cultivation, with olive groves in the east which extend into the Sahel.

When Arabs from Tripolitania invaded and conquered *Ifriqiya*, their route lay across the plains, unusual in a country where danger always came from the sea. They founded **Kairouan**, North Africa's first Islamic capital, at the heart of the lower plains, choosing this harsh land for its central location and strategic importance.

The Sahel, the humanised edge of the plains

The Sahel forms part of the region of the low plains, but their steppe-like character is modified by Mediterranean influences, with rainfall in the Sousse area reaching about 350mm per year. Forty per cent of the frequently torrential rainfall is recorded in the autumn, and precipitation of 50mm in a single day is not uncommon after months without a cloud. This lack of water is partly balanced by the Mediterranean's contribution to humidity, in the form of mist or dew. With its high temperatures moderated by sea breezes, the Sahel is highly favoured as a holiday region.

The identity of the Sahel is derived as much from historic and structural factors as from its geographical setting and climate. The province corresponds to the ancient Roman province of Byzacena; despite its unfavourable climate, the Romans developed olive-growing on a grand scale, because olive trees can withstand years of drought. The production of olive oil was expanded further under the French protectorate, and today the Sahel is still characterised by its great olive plantations. The area has always been open to the sea and the outside world, and ports (Sousse, Mahdia, etc) and other urban settlements developed at an early date. To this has been added a wide range of industrial and service activities, above all coastal tourism. Highly dynamic in economic terms, the Sahel illustrates Tunisia's structural imbalance between a developed coastline and an underpopulated and impoverished inland area.

The legendary South

The fascination of the Tunisian South dates back to the origins of tourism in this country, when in 1910-20 the first groups of Westerners were attracted by the ruins of Carthage and the exotic atmosphere of oases and dunes. Today, with the fashion for off-road-vehicle expeditions and camel trips, this impoverished region is taking on greater importance under the watchful eye of the State, for tourism brings in one-third of its currency resources. It has every ingredient to attract foreigners in search of authenticity and the exotic: the Sahara, oases, unexpected types of settlement (the fortified granaries known as *ksour* and cave dwellings), a mythical island and a welcoming people.

The land south of the line between Gafsa and Gabès has virtually no trees. This is the beginning of the Tunisian South, a sub-desert zone which stretches as far as the great *chotts* with the true Sahara beyond. To the north of the Chott el Jerid lie the **mountain oases**: Chebika, and above all Midès and Tamerza, abandoned after torrential rain. The finest oases, however, are at **Jerid**, with its two offshoots of Tozeur and Nefta. In Arabic, *Jerid* means "palms", the palm being the royal tree of the oasis.

A true inland sea, but dry for most of the year, the **Chott el Jerid** is crusted with salt bloom – a crystal surface which confuses and teases the traveller with disturbing glimpses of mirages. This vast depression lies below sea-level, and in the 19C Ferdinand de Lesseps had the wild idea of linking it to the Mediterranean by canal. Annual rainfall around the great *chotts* drops below the all-important 100mm mark: this is the ultra-arid world of the Sahara. The south-east consists of a coastal plain, the **Jeffara**, and the chalk and sandstone plain of the **Dahar**, a hostile environment which throughout history has provided the Berber peoples with a natural stronghold. The *ksour* and cave dwellings of the Dahar show how well they adapted to their environment. The income earned from livestock (camels, goats, sheep) and the traditional activities of the oases (dates and market-gardening) has been increasingly supplemented by tourism, which has developed until it is now of major economic importance. Outside the oases, the modest crops are restricted to the wadi beds and valley-bottoms, where a system of small terraces, the *jessour*, makes irrigation possible.

To the west, the Dahar fades away, and the **Great Eastern Erg** begins, the desert of everyone's imaginings. The ergs are sandy masses, dunes of different types that make up most of the Tunisian Sahara, the most spectacular dunes being the crescent-shaped *barkhans*. In the Great South, the climate becomes truly extreme: rainfall is less than 50mm per year, with very marked temperature contrasts between day and night, and high rates of evaporation.

Jerba is the ancient island of the Lotus Eaters, which exercised such fascination on Odysseus that he nearly ended his travels there. Al-

Controlling water

Pliny reports how there was a skilful system of water management in Gabès in ancient times: "Within a radius of approximately three thousand paces, water flows abundantly from a spring but is distributed to the inhabitants only at fixed hours." This kind of system still operates in Ouedref, Chebika and El Jerid. Where there were no springs, wells were dug down into the deep strata to find water. The low stone walls known as "Jessour" were built along slopes or in wadi beds to hold back run-off water; they retain not only surface water but also the land itself when violent winter storms wash away the top-soil. Hill dwellers cultivate barley, wheat, olives, figs and palms on these terraces.

though it is only the extension of the pre-desert plain, its Mediterranean setting endows it with particular climatic conditions, with cooler temperatures and rainfall of between 100 and 200mm per year. None the less, water is still the great preoccupation of the people of Jerba. The road linking the island to the mainland, 6.5km long, runs beside a canal which brings the water necessary for both tourists and residents. The skilful system of cisterns installed inside their traditional houses, the *menzel*, is only practical for domestic purposes; water from the wells is too salty to make it suitable for irrigation. In Jerba as well as in the Zarzis area on the mainland, olive trees have secured a final stand before giving way to the desert and its occasional palm-trees.

Dates	Events	Sites
Classical Times		
814BC	Foundation of Carthage	*Carthage*
420-264BC	Conflicts between Greece and Carthage over land and trade	
264-146BC	First, Second and Third Punic Wars, ending with the total destruction of Carthage by the Romans	*Carthage*
1-2C AD	Roman expansion	
3C	Christianity expands in northern Africa	
429	Vandal invasion	
534	The Byzantines expel the Vandals	
646	First great Arab invasions	*Sbeïtla*
The Islamic Era		
647-670	Conquest of Ifriqiya by the Arabs	*Kairouan*
800	Foundation of the Aghlabid dynasty	*Kairouan*
909-972	The Fatimids overturn the Aghlabids impose Shiism. They settle in Cairo in 972 after conquering Egypt	*Mahdia*
1048	The governor of Ifrqiya breaks away from Fatimid control and founds the Zirid dynasty	*Mahdia*
11C	Ifriqiya is destroyed by the Beni Hilal	
1159-1230	The Moroccan dynasty of the Almohades dominates the whole of the Maghreb and Spain	
1230-1574	Hafsid reign, with Tunis as capital	*Tunis*
The Ottoman era		
1534-1574	Spain and Turkey quarrel over Tunisia, which finally falls to Ottoman control	
17-18C	Pirates roam the Mediterranean	*La Goulette*
1705	Foundation of the Husseinite dynasty, under the symbolic authority of the Sultan of Constantinople	*Tunis*
1881	French military intervention. Signing of the Treaty of Bardo	
Modern Times		
1934	Habib Bourguiba creates Néo-Destour, the independent party of opposition	
1942-1943	The Axis forces occupy part of Tunisia The Allies crush the Italians and Rommel's army	
1956-1957	Declaration of independence. Bourguiba becomes President	
1974	Bourguiba becomes President for Life	
1987	Bourguiba is removed for health reasons Ben Ali, the Prime Minister, takes over temporarily	
1989	Ben Ali is elected President	

A SMALL STATE
AT THE HEART OF MEDITERRANEAN HISTORY

By far the smallest country in the Maghreb, Tunisia is the oldest political entity in Africa (together with Egypt): its eastern and western frontiers, despite having no geographical basis, are almost the same as they were 2 500 years ago. The country's very survival is surprising after so many invasions from east, west or north – from the south, Tunisia has never had anything to fear except the advance of the desert. Under the yoke of Phoenicians, Romans, Byzantines, Arabs, the Ottoman Empire and then the French, she has always managed to retain her individuality and has achieved independent statehood. It is not for nothing that this little promontory was once known as Carthage, an empire to rival Rome.

Human remains have been found in Tunisia that date back to palæolithic times, but the first known inhabitants were the **Berber** tribes, nomad or settled, who were very soon joined by peoples from other regions.

Classical Times

From the Phoenicians to the Carthaginians

Originating in what is now Syria and Lebanon, the **Phoenician** traders not only dominated the eastern Mediterranean from the 12C BC, but also established trading-posts along its western coasts. **Utica** is generally considered to have been the first colony of Tyre, in the territory of modern-day Tunisia, but it was Carthage ("the new city"), founded in 814BC, which was destined to have the most dazzling future.

In the 6C BC, under the Magonid kings, **Carthage** supplanted its mother country on the African coast and in the western Mediterranean. Having become one of the most powerful cities of the western Mediterranean, it carried on the Phoenician legacy. Enterprising traders, the Punic people (the Latin derivation from "Carthaginian") extended their area of influence, created other trading posts and established commercial links with Egypt, Etruria and Greece. *Hanno's Journey* recounts the epic of a 5C king of Carthage who ventured out with sixty ships beyond the legendary Pillars of Hercules (the Straits of Gibraltar) to explore the Atlantic coast of Africa.

This was when **rivalry with the Greeks** began over Sicily, which was to continue in the following century. After a stinging defeat at Himera in 409BC, the Carthaginians were content to consolidate their positions. When they finally managed to establish a footing in Messina, in 270BC, they found themselves facing a new enemy – the Romans.

Hannibal's return

The history of Tunisia as it used to be taught began with the Arab conquest in the 7C BC. Nothing was said of the Carthaginians, the Romans, the Vandals or the Byzantines: the only history was Islamic. This has now changed, and Hannibal seems likely to become the first Tunisian hero. President Bourguiba once declared that Hannibal "was the only representative of Tunisian independence" before him. President Ben Ali recently named an influential political club after the Carthaginian general, and Tunis also plans to erect a monument to his memory, as victor at Lake Trasimeno and Cannae. Some even whisper of bringing his ashes back from Turkey... but where are they?

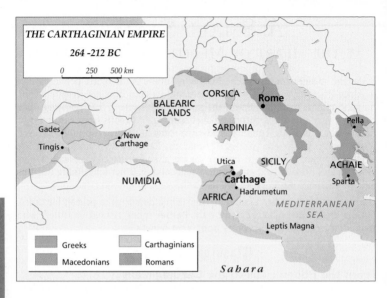

THE CARTHAGINIAN EMPIRE
264 -212 BC

0   250   500 km

CORSICA · **Rome**
BALEARIC
ISLANDS
SARDINIA
Pella
Gades ·
· New
Tingis · Carthage
Utica SICILY
· · ACHAIE
NUMIDIA **Carthage** Sparta
· Hadrumetum
AFRICA MEDITERRANEAN
SEA
Leptis Magna ·

Greeks   Carthaginians
Macedonians   Romans
Sahara

During the long years of the **Punic Wars** the Romans and Carthaginians struggled for domination of the western Mediterranean *(see page 163)* Although Hannibal and his elephants were able to threaten Rome for a time, the conflict was resolved by the total destruction of Carthage in 146BC. The Romans razed the site and spread salt to make it sterile, hoping to erase the very memory of that great rival – in vain.

Roman Domination

The conquered territories formed the Roman province of Africa, bordered on the west by the kingdom of Numidia. Aware above all of the province's strategic importance – control over the straits of Sicily – the new masters initially neglected to make good use of it. After **Caesar** captured Numidia (46BC), Carthage was rebuilt under **Augustus** and established as the capital of an extended province that included Tripolitania. The ruins of **Sbeïtla**, **Makthar**, **Dougga**, **El Jem** and **Bulla Regia** are proof of a very advanced degree of town planning in the Roman era. Water was brought to Carthage and its 300 000 inhabitants along a 132km aqueduct. The province prospered from the export of grain, oil and wine to in Italy, and in return most of it was substantially Romanised.

Few people realise that Africa was one of the most whole-heartedly Christianised regions at a very early stage. A dazzling intellectual centre, it saw the flowering of some of the greatest theoreticians of the Roman church: **Tertullian** (155-225), **St Cyprien** (c 200-258) and later, **St Augustine** (354-430). Among its other contributions, it is to the Church in Carthage that we owe the adoption of Latin as the language of western Christianity.

In the 3C, the province was shaken by serious social disturbances, but subsequently recovered. It was during the 4C, at the time of the **Donatist heresy**, resisted by St Augustine, that it began its irreversible decline. The immediate reason lay in the election of a bishop, but the causes ran deeper than this. The scale of this schism, both political (conflict between clergy of the African tradition and the Emperor Constantine) and social (violent rebellion by the ordinary country people against the great landowners), left the Church of Carthage deeply divided.

After capturing the city in 439, the **Vandals** took over its existing institutions and persecuted the Catholics. Attacked by the Berbers and weakened by rural uprisings and internal divisions, their kingdom collapsed quickly on the death of their brilliant leader **Genseric** in 77.

The Byzantine dream

The Byzantine emperor **Justinian**, who reigned from 527 until 565, dreamed of recreating a universal empire in the Roman tradition. His brilliant general **Belisarius** encountered little difficulty in throwing the Vandals out of North Africa (in 534), and he also managed to bring Italy and part

GIRAUDON

St Augustine
St Augustine was born in 354, at Thagaste (Souk Ahras, in Algeria), but spent his student years in Carthage. His youth was turbulent, and he was not blind to the attractions of the opposite sex. Tempted at one time by Manichæism, he was finally converted to Catholicism through the influence of his mother; and he was baptised in Milan in 387, at the age of 33. He returned to Africa, to Hippo (Annaba in Algeria) where he was ordained as a priest, and became bishop there in 395. In his theological struggles with Donatist, Pelagian and Manichæan heretics, Augustine established the foundations of Catholic belief, and confirmed the future universality of the Church's vocation. Augustine died in 429, at a time when the Vandals were beginning their conquest of Africa.

of Spain back into the empire. However, the military forces inherited by Justinian's successors were too widely scattered to ensure the security of such vast territories. They were unable to prevent either the invasion of the Lombards in Italy or that of the Slavs in the Balkans.

The many fortresses that they built in North Africa did not survive the onslaught of the Arab conquerors. After some devastating raids, such as the attack on Sbeitla in 646, the Arabs returned and established permanent settlements. **Kairouan**, founded by Uqba Ibn Nafi in 670, became the rear base for the invaders' military campaigns. The capture of Carthage in 698 marked the end of the Latin presence in this region, nearly 850 years after the Roman conquest. It was a turning-point for the Mediterranean.

Gradual Islamisation

A difficult pacification

For the new occupying forces, the Berbers were far more to be feared than the Byzantines, and the Arabs found it very difficult to pacify the region. In 702, on the death of **Kahena** – a Berber princess who had led the struggle against the invader *(see page 276)* – the **Ummayad** caliph of Damascus was finally able to extend his authority over the whole region, which became the province of **Ifriqiya** (taking in the east of present-day Algeria). The foundation of **Tunis** dates from this period. Converted to Islam, many Berbers joined the army. They provided the majority of the troops in the Arab attacks on Spain and Gaul.

In 750, the **Abbassids** of Iraq succeeded the Ummayad. Tunis, Kairouan and Sousse expanded considerably through their trade with the Orient. At a cultural level, the rapid advances of Islam and of Arab culture marked a permanent break with the Roman past. However, the Berbers did not take easily to the humiliating status of vassal, and proved once again that they were not docile subjects. They turned to **Kharijism** *(see page 56)*, a strict heresy that was hostile to the central government, and twice seized hold of Kairouan.

In 800, the Emir Ibrahim el Aghlab founded the **Aghlabid** dynasty, under the nominal authority of the Abbassids. In 902 the Aghlabids conquered Sicily. Religion was dominated by the **Malekite doctrine** which preached a tolerant and peaceful Islam. Substantial communities of Christians and Jews lived in Tunis and Kairouan at this time, contributing to the country's prosperity. Intellectually and architecturally, this era is seen as a Golden Age: the reconstruction of the Great Mosque of Kairouan dates from this period.

In revolt against the arbitrary power of the Emirs and the burden of taxes, the indomitable Berber tribes adopted the **Shiite** heresy and ranged themselves behind a new invader, Obaïd Allah, who claimed descent from Fatima (the daughter of the Prophet). With the help of the Berbers, he overthrew the Aghlabids in 909. The **Fatimid** dynasty was born, and set out to conquer the Arab world and convert it by force to Shiism *(see page 56)*, with *Ifriqiya* becoming merely a stage along the way.

The Second Arab Invasion and the Berber Dynasties

After the conquest of Egypt, the Fatimid caliphs settled in Cairo (972) and handed *Ifriqiya* over to the Berber tribes of their ally Buluggin Ibn Ziri, the founder of the **Zirid** dynasty. Under their power, the province enjoyed a period of prosperity and adopted the Sunniism of the Malekite scholars. Considering themselves powerful enough, the Zirids rejected Fatimid protection (1048) and acknowledged the more distant and less restrictive Abbassids of Baghdad as overlords.

The reaction of the Fatimid caliph was to hand the country over to a troublesome and aggressive group of **Beni Hilal**, Bedouins from Upper Egypt. This second Arab invasion permanently disrupted the region's stability. The cities of the south and the centre were pillaged and irrigation systems ruined, returning vast irrigated lands to the desert. In the plains, agriculture receded and stock-rearing expanded, the population deserted the countryside and took refuge in the mountains and fortified villages. The coastal regions of the east seized their freedom and formed small independent principalities. Arab culture intensified and Christianity vanished almost completely. The **Genoese** and the **Pisans** (11C) and then the **Normans** (12C) profited from the chaos to settle in various cities along the coast and to levy tribute.

The Normans had barely established themselves before they were thrown out in their turn by the **Almohads** (12C), Berbers from Morocco. Their caliph, Abd el Moumin, then achieved a great coup when he united all the Muslims of the Maghreb and Spain; but this vast empire grew beyond his control and he was faced by the demands of Beni Ghaniya's **Almoravids**, allied to the Hilalians and the Turks of Tripolitania. It needed a Moroccan governor based in Tunis, Abu Hafs, to normalise the situation. Aware of his strength, his successor broke away from the Almohads and adopted the title of Emir (1230). The **Hafsid** dynasty was to rule for three hundred years.

Despite frequent internal crises, Arab revolts and several **crusades** (including one in 1270 led by St Louis, King of France), *Ifriqiya* enjoyed some periods of peace and prosperity. It took in the Muslims and Jews who were expelled from Spain at the Reconquest; they brought with them an advanced culture and great agricultural and craft skills. Tunis became a famous intellectual centre throughout the Muslim world, a revival illustrated by the career of the historian and philosopher **Ibn Khaldoun**, born in 1332.

At the end of the 15C, Spanish and Turkish attacks brought about the collapse of a dynasty that was already in decline. The Middle Ages were well and truly over.

St Louis lands at Carthage: wood engraving, 1518

Under Turkish Rule

Sixteenth century Tunisia was a turbulent place, a major pawn in Mediterranean trade caught up in intrigues between the two great powers of the day – Spain and the Ottoman empire.

A distant Ottoman province

Pirates became so powerful in the western Mediterranean that in 1534 the most famous of them, a Turk known as **Barbarossa**, seized Bizerte, Tunis, La Goulette and Kairouan for Constantinople. In the following year the **Emperor Charles V** recaptured Tunis, restored the Hafsid sultan, and took advantage of the occasion to establish a protectorate. The Turks did not give up easily, however, and after several decades of fierce struggle the region finally returned to Ottoman control in 1574. The Turkish administration installed the "Regency of Tunisia", headed by a **Pasha** appointed for three years and supported by a **Divan** (council) of militia officers. These officials – Turks, then Muslim Levantines and *Kurughlis* (sons of Turkish fathers and local Tunisian women) – were commanded by an **agha**.

The junior officers **(deys)** were sickened by the Pasha's abuse of his powers. In 1590 they revolted and imposed one of their number to operate alongside the *agha*, the *qahtan* (naval commander) and the **bey** (the head of the army, responsible for collecting taxes). The dey, elected by his peers, quickly took power into his own hands.

Privateering *(see page 209)* was the true economic driving force at this time, benefiting from the authorities' tacit approval and feeding goods and slaves into the souks. Tunis was a prosperous and cosmopolitan city, the meeting point for Jewish merchants and traders from Marseille, Moriscan craftsmen (Spanish Muslims forcibly converted to Catholicism), and renegades (Christians who had converted to Islam, who sometimes had attained high government ranks). One Corsican renegade, Murad, reached the office of Bey and won the right to pass it to his son – he in turn took power in 1640 and founded the **Muradite dynasty**. A military coup d'état brought it to an end in 1702.

Virtual independence

The Agha Hussein Ibn Ali had himself proclaimed bey in 1705, after a period of transition. He abolished the title of bey and founded the **Husseinite** dynasty which remained in power until independence in 1957. The bey recognised the Sultan of Constantinople as overlord, but only in symbolic terms: legally the Sultan's ultimate power came to an end with the signing of the Treaty of Sèvres in 1920. In this land where privateers and the militia were the real rulers, the Husseinites did their best to create a modern state. In the 18C the Regency, undermined by debilitating internal squabbles, faced uprisings as well as frequent conflicts with Algeria. Tunis developed commercial trade with the European powers, particularly France. Gradually, in the guise of commercial agreements, Tunisia lost her independence. Economically too the country lost strength, and was gradually forced to give up privateering under pressure from the western powers.

On two occasions, in 1811 and 1816, the janissaries revolted. The beys took advantage of these incidents to reduce the influence of this élite corps which threatened their power.

Henceforward the unchallenged leader, the bey was supported by a grand vizier, while the middle classes were kept out of state affairs. Locally, government was run by Caïds who were responsible for collecting taxes and keeping order. In the northern regions, closely supervised by the authorities, their authority was much resented, but in the south, on the edges of the desert, the tribes retained their independent traditions.

European Envy

French colonial ambitions had for long been focused on Algeria. Once Algiers had been captured (1830), these ambitions found a new target in Tunisia. In 1836 French troops were despatched to Tunis' port of La Goulette to protect the Tunisian government against a possible Ottoman landing.

Competition from European products, a crippling fall in the price of olive oil and the end of piracy provoked a severe economic crisis. But, far from curbing its expenditure, the Tunisian court threw itself into an orgy of extravagance, paid for by extra taxes imposed on a populace already suffering from an epidemic of the plague. France took advantage of the situation to increase her influence. The beys undertook various political reforms: the principle of equality before the law was adopted in 1857, and a constitution promulgated in 1861. All such moves to improve financial conditions were long-term in their effect, however, and the nation had plunged so far into debt that it risked bankruptcy. In 1869 Mohammed el Saduq accepted the protection of a Franco-Italian commission under French leadership. He tried in vain to play on the rivalry between these two powers. Italy remained aloof when, in 1881, a French force 30 000 strong invaded Tunisia on the pretext of repelling an attack on Algeria by Kroumir tribesman. A largely uneventful 3-week campaign ended with the French firmly installed in Tunis. A few months later France won the right to be involved in defence and diplomacy under the **Treaty of Bardo**, which confirmed the end of Tunisian independence.

The French Protectorate

A model colony

French troops were involved once more in the same year, 1881, to subdue a nationalist rebellion among the southern tribes: Sfax was occupied in July, Kairouan in October, Gafsa and Gabes in November. The French **Resident General** won full control under the **Convention of La Marsa**, which was imposed on the bey in 1883, and he established a parallel administration made up entirely of French civil servants. Paris decided to create a model of colonial development in Tunisia: eliminating fraud and corruption from the financial system, reforming education along French lines, building hospitals and improving health and hygiene (eradication of cholera and typhus). Finally, the agricultural and mineral resources (phosphates and iron) were fully evaluated and exploited through the modern infrastructure (port and railway systems). Progress of this type benefited only the new colonials from Europe and a small section of the local middle classes, however; and French settlers were fewer in number (48 000) than the Italians (with 88 000).

The beginnings of Tunisian Nationalism

In 1907, Tunisian leaders were admitted to the heart of the consultative body. But this concession was too limited to halt the surging wave of demands for recognition. Inspired by the example of the Young Turks and emerging Arab

ROGER-VIOLLET

The Marriage of the Bey's Son, illustration 1903

nationalism, the **Mouvement des Jeunes-Tunisiens** (Young Tunisian Movement) came to the fore as the standard-bearer of nationalism. In 1911 and 1912 riots in Tunis were repressed with severity, the leaders arrested and expelled, newspapers banned and a state of emergency declared from 1914 to 1921.

Impatience grew steadily after the **First World War**, when 60 000 Tunisians fought on French battlefields. All claims for representation and freedom of expression formulated by **Destour** (the "Constitution" movement established in 1920) were rejected – indeed, the leaders of the UGTT (the *Union générale des travailleurs tunisiens*, the general union of Tunisian workers, founded in 1924), were accused of stirring up social agitation and put in prison. Tensions came to a head in 1930 when a statue of a Roman Catholic Cardinal was erected in front of the Tunis medina, the old Arab quarter. Nationalist claims appeared to die down after this.

The calm was only temporary. In 1934 the most radical elements of Destour split off to form **Néo-Destour**, led by **Habib Bourguiba**. The new party adopted a secular and modernist line and looked for support among the working classes and the poor. In the same year Bourguiba was arrested and sent into internal exile. Any hopes roused when France's Popular Front party gained power were quickly disappointed, for Léon Blum's government, weighed down under vast economic and social problems, pushed colonial affairs into the background.

In 1937-1938, a fresh wave of rioting led to the banning of Néo-Destour, its leaders were arrested, freedoms suspended and a state of emergency declared.

During the **Second World War**, Tunisia was partially occupied by the Axis powers. While asserting his neutrality towards both sides of the war, **Moncef Bey** took up the torch of nationalism once more under the Vichy government and demanded a return to the spirit of the protectorate treaties. After the war the French did not forgive or forget this approach: convicted of collaborating with the enemy, Moncef Bey was deposed and replaced by his cousin **Lamine**. Bourguiba was more far-sighted; he resisted the intense pressure put on him by the Italian fascist government and always insisted on Tunisian independence as a precondition for any negotiations. Quite apart from his personal preference for the democratic forces represented by the Allies, as an experienced politician he had calculated on a German defeat.

Bourguiba in 1942

"The naive belief that the defeat of France is a punishment from God, that her domination is over and that we will gain our independence from an Axis victory, is rooted in many minds... So I assert that this belief is wrong, profoundly wrong, that it will cost us dear if we adopt it... The blinding truth is that Germany will not win the war, that it cannot win it, that time is working against her and that she will be crushed with mathematical precision. It is no more than a question of time. In these circumstances our role, your role, the role of anyone with some sort of authority over the masses, is to operate in such a way that at the end of the war the people of Tunisia, and more specifically its leading wing, Néo-Destour, does not find itself among the defeated, in other words compromised by association with the German-Italian camp."

The Struggle for Independence

In the immediate post-war period, the nationalists did not press their claims. Returning to the country in 1959, Bourguiba found his popularity unimpaired and took up the struggle once more, basing himself in **Farhat Hached**'s UGTT. In 1950 the French cautiously acknowledged his proposals for independence and **Salah Ben Youssef**, a member of Néo-Destour, was brought into the government in the same year. Two years later, tensions came to a peak when the Resident, Louis Périllier, was replaced by Jean de Hauteclocque, who ordered the arrest of Bourguiba and other nationalist leaders and then dissolved Ben Houssef's government. After the assassination of Farhat Hached by extremist French settlers the country, shaken by a wave of terrorist attacks, seemed to be descending into violence as the **fellaghas** embarked on armed struggle in the rural areas.

Faced with a deteriorating situation, the French Premier, Pierre Mendès France, spoke in favour of "internal independence" (July 1954) and opened negotiations with Bourguiba and the government. The independence agreement of June 1955 enabled Tunisians to take over management of the country's internal affairs; for some time Salah Ben Youssef, who considered these measures inadequate and therefore rejected the agreement, led an armed conflict in the south before escaping abroad. In 1961 he was assassinated in Frankfurt; his rival, Bourguiba, had gained total victory and forced through plans for a modern and social republic, in contrast with Ben Youssef's Islamist pan-Arabism. Independence in Morocco accelerated independence in Tunisia, which was finally recognised by France on 20 March 1956.

The French Protectorate

25

The Young Republic

In the elections of April 1956 Néo-Destour, with practically no opposition, won all the seats in the constituent assembly. On 25 July 1957 the Bey was removed from office and the republic proclaimed, with Bourguiba as president.

Creating a modern state

The **1959 Constitution** guaranteed equality and citizens' rights, but in reality Néo-Destour was installed as a single party, inescapable at every level of government and civil society. As all-powerful president, Bourguiba set out to modernise and to secularise teaching and the legal system. However, it was the code of individual status, promulgated in 1956, which had the greatest effect on Tunisian society and which still today endows it with a specific and separate place in the Arab world; it emancipated women by abolishing polygamy and by replacing marital repudiation with legal divorce *(see page 62)*.

In the 1960s, as a result of the rising tide of social problems and the demographic explosion, the régime adopted a dictatorial policy. Néo-Destour changed into the Destourian Socialist Party (PSD) and the State concerned itself with every aspect of life – social (religion, culture) and economic (agriculture and trade). The spread of cooperative organisations in trade and agriculture did not achieve the hoped-for effects – rather the contrary. The deepening economic crisis and external dependence led to the dismissal of the Minister of the Economy, **Ahmad Ben Salah**, former General Secretary of the UGTT, who was soon condemned to ten years in prison.

A new policy of liberal inspiration, **infitah** ("openness") was introduced while, paradoxically, power became more autocratic: Bourguiba was named President for Life in 1974, the general strike in 1978 was repressed and the UGTT closely controlled. At the same time, the Islamist movement began to enjoy unprecedented influence among younger members of the population who were qualified but unemployed. The vulnerability of the Tunisian state was revealed by the Gafsa incident of 1980, when a group of armed men (probably Tunisian exiles from Libya) took over the town and were only dislodged after several days' fighting. The government was forced into a political approach from which Islamists were excluded and which came to an end in 1984, during riots over a rise in the price of bread, leading to many deaths. In April 1987, clashes between government forces and Islamists claimed many victims in Tunis.

The Ben Ali Era

In November 1987 the old leader Habib Bouguiba was replaced, on the grounds of medical incapacity, by his new Prime Minister, **General Zine el-Abidine Ben Ali**. In accordance with the Constitution, the General succeeded Bourguiba as head of state until the end of the parliamentary term. This turning point was greeted as a promise of openness by most of the opposition and intellectuals. Democratic reforms were quickly introduced by the new Head of State: political prisoners were released, the office of President for Life and the Court of State Security were abolished, and plurality of political parties authorised. The PSD changed its spots and became the Democratic Constitutional Assembly (RCD).

The presidential election in 1989 was the moment for Ben Ali, supported by 99 % of the votes, to strengthen his authority. At the election, the Movement for Social Democrats (MDS) was virtually eliminated, while the Islamist movement won 13 % of the votes. Re-elected in the 1994 election, Ben Ali has managed to restrain the Islamists' advance by various measures. On 24 October 1999, President Ben Ali won a third term in office, with 99.44 % of the vote. A landslide result was also recorded at the legislative elections held at the same time. Out of the 182 seats in parliament, the RCD won 148, the 34 remaining seats having been allocated to the opposition parties before the announcement of the election results, by way of improving political pluralism in the country.

Foreign Policy

During the first years of independence, in a context dominated by the Algerian War, relations with France were very tense. The tension came to a peak in 1961 with the Bizerte crisis, when the French army fired on demonstrators and killed nearly 1 000 people *(see page 210)*. Relations between the two countries gradually became more normal, and Tunisia has received substantial aid from France. Bourguiba has also supported American foreign policy and the United States also contributed to the country's economic expansion.

This pro-West policy inevitably stirred up various strands of friction with the Arab countries and, concerned to maintain balance, Tunisia therefore confirmed her status as an ardent defender of the Palestinian cause. After the signature between Egypt and Israel of the Camp David peace agreement (1978), the **Arab League** transferred its headquarters from Cairo to Tunisia. This was copied by the leaders of the **PLO**, after the Israeli invasion of Lebanon (in 1982). During the **Gulf War** (1990-1991), Tunisia refused to take part in the Allied military intervention in Iraq; most of the population disapproved of the war.

At the present time, Tunisia's main foreign policy concern is with the situation in the Maghreb. The setback to the proposed union with its ebullient Libyan neighbour, in 1974, led to a distinct cooling of relations between the two nations. Ghadaffi added more fuel to the fire by supporting rioters in Gafsa at the beginning of the 1980s, and by expelling 30 000 Tunisian workers in 1985. In 1989 Tunisia signed the **Great Arab Maghreb** Treaty of Union, designed to bring Morocco, Algeria, Tunisia, Libya and Mauretania together in a single economic zone. Today this project is virtually dead, particularly because of the civil war in Algeria. Militant Islam represents the greatest challenge to the young republic in the forthcoming years.

MODERN TUNISIA

The Political System in Tunisia

A Presidential regime

The Constitution of 1 June 1959 is still in operation, but with some amendments. It is a fairly short document, designed specifically for its first office-holder, Habib Bourguiba. The **Chief of State** is elected for a term of five years, which is renewable for two further consecutive five-year terms; in 1974, with his mandate no longer available for renewal, Bourguiba was named President for Life. The **Legislative Assembly** election, under universal suffrage and also for five years, takes place at the same time as the presidential election. As in the United States, the government is nominated by the president and is answerable only to him.

Essentially liberal, the Constitution guarantees public freedoms (press, assembly, opinion, expression, association) and the equality of citizens under the law. From the moment he came to power in 1987 President Ben Ali has sought to modernise the regime, abolishing the position of President for Life and creating a **constitutional council**. In the case of a lapse in the presidency, it is the president of the assembly (and no longer the prime minister) who takes charge in the interim: it is he who must organise a fresh election, and he cannot stand for the office himself.

In **administrative** terms, the territory of Tunisia (163 610sqkm) has been divided since 1986 into 23 **governorships**, each bearing the name of its principal town. Lower levels are the concern of delegations, communes and *cheikhats*.

The Ben Ali era

A lack of variation

In reality, Tunisia only discovered the multi-party system in the mid-1980s, and has still never experienced a change of government. The principal political forces are the **RCD** (*Rassemblement constitutionnel démocratique*, the formerly Destourian democratic constitutional assembly), and the trade union **UGTT** (*Union générale des travailleurs tunisiens*, the General Union of Tunisian Workers).

In reality, Tunisia only discovered the multi-party system in the mid-1980s, and has still never experienced alternance of power. The main political operators are the **RCD** (*Rassemblement constitutionnel démocratique*, the formerly Destourian Democratic Constitutional Assembly), and the trade union **UGTT** (*Union générale des travailleurs tunisiens*, the General Union of Tunisian Workers), close to power. In the early 1980s the **PCT** (*Parti communiste tunisien*, the Tunisian Communist Party), the **MDS** (*Mouvement des démocrates sociaux*, the Social Democrat Movement) and the **MUP** (*Mouvement pour l'unité populaire*, Movement for Popular Unity) formed a coalition alliance, but their political weight remained negligible. Since the elections of October 1999, five parties – the **MDS**, the **PUP**, the **UDU**, **Attajdid** (formerly the PCT) and the **parti social libéral** (the Social Liberal Party) – share the 20 % of parliamentary seats reserved for the opposition. The islamic movement **Ennahdha**, meanwhile, remains banned.

An emerging economy

Although still classed as one of the developing economies, Tunisia has grown rapidly since the end of the 1980s (around 4.5 % per annum on average). Lacking natural resources, the country has had to concentrate on services (50 % of GNP), and above all undertake a thorough-going modernisation of its economy.

Breaking with its *dirigiste* traditions, since 1989 Tunisia has been engaged on a programme of **economic liberalisation** under the guidance of Ben Ali. A vast programme of privatisation has been set in motion (nearly 100 enterprises were denationalised at the beginning of 1997, out of 250 planned), while the country opened up to the outside world. Stability and solvency are its two distinctive advantages in attracting **foreign investment**. Money comes from the Gulf, but above all from France, which remains Tunisia's leading economic partner. In addition, most of the great French industrial undertakings and services have a base here. The former colonial power is particularly in evidence in the two main strands of the national economy: **textiles** and **tourism**.

Nearly three-quarters of Tunisia's **trade** is with the countries of the European Union, and entry into the European free trade zone, planned for 2008, should increase this element. Textiles, oil and its derivatives and olive oil are the leading elements of Tunisian exports. In comparison, the figures for trade with the Maghreb (6 % of the total) look trivial.

But in order to become the Mediterranean Singapore that some claim to see in her, Tunisia needs to concentrate on training a skilled labour force, and develop a high-added-value industrial sector which will mark it out from competition from nations with medium-scale economies (Eastern Europe in particular). In addition, the revolution in attitudes in business and the modernisation of economic structures remains to be achieved, no doubt at the price of an increase in unemployment, which already affects more than 15 % of the working population.

However, recent years have seen the emergence of a new middle class of engineers, teachers, middle managers, senior civil servants and professionals. Devotees of consumerism and hire purchase, their lifestyle contrasts with that of most of their fellow Tunisians, nearly half of whom still live in the countryside.

ART AND ARCHITECTURE

The Punic Era

It is one of history's ironies that, despite their invention of the alphabet, the Phoenicians have left us very few written records. Cato's constant repetition of the slogan, "Carthage must be destroyed!" was unfortunately carried out very thoroughly, and the Punic libraries were burned and looted. Only **Mago's** famous treatise on agriculture survives, in the form of a few fragments of Latin translation. The present-day archeological site gives only a feeble notion of the luxury of the Punic capital, the most powerful Mediterranean city of the 6C BC – the Romans left no stone standing in the city, and raids and pillaging did the rest. The ruins were superficially excavated in the 19C to supply material for European museums, and in the 1970s Carthage narrowly escaped being over-whelmed in the urban expansion of the Tunisian capital. It was rescued at the last moment by a UNESCO programme.

A syncretic art

From what we know of it, Punic architecture resembled the Eygyptian style in its massive volumes, stylisation and moulded cornices, together with Mycenian, Cypriot and Greek echoes, a taste for syncretism which displayed an early "baroque" or "mannerist" approach.

For lack of evidence, **Punic temple design** is largely a matter of supposition. In its final period (320-146 BC), architectural design continued to be characterised by eclecticism: Doric and Ionic orders next to cornices or moulded Egyptian style. Built on a hillside, the **Byrsa citadel** at Carthage consisted of an enormous temple, the "most handsome and the richest in the city" according to Appian, dedicated to the Greek god **Euchmon**. The temple of Tharos, in Sardinia, gives an indication of what the religious buildings may have looked like at this period: the *cella* (the inner sanctuary) stands in the courtyard, on a podium with a Doric colonnade approached up central steps. In his account of the Roman's destruction of Carthage, Appian also offers some idea of the internal decoration of the sanctuaries: "The soldiers made their way into the area sacred to Apollo, with the gilded statue of the god; the building in which it stood was covered with leaves of gold each weighing 1 000 talents."

A very few funerary monuments have escaped the ravages of time and destruction, examples of what has come to be called **"Numidian royal architecture"**. Here too, a kind of eclecticism is the prevailing feature. The **Libyo-Punic tomb at Dougga** *(see illustration page 47)*, built for a Numidian prince, forms a square three-storey tower; the lowest level is set on a pedestal with five steps, the second is decorated with Ionic half-columns and an Egyptian-style moulding and the third bears decorative bas-reliefs. The monument is topped with a pyramidion with winged female figures set at the four corners, and a seated lion on top *(see also page 180)*.

Although there are few ruins, there is an abundance of **funerary furnishings** which also reveal a very wide range of external influences. Most of the objects discovered in the tombs are imported or copied to a greater or lesser degree: Greek lamps and vases, Egyptian amulets, Ionian amphorae, etc. Only some little **glass paste masks** are proof of a genuine originality and skill among the

Carthaginian glass-makers. The burial grounds also contained **sarcophagi** from the 4 and 3C BC. They too are the end result of a triple influence: Etruscan in their representation of the dead person on the sarcophagus, Greek in the rules of the statuary, Punic in the pose.

Town planning and housing

Archeological evidence shows that early Carthage was not a simple trading post, but a true city, with the whole range of urban functions.

The houses on **Byrsa Hill** (first half of the 2C BC) were grouped in blocks linked by broad avenues, 6-7m wide, which cut across each other at right angles. The individual houses sometimes consisted of rooms set round a central courtyard, with large quantities of **paving mosaic** (*pavimentum punicum*) made of marble splinters, stone and pottery set in grey mortar. The fragments of frieze or cornice made of brightly coloured ceramic and slender columns covered with plaster betray a taste for Egyptian design. Finally, the solidity of the walls and the absence of bedrooms support the theory of the existence of an upper floor. In houses discovered at **Kerkouan** some of the rooms are laid out round a terrace which communicates with the street by a passage.

Symbols of Carthaginian power

Nothing remains of the 34km **sea ramparts** of Carthage apart from a few blocks scattered along the sea-front, and a trench. Inside, the walls had two levels, with the lower one serving as an elephant shelter. The **ports** were the Carthaginians' finest technical achievement, forming the key to their

A Punic interior
The vestibule, which leads from the road to the courtyard of the house, is always angled to protect privacy. Life is organised round this central courtyard with its well and oven, and all the rooms open on to the courtyard. Niches have been set into the walls of the rooms for shelving. The main room (7m x 4.50m) is elegantly decorated with red, pink or blue plaster-work, with Egyptian moulding and moulded relief plinths. The ground is covered with a somewhat unsophisticated mosaic, a layer of cement encrusted with fragments of pottery, white marble and murex shells. Behind this formal room is the "thalamos", a small windowless room of unknown purpose; perhaps a rest-room for the master of the house? The bathroom, oddly placed close to the entrance passage-way, still has a "washing bowl" and a bath-tub lined with a red coating.

power in the western Mediterranean. Consisting of two parts, one civil and the other military, they are only known to us in a description dating from the 2C AD, but the harbour basins are still visible (*see page 164*).

The Roman Era

Roman Carthage: a model of town planning

Several decades passed after the destruction of Carthage in 146BC before Emperor Augustus built a new city close to the old one. It was a remarkable example of a grid layout applied to a pre-existing town plan. This plan, conceived under the initiative of Augustus, was repeated in the rest of the province. The area to be developed was divided into blocks *(insulae)* of 5 000sqm, while the rural area beyond was divided into *centurion* sections of 50 ha. Under Augustus' orders, Byrsa Hill was levelled and a new acropolis built there, with a basilica (a secular building used as a tribunal), a large temple (capitol or sanctuary of Concordia), a second sanctuary and a gallery of statues of emperors. The architects also laid out a vast public square there, measuring 233m x 336m and divided into two open esplanades with portico, one of which was the forum.

The lower town adopted the layout of the Punic city, and recent archeological investigations appear to indicate that the famous maritime quarter, near the ports, occupied the site of the Punic public *agora* (meeting place).

As in Rome, the city then built itself an enormous theatre, vast public baths, a covered auditorium, a theatre and a circus capable of seating 60 000 people – making it the Empire's second city in its splendour.

Colonising the province

The Romans also laid out 20 000km of roads, constructed bridges and aqueducts, and colonised the rest of the province. The new settlements, inhabited mainly by retired soldiers, were built to the same partial or total grid layout, and had a similar monumental character. In this respect, **Sbeïtla** is a prime example of the ideal Roman city built to a pre-determined plan with no regard for the local topography or previous urban settlement *(see page 272)*.

An ostentatious style of architecture

When a citizen acquired a position – as priest, decurion or magistrate – he would usually hand over a sum of money ("summa honoraria") to the city treasury and pay for a banquet, a statue, or the cost of building a public monument. In the province of Africa, the accession of a large number of locally-born people to Roman citizenship – particularly from the time of the reign of Septimus Severus – led dignitaries to compete in expressing their liberality. The cities were heavily endowed with elaborate monuments, ostentatious and sometimes excessive facilities, with no relation to genuine local needs. Dougga is a notable example.

The luxury of patrician houses

Even in ruins, the patrician houses lived in by the province's elite have something of the scale and grandeur of official buildings and monuments; they leave a strong impression of a luxurious and refined lifestyle.

The entrance is approached through a colonnaded porch, and the living rooms are laid out round one or more colonnaded courtyards, some paved and others with a garden, fountains and pools. The floors are covered with mosaic, the finest generally in the *oecus* (grand reception room) or in the *triclinium* (dining room). The most luxurious villas had private baths opening out on to a courtyard. In Bulla Regia, the wealthiest citizens went to great lengths for coolness and comfort in summer, building themselves sumptious suites of underground rooms arranged around a courtyard. In Carthage, the Romans built a complete residential quarter on the hillside where the covered auditorium was located. The villas, set on platforms, had a view over the sea, like the house known as **"The Birdcage"** which had a large reception room paved with marble, superb mosaics, a peristyle, a garden, and a large decorative pool.

The plastic arts

After the total destruction of the Punic civilisation by the great western power of the day, one can hardly reproach Romano-African art for being provincial and somewhat derivative. It was an imported art, an art which looked to Rome instead of drawing on its own roots. The sculptures are strongly classical, like the Victory figures which came off the production line to be despatched to cities throughout the empire. With time, the lack of originality resulted less from a certain provincialism than from a uniformity of style across the whole empire. The art reflected the period. In the 2C AD – when the province of Africa was at its peak – the various races were already so well assimilated that there was nothing to stop Septimus Severus (from Libya) and his wife Julia Domna (from Syria) taking power. Nor did art escape the mood of the day and a cerain "globalisation": the **sculpture** workshops of Aphrodisias were established at Leptis Magna, in Libya, and African mosaicists sent their works as far as the Rhineland.

Creativity no doubt suffered – the same designs and the same subjects were reproduced everywhere – but the execution was remarkable. In the era of Severus, provincial artists achieved a mastery wholly comparable with that of their Italian equivalents. In particular, the **wall paintings** of North Africa or Syria match those in Rome.

The Africans also stood out in the domain of **mosaic**. This craft, which sometimes approaches true art, requires a very complex technique that they acquired only at a fairly late date. The great vigour of mosaic in the province dates from the 2C AD, and there is little doubt that, initially, the most elaborate works were imported from Italy. The great period of African mosaic extended from the 2C to the 5C: the **God Neptune and the Four Seasons**, which can be considered the masterpiece of the Bardo museum, dates from the 2C, and the **mosaic of Lord Julius**, another of the museum's masterpieces was probably completed in the 4 or 5C.

Mass production of mosaic

In the 3C BC the invention of tesserae of stone, brick, marble or glass paste revolutionised mosaic. The "opus tesselatum" (1-2cm cubes) was kept for the geometric framing designs. The "opus vermiculatum" made it possible to compose the scenes with figures at the centre. For this, the tesserae were trimmed very delicately and selected for their colour, so as to achieve blends close to pictorial art. It was the master craftsmen who carried out the central sections, with the surrounding area undertaken by the less skilled workers. Although there were some genuine artistic creations, the subjects and designs were often repeated from one piece of work to another and carried out in almost identical ways (for example the theme of "the Ocean god"). No one doubted that the mosaicists had a range of "standard issue" ornamentation and representation, from which the client could take his choice.

Paleo-Christian and Byzantine Art

Classical heritage and change

Christianity spread quickly through the province of Africa, but Christian teachings did not touch only the oppressed and the humble, as has sometimes been claimed – by the 2C the new faith was finding converts among the patricians and the intellectual élite. **Tertullian** (Carthage, 150-222) one of the most brilliant writers of his century, was one of those cultivated minds which achieved a perfect combination of Classical culture and Christianity. Two centuries later, in the "literary salons" of Carthage, **St Augustine** was to discuss rhetoric and philosophy with other men of letters, some pagan and some Christian, with all this intelligentsia sharing the same intellectual assumptions.

The plastic arts developed in similar ways. Christianity borrowed motifs from paganism, but did so in order to redirect their meaning. This is what happened with the **Bon Pasteur** ("The Good Shepherd"), a recurrent figure in classical iconography which was transmuted into Christological representation (the catacombs of **Sousse** have an example).

The mosaicists also drew inspiration from Christian symbolism and martyrology: "two stags flanking a baptismal font", **"Daniel in the lions' den"**, etc. The use of mosaic also changed – from being purely decorative it became **funerary** as well. From the 4C, the church permitted burial inside religious buildings: mosaic work on the tombs bore the earliest symbols of Christianity with an inscription showing the dead person's name and age, and perhaps his role in the church hierarchy. These funerary mosaics are sometimes set at the centre of paving with geometric or floral designs, and detract from the overall coherence of its design. For secular use, mosaicists continued for a time to create beautiful works based on mythology, but gradually their work lost its content and meaning, until they became purely ornamental.

The earliest Christian sanctuaries date from no earlier than 312. Originally they were simply a space set aside in the house, but soon the **basilicas** which served as courts of law were converted to this religious purpose. Their rectangular layout with three aisles and an apse was to inspire the design of churches; the selection of this type of building was based on the fact that it was a meeting place, in contrast to the classical temple, a place in which to preserve the idol and which was reserved for the priesthood alone. Carthage had twelve churches in the time of St Augustine: apart from one vaulted chapel, a galleried rotunda and a church at the location known as **Damous el Karita**, they were destroyed by the Vandals. One of the masterpieces of paleo-Christian sculpture has been found here: two bas-reliefs representing the Adoration of the shepherds and the Magi.

Nothing remains of the **Vandal period**, which lasted for nearly a century (439-533). Only their destructive efforts, for

Mosaic: The "Lady of Carthage"

Musée de Carthage/GIRAUDON

Art and Architecture

which their name is still known, have survived them. This reputation is not wholly accurate, for even if construction did not continue with the same dazzling display, the workshops of Carthage continued to produce their work and export it. The beautiful mosaic of **La Dame de Carthage** (The Lady of Carthage) even appears to show a Roman influence at work in this Germanic Christian tribe.

The Byzantine era

The Byzantines, who arrived in 534, saw themselves as heirs of the Romans. In fact, by re-occupying part of the former Roman provinces, Justinian restored the basic meaning of "empire" in its full sense; but although the structure of the State was Roman, its culture was now predominantly Greek and its faith Christian. In Byzacena itself Latin gave way to Greek as the official language in the reign of Heraclius (610-641). Although a universal art had emerged from the 2C, with its centres of production spread across the whole empire, by the 4C Byzacena was to be the focus of all the artistic and intellectual creativity of its day.

The changes begun in the palæo-Christian era continued and became established. The basilica layout, with three or five aisles, was adopted throughout the whole of the Christian world for places of worship. In the 5C it underwent a particularly significant development: in Carthage the church of Damous el Karita was restored and an apse and an atrium added. The churches had mosaic floors and mosaic also appeared on the walls for the first time.

The **cult of martyrs** also took on considerable importance, and basilicas were built to house a relic or a corpse. The body of a decapitated man has been found in the apses of the church of Vitalis (5-6C) in **Sbeïtla**... clearly a martyr. Most of the many fragments of inscriptions relating to the martyrdom of St Perpetua and St Felicity date from the Byzantine period.

The Byzantines restored the ports of Carthage, but above all they built numerous citadels and fortified suitable towns, reinforcing Roman constructions in some cases or demolishing them in order to reuse the materials.

Islamic architecture

The Arabs took possession of *Ifriqiya* in the 7C. Unlike the Vandals, they eliminated the past, using the cities of classical times as sources of stone to build their mosques. Yet the link with classical culture was not completely broken: many Moslem artists had been trained in the school of Byzacena and to build their first mosque – of the Prophet, at Medina – the Caliphs called on Greek architects.

The mosque as a place of prayer

One may wonder at the need for the mosque as a place of prayer, since Islam is a religion without priests: the Moslem can pray alone and anywhere, provided that he has undertaken his ablutions and that he turns towards Mecca. The origins of the building should no doubt be sought in the tribal structure of Arab society, and in the theocratic nature of Islam. Among the earliest Moslems the sense of community was extremely powerful, and collective prayer was the occasion of true group communion. Public prayer was to some extent more valuable than solitary prayer (a conviction still shared by present-day Moslems), hence the need of a place in which to meet. The principle of such a building was also political. On Friday at midday the faithful were to gather in a single place under the authority of the Imam; he would not deliver a sermon but would consider all the community's material, strategic or political problems. Each Islamic town therefore had its Friday **"Grand Mosque"** as opposed to other religious places used only for prayer. It was generally at the centre of the medina, a focal point in the life of the community.

Principles of religious architecture

The layout of the house of the Prophet in Medina formed the basis for the design of all subsequent mosques. This house must be imagined as a simple building made up of small rooms (bedrooms for the wives) opening on to a square walled courtyard. This open space was used as a place of prayer and, to provide a little shade, Mahomet built a light palm-leaf shelter along the north wall. When the Medina mosque was built in 706, on the very spot where the Prophet had lived and where his body was preserved, the builders took great care to recreate the main lines of the holy dwelling: a general layout forming an approximate quadrilateral, a courtyard and an enormous room giving shade and coolness, the whole making up an enclosed area.

The mosque is always oriented towards Mecca, to which Moslems turn to pray. This direction is indicated by the **mihrab** *(see the architectural plan, page 45)*, a niche set in the middle of the wall known as the **qibla**. The meaning of *mihrab* is disputed, but it is thought that this empty niche – which in some ways recalls the apse of palæo-Christian churches – might symbolise the physical presence of the Prophet, since Moslem art does not allow any figurative representation *(see page 40)*. The *mihrab*, the most richly decorated feature of the mosque, is aligned on the central aisle. Its location is marked on the outside by a dome and it is the point towards which everything converges. Next to it is the Imam's pulpit, the **minbar** *(see architectural plan, page 45)*, the symbol of spiritual authority and theocratic power. The earliest pulpits were made of carved wood, but later they were made of marble.

The architectural prototype of the mosque is the Great Mosque of the Ummayads, at Damascus (715): a **pillared prayer hall** opening onto a **portico courtyard** *(sahn)* as in many Græco-Roman buildings.

Enclosed within their high walls, the mosques sometimes look like fortresses – which is what they were at the time of the Arab conquest. Many of them retained this defensive appearance, although any threat has long since vanished, shifting their role as the **fortresses of Islam** to a symbolic level. The **minaret**, derived from the Christian belfry, also relates to the watch-tower of Byzantine and Roman forts. In some countries (Turkey, Afghanistan), the minaret was to evolve into aesthetic forms far removed from military architecture, but the **Almohad minaret** (Maghreb) remains a sentinel of the faith: a square tower, often crenellated at the top.

The medersa is a Koranic school or university. The rooms (courtyard rooms, sleeping accommodation for the students, prayer room, class-rooms) are set round a courtyard with a portico. The zawiya is a religious foundation established close to the tomb of a holy man *(marabout)*. The ribat is a fortified monastery built on the model of Byzantine forts. *(see page 244)*

Housing and town planning are covered on page 60.

Pre-classical Islamic architecture

The Kairouan model

The **Great Mosque of Kairouan**, the oldest place of prayer in North Africa, was founded in 666 at the same time as the town. It was completely rebuilt in 836 under the reign of the **Aghlabids**, and its layout was repeated throughout the Maghreb. It is characterised by its strongly defined **T-shaped layout**: the central aisle and the aisle running along the wall of the *qibla* are wider and noticeably higher *(see plan page 267)*. The central aisle is also topped with two domes at each end, adding emphasis to the axis that leads to the *mihrab*. Like in the mosque of the Prophet in Medina, it has seventeen aisles. Another feature is the **horseshoe arch** *(see architectural plan, page 44)*, a style with very few known examples from this early period.

From outside, the mosque displays all the features of a fortress; outer walls reinforced with powerful buttresses and square crenellated towers. The minaret, possibly from the Ummayad era, is similar to the lighthouses of the Roman period. Its battlements and massive appearance make it look more like a military building than a place of worship.

The **Great Mosque of Tunis** (856-863) is directly inspired by the Kairouan mosque: the same T-shape, the same ribbed domes at each end of the central aisle, etc. Its exterior appearance differs in the greater richness of its decoration and above all in its later additions: the Ottoman period gallery, and the Almohad-style minaret dating from 1834.

In the 10C, Obaïd Allah, chief of the Fatimids, founded a short-lived capital at **Mahdia**. He surrounded it with a town wall and built two palaces, a port, an arsenal and a Great Mosque. This reproduced the T-shape of the Kairouan mosque but introduced several significant new features, such as the projecting porch inspired by the design of Moslem palaces. Another innovation was the monumental entrance reserved for the sovereign, which underlined the semi-divine status of the Shiite Caliph.

The **Great Mosque of Sfax** (late 9C) originally looked very similar to the Kairouan mosque, although this resemblance is barely discernible today: the building was reduced in the 12C and then partly reconstructed in the 18C. The minaret, built under the Zirid reign, is not unlike the Kairouan minaret, but higher. It also differs in the curving lines of its windows, its decorated horizontal bands and the design of the decorative merlon parapets.

Classical Islamic architecture

After expelling the Almoravids, the **Almohad** Berbers took power throughout the whole of North Africa and in Spain in the 12C. Almohad architecture (Hispano-Moorish) expanded particularly in Morocco and Andalusia; it is distinguished by its many domes and the care lavished on the design of its increasingly large courtyards. The richly decorated **Almohad minaret** is as much an expression of the glory of Allah as of the dynasty *(see the architectural plan, page 45)*. More puritan than the Almoravids, the Almohads renewed the Moslem aesthetic with a taste for the purity of line and decoration. They continued the tradition of aisles at right angles to the *qibla* together with a wide central aisle, but reinforced the T-shape plan by increasing the size of the aisle beside the *qibla*, and by topping it with three or five domes.

Muqarnas

Made of stone, brick or plaster-work, "*muqarnas*", or stalactites, are an essential feature of Moslem art, cell motifs that embellish the curving surfaces of buildings (domes, squinches and pendentives). The first appeared in Iran in the 11C, but it was above all in North Africa and Spain that they were most popular. In Ifriqiya the oldest are in Algeria in the Q'ala of the Bani Hammadids, a branch of the Zirid family. With time they developed into increasingly complex forms, as in the Alhambra in Granada (14C).

From the 13 to the 15C Tunisia took in Andalusians expelled from Spain after the Reconquest. The great craft and artistic skill these refugees brought with them was to make a permanent mark on the buildings of North Africa. Andalusian art tends towards the abstract and the geometric: interlinked vaulting, ribs, muqarnas, multiple arabesque ornamentation, trees of life, etc.

The Ottoman era

Tunis fell into Ottoman hands in 1574. This marked the beginning of a prosperous period, mainly the result of piracy (*see page 209*) which supplied the finance for numerous architectural projects: the Hammouda Pasha and Youssef Dey mosques (17C), several 18C *medersas* (Moslem colleges), the Turkish souk, etc. Above all they left an impressive number of forts and barracks. In decorative terms, the Turkish style is characterised by a taste for floral designs on painted ceilings and pottery. The mosques built by the Ottomans differ noticeably from the Maghreb pattern. The **Ottoman minaret** of the Hanefite rite is octagonal and much taller than that of the Almohad style (*see the architectural plan, page 45*). The mosque courtyard is divided into several sections around the sanctuary, as in the Hammouda Pasha mosque. These mosques are often associated with the tomb (*tourbet*) of their founder and his dynasty.

The 17C **Sidi Mahrez** mosque in Tunis is a different matter. It was directly inspired by the mosques of Istanbul and has no features in common with earlier buildings in Tunisia. Among other features that mark it out are its many domes – the largest one is above the prayer hall – and its narrow L-shaped courtyard. In the 18 and 19C the **Husseinite** princes in their decline still financed fine examples quite distinct from the Turkish style but showing strong western influences. One example is the **Youssef Sahib and Taba mosque** (1812), where the Italian influence is particularly apparent.

Representation in Islamic art

From idols to pictures

The conventional wisdom is that Islam rejects figurative representation, and more particularly that of living creatures. This view deserves to be examined, for there is nothing in the Koran that prohibits pictures, painting or statues. The few denunciations on this subject focus very specifically on idols alone.

In the earliest days of Islam, princely palaces were decorated with mosaics, mural paintings and statues but, with a few exceptions, the mosques remained bare of all figurative ornamentation. This must be seen as bringing the weight of a ban – inherent but unspoken in the sacred text – that the doctors of Islamic law

The Great Mosque, Kairouan:
the oldest place of worship in the Maghreb

Art and Architecture

took pains to make manifest in their *hadiths*, the texts which formed an appendix to the Koran. Moslems profess an absolute monotheism *(see page 55)*, and in these early days of Islam paganism remained a threat; the Arab theologians feared that the faithful would come to venerate pictures of Mahomet, like Christians who addressed their prayers to effigies of Jesus, Mary and all the saints of Paradise. God alone is the object of worship and it would be vain to seek to represent God.

At certain times intransigence among the Imams on this subject was equally encouraged by the social and political context: reaction against Greek culture, condemnation of the frantic luxury of the Caliphs, princes and other prosperous figures.

Towards an art of the abstract

The banning of figuration was to be spelled out in the anthologies of *hadith*, the words of Mahomet, the main examples of which date from the 9C. A ban on representation was gradually extended by the theologians to secular art: the imitation of animate creatures was an act of sacrilege, an imitation of God in giving life to creatures and to measure Man against God. And yet, outside the sphere of the sacred, artists managed to get round the ban, as can be seen in the impressive surge of Islamic painting, notably in the 13–18C. They succeeded in this by turning towards stylised and abstract art forms. By moving away from any realistic representation, the artists demonstrated their humility in the face of creation. They abandoned everything in their art which could give an impression of reality: perspective, depth, shadows, modelled forms... everything that had established the greatness of Græco-Roman art and which was very familiar to Moslem artists. For the same reasons the art of portraiture is virtually non-existent. When a man is shown, he is never an "individual" but a "type", a human or universal representation or an idea. It is very rare to find figures of Arab princes, or a set of portraits of a whole dynasty. Only the Turkish sultans commissioned their own portraits (undertaken by European artists), and even those were created in secret.

Decorative Art

Once the doctors of the law had pronounced against figurative art, the decorative arts came to the fore. "Decoration" was no longer a frame or a filler in such representation – as in Græco-Roman and Byzantine art – but formed a major element in all artistic composition.

Arabesques

Geometric tracery uses the polygon as its basic form, more particularly the octagon and the hexagon. In the 18C polygons, triangles, lozenges and stars were combined and superimposed in complex compositions.

Curving or floral tracery is based on the same prinicples as geometric tracery but it uses the sinuosity of the curved line. The line unfolds to form very stylised floral motifs: scrolls, fan-shapes, leaves, pine-cones, etc.

Calligraphy

Calligraphy is one of the most characteristic features of Islamic art and expression. Through Mahomet God expressed himself in Arabic, and his words were taken down in Arabic characters. The word of God and Arabic language and writing co-exist in a state of consubstantiality, and indeed the Koran states very explicity that the art of writing is essentially divine (Sura 96, 4).

In Islamic regions calligraphy is a major art, the only one considered worthy of ornamenting the verses of the Koran. This art became established on the basis of certain characteristics unique to Arab writing, each one of the letters of the alphabet acquiring a specific form according to its position in the word – initial, median or final. Calligraphy is the art of representing these variations. Initially designed to accompany text, the art of the calligrapher gradually broke away to become a wholly decorative art-form, independent of the meaning of the signs expressed; in fact, in its most extreme and ornamental forms, calligraphy is illegible.

Arab calligraphy is divided into two main styles:

Kufic writing, which is characterised by its vertical strokes, the uniform thickness of the letters, its right-angles, its serious and monumental effect. From the 11C onwards Kufic lost its original sobriety: the ascending and descending strokes of the letters became more elongated, crossed over each other, and acquired plant-based features **(floral Kufic)**. **Cursive writing**, which appeared in the 11C, can be recognised by the suppleness and delicacy of its letters, drawn in upstrokes and downstrokes. In the end it completely took over from the Kufic style.

Calligraphy was also used for **epigraphic design** on monuments – carved into stone or plaster-work, or featuring in ceramics. The serious and substantial Kufic is particularly suitable for epigraphic use. This use of the style was never wholly supplanted by Kufic, in contrast to the usage for books.

ARCHITECTURE OF ANTIQUITY

THE TEMPLE

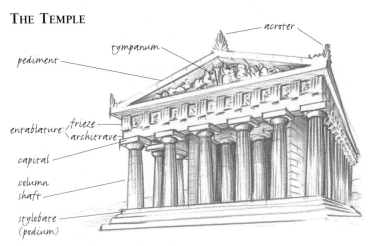

- acroter
- tympanum
- pediment
- entablature: frieze
- architrave
- capital
- column
- shaft
- stylobate (podium)

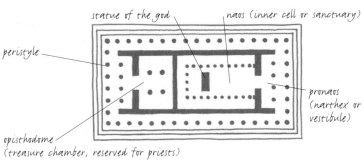

- statue of the god
- naos (inner cell or sanctuary)
- peristyle
- pronaos (narthex or vestibule)
- opisthodome (treasure chamber, reserved for priests)

THREE CLASSICAL ORDERS

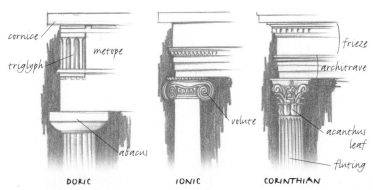

- cornice
- metope
- triglyph
- abacus
- volute
- frieze
- architrave
- acanthus leaf
- fluting

DORIC   IONIC   CORINTHIAN

H. Choimet

THE ROMAN AMPHITHEATRE

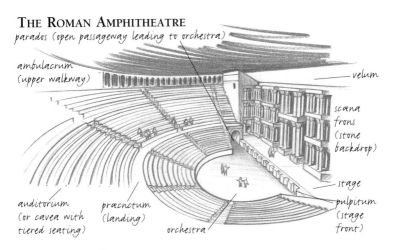

parados (open passageway leading to orchestra)

ambulacrum
(upper walkway)

velum

scæna
frons
(stone
backdrop)

stage

pulpitum
(stage
front)

auditorium
(or cavea with
tiered seating)

præcnctum
(landing)

orchestra

THERMAE OR BATHS

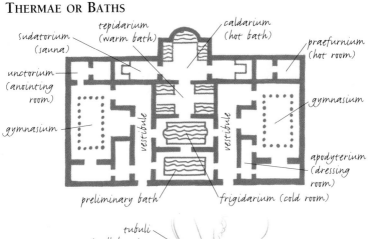

sudatorium
(sauna)

tepidarium
(warm bath)

caldarium
(hot bath)

praefurnium
(hot room)

unctorium
(anointing
room)

gymnasium

vestibule

vestibule

gymnasium

apodyterium
(dressing
room)

preliminary bath

frigidarium (cold room)

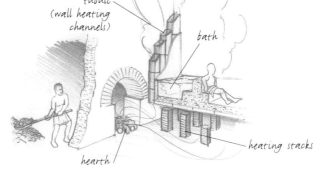

tubuli
(wall heating
channels)

bath

hearth

heating stacks

HYPOCAUST HEATING SYSTEM

H. Choimet

43

FROM CLASSICAL TIMES...

THE ROMAN BASILICA

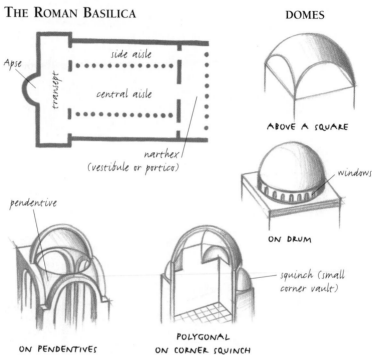

Apse

transept

side aisle

central aisle

narthex
(vestibule or portico)

pendentive

ON PENDENTIVES

POLYGONAL
ON CORNER SQUINCH

DOMES

ABOVE A SQUARE

windows

ON DRUM

squinch (small corner vault)

ARCHES

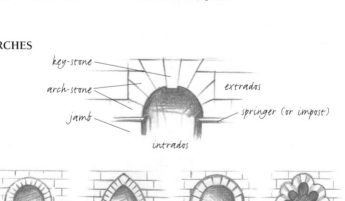

key-stone

arch-stone

jamb

extrados

springer (or impost)

intrados

ROUND-HEADED

POINTED

HORSESHOE

MULTIPOIL

H. Choinet

...TO ISLAM

THE MAGHREB MOSQUE

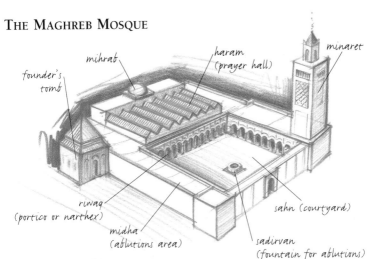

founder's tomb

mihrab

haram (prayer hall)

minaret

riwaq (portico or narthex)

midha (ablutions area)

sadirvan (fountain for ablutions)

sahn (courtyard)

MINARETS

THE MIHRAB THE MINBAR (PULPIT)

MUQARNAS ('STALACTITES')

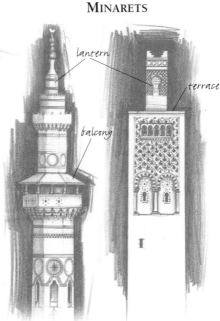

lantern

balcony

terrace

OTTOMAN (MAGHREB AND MIDDLE EAST)

ALMOHADE (MAGHREB)

H. Choinet

Brief glossary of architecture

Apse	Semi-circular hall forming the head end of a church. It rounds off the choir where the clergy sit.
Acropolis	Upper town in Greek cities, used as fortress or place of worship.
Atrium	The court inside the entrance of a Roman house or building. A courtyard usually with a pool for rain water.
Basilica	Rectangular civic building with three aisles, used as a court or meeting place. The name was later given to the earliest Christian churches built to the same design.
Bond	Pattern in which bricks are laid (in Latin, *opus*) (see also *dressing*).
Cardo	The north-south street in a Roman town. The *cardo maximus* is the main axis at right-angles to the *decumanus* (see below).
Decumanus	East-west street in a Roman town (see also *cardo*).
Dressing	The style in which stone is trimmed and prepared for building use.
Epigraph	Inscription on a monument. Epigraphic design uses Arab calligraphy.
Forum	Public square in Roman towns, the market-place and centre of political life.
Hammam	Turkish steam baths, in the tradition of Roman baths.
Hypostyle	A temple, mosque or palace in which the roof is held up by columns.
Insula	Section or bloc of a classical city.
Limes	Fortified frontier zone, designed to protect the provinces of the Roman Empire from barbarian attack.
Maqsura	Wooden panel separating the Imam from the faithful.
Marabout	Holy place, a tomb which is the object of veneration (see also *zawiya*).
Medersa	Koranic school.
Merlons	Decorative crenellation.
Mihrab	Niche in a mosque indicating the direction of Mecca.
Minbar	Pulpit in a mosque, approached up stairs, from which to preach on Fridays.
Muqarnas	Architectural decoration in brick, stone or plaster-work in a stalactite-like form.
Nymphaea	Natural spring or fountain dedicated to nymphs. In a Roman city, monumental fountain symbolising its power and wealth, often dedicated to an emperor.
Odeon	Small theatre, usually covered, used for concerts and public readings.
Œcus	Reception room in a Roman house.
Peristyle	Gallery or portico with columns surrounding a temple or courtyard.
Pilaster	Square pillar, half set into a wall.
Portico	Covered gallery supported on pillars. Porticos round the forum housed shops.
Qibla	Wall of the mosque that faces Mecca.
Ribat	Fortified monastery.
Stucco	Plaster coating used for embellishing walls and ceilings.
Tessera	Small cube of coloured stone or glass, used to make mosaics.
Triclinium	Dining room in a Roman house.
Tophet	Expression taken from the Old Testament to designate sanctuaries where infant sacrifice was practiced.
Tourbet	Moslem tomb.
Zawiya	Religious foundation built close to the tomb of a holy man.

G. Dageorge

The Libyo-Punic tomb at Dougga

Meeting the People

Cafés are a
Tunisian institution

IDENTITY AND CHARACTER

Legendary hospitality

The people of Tunisia are known as the most gentle-natured and welcoming of the inhabitants of the Maghreb. Melting-pot of civilisations, land of invasions, Tunisia is the product of many and varied influences – and although it may not have a marked character of its own it has a rare spirit of openness, with an equally rare natural sense of tolerance. Visitors are often invited to sample a couscous dish or to join in a family celebration. They may even be invited to a traditional wedding, particularly in the south. Guests always receive more attention than the master of the house, and hospitality can often be overwhelming.

A homogeneous population

Tunisia has about nine and a half million inhabitants. Although it has been more exposed to foreign influence than any of the other Maghreb lands it is also, para-doxically, the land with the least variation among its people: 98 % Arab, 99 % Sunni. Divisions are therefore neither ethnic nor linguistic (between Arab and Berber, for example), nor are they religious (between Sunni and Shiite). The dif-ferences lie rather between the 53 % who are town-dwellers and the 47 % who live in a rural setting, between a highly Europeanised urban middle class and a peasant society which maintains a traditional way of life, between the tourist areas by the sea and the inland regions, between north and south.

Regional differences

As everywhere, distinctively regional elements are dying out with the spread of rural depopulation and universal education – yet each province still retains its own characteristics which the Tunisian never forgets, which stay with him no matter where he goes. The Jerbian is a hardworking trader whose grocery shop is often open until late in the evening, the people of Sfax are known everywhere as merchants and dealers, the inhabitants of the Kef region love the land and tackle their work with gusto.

Each province also also has its own distinctive style of clothing. In the cities these differences are lost in the generalised European styles, but it is not unusual to meet a venerable old man wearing his *chechia* with his three-piece suit, and outside office hours the average Tunisian may well wear a *jebba*, a lightweight, loose-fitting form of *jellaba*, or tunic. Clothing is generally more traditional in the countryside, with the peasant huddled in the cape of his *kachabiya* and the women in their bright dresses in the fields, but regional clothes, head-dress and jewellery are now brought out only for ceremonial occasions or festivals (*see under Finery and Clothing, page 66*).

Tunisians of town or country

It is in economic terms that the differences and inequities between the provinces are most obvious. You only need to leave the smart suburbs of Tunis or the tourist areas and venture a few kilometres inland to discover another Tunisia, agricultural and with few modern facilities, a situation reflecting a division which dates from classical times. The city of Carthage maintained its power by constructing a whole series of trading centres and towns along the coast, but the inland areas remained outside its control. The Romans settled more extensively in the interior, but they established an essentially urban way of life, with the nomadic tribes pushed back beyond the military frontier. Furthermore, the principal Roman settlements were basically port cities like Carthage, Hadrumetum and Utica. This division between coast and the interior was maintained under Arab rule, with one notable exception – Kairouan, founded at the heart of the plain. Colonial activity under the French Protectorate was focused on the ports (Bizerte, Sousse, Sfax) and the north of the country. The development of tourist resorts after independence only served to accentuate the imbalance between the coast and the interior of the country. At the present time, 60 % of the population lives in a narrow coastal strip from Bizerte to Jerba and the Sahel, which has always been alert to trade and wider opportunities, and is the most dynamic region of Tunisia, combining tourism, industry and service industries. It is a focus of attraction for young people in search of employment.

The different communities

Tunisia has been formed by the events of successive invasions. The ancient foundation formed by the Berber population (Numidian) has absorbed waves of Phoenician (Punic), Roman, Vandal, Arab, Turkish and European immigration, while over several centuries the slave trade added a steady flow of black Africans and captive Christians. For a long time Tunisia was also open to Jews and traders of all nations: Maltese, Neapolitan, Sardinian, English and French.

The Arabs

The Arab conquest of *Ifriqiya* in the 7C marked a complete break with the Roman-Punic past, although the process of Arabisation and Islamisation in the Maghreb began slowly; it did not become permanent until the 11C, during the second Arab invasion under the Beni Hilal people who put the land to fire and the sword (*see page 20*). The Christian communiy which coexisted with the Moslems vanished almost completely at this time; the periods of Turkish and then French domination did not affect this situation.

The Berbers

Their name is derived from *barbarus*, "that which is foreign to the Græco-Latin civilisation", and their presence in North Africa has been known since the dawn of history. There is no single Berber race, for the group includes a range of ethnic elements – their only common denominator is that they are Berber-speaking and that they share the same spirit of independence which has always made them rebels. From the most remote classical times the story of the Berber peoples has varied between resistance and assimilation into dominant civilisations. Although the Berbers more or less managed to preserve their identity from Punic, Roman and Byzantine influences, the Arab conquest was to be a fatal factor; it has been estimated that from the 12C they were all definitively converted to Islam. Their opposition to Arabisation and to orthodoxy was then expressed by their support for dissenting religious elements such as Kharidjism or Shiism – as when the Berbers helped the Shiite Fatimids to overthrow the Aghlabid dynasty and to take power. Fleeing into the mountains of Aures, the Rif and the Atlas, the Berbers resisted Arabism better and retained their own language and customs. In the absence of precise figures, it has been estimated that there are more than 4 000 000 Berbers in Morocco and some 2 000 000 in Algeria. In Tunisia, where the mountainous landscape is on a much smaller scale, assimilation has been almost complete, and the Berbers probably only represent some 1-2 % of the population, scattered across Jerba and some villages in the south.

The Bedouin

In nomad mythology, houses are graves in which human beings are buried alive, while city dwellers in contrast have always mistrusted the Bedouin, seeing them as warlike and prone to pillaging. It would be inaccurate, however, to speak of true antagonism between the sedentary life and nomadism in the Maghreb: the two ways of life were complementary, with the Bedouin tribes maintaining the security of oasis settlements in their area as well as commercial trade. It was a fragile balance which could break down in periods of shortage or invasions by enemy tribes.

It was this same fear of the Bedouin that led the colonial authorities to try to turn them into a settled race. But other factors are influential too, increasingly so since independence. Developments in transport, the need for security in the more remote areas and changes in land use like the extension of arabic farming – all have made the nomadic way of life obsolete. People are encouraged to settle by the need for security in the more remote areas and changes in land use like the extension of arable farming, the sinking of artesian wells and the opening of schools and health institutions. Nonetheless, there may still be around 15 000 who follow the tracks of their forebears across the Chott el Jerid and the Great South.

The Jews

The Jewish community is one of the oldest in Tunisia, as can be seen from the graves in the Jewish cemetery at Gammarth which dates back more than 2 000 years. There are even claims that Jews reached Jerba in the company of the Phoenicians who founded Carthage, before the destruction of the first temple in Jerusalem. Tunisia also experienced later waves of immigration, particularly in the 14 and 15C when the Jews were expelled from Spain. They played a substantial role in trade, finance and the liberal professions. Under Islamic law, the Jews belonged to the category of *Dhimmis*, a legal status which enabled them to be integrated into Islamic society but which was not without its constraints and irritations. These were not abolished until 1859, by the reforming Ahmed Bey.

The vagaries of independence and development in the Arab-Israel conflict drove the great majority of Tunisian Jews into exile – the population has fallen from 120 000 in 1947 to no more than 2 000 today, the great majority in Jerba.

The Dhimmis

Theological links between the Judæo-Christian and Islamic religions created a particular status for the Jews and Christians which enabled them to take their place in Islamic society. They fell into the category of "dhimmi" or "protected people", a legal status recognised in Islamic law. The dhimmis enjoyed relative religious freeedom and their lives, possessions and sanctuaries were in theory protected. Nevertheless, "dhimmi" status included certain discriminatory measures, such as the ban on building new places of worship, on bearing arms or travelling on horseback. They also had to wear distinctive clothing and avoid any ostentation. A Moslem could marry a "dhimmi" woman, but "dhimmi" men could not aspire to a Moslem bride. They were also subject to additional taxation.

An element of intermarriage

The trade in black slaves lies behind the interracial blending visible in Cap Bon and the Tunisian south. For many centuries slavery was of great economic importance, particularly in the market of Kebili, which used to be the focus of the trade in slaves from the Sudan. This lucrative trade continued into the 19C.

E. Valentin/HOA QUI

A Bedouin of the Great South

RELIGIONS

Islam

The word *islam* means "submission to the will of God". A Moslem, or *moslim,* is one who submits to Allah. Under Article 1 of the constitution, "Tunisia is an independent State in which the religion is Islam", but religion has less impact on the country's life than in other Arab countries.

Origins

Mahomet (Mohammed Ibn Abd Allah) was born at **Mecca** around 570, at a time when the city in the Arabian peninsula was an important centre in the caravan trade. Like most of the inhabitants of Mecca, Mahomet belonged to the Qoraychite tribe, but he was an orphan and poor. Tradition has it that he was a shepherd in his younger days, but later he was employed by a rich widow for whom he organised caravans which he may have led as far as Syria. Having won the confidence of this woman fifteen years his senior, he married her.

Around the year 610, during a retreat in the desert, he experienced his first visions: in a visitation from the Angel Gabriel the word of God was revealed to him. Then came three years of doubt, during which Mahomet received no more divine manifestations. The revelations began again around 613, and for about ten years the prophet preached that Allah is all-powerful, that he is the one God, and that mankind must prepare for the Last Judgement. From the outset Mahomet had a following, a small group of faithfuls who believed in his mission, but the authorities in Mecca were polytheistic pagans, disturbed at this new sect which no doubt appeared likely to threaten their economic interests. In 622 Mahomet and his disciples were forced to leave for **Medina**, an oasis lying about 350km to the northwest. This "emigration", the **Hegira**, marks the year Zero of the Islamic era.

In Medina, Mahomet gradually gathered power and set up a veritable theocracy: by now the Prophet was more than a spiritual leader, he was also a politician, a legislator, and soon a soldier. He and his devoted supporters attacked the caravans of the Qoraychites and extended their influence across the whole Arab peninsula. In 630 the "Moslems", as they would henceforward be known, entered Mecca as victors. Mahomet penetrated into the temple and overturned the idols but showed mercy to his old enemies. Before he returned to Medina, where he died in 632, he instituted the pilgrimage to Mecca.

The Koran

Like the Christian *Bible* or *Gospels,* the *Koran* is a book of revelation, the word of God revealed to man through the mediation of his prophet Mahomet. In Arabic, the word *Koran* means "recitation": Mahomet was invited to recite the text which God had dictated to him, and by extension it is the "sacred text which is recited". These revelations are presented in the form of verses which the faithful have gathered in chapters or **sura**, without concern for chronology.

The Koran is the prism through which the Moslem interprets the world, a book of spirituality as much as a moral or legislative code. It is also valuable as a guide to rhetoric and grammar. Arabic, the language of revelation, should not be corrupted in its usage, and there is therefore a split between the different dialects of the spoken language and the classical Arabic of the *Koran,* which is fixed in its sacredness (see under "Languages", page 74, and "Calligraphy", page 40.)

The **Sunna** (or "tradition") set out in the **hadiths**, the sometimes legendary narratives of the life of Mahomet, clarifies certain obscure points from the *Koran*, completes the precepts that it outlines, and deals with questions of modern life.

The "five pillars" of Islam

The Koran specifies five essential obligations:

The profession of faith (*chahada*), which consists of affirming the singleness of God: "I believe that there is no God except Allah and that Mahomet is his Prophet." This is the essential act of conversion to Islam.

Prayer: the Muslim believer turns towards Mecca five times every day to pray. He may be alone or with others, but he must follow a very precise ritual. First there are ablutions for purification. Prayer begins with the incantation, *"Allah Akbar"*, "Allah is great". Standing, the believer then recites the first sura of the *Koran*, followed by verses of his own choice. Next, he bends forward and stands upright again before prostrating himself as a sign of adoration, his forehead to the ground. After this he remains kneeling, sitting back on his heels. He proclaims the singleness of God (*chahada*) before prostrating himself again, and then standing up.

Prayer at midday on Fridays brings all the men together at the mosque; it is preceded by a reading from the *Koran* and a sermon.

Legal alms, a contribution in kind or in monetary form towards the cost of good works.

Ramadan, corresponding with the ninth month of the lunar year. This was the date when the first *sura* of the *Koran* was revealed to Mahomet. For a month all adult Moslems – with the exception of the sick, pregnant women and people undertaking a long journey – are required to fast from dawn until sunset, to commemorate the event. They also abstain from drinking, smoking, and sexual activity. Life is resumed at nightfall, in an atmosphere of festival and family dinners.

The Pilgrimage to Mecca (*haj*) which every Moslem should undertake at least once in his life if he can afford it. By undertaking this pilgrimage, the believer ensures the remission of all his sins; it is the occasion of numerous prayers and rituals, of which the most spectacular consists of making seven circuits of the Kaaba on foot.

Dogma: similarities and differences

Christianity and Islam share many points of dogma: belief in the Resurrection, the Last Judgement, Hell and Paradise, and angels. On the other hand, Islam, which preaches a strict monotheism, does not recognise belief in the Trinity or in the incarnation and redemption. Jesus is not the Son of God but a human being, purely a prophet. Similarly, the Moslem paradise is largely concerned with material rewards, including "houris", women promised to the chosen. This is a joy which few Moslems interpet in symbolic terms. Nor does Islam include the dogma of original sin: man is good, and it is right that he seeks the goods of this world. Asceticism is not required and celibacy is disapproved of. Islam is a religion without priests, and although there are Imams who direct prayer, any believer can in theory undertake this function.

The Moslem religion also specifies a certain number of things which are **forbidden**. No consumption is permitted of alcohol, pork, blood or unbled meat (and thus of game). Games of chance and usury are also banned. In theory, lending at interest is forbidden.

Major dates in religious life

Civic life in Tunisia follows the Gregorian calendar but religious life is ruled by the Moslem calendar, which is calculated according to the twelve months of the lunar year. Each month begins with the new moon and consists of 29 or 30 days alternately; a lunar year consists of only 355 days and is thus twelve days ahead of the solar calendar. Year 1 of the **Hegira** began on 16 July 622 (*see above, page 54*).

Calendar of Muslim Festivals				
Year of the Hegira	1421	1422	1423	1424
Ras el Am	5 Apr 2000	25 Mar 2001	14 Mar 2002	3 Mar 2003
Achoura	15 Apr 2000	4 Apr 2001	24 Mar 2002	13 Mar 2003
Mouloud	14 June 2000	3 June 2001	23 May 2002	12 May 2003
Ramadan begins	27 Nov 2000	16 Nov 2001	5 Nov 2002	25 Oct 2003
Aïd es Seghir	27 Dec 2000	16 Dec 2001	5 Dec 2002	24 Nov 2003
Aïd el Kebir	5 Mar 2001	22 Feb 2002	11 Feb 2003	31 Jan 2004

As the calculation of the lunar calendar is quite complicated, these dates may vary by one or two days.

Main Festivals

Mouharem or **Ras el Am**: Islamic New Year.

Achoura: Day of mourning and meditation in cemeteries, in memory of the assassination of Hussein, grandson of the Prophet.

Mouloud: anniversary of the Prophet's birth.

Aïd es Seghir ("little festival"): celebration of the end of Ramadan. Children are dressed in new clothes. Alms-giving is one of the duties of the festival.

Aïd el Kebir ("great festival"): commemorating the sacrifice of Abraham, during which a sheep is sacrificed.

Sunnites, Shiites and Kharijites

99 % of Tunisians are Sunnites, but historically this has not always been so: in the 8C the Kharijite sect converted many members of the Berber tribes who captured Kairouan in 745. Orthodoxy did not return until around 800, when the Aghlabids came to power. Shiism was introduced into Tunisia on approximately similar conditions: here too it was the Berbers who embraced the new "heresy" and installed the Fatimid dynasty on the throne of *Ifriqiya*. Disinclined by nature to support the intransigence of Shiism, the people rejected the Fatimid rule in 1048 (*see page 20*).

The origin of these struggles lies in the question of the legitimacy of power. Who has authority over the Moslem community? According to the **Sunnites** ("those who follow tradition"), the Caliph should be a member of the Qoraychite tribe, Mahomet's tribe. For the **Shiites** only direct descendants from the Prophet, the issue of his daughter Fatima (hence the name of "Fatimids") and his son-in-law Ali, are worthy to take power. The **Kharijite** heresy, on the other hand, is based on an egalitarian claim: that it is for the most meritorious of the faithful, whatever his status or race, to preside over the fate of the community.

The Koran is the prism through which the Moslem interprets the world

A modernist Islam

The Tunisians' choice of a progressive and democratic form of Islam reflects their historical dislike of intolerance and fanaticism. The Fatimid dynasty's failure to impose Shiism in Tunisia was partly the result of its religious intransigence.

Bourguiba's attitude towards religion was therefore welcomed by Tunisians; he saw the decadence of Tunisia under the Beys as the consequence of certain Islamic traditions, and undertook the creation of a secular society despite the continuing acceptance of Islam as the official religion. Polygamy was forbidden, women could initiate divorce and have access to education (*see page 62*). The old theological university of Zitouna, which dispensed its knowledge in the shadow of the Great Mosque of Tunis, was closed in 1955, giving way to a modern style of campus.

When Ben Ali came to power, one of his first actions as President was to reopen Zitouna. This was a concession to traditionalists, but its teaching of theology and Islamic law is designed to promote the elements of Islam which favour universalism and tolerance. Among other concessions, the call to prayer is shown on television several times daily, in civic offices the hours of work have been adapted to allow the observance of fasting, and facilities are available for prayer, etc. On the other hand, the rights of women appear to have gained definitive confirmation and it would be very unpopular to question them.

The approach of the "*intégristes*", or strict traditionalists, is less radical than in other Arab countries. It makes gestures to both Islam and progressivism, to show for example that it is possible to wear the veil and still be a modern young woman. The argument is less than convincing, to judge by the skin-tight jeans and short skirts of the girls in Tunis or Sfax.

Judaism

The local traditions developed down the centuries by the Tunisian Jewish community are very similar to those of the Moslems. In Tunis, for example, the Jews venerate the Moslem *marabout* (holy man) Sidi Mahrez, who interceded with the authorities of his day to allow the first Jews to settle inside the city. Now that there are very few Jews in Tunisia, their presence in Jerba is all the more noticeable. The **Pilgrimage to El Ghriba** is one of the island's greatest festivals: according to legend, the synagogue was founded on a stone taken from the first temple of Jerusalem, 2 500 years ago (*see page 300*).

Specifically Tunisian Jewish Festivals

The **Jewish Easter** or **Pessah** took on a distinctive character in Tunisia and became the occasion for a *rapprochement* between the two communities, the Jews and the Moslems. On the first day of Easter the Jews gave their Moslem friends the traditional *matzos* (wafers of unleavened bread), and honey cakes. On the last day, it was the Moslems' turn to present them with baskets full of fish, bread, fruit and vegetables.

The **girls' festival** or **Rosh Hodesh el-Bnat** is celebrated around December. Young girls are honoured, and those who are engaged to be married receive their first piece of jewellery. The origins of the festival remain uncertain: it may commemorate the heroism of Judith, who saved her nation from Holofernes,

King Nebuchadnezzar's Persian general. According to another tradition, the festivities celebrate the memory of Queen Esther who pleaded with King Ahasuerus on behalf of her people. Whatever the original reason, it is an occasion for celebration and feasting.

The origins of the **boys' festival** or **Se'udat Itro** ("Jethro's banquet") are also unknown. The name evokes the meal presented by Jethro, father-in-law of Moses, after many sacrifices to God, but according to another theory it celebrates the sudden end of an epidemic which affected boys particularly severely. It is also, however, the day when little boys recite the Ten Commandments by heart for the first time. For this occasion, around February, miniature feasts are prepared for the smallest boys: a pigeon replaces the chicken, and the meal ends with pastries soaked in honey. Everything is served in dolls' dishes.

A Jew from El Ghriba, Jerba

P. Dannic/DIAF

DAILY LIFE

Housing

Housing is designed according to the "principle of closeness" required by Islamic law. This is expressed by enclosed spaces which are inward-facing and closed off from public view.

In the medina

The word "medina" designates the traditional Arab city. It is usually set inside ramparts, only accessible through gates (*bab*), which were normally closed at night with heavy doors. They were also closed on Fridays, for fear of surprise attacks during prayer hours. The walls enclose a maze of alleys and winding lanes which sometimes lead to dead ends. Around the **Great Mosque** which stands at the centre of the city are the great **souks** (bookshops, jewellers, perfumiers, weavers, etc.) and the *médersa* (Koranic schools). The souks are sometimes covered with barrel vaulting which adds to the "antheap" impression of these lanes teeming with activity. The trades which create greater pollution (blacksmiths, tanners, etc.) are relegated to the outer edges.

To avoid noise and other problems, **residential** and commercial districts are kept separate. Housing lies in quiet lanes with blind walls, for the Tunisian house, or **dar**, turns its back on the street. It has very few windows or none at all, and can be identified only by a substantial painted door beneath a lintel of carved stone. The only external sign of wealth, the doorway is more or less richly decorated according to the owner's social status. The *dar* is built in traditional style: a quadrilateral arrangement of cellular units round a central court, a plan which can be found in many different types of building: palace, *médersa* or *fonduk* (a building used as warehouse and accommodation for foreigners). The architect was often merely a builder or skilled craftsman who copied traditional style, and rather than architectural design it was the decorative arts (painted or carved wood, stucco, tiling) which took pride of place. Inside, the house opens on to the inner courtyard which is completely hidden from passers-by. Any rare window that opens on to the street is protected by *moucharaby*, wooden or wrought-iron grilles which allow the women to see without being seen. The ground floor has the general family rooms, kitchen and stores, with bedrooms on the first floor. The importance of the house is judged by the number of storeys or inner courts. The roof, often a terrace, is used for drying linen and pimentoes in summer.

In colonial times the medinas were affected by a process of social downgrading which still continues despite the proliferation of **Preservation Associations**. Leading members of society and the middle classes left their centuries-old palaces and their grand houses to settle in the European town built at the gates of the medina (as in Tunis, Sousse and Sfax). Living in the European area conferred a certain prestige, while the medina was considered shabby and outdated. The old town was then taken over by impoverished rural newcomers who divided up the houses and former palaces with flimsy partitions. There were few who could afford to renovate the houses, or even keep them in good condition.

The European city

The city of the colonial era was originally laid out by engineers rather than town-planners or architects – which explains the grid design and the great traffic arteries which cross each other at right-angles. In contrast to the medina, the European city turns outwards: façades are monumental in character, designed to be seen from the street. The architectural style is often eclectic: Beaux-Arts, Art Nouveau, Art Deco, neo-Moorish. Following independence, fomer French apartments were taken over by Tunisians from the lower social classes. Today the westernised upper middle classes live in the smart suburbs (Carthage, La Marsa, etc.) where they have built villas fitted with satellite dishes and all modern comforts. The influx of an immigrant population of rural origin has also had a "shantification" effect on the outskirts of some of the large cities.

In the countryside

In the **north**, the poorest people still live in the traditional **gourbi**, or shack, a structure half-way between a conventional house and a tent, built of branches and covered with thatch. Some more elaborate gourbis consist of stones or clay covered with daub or constructed with bricks of earth and straw baked in an oven or dried in the sun. Both Gourbis and modern houses are dotted about in the middle of gardens and fruit-trees, preferably close to a spring.

In the **south**, fortified villages are visible from far away, perched on the heights and difficult to reach. These are the **ksour** (plural of *ksar*), built in earlier times by the Berbers to protect themselves against Arab raids. Each *ksar* has a **ghorfa** above, an attic for grain which may be decorated with geometric wall paintings or hand prints on the clay. These ghorfa could be compared to the cells of a beehive: each cell corresponds to a room with its own doorway opening. When no longer required for grain they provided housing space until they were gradually abandoned during the French Protectorate. Unfortunately, many of them were demolished in the modernising enthusiasm of the young Tunisian Republic in the late 1950s – nearly 30 *ksour* and 6 000 *ghorfa* were probably destroyed at this time, in the region of Medenine.

The area round Matmata has **troglodyte** houses, cave dwellings: set round a central light-well which replaces the traditional courtyard, several storeys of niches are used for living space or for storage. Some courtyards are as much as 10m beneath ground level, interconnected by tunnels. The southern mountain area also has a different type of cave dwelling, hollowed out into cliff faces, with the house subsequently closed off with a simple brick wall, creating a courtyard for the domestic animals. The peasants of these regions boast of the "natural air-conditioning" of this type of housing – although this does not stop the younger generation from leaving the villages for urban areas which may not be smart but which are certainly more modern.

The individual and the family

The family structure becomes tighter

Family names were made obligatory under a decree of the Bey in 1908 which was designed to create a civic state. The absence of a family name had been based on the importance of belonging to a clan, the primacy of the tribe over the individual. The extended family came under the undivided authority of a patriarch (the *sheik*), in which polygamy was standard practice (up to four wives), and a husband could repudiate a wife through a simple public declaration. Judging that this was inhibiting modernisation of the country (and no doubt its control by the State), Bourguiba wanted to see the family structure develop along the western lines of the nuclear unit focused around parents and children. Immediately after independence he therefore introduced monogamy, and civil divorce was legalised. Equality between husband and wife was also strengthened in 1993, and from that date the inheritance of Tunisian nationality could be derived through the mother as well as through the father. The father's authority, hitherto all-powerful, now became shared with his wife who increasingly often undertook paid work. The family was also tending to become more tightly focused under the pressures of the rural exodus and the high cost of rents in urban areas. The time when a whole family from grandparents to grandchildren, and not excluding nephews and nieces, would live under the same roof (or the same tent) seems to have gone for ever.

Women's emancipation

Women's emancipation is more than a simple theme for electoral speeches: it has been part of daily life for several decades, overturning centuries of restriction and prohibition; yet Tunisian women have long been ahead of their times and it was not surprising to see the Bey's wives riding their bicycles at the beginning of the 20C.

Since 1956 and President Bourguiba's promulgation of the **Code of Personal Status** (CSP), Tunisian women have been among the most emancipated of the Arab world. The time is long gone when they lived in cloistered conditions at home, watching the world through the narrow openings of their *moucharaby*. Often wearing European dress, Tunisian women are active in all trades and professions – they have even penetrated the army and the police, where they are particularly numerous. Their elegant uniforms are to be seen at every street corner.

In a bold move, the Code of Personal Status tackled the *sharia* code of Islamic law and abolished polygamy, set the minimum age for marriage at 17 for girls, and gave guardianship of children to the mother in the case of the father's death. In 1957 women won the right to vote, and ten years later abortion was legalised – an area in which President Ben Ali has followed the policy of his predecessor. The national pact signed in 1988 gave added strength to women's civil rights. 1992 brought new amendments in the same spirit: wives could now expect to be granted management of the household and of children's affairs in the case of divorce. These important regulations still include shadowy areas, particularly where inheritance is concerned: if her husband dies, a wife has a right to only one-eighth of his estate, the same as his mother.

Important moments in personal life

Circumcision

Already practised by the ancient Egyptians, the removal of the prepuce is still undertaken by Copts, Jews and Moslems. More tradition than Koranic prescription, this is the great event of the child's life; it used to mark his passage into adult life, but is now undertaken at an increasingly young age, sometimes in the very first months of life. The operation is now performed by doctors, who have taken over what used to be the role of the village barber. For the occasion the infant is dressed in traditional costume, and it is a time for great family rejoicing.

Marriage

Once, marriage was arranged by the parents without any consultation with the young couple, but the young woman's consent is now required by law. Maghreb marriage traditionally consisted of a series of rites which in some cases probably dated back to classical times: rites of protection, of passage (from the state of young girl to womanhood), of purification, etc. Purification is undertaken in the hammam, or Turkish bath, and lasts two days. The future bride is accompanied by her relatives and friends, with joyful and strident, ululating cries. On the first day she washes herself clean, since an unclean body denotes an unclean soul. After cleansing her skin with energetic friction rubs, all her body hair is removed – before marriage, tradition forbids epilation above the knee. On the second day the bride is marked with henna on her hands and feet, and her hair is coloured: cosmetics are considered to be protective but above all erotic. The young girl is also symbolically liberated by her parents or neighbours from the "lock" which has hitherto protected her virginity. On the wedding night, two friends of the bridegroom are posted outside the wedding chamber. It is their task to receive the night-dress marked with blood, proof of defloration, and to present it to the assembled guests.

J.-P. Garcin/DIAF

A young bride in traditional costume

Marriage is still often accompanied by traditional feasting, particularly in the south, but it now tends to be more westernised like the rest of society, with a procession of vehicles, blaring car horns and European dress. The age for marriage has also changed noticeably: in 1956 brides were generally around 19, while in 1984 the average age was 24. As a result of unemployment and practical difficulties, young men are marrying later and later, and tend to remain in their parents' house until they find work.

Mourning and death

When there is a death the body is buried as soon as possible, after a night when it remains with the family long enough to be washed and perfumed after the final ablutions. The family must not cook before the burial. Three days after the death the family invites those who have not been able to attend the funeral to a day of prayer. They then prepare a meal (the first *fark*), part of which is served to the poor. On the seventh day they prepare a second *fark*, with a final day of prayer on the fortieth day after the death.

The *Achoura (see page 56)*, the commemoration of the dead, is less a day of sadness than an occasion to honour the life of a person before their God. The cemeteries are not devoid of life, as in the west; people meet there and gossip round the tomb of the loved one, and sometimes children even go there to play.

Education

Together with women's emancipation, education is Bourguiba's greatest achievement. Tunisia has emphasised this sector since independence, and has devoted a quarter of its national budget to it. In an initial development under the Protectorate, traditional Koranic teaching (juridical and theological) was replaced by secondary and further education on French lines. Teaching in French gave young Tunisians access to a vast field of European culture, particularly in scientific and technological areas, but this education was restricted to a select few: in 1956 only 10-15% of the population knew how to read and write, compared with 66% today. In 1966 fewer than 10% of the working population had received secondary or higher education, against 25% in 1984. School attendance has been obligatory up to the age of 16 since 1992; before then, education for girls frequently lasted only a few years, particularly in the rural areas where girls were engaged on domestic and farming work from a very young age. At the present time, virtually as many girls as boys attend school, and the classes are mixed. Bilingualism (French/Arabic) is normal everywhere.

With few raw materials, Tunisia concentrates on its intellectual resources. 130 000 students are currently engaged in further education, and numbers are expected to double during the next decade; in particular, the number of science and technology students will expand. Unfortunately the job market is not keeping pace, and it seems likely that these educated but embittered unemployed may turn to fundamentalism in order to find a solution to their problems.

Social life and customs

Chicha

The *chicha* is a type of *hookah*. A pipe filled with *tombac* (a sort of tobacco) is attached to a long tube which passes through a flask of flavoured water. It can be smoked alone but it is more often a social pastime, and in cafés it is not uncommon to see the *chicha* being passed from one mouth to another.

The souks

The souks are still a setting for social life and talk, even though they are now heavily angled towards tourism. It is in the souk that young girls gather to gaze at rings and pendants in jewellers' displays, and where mothers buy the traditional clothes for the circumcision of their latest baby. Every souk has one or more cafés, where craftsmen and tourists can meet – but it is no good getting up too late, for everything in the souk happens in the morning.

Cafés

If there is any single feature which reflects the essence of Tunisian life, it is the open-air cafés which take advantage of the shade provided by an angle in the wall, an overhead canopy, or a clump of trees. Always full no matter what the

J.-F. Galmiche

A Tunisian café

hour, this is where the men meet to sip a glass of mint tea, smoke the *chicha*, or play cards or dominoes. There are never any alcoholic drinks in Tunisian cafés. Nor any women.

The hammam

A session in the hammam is a good way of getting to know Tunisia. Despite the great increase in private bathrooms, the hammam is still a sociable place where you can meet friends while attending to your physical well-being.

The same hammam is used for both men and women, but at different times: men in the morning, women in the afternoon. Tunisians go there with a full bag, suitcase or sports bag with several thick towels, a cotton wrap to cover the body from waist to knees (*fouta*), a pair of plastic sandals, a friction glove (*kessa*) or one of those acid green or pink synthetic gloves on sale in the souks, and of course soap, shampoo, brushes and comb. The prudent Tunisians complete this equipment with long-handled cups to pour water over themselves; the only alternatives available are large plastic buckets or empty jam pots.

You step straight into the great central hall (*mahress*), with its decorated ceiling and windows in its dome. The water-spouts of the fountain at the centre are almost always turned off. The room is lined with stone benches covered with mats (*doukanas*) and large numbers of lockers overhead, complete with padlocks, for the visitors' clothes. The *beya*, or manageress of the hammam, directs an army of *harzas*, staff who will help you through the various phases of your stewing in return for payment.

Wrapped in your *fouta* and wearing the hammam's wooden clogs (if you have forgotten to bring your own sandals), you finally enter the hammam itself. It consists of a series of halls with progressively greater temperatures until you reach the hottest room, its temperature maintained by a great basin of almost boiling water which gives off clouds of steam. After a good sweat, you rub yourself vigorously with the *kessa* to slough off dead skin, then rinse yourself before going back into a cooler room to wash your body and hair. Wealthier patrons pay a few extra dinars for a massage with *tfal*, a kind of scented clay. Once thoroughly cleansed, you return to the *mahress* to rest for a while before getting dressed again. You go out into the heat outdoors with the sensation of being clean for the first time in your life.

Jasmine

Jasmine, Tunisia's symbolic flower, is everywhere. Since its first introduction by the Andalusians in the 16C it has been an integral part of Tunisian culture: as soon as night falls, traders set up their stands in the streets and begin to make up little bunches to fill the evening with perfume. Some street hawkers try to pass off orange-flower buds as jasmine – but the perfume is much less subtle. The scent varies with the region. In Tunis and the resort towns around it, some thirty flowers are gathered on a stem and bound with a coloured thread, which should be undone so that the bunch can breathe out its full fragrance. In the Sousse and Monastir regions the bunches are enormous, and are made up in complex designs where jasmine is often mixed with orange flowers. In El Jem it is presented on a single stem with flowers set along its entire length.

Jasmine is a language which requires its own interpretation: the man who wears it on his left ear is hoping to share his heart, while the woman who accepts a necklace of these little flowers has already said "yes".

Finery and clothing

Festivals are the time for traditional costumes to be brought out, made of the finest woollen thread, embroidery, gold and silver thread. This richness can still be seen in rural regions or during displays of traditional folklore, but it is disappearing from the towns where sober European clothing has infiltrated all ceremonies.

Men's clothes

Villagers and country folk now consider the *jebba* as something to wear on ceremonial occasions. White in summer, grey in winter, this is a sleeveless tunic which men wear over a shirt with a waistcoat and baggy trousers, the *serwal*. The

jebba is soberly embroidered, always with silk thread. For everyday wear the men make do with plain trousers and shirts, over which they sometimes put on a *kadroun*, a woollen tunic cut narrower than the *jebba* and with long sleeves. In winter they wear a woollen *burnous*, except in the north where they prefer the *kachabiya*, a brown and white striped woollen coat with a hood.

Three men of fashion in earlier times

In towns, ceremonial wear consists of a linen shirt with a stand-up collar and long sleeves. The cloth *serwal* is decorated at the ankles and on the pockets with a little discreet braid or embroidery. A broad belt of the same fabric retains the folds and holds the *serwal* at the waist. A silk and woollen *jebba* completes the outfit, with an elegant braided *burnous* added in winter. Shoes, bright yellow slippers, leave the heels uncovered. The fashionable hairstyle is with a red *chechia* decorated with a tassel of black thread.

When the modern urban resident wants to feel relaxed and comfortable in his leisure time, he may simply put on a *jebba*.

Women's clothes

In the east as in the west, women's clothes are much more varied than those of the men. **In towns**, most of the young women have adopted European styles, but older women, even in the towns, always wear a *sefsari*, the white veil of silk or fine wool which covers the head and which they wear over a blouse and baggy trousers – this is what gives the Tunisian woman her unforgettably graceful walk. Their silhouettes with their *sefsari* floating out in the breeze form part of the classic image of Tunisia, like the blue and white houses of Sidi Bou Saïd. Women even risk riding on the back of motor scooters, *sefsari* clenched between the teeth.

In the country, women and even some girls still continue to wear brightly coloured dresses. This is where you will meet the Berber or Bedouin woman dressed in her *melhafa*, a length of blue or red cotton fabric which is typical of her region or village. The fabric is open down the sides, held at the waist with a belt and at the shoulders with two pins. The women often wear large jewels, roughly cut and shaped.

Costumes for festivals and ceremonies vary somewhat from one region to another. In the towns and villages of the Sahel, the supreme item of clothing for celebrations consists of a **draped dress** of wool or cotton. This is worn over a bodice embroidered with silk and silver, a velvet waistcoat decorated with gold, lace trousers, and a silk belt. The clothes of the Madhia women are the most striking. Until the mid-19C, the young brides of Tunisian aristocrats wore **caftans**. Made of velvet, brocade or silk, they were richly embroidered with gold and decorated with fine jewels. In modern times the traditional brides in Hammamet and Sousse still wear an elegant caftan with three-quarter length sleeves, open in front, varying in length from knee to mid-calf.

The richness and distinction of the clothes lie less in the cut or the fabric than in the woven designs or **embroidery** which sometimes cover it completely. This embroidery uses gold and silver thread, or a contrasting design of red, blue and black thread. The most unexpected are the Raf Raf costumes, made with silver thread on waistcoats and trousers of violet silk.

Wearing the veil is not very widespread in Tunisia. In its day, this modest square of cloth brought down Bourguiba's tirades. "I beg you, take away this heavy burden. It is not worn any more. Women's faces have greater need of contact with the fresh air. You have no more aggression to fear. The State sees to that." In fact the State forbids the veil in schools and offices. The same applies to the Islamic scarf, or *hijeb*.

Jewellery

For a woman, her jewels are her bank account. Traditionally, the bridegroom presents his bride with jewels as a dowry to be kept by her if they separate. Even now it is not unusual to see a peasant women with heavy necklaces of gold or silver round her neck. This finery was more an expression of belonging to a community than the social standing of the individual who wore it, and the number of items was fixed by ancestral custom. Exterior signs of wealth used to lie in tiny variations which were only visible to the tutored eye: the size and weight of the stones, their greater or lesser quality or their setting, etc.

Not all the jewels are sold already mounted. The women often buy the separate elements which they then assemble as necklaces, headdresses or sets for the brow or the chest. For this they use needle and thread, where a jeweller uses links and rings. There are few variations in these basic items: rings, chains, copies of coins, fish, Hands of Fatima, pierced rose patterns, coral and glass beads.

The hand and the fish

The Hand of Fatima (khomsa) and the fish (houta) are the two symbols most frequently seen in Tunisian culture. Their origins probably date back to the most distant classical times, and their chief virtue is to provide protection against the evil eye. The fish is often shown in stylised fashion on plates, chests and wooden shelving; it can be seen in the form of a geometric design in the patterns on rugs and blankets, sometimes reduced to a simple spine embroidered with gold or silver thread on a rich silk costume or hanging. The khomsa is always seen in the form of an open hand; it is used above all in jewellery and in house decoration, particularly on the façade or beside the entrance door.

The *rihana* is a silver necklace made of flattened rings. The *khelala* or brooch, is an enormous dress-pin decorated with the signs of Tanit (pierced triangle or crescent). The *dibleg* is jewellery for the temples, fixed onto the hair: it forms a triangle with little *rihana* chains hanging from it, ending in small Hands of Fatima. *Menaguech* are triangular or semi-circular earrings. The *Khomsa*, worn as a pendant, represents the hand of Baal which was used as an amulet by the Carthaginians; the Islamic version is the Hand of Fatima which protects mothers and their children. The *hedeyed* are broad bracelets, generally made of carved silver. The *khokhal* is a ring for the foot, delicately carved with designs of flowers, fish and hands of Fatima; a pair may weigh up to a kilogramme. In the days of Carthage these foot rings were a symbol of chastity.

Perfumes

For Tunisians, perfume is more than a simple item of toilette, it is evidence of good taste and civilisation. People use perfume for all occasions, particularly on the evening before Friday, prayer days, and for religious or family festivals. Guests are perfumed at the end of the meal or a marriage contract, and bodies are perfumed at the end of the final washing after a death.

G. Degeorge

For women,
jewellery is as good as a bank account

CULTURE

Music

Births, marriages or religious ceremonies – music is always part of the occasion. In Tunisia it is the result of a musical blending that has developed down the centuries. The *malouf* is music of Andalusian origin, its piercing charm a vivid interpretation of the sweetness of life for a whole nation. Traditional songs are also part of the image of this cultural mix. Introduced by the Turks in the Ottoman period, the *chgoul* is an integral part of these songs which set the rhythm for family ceremonies, while *rbouks* accompany the workers' feast-days. In terms of instruments, town and country each have their own style. In urban settings, they are stringed instruments (violin, lute or zither), and percussion (*tabla* or *darbouka*). While Bedouin songs are usually accompanied by wind instruments such as the bagpipe, the *fhal* (a kind of metal flute) or the *gasba* (a reed flute).

Musicians at Nefta

G. Degeorge

Tunisian performers do not attract great crowds. Only **Saliha**, in the 1930s, won a public with a remarkable voice which can still be heard regularly on Tunisian radio programmes. Apart from Saliha, the most famous Tunisian musicians and singers include Khemais Tarnane, Raoul Journou, Ali Riahi, Hedi Jouini, Hammadi ben Othman and **Lofti Bouchnak**. Other musicians represent the renewal of Tunisian music today, including **Fawzi Chekili** and **Anouar Brahem**. The latter, who is known as the "prince of the *wadi*" has played with the saxophonist Jan Gabarek and the French accordeonist Richard Galliano.

Literature

Tunisia in Literature

In the wake of the French Protectorate, it is hardly surprising that European literature is more likely to be in French than any other language, and indeed Tunisia has been a particular source of inspiration for French writers. **Flaubert** heads the list with his novel *Salammbô*, which he based on historical fact: the Carthaginian campaign against its own merchants at the end of the First Punic War. Flaubert spent a month in the "land of dates" and based his characters on what he perceived of African psychology. Other French writers who used this

Culture

exotic extension of their own land as a literary setting include **Chateaubriand** (*Itinéraire de Paris à Jérusalem*), while **Guy de Maupassant** transposed actual events from Tunisia to Morocco for *Bel Ami*. **André Gide** travelled in North Africa in 1893, at a time of profound psychological distress; the initiation of the senses he experienced there is evoked in *Les Nourritures terrestres*. **Henry de Montherlant** and Georges Duhamel also set novels in Tunisia.

Long before these writers, classical authors brought Tunisia into their writing, the most famous being Virgil, in *The Aeneid*: Books I and IV tell the tragic story of Dido, Queen of Carthage, and her love for Aeneas. In the early 20C Aldous Huxley and Norman Douglas wrote colourful and idiosyncratic descriptions, and more recently Paul Theroux has described his travels in Tunisia; and works on Islam and Moslem society by Edward Said, Ernest Gellner and Edward Mortimer help to set the scene for the modern visitor. English novels set in Tunisia are rare – two names to look out for are Patricia Highsmith and Paul Bowles.

Tunisian writers

Ibn Khaldoun, born in Tunis in 1332, is one of the greatest thinkers of the Arabic language. Historian and philosopher, he is also seen as a forerunner of sociology, best known to Europeans for his book *The Muqaddimah* (published in English in 1978). His name is commemorated in La Khaldounia, a school founded in 1896 which teaches modern sciences.

French-speakers can read 20C Tunisian poetry such as *Chants de la nuit* by **Abou Kacem Chabbi**, from Tozeur, who died in 1934 at the age of 25, or the work of **Tahar Bekri**, the most famous name in Tunisian poetry: born in 1951, he has lived in Paris since 1976. He writes in French and Arabic, and several of his collections of poetry have been published in France (see *page 113*). He is also a well-known literary critic and essayist. A good introduction to Tunisian literature can be found in his *Littératures de Tunisie et du Maghreb*.

Among Tunisian novelists writing in French, **Albert Memmi** (*La Statue de Sel*, with a foreword by Albert Camus) and **Nine Moatti** (*Les Belles de Tunis*) are the most typical. Memmi, a Tunisian Jew who has taken French citizenship, examines the mechanisms of racism and the relationships of domination in all his work. Two of his books, *Colonizer and the Colonized* and *The Pillar of Salt*, were published in English in the early 1990s. Two other Tunisian novels published in English at the same period are Mustapha Tlili's *Lion Mountain* and Gisèle Halimi's *Milk for the Orange Tree*, about children in Tunisia. Publication of new Tunisian talents in French is currently being planned: Ali Abassi, Ali Bécheur, Emna Belhadj. Like many writers of the Maghreb, they evoke the fracturing and dismembering of the self, representing the split between tradition and modernity. Another modern writer, Hélé Béji, takes the "deception" of cultural blending as his target.

Painting

Tunisia in western art

Alexandre Roubtzoff, a Russian aristocrat who became the most important painter of Tunisia, was 30 years old when he reached Tunis in 1914, the recipient of a substantial bursary from the Imperial Fine Arts Academy of Saint Petersburg. Personal preference led Roubtzoff to settle permanently in Tunisia even before the Great War and the October Revolution forced him to remain there. Like so many other artists, he was fascinated by the quality of the light in this land where he was to remain until his death in 1949: Tunisia in all its variety was the sole source of inspiration for more than 3 000 pictures. It is a body of work that defies neat classification – in turn orientalist, academic and neo-Impressionist – but whatever the school of his inspiration, his work endures as irreplaceable evidence of a Tunisia which has almost completely disappeared.

Paul Klee (1879-1940) and **August Macke** (1887-1914) came to Tunisia in 1914 on a visit which marked a turning-point in their art. Their experience of Tunisia helped them develop their ideas on light and colour which had already been influenced by Cézanne, Cubism and their meeting with Robert Delaunay in 1912; Klee translated Delaunay's book *L'Essai sur la lumière*. While in Tunisia, August Macke executed a series of Cubist-style watercolours, experimenting with intersecting planes and a very rich chromatic range. The same revelation of colour and light also affected Klee, but in his case the change was even more radical: the artist went so far as to write in his diary, "Colour and I are one. I am a painter".

This encounter with the east was far removed from the surface exoticism of the orientalists, and found its meaning in the very sources of artistic creation.

Tunisian painters

The **Tunis School** was created in 1949, on the initiative of a group of French and Tunisian painters: Pierre Boucherle, Abdelaziz Gorgi, Hedi Turki, Zoubeir Turki, Jellal ben Abdallah and Mosès Lévy. Rejecting colonial folklore and orientalism, the Tunis School launched itself in search of a genuinely "Tunisian" school of painting. Some of its members felt that it was to be found by returning to the sources of Arab-Islamic aesthetics: miniatures, tracery, Islamic architecture, etc.

The following artists are among the best known of the group:

Abdelaziz Gorgi, born in Tunis in 1928 and a student at the Tunis School of Fine Arts. Co-founder of the Tunis School, he has led the group since 1968. Today he also expresses his art in tapestry and ceramics.

Ammar Farhat (1911-1988), an illiterate artist who was a baker and occasionally a boxer. He painted scenes of everyday life (ceremonies, mourning, feasts) in a bright and simple style. Before the Second World War, he exhibited at the Tunis Salon and won the Young Artist prize.

Mosès Lévy, born in Tunis in 1885, lived in cosmopolitan and prosperous circles; his mother was Italian and his father British, a business man and adviser to the Beys of Tunis. Lévy studied painting in Italy, at Lucca and at the Florence Academy of Fine Arts. He exhibited at the first Venice Biennale in 1923 and went on to a brilliant international career, his art forming a bridge between the northern and southern shores of the Mediterranean. Mosès Lévy died in 1968 in Italy, where he had spent much of his life.

Cinema

Tunisian productions remain rare and little-known, although some have had considerable success with critics outside Tunisia. Among the best known and the most recent films, it is worth noting *Un été à la Goulette* (1996), by Farid Boughedir. In flash-back this comedy presents the little community of La

Goulette, a working-class Tunis suburb, in a vanished period when Moslems, Jews and Christians lived side by side in tolerance and good humour. *Halfaouine, l'enfant des terrasses* (1990), also by Boughedir, was undoubtedly the Tunisian film industry's greatest success, showing a child in Tunis in the 1960s with great sensitivity. Nouri Bouzid brings a clear unsentimental eye to Tunisian reality: in *L'Homme de cendres* (1986) he dealt with prostitution and relationships between the Moslem and Jewish communities, while in *Bezness* (1991) he focused on sexual tourism. *Les Silences du palais*, by Moufida Tlatli (1994), won several prizes at international film contests. The first Arab film directed by a woman, it shows life in an aristocratic Tunis house through the eyes of a young girl.

For several years, Tunisia has strived to become a minor Mediterranean Hollywood. The producer, Tarak Ben Amar, Bourguiba's nephew, has persuaded the greatest directors to use his Monastir studios. Polanski filmed *The Pirates* there, and Zeffirelli his *Jesus of Nazareth*; and George Lucas was entranced by the natural settings and cave dwellings of the Tunisian deep south, where some scenes of *Star Wars* were filmed. Part of the success of *The English Patient* can perhaps be attributed to the spectacular desert scenery filmed in southern Tunisia.

The Press and the Media

The Press

Tunisia has a wide range of newspapers and periodicals in French. Reading the daily papers is a good way of getting to grips with life in Tunisia, regardless of the journal's ideology. There are three national dailies: *La Presse* (state-owned), *Le Renouveau* (the organ of the ruling party, the Rassemblement Constitutionnel Démocratique) and *Le Temps* (an independent and liberal-minded newspaper). *La Presse* contains a large amount of practical information: train and air time-tables, useful telephone numbers, the weather forecast, etc. Of the weekly papers, the main ones are *L'Observateur* and *Réalités*. Sports fans can rely on *Le Sport*, a source which always supplies a good talking point.

The principle daily newspapers of most European countries are also available, a day late, in the larger towns. Some foreign daily newspapers are sometimes absent from the news-stands when they are unfortunate enough to displease the government of the day.

Television

Many hotels have satellite TV with a number of European and American channels; Egyptian soap operas are popular on national TV and give an interesting portrayal of life in an Arab country.

LANGUAGES

Arabic as a universal language?

As the language of the tribes in the north of the Arabian peninsula and the adjacent areas of Syria and Iraq, Arabic became a language of religion as a result of the *Koran*. Following the conquests of the 7C it achieved the status of universal language in an area stretching from Morocco to Central Asia. Membership of this vast empire is defined linguistically: an Arab is someone who speaks Arabic. From its earliest days Arabic evolved in terms of its vocabulary as much as in its meaning and grammar. Like all languages it retreated in the face of other and more dominant cultures, and developed through borrowings: from Hebrew and Greek, Persian in the 9C, Turkish – which remained the language of the rulers until the First World War – French until the 1960s, English for the last thirty years. Depending on the region, from one town or village to another, Arabic also takes on different dialect forms. Today, an Algerian would have the greatest difficulty in making himself understood by a Syrian: yet there is a generally widespread fiction, in Arab lands and elsewhere, that an authentic Arab language exists which is independent of historical development and its various dialect forms of expression. This unchanging and sacred language is that of the *Koran* which, in this perception of the language, has the privilege of being understood by the whole of the Moslem community. In reality, however, national forms of the language are very far removed from the Arabic of the *Koran*: this classical Arabic can only really be read by those who have undertaken specialised Koranic studies; nevertheless it remains the language of preaching and religious ceremonies.

Contemporary speech, on the other hand, tends towards uniformity, towards a **standard** Arabic which is becoming accepted through publishing and the media and gradually blurring national and regional differences. Arabic as spoken in Egypt is the most widely recognised form of the language, a result of the very large audience for Egyptian music, television and film.

Writing – Arabic is written from right to left and from top to bottom. For this reason books, exercise books and magazines are bound on the right and the first page is the equivalent of our last page *(see also under "Calligraphy", page 40).*

Franco-Arabic bilingualism

The majority of Tunisians speak very good French. After a short break when President Ben Ali came to power, French became compulsory once again in schools, a principle established by Habib Bourguiba at the time of Tunisian independence. This bilingual approach, which begins in the primary schools, continues throughout the education system.

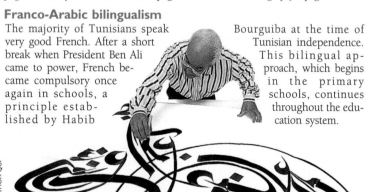

Calligraphy is an abstract art

CRAFTS

Tunisian craftsmanship derives its richness from contact with the different cultures which have succeeded each other across its territory. The Berber foundation has been overlaid with successive influences – Punic, Roman, Arabic and above all Andalusian. In contrast with western civilisation, Islamic culture recognises no difference between art and craft, fine arts and the minor arts. Creativity is expressed in the production of objects which are essentially functional, even if in many cases the decorative element has become more important than the utilitarian. The development of crafts has been helped by the establishment, shortly after independence, of a National Craft Office. Today, craft skills no longer pass from father to son: production is based on the workshop or studio. Standardised production restricts individual creativity, but has achieved higher standards of quality.

Metals

In classical times, metal working consisted only of cast bronze. The oriental nations – Chinese, Persians and Ottomans – were the first to use leaves of copper beaten by hand to create tools and containers. Tunisian craftsmen have inherited something from all these techniques.

Techniques of **beaten metal ware** were used to produce numerous objects in solid bronze: mortars and pestles, door-handles, candelabra, scabbards, and crescents for the top of minarets.

Coppersmiths supplied **cauldrons** for heating bath-water and basins for hand-washing or preparing couscous, as well as the utensils that were essential items in a young girl's trousseau. Although couscous pots and stew-pots are never decorated, cake-dishes, coffee services, bowls and ewers frequently bear finely carved decoration; cypress trees, circular rose patterns, and delicately outlined curves which recall the Turkish origins of Tunisian copperware.

These crafts continue to be practised today, though most of their products are destined for the tourist market *(see page 109)*.

Cabinet-making and woodworking

In town...

The traditional house has little in the way of furniture, armchairs, upright chairs, tables or other bulky furniture, and the family takes its meals sitting at floor level. The only piece of furniture is very often the trunk which was used for the bride's trousseau, and which now contains clothing. Other storage consists of shelving for books, weapons and kitchen equipment. Chests and sets of shelves were very often decorated with motifs showing baskets of fruit, bowls of flowers, fish, or hands of Fatima. These traditions remained very vigorous in the city of Sfax until very recently.

The houses of important people were embellished with painted and carved ceilings, sometimes gilded, with geometrical and floral motifs. The doors were also decorated.

Nineteenth century Tunisia, and particularly Tunis itself, was powerfully affected by Italian influences. Houses were adorned with gilding and filled with furniture, disturbing the harmony of earlier styles of decoration which consisted of a blend of panelling, hangings and rugs. Widespread contemporary enthusiasm for western patterns of living means that the most prosperous Tunisian houses tend to be crowded with furniture. Cabinet-makers have responded, and offer furniture of European inspiration, but adapted to eastern taste, in a somewhat heavy style.

Lace-like clay decoration in the furniture of a cave-dwelling

...and in the country

In the Tabarka and Aïn Draham regions of the north, oil measures, bowls and basins are made of olive wood. In the south, palm-wood is the basic material, used to make, amongst other things, the doors of traditional houses. In cave dwellings the furniture is built into the structure, and is designed in a truly lace-like style. It falls to the women to assemble the branches of olive-wood or palm-wood used to construct the wooden trellis which supports the bed or storage fixtures. Once attached to the ground and walls, the wooden structure is covered with a mixture of clay and husks which is then whitened with gypsum plaster.

Textiles

The women who weave the textiles, for use as hangings or as rugs, are often illiterate (at least the older among them), and textile weaving offers them a form of expression. They allow themselves great freedom and give full rein to their creativity. As a visible sign of wealth, textiles and rugs are an essential element of the future bride's trousseau, although in Oudref it is the bridegroom's task to supply the household linen. For their sons' weddings the mothers create a *hanbal*, a large blanket of dark colours, deep blue or claret red, enlivened with geometric motifs in light colours. These rugs are not available for purchase or order from a craftsman – each one forms the central item in the household inheritance, destined to remain in the family.

These very long pieces of fabric are used for multiple purposes. Folded, they can be used as a mattress, and for festivals they are hung on the walls of the houses. Washed and dried at the end of the cold season, they decorate the plaster bed-heads of traditional houses in remote villages.

Leather

Today, *Malaab* or *"fantasias"* – elaborate sets of saddlery – are the last examples of the great art of the Tunisian **saddlers** who until quite recently occupied an important place in the souks. Embroidered with silk and gold and silver thread, the saddle was a source of pride for every horseman, a worthy accessory to his Arab steed. It came complete with head-collar, bridle, girth and highly-wrought spurs. Nowadays most of the master saddlers have turned to making goods for the tourist trade *(see page 109)*.

Shoemaking owes much to the Carthaginian influence, which produced the famous *"cothurnes"*, shoes with elevated soles. These were followed by *babouches* or Turkish slippers, the most popular shoes in Tunisia. Today the babouche-makers are adapting to modern demands, and Sfax has become the great city of both hand-made and mass-produced shoes.

Dressed Stone and Stucco

Recent years have brought a considerable revival in craftsmanship in stone, and the dynamism of Dar Châabanne on Cap Bon has made it a masons' Mecca. This is a surprising new trend, for it is a form of expertise that virtually disappeared when the Tunisians developed a passion for modern apartment-style life and abandoned the medinas. Traditonally, even the most modest of owners was determined to decorate his house with a door-frame carved out of the softest limestone, or in a pale pink hard sandstone. The craftsmen carved inscriptions on the lintels to invoke God's blessing, as well as geometrical and floral motifs, a hand set inside a frame of fish, or the star and crescent of the national flag. The wealthiest proprietors also embellished their establishment with tiles and columns in stone or marble.

After a gap of several decades, a style of building is developing which is supposed to be "traditional" but which is closer to pastiche, with "Arab-style" arches and columns, door- and window-frames. It can be seen on public buildings as well as private houses. This kind of kitsch reaches its fullest development in prosperous villa quarters, where masons have given themselves a free rein, with barley-sugar columns and bloated curves of classical inspiration.

Decoration inside the houses is of plaster, with geometric designs chiselled directly on to the wall.

Rush Matting

In a land where the traditional furniture is so simple, rush matting has acquired a particular significance. In winter, the mats were used to keep rugs away from direct contact with the ground, while cushions provided protection from contact with damp walls. In summer, rush matting provided a cooler surface than wool, and was more hygienic than the ground itself. Rush matting has developed in several regions. In the rural areas it is the women who weave the esparto grass on a vertical loom, while in the towns men work with reeds on horizontal looms set a few centimetres off the ground. The most elaborate mats are made in Nabeul. Their decoration, inspired by textile hangings, uses reeds dyed blue, red, brown or green *(see page 109)*.

(see page 109)

Painting on glass, a popular art

Painting on glass

Painting on glass is one of the few items of popular craftsmanship where the function is purely decorative. Known in Europe from the 14C, it appeared in Tunisia in the 19C. The craftsman creates his work on the back of a sheet of glass. These artists transgress the sacrosanct Islamic rule of no figurative representation, and take their inspiration from old tales, legends and the great deeds of Arab chronicles: the conquest of *Ifriqiya* by the Moslems, the Prophet's ascension on a winged horse, etc. The most interesting images make use of the infinite richness of calligraphy: lettering becomes an element of design and poetry is transformed into a birdcage, or a rustic scene. Some of these items were the work of true artists, whose names are sadly unknown – popular art is frequently anonymous.

Pottery and Ceramics

Archeological excavations have provided evidence of the presence of potters in Tunisia from the earliest days of antiquity. Production sites have shifted over the centuries, with Kairouan succeeding Carthage and Tunis taking over from Kairouan; finally, Nabeul has supplanted Tunis and Guellala where potters had practised their art for a thousand years. Each period, each city, has contributed to the wealth of the common heritage. For a long period, one of the principal centres existed in the very centre of Tunis itself; drawing on both Moorish and Spanish influences, the city's craftsmen were particularly prolific. Today, nothing survives from the substantial community of potters except the name of the Qallaline quarter (from *qolla*, meaning "water pitcher"), not far from the Place Bab Souika.

Nabeul

Today, Nabeul is the largest centre of pottery and ceramic production in Tunisia – yet the pottery of Nabeul as we know it today dates only from the beginning of the 20C. Historians attribute the birth of a craft centre to the Jerbians, attracted by the existence of high-quality clay around the city. Today, the "Jerbian quarter" is still the place to find the potters.

Although the influence of the Jerbians is indisputable, the arrival and permanent settlement of French master craftsmen, determined to rediscover old forms and the old-style manufacture of enamels, was equally significant. Thus, the studio of Louis and Lucienne Tisser was where the Kharraz father and son, the Abderrazaq twins and others were to be found, who still today give their name to the most famous manufacture. By the 1930s the reputation of Nabeul pottery was already spreading far beyond Tunisia. Tiles with Andalusian or Turko-Persian designs were exported to adorn several Californian houses, including that of the razor-blade tycoon Gillette. The dynamic craftsmen of Nabeul continue to adapt as their country and their clientele develop *(see also page 109)*.

Sejenane

Distinctive, ochre-toned pieces, with easily identifiable geometric designs can be found in the souks or at the roadside between Bizerte and Tabarka.

These are the work of women from the country town Sejenane, who decorate pots, goblets and fat-bellied jugs using camel-haired brushes dipped in mastic-tree juice, tar, or red ochre. It is a primitive and mysterious type of Berber pottery resembling naive art, and its most original creations are little figurines: dolls, birds or camels. They should be handled with care, for they are made of a very fragile clay baked in the sun.

Guellala

Earthenware from Guellala, in the south of the Isle of Jerba, dates back to times immemorial. Craftsman there have established a speciality in unglazed pots of very pure form, mainly amphorae or other large items. These jars, with a capacity of some 200 litres, were in use for centuries as essential items in the Tunisian household, for storing olive oil, cereals or pasta.

Jerba craftsmen also make glazed pottery, some of it reminiscent of Spanish ware from Cordoba. The usual colours are green and ochre, but the range has suffered from competition from the more vivid colours of the pottery produced in Nabeul.

Moknine

As in Guellela, pottery made in Moknine is unglazed but its main characteristic is its porosity. The water coolers, which were always an essential item of daily life came from here. Before refrigeration, these water jars were essential for water carrying. Today the market for them is very much reduced, and the craftsmen are seeking an alternative outlet by learning the techniques of enamelling.

Rugs and Carpets

Tunisia has two types of rug, the smooth *mergoum*, and the knotted *zerbia*.

Smooth rugs

Mergoum, which are of Berber origin, take various forms. The best known are *kilims*, combining taffeta weaving and knotted threads; they can be found in the regions of Oudref, Jerba and Sbeïtla. Smooth rugs from Gabes, Matmata, Kebili, Douz and Gafsa are also well-known, but the strangest are the macramé *bakhnoug*, a kind of braiding in fashion at El Jem, Tataouine and Thibar. Whatever their source, they are immediately striking in their extraordinary richness of colour and form. No two rugs are ever alike, although the design features are limited to squares, rectangles, lozenges, crosses, chevrons and wide bands or narrow strips: curved lines are very rare. Colours vary with the region and occasionally the village, and no craftsman would be in any doubt over the origin of a rug; around Gafsa, for example, the *mergoum* have warm colours and imaginative designs, Tripolitanian influences can be seen around Redeyef, Mdhila and Metlaoui and the rugs are characterised by zoomorphic motifs, and sometimes even anthropomorphic designs which are unique in style.

Knotted rugs

Although Kairouan rugs are now highly prized, their origins remain obscure. According to some experts the first *zerbia* was made in the 19C, when the governor of the city was supposed to have introduced the weaving of a rug made with deep wool pile to donate to one of the mosques. Others evoke the influence of a young Tunisian of Turkish origin, the daughter of a curator of the *habous* of Kairouan. Whatever the legend, the "Kairouan" has become a veritable national industry which employs a large number of workers.

The *zerbia* takes its inspiration from Turkish rugs and, in contrast to the *mergoum*, its design is often placed centrally, surrounded by framing borders. The background is traditionally red, green or blue, but the designs use a broader range of colours. Currently, the most highly valued rug is the *alloucha* (*alloucha* means "sheep") which preserves the natural colours of the wool, making good use of its white and brown shades *(see also page 109)*.

Rugs with designs inspired by animals

Crafts

MANNERS

How to get on with local people

The Tunisian people are in general very welcoming. The long association with France means that many people are familiar with western ways and do not allow their natural sense of hospitality to be affected by occasional political tensions between the West and the Arab world. Nevertheless, Tunisia is an Islamic nation, with the majority of its inhabitants respecting Islamic laws and precepts, even though prayer times do not interrupt national life. The traveller should be aware of this – particularly, women travellers – for Tunisians may often think that a European woman has come to Tunisia in order to find adventure. Given the weight of sexual restrictions which weigh upon the population, this is an opportunity that some male Tunisians may be anxious to exploit.

Public transport – This is a good way to meet people. In trains or collective taxis, passengers and driver will not hesitate to start up a conversation, out of straightforward curiosity.

Hitch-hiking – Few households own a car, particularly in the countryside. For this reason, hitch-hiking is a normal way of getting around for everyone. Giving people a lift can lead to all sorts of interesting conversations, even to an invitation to come and share the family meal.

Cafés – Cafés are basically places for men. A woman on her own there may well feel uncomfortable *(see page 64)*.

Festivities – True to their sense of hospitality, Tunisians are quick to invite foreigners to share in their family ceremonies. They will often be treated better than the master of the household himself.

Good manners

Meals – Table manners are the same as in Europe. All restaurants, even the most simple, serve meals with conventional place settings. If by chance you are invited to share couscous with country people, remember that you should use only the three fingers of your right hand to transport food to your mouth.

Tea – Green tea is offered as a sign of hospitality; it's bad manners to refuse, however heavily sweetened it may be. Among families of modest means, there will be a teapot constantly kept hot: the tea, which boils and infuses for hours, is undrinkable – here, too, it is difficult to refuse.

Invitations – If you are invited to a family home it is polite to take a small gift, which is always more acceptable than money *(see also page 93)*. Only remove your shoes if your hosts do so.

Responding to conversation – Always remember to take off your **sunglasses** if you speak to someone.

Salaams – Tunisians are fond of interminable **forms of social politeness**, particularly when you meet. If you can demonstrate interest in them with some expressions in Arabic you will be accepted more easily *(see the "Glossary", page 114)*.

Pitfalls to avoid

Clothing – Summer heat is an invitation to light clothing, but **outside seaside resorts**, women should avoid very short skirts. In **sacred places** shorts (even for men) and skirts shorter than knee-length are forbidden; you will be lent a *jebba* (a full tunic) at the entrance if necessary.

On the beach, topless bikinis and nudism are generally not allowed. Bikinis are permitted everywhere, but are more acceptable in the grounds of international hotels or in heavily tourist-oriented areas. Tunisians, including young folk, generally swim in one-piece bathing costumes, and it is not unusual to see women go into the water clad in a T-shirt and long leggings. Many of them also keep their dresses on while they are on the beach.

Ramadan – During the month of Ramadan, you should not smoke, drink or eat ostentatiously in public places, except in tourist hotels or restaurants.

Time for tea: Matmata Berbers

Manners

FOOD AND DRINK

Hospitality, Tunisian-style

Tunisians have long been in the habit of taking their meals in western style, seated round a table laid in the dining-room. It is only rarely that some families outside the major cities retain the custom of a single dish served on a rush mat.

Some people are nostalgic for old-fashioned gatherings. During hot summer evenings, middle-class families receive their guests on their terrace, while in cooler weather they use their main room, its floor covered with richly decorative rugs. The food is served on low tables covered with the finest cloths. The housewife brings out delicate embroidered table-napkins, and the incense-burner breathes out delicate scented fumes of incense or sandalwood. Glasses are filled with cold water and the *chorbas* arrive, then the *briks* and finally the *méchouïa* and fish dishes. Couscous follows afterwards, and the meal ends with plates of cake or creams, always served after fruit.

The guests then wash their hands in water before being offered orange-water, rose-water or jasmine-water which is poured gently over their fingers. Musicians arrive and play while the guests sip their Turkish coffee or black tea flavoured with amber.

A la carte

Seasoned with harissa and flavoured with spices, *carouïa* (caraway), *kamoun* (cumin) or coriander, the food is often simmered in olive oil. Some dishes are also concocted on a base of tomato sauce which may be fresh or preserved.
Generally speaking, the ingredients used are very fresh: guests may be offered a freshly ripened peach and the vegetables will often have been freshly cut that morning. Tunisia offers the visitor flavours and aromas which are often forgotten in European settings.

Starters

Méchouïa (the "mixture") is the national salad, available in every restaurant and on every domestic table. Tomatoes and chilli peppers are grilled on the barbecue, together with garlic. The ingredients are chopped finely and seasoned with lemon, and often served with finely-chopped tuna, hard-boiled eggs and black olives. The Tunisian **tajine** bears no relation to the Moroccan dish of the same name: served at the beginning of a meal, this version is based on eggs, cooked with mutton, cheese or brains. The **chorbas** (soups) are delicious thick soups, often spicy, to be tasted with a touch of lemon. **Briks**, savoury fritters made of very delicate pastry, may be of various kinds: most often with egg and tuna, but also sometimes with beef, mutton or chicken.

Main dishes

Markas, or stews, are an alternative to couscous. Often based on haricot beans and tomatoes, they are prepared with mutton, or more rarely with chicken. Other stews are made in different ways, including **akoud** (*see below*) and **mloukhia**. *Mloukhia* is a festive dish based on beef and chicken with powdered leaves of corchorus, a strongly-scented aromatic plant which lends a strange green tint to the dish.

A land of flavours

Spicy or not spicy?

Many Tunisian restaurants have adapted to western tastes and prepare dishes which are noticeably less spicy than the traditional cuisine – but tourists should be wary if they venture too far off the beaten track. It is better to seek advice from the restaurateur before embarking on a particularly fiery "méchouia" salad. With peppers, the smaller they are the more spicy they are likely to be. The "tourista" stomach from which many Europeans suffer when they travel is very often no more than the result of food which is too heavily seasoned.

Meat and **fish** are often grilled and served with a wedge of lemon. Tunisia is the land of the **merguez**, spicy sausages made of beef or mutton; since minced meat goes off quickly in hot conditions. It is best to make sure that they are fresh.

Couscous

As elsewhere in the Maghreb, it is couscous which is the unchallenged master of every table. Originally the word indicated semolina made from hard wheat, rolled and steamed, but the name is now used for all dishes of meat or vegetables made with this cereal – the best known versions are of course couscous of chicken and of lamb. **Fish couscous** exists as well, with a mixture of spices accentuating its flavours. Couscous varies with region and even from one family to another.

Some Judeo-Arabic specialities

Although most dishes are common to all Tunisians, some are more specifically Jewish.

One place where a good range of Judeo-Tunisian specialities can be found is along the avenue Franklin Roosevelt at La Goulette. The meal will begin with a substantial **menina**, a starter made up of little portions of salads, haricot beans with cumin, or omelette. Gourmets will seek **boutargue**, dried mullet eggs to be eaten in slices sprinkled with lemon juice. The best are the freshest, pale in colour: you should be able to see the light through them despite the protective layer of wax. The next course frequently consists of a **whole fish**, a slice of mullet garnished with **tastira**, a salad of tomatoes and cooked peppers or perhaps **Akoud**, a casseroled dish of tripe with tomato. Feast days are honoured with **bkayla**, a stew based on fried spinach, beef and **osbane**, a type of sausage spiced with mint. Couscous is served with all these dishes.

Desserts

Patisserie – more than most of its Arab neighbours, Tunisia is a land of cakes and pastries. Among typical Tunisian products are **makhrouds** (cakes soaked in honey and stuffed with dates), **cornes de gazelle** (based on almonds and sesame), **briks** (sweet fritters of dried fruit) or **harissa** which is made of semolina soaked in honey and flavoured with orange-flowers. Some confectioners specialise in cakes of Turkish origin, such as **baklaouas, caaks or k'taifs**, filled with a paste of almonds, pistachios or hazelnuts and sprinkled with honey or syrup. France has also left a sweet imprint: in La Marsa there are still excellent **millefeuilles**, a final memento of what was once, not so long ago, one of the great Tunisian specialities.

It is only in sadly few restaurants, or at family tables, that you can still enjoy **entremets**, sweet side dishes, and other confectioners' creams based on cereals and dried fruit. Often industrially prepared, **ice-cream** is rarely special, except for **granita**, a particularly delicate lemon sorbet which melts on the tongue. This is one Italian legacy, another is the delicious **vacherin** (made of meringue and ice-cream) or **"ice-cream sandwich"** made with two delicate *sablé* (shortbread-type) biscuits.

Breakfast

Traditionally, Tunisians begin their day with **Laglabi**, puréed chick peas with harissa and olive oil, although there is an increasing tendency to have bread, butter and jam.

Wines and Spirits

Carthage produced wine which it exported throughout the Mediterranean world, even to its greatest enemies, the Romans. The Arab conquest did not mean that all the vines were torn out, but wine drinking fell out of favour and it was not until the days of the French Protectorate that wine production expanded once again. Work continued in the vineyards even after the departure of the French and very satisfactory wines are available from the vines at Cap Bon (which has 85 % of the country's vines), Carthage, Mornag and Tébourba. Good red wines include **Vieux Magon** or **Haut-Mornag**, while **Kelibia** is a modest dry muscat.

Nor has Islam interrupted the production of spirits: **Thibarine** is a liqueur prepared with aromatic plants and sugar, and **boukha** is a fig brandy served very cold as an aperitif. Another novelty is **lagami**, palm-tree milk of greater or lesser alcoholic strength according to its preparation *(see also under "Alcohol", page 105)*.

Lagami

Lagami, palm-tree milk, is obtained by cutting into the bark of the tree. It can be drunk raw (and in oases it most often is), but people from the Kerkennah islands prefer it fermented (a little stronger than beer). Every morning they add the freshly collected milk to a large jar which already holds fermented lagami. The taste is light and slightly sweet. Some add pastis, whisky or boukha. It cannot be found on sale commercially: anyone wishing to buy some should ask local people and bring their own bottle. It costs around TD1 a litre.

The best North African pastries

J. D. Vallet/PIX

A la carte

Practical Information

The beach
at Sousse

BEFORE GOING

- ### How to call Tunisia
00 + 216 + city code (without dialling 0) + the number you wish to call.

- ### Local Time
Tunisia is on Greenwich Mean Time (GMT) and 5 hours ahead of Eastern Standard Time (EST).

- ### When to go
The Mediterranean climate in the north and along the coast gives way to semi-arid, even dry, conditions in the interior of the country and the south. For most of the country, the best season is May through to mid-October, with the exception of the south.

Spring has cool temperatures, especially in the north where there is much wind and frequent rainfall. In May and June, the temperature is pleasant everywhere. The **summer** is hot and dry, but is bearable on the coast, thanks to the sea breeze. Beach-goers will enjoy relaxing in 23°C (73°F) waters, but in the south of the country, summer temperatures can be truly hellish. By contrast, Kroumiria in the far northwest is a haven of freshness. The climate remains good until mid-October. If you are not sensitive to the cold, swimming is possible in **autumn**, especially in Jerba. In **winter**, weather is mostly windy and rainy in the north, and snow is frequent in the Kroumirian mountains. In the south, temperatures remain warm, particularly in the Tozeur region's oases and in the deep south. Although the light may be ideal, nights, on the other hand, can be very cold.

Sea temperature averages 10-15°C (50-59°F) in the winter and spring months. It rises to 20°C (68°F) in June and reaches 23°C (73°F) in July and August. It remains at about 21°C (70° F) until the end of October.

- ### Packing List
If you are planning an excursion to the desert, here are some things to keep in mind. Equip yourself with hiking boots to avoid sand between your toes… not to mention scorpions. Wear loose clothing (avoid jeans) if you are planning to ride on a camel. Nights are often cool in the desert; warm clothing is highly recommended. Bring a bathing suit if you are planning to go to Ksar Ghilane – it's a real treat to bathe in the springs of the oasis. Don't forget sunglasses, a hat, sunscreen, lip protection, a sheet sleeping bag, a flashlight, a water-bottle and plastic bags to protect your belongings from the wind that blows in everywhere. For anyone wanting to follow in the footsteps of Lawrence of Arabia, a compass is a must.

See the section "What not to do" for additional clothing advice (page 83).

- ### A trip for everyone
Travelling with children
Children are treated like royalty in Tunisia. Hotels offer special activities for children as well as discounts for additional beds in parents' rooms.
Women travelling alone
Tunisia is one of the rare Arab countries where a woman can travel alone without being constantly bothered. On the other hand, women do not go to restaurants alone (other than in hotel restaurants).

Elderly people

Elderly people should experience no particular difficulty when travelling in Tunisia. Many hotels are air-conditioned and can provide special services.

Disabled persons

Tunisia is very short of facilities for the disabled. Many Tunisians will go out of their way to help people in need, though such kindness cannot always be relied on in the case of hotel staff.

• Address book

Tourist Information Offices

United Kingdom – Tunisian National Tourist Office, 77a Wigmore Street, London W1 ☎ 0207 224 5598, Fax 0207 224 4053, tntolondon@aol.com

USA – Embassy of Tunisia and Tourist Information, 1515 Massachusetts Avenue, NW Washington D.C. 20005 ☎ 202 862-1850, Fax 202 862-1858.

Canada – Tunisian Tourist Office, 1253 McGill College, Office Suite 655, Montreal, Quebec, H3B 2Y5 ☎ 514 397-1182/0403, Fax 514 397-1647.

Embassies and Consulates

United Kingdom – Embassy of the Republic of Tunisia, 29 Prince's Gate, London SW7 1QG ☎ 0207 584 8117, Fax 0207 225 2884.

Open 9am to 4pm Monday to Friday; 9.30am to 1pm (visa enquiries).

USA – Embassy of the Republic of Tunisia, 1515 Massachusetts Avenue, NW Washington D.C. 20005 ☎ 202 862-1850, Fax 202 862-1858.

Consulates in Miami and San Francisco

Canada – Embassy of Tunisia, 515 O'Connor Street, Ottawa, Ontario K1S 3P8 ☎ 613 237-0330 / 2, Fax 613 237-7939.

Australia - Consulate of Tunisia, 37 Miller Crescent, Mount Waverley, Victoria 3149 ☎ 03 9807 5023 / 03 9807 070, Fax 03 9807 3876.

Level 5, Edgecliff Centre, 203-233 New South Head Road, Edgecliff, New South Wales 2027 ☎ 02 9363 5588, Fax 2 9327 8666.

Web Sites

Surfers may find the following websites useful:

Travel Cities: www.travelocity.com

Travel & Tourism Guide to Tunisia: www.tourismtunisia.com

Tunisia Online: www.tunisiaonline.com

Country Information: www.multiasking.com/pmena/country.htm

Tunisia Welcome: www.idsonline.com/tunisia

Arabnet: www.arabnet.com

To listen to Tunisian Radio direct:

Radio Tunis: www.radiotunis.com

For an internet provider on site:

ATI (Tunisian Internet Agency): www.ati.tn

• Formalities

Identity Cards

A **valid passport** is needed for all individual and group travellers. **Visas** are not necessary for stays of up to 4 months.

Customs

Upon arrival in Tunisia, you will need to complete a form declaring the amount of money and the valuables you possess. Don't misplace it – the customs officials will ask for it when you leave the country and will question you, often rudely, about the amount of money you have remaining. It is wise to keep your money exchange receipts in order to change back your dinars before leaving the country. Also keep receipts for photographic equipment, in case of checks made on your return. Consult your country's customs regulations for the amount of non-taxable goods you can bring home.

Health Regulations

There are no particular health regulations governing entrance to Tunisia.

Vaccinations

No vaccinations are needed to enter the country but it is advisable to get vaccinations against tetanus, typhoid fever and paratyphoid fever, particularly if you plan to travel in the south (*see "Health" section page 111*). Consult your doctor for details.

Conditions of entry with a car

If you plan to enter Tunisia with your car, be sure to have your driver's licence, registration card and proof of insurance. If the vehicle is not your own, request a letter from the owner, duly authenticated. Customs services will grant you a special permit that must be returned when you leave the country.

• Currency

Cash

The Tunisian dinar is the national currency. It is divided into 1 000 millimes. Coins come in the form of 10, 20, 50 and 100 millimes and 1 dinar. Notes are 5, 10 and 20 and 30 dinars. At present both old and new notes are in circulation which may cause some confusion for first time visitors. In early 2000 the exchange rate was about TD1 = US$0.80 and TD1 = £0.50.

Money Exchange

It is impossible to change money into dinars outside Tunisia. You will need to exchange your money **upon arrival** in the country, in the foreign exchange office at the airport or in banks or post offices in the city centre. In addition, numerous hotels and clubs offer exchange services to their patrons. Exchange offices at the border will take back up to 30 % of the amount converted into dinars, if you can present the receipt from the original transaction (*see the "Customs" section below*). It is best to change money as and when you need it.

Banks generally do not take a commission, except occasionally on travellers' cheques. Post offices accept postal cheques.

Travellers' Cheques

Travellers' cheques are generally accepted in shops and hotels.

Credit Cards

Use of credit cards (Visa, Eurocard, American Express) is prevalent in upmarket hotels and restaurants, as well as in some tourist shops, particularly in state-run artisan's stores (SOCOPA). SOCOPA shops and airport duty-free shops only accept payment in cash or by credit card. In principle, shopkeepers don't take commission on payments made with a credit card.

The country exercises strict exchange control, but withdrawing money is extremely easy. Visa and Mastercard cash cards can be used to withdraw cash from a number of banks and an increasing number of cash machines.

• Spending money

Life is less expensive in Tunisia than in the UK, USA or Canada, even if prices fluctuate with the seasons. Calculate approximately **US$75** for two people travelling mid-season – from September to the end of October, and from April to the end of June – assuming that one of two meals is taken in a good restaurant and the other in a more simple establishment. High season is from 1 July until 31 August. In seaside resorts the price of hotels – palaces included – can decrease from 20-80% in the mid- and low seasons. On the other hand, the price of hotels in the cities remains the same throughout the year, particularly in Tunis. In the southern oases, prices increase during end of the year holidays *(see the "Hotel" section, page 103)*.

• Booking in advance
It is a good idea to book car hire in advance. Unfortunately, the discounts that can often be obtained from international rental agencies are not guaranteed on site. Local representatives apply their own rates that may be negotiable.

• Repatriation insurance
Emergency / repatriation insurance is often included in the price of organised tours. If you plan your own trip, obtain an insurance policy through a specialised agency or contact your bank for information. Some bank cards grant special insurance policies.

• Gifts
The choice of imported goods is limited and the prices make them prohibitive. Tunisian friends will be pleased if you bring fashion accessories, electronic devices or household appliances. A selection of cakes from the choice local cake shop is bound to go down well with your host, or some may prefer a bottle of good whisky. If you are on a more modest budget, think about small items to offer children. Everywhere you go in Tunisia, from archeological sites to medinas or remote villages, children will request a pen, your sunglasses, a key fob or a watch. Bring along a packet of pens – you'll make a lot of kids happy.

GETTING THERE

• By air
Scheduled flights
97% of travellers arrive in Tunisia by air. Most of the major European airlines fly to Tunisia's 6 international airports (Tunis-Carthage, Monastir-Sousse/Bourguiba, Sfax-Thyna, Djerba-Zarzis, Tozeur-Nefta and Tabarka) several times a day or per week.

Those travelling from North America will find it easiest to fly via Paris or London.

British Airways (☎ 0845 72 22 111), **Tunis Air** (☎ 0207 734 7644) and **GB Airways** (☎ 0875 111 666) fly regularly from London to Tunis. You can also fly direct from Birmingham, Manchester, Newcastle and Belfast.

Tunis Air (☎ 0207 734 7644) and **Air France** (☎ 0845 084 5111) fly direct from Paris, Lyon, Nice, Marseille, Strasbourg, Lille, Bordeaux and Toulouse. Tunis Air also flies from London to Tunis 4 times a week.

Sabena Air (☎ 0845 601 0933) flies from Belgium to Tunis and Monastir.

Swissair (☎ 0208 754 8594) flies from Geneva to Tunis.

Lufthansa (☎ 0845 773 7747) flies from Frankfurt, Germany to Tunis, Monastir and Djerba.

Alitalia (☎ 0207 602 7111) flies from Rome to Tunis.

Charter flights

While there are no charter flights to Tunisia from the USA, Canada, or Australia, a number of charter companies operate flights from the UK, among them:

Monarch ☎ 01582 400 000

Aer Lingus ☎ 0645 737 747

Britannia ☎ 01582 424 155

Airtours International ☎ 01706 260 000

Caledonian ☎ 01293 535 353

Flying Colours ☎ 0161 489 5757

Sunworld ☎ 0113 215 1500

Confirmation

To be on the safe side, reconfirm your flight 24 hours before departure. Also, be sure to keep enough money aside to pay for taxis, departure taxes, etc.

● By car

The documents you need to bring your car into the country are mentioned on page 92. Contact the SNCM for information on how to bring your car aboard ferries from France. Don't forget to make reservations in advance (*see below*).

● By boat

To and from Italy

Serena Holidays, 40-42 Kenway Road, London SW5 0RA, ☎ 0207 373 6548 and **Viamare Travel**, Graphic House, 2 Sumatra Road, London NW6 1PU ☎ 0207 431 4560 can reserve places on ferries and jetfoils connecting Tunisia to Italy. Ferries arrive and depart from La Goulette (approximately 15-20min from Tunis by tram) and go to Trapani, on the western tip of Sicily, Catania in eastern Sicily, Genoa in northern Italy and Cagliari in southern Sardinia. A one way ticket to Trapani and Catania costs around US$50 (car an additional US$100) and one way to Genoa costs about US$100. The jetfoil service is dependent on weather conditions. It connects Kelibia on Cap Bon (2hr from Tunis by bus or group taxi) to the Italian island of Pantelleria and to Trapani. Jetfoil rates are slightly higher than the ferry.

To and from France

SNCM Ferryterranée, 12 rue Godot-de-Mauroy, 75009 Paris, France (information and reservations ☎ 33 1 49 24 24 24, Fax 33 1 49 24 24 09. In the UK, travel on the SNCM can be booked through Southern Ferries Ltd, 179 Piccadilly, London W1V 9DB, ☎ 0207 491 4968. There are two connections per week between Marseille and Tunis (from La Goulette) in the low season, and the service operates almost daily during the high season. The crossing lasts approximately 24 hours. Check-in time is 4 hours prior to departure in the summer and 2 hours during low season. Fares are approximately US$150 per person one way and around US$300 for a car one way. Ask about the "Jasmin" rate which gives a 35% discount (available during the off season with a minimum of 2 passengers) and the "group" rate (for minimum 10 persons or 4 cars). During the high season, you must purchase a return ticket.

• Package deals

Nearly 80% of tourists travel to Tunisia on organised tours. The majority of them offer all-inclusive stays as well as excursions. Below are some tour operators or organisations:

Special Interest

Andante Travels, The Old Telephone Exchange, Winterbourne Dauntsey, Salisbury SP4 6EH, ☎ 01980 10555, andante.travels@virgin.net

Aspects of Tunisia, 122 Wigmore Street, London W1H 9FE ☎ 0207 486 4425 Prospect Music & Art Tours, 454-458 Chiswick High Road, London W4 5TT, ☎ 0208 995 2151.

Martin Randall Travel, 10 Barley Mow Passage, Chiswick, London W4 4PH, ☎ 0208 742 3355, info@martinrandall.co.uk

The British Museum Traveller, 46 Bloomsbury Street, London WC1 3QQ, ☎ 0207 323 8895.

TunisUSA, 155 E. Lancaster Avenue, Wayne, PA 19807, ☎ 610 995-2788 / 1-800-474-5500, Fax (610)964-0438, info@TunisUSA.com

Cultural Tours/Fair Winds Travel, Inc., 7758 Wisconsin Avenue, Bethesda, MD 20814, ☎ 1-800-826-7995 and (301)718-7273, Fax (301)718-2851, fairwainds@fairwindtravel.com, www.fairwindtravel.com

Hiking

The following agencies organise treks and jeep expeditions through the eastern Erg desert. Visit the ksour and the oases, at the gateway to the desert, where life is lived in bivouacs or on camel-back. Bags are usually carried on the camel's back.

Explore Worldwide, 1 Frederick Street, Aldershot, Hants GU11 1LQ, ☎ 01252 319 448 / 344 161, www.explore.co.uk, info@explore.co.uk

Dragoman, 99 Camp Green, Debenham, Suffolk, IP14 6LA, ☎ 01728 861 133, www.dragoman.co.uk, info@dragoman.co.uk

Worldwide Adventures Abroad, 7 Delamere Close, Beighton, Sheffield S20 2QE, ☎ 0114 247 3400.

Incredible Adventures Inc., 6604 Midnight Pass Road, Sarasota, FL. 34242, ☎ 1-800-644-7382 / 941-346-2488.

Diving

Aquatours, Shelletts House, Angel Road, Thames, Ditton, Surrey KT7 0AU, ☎ 0208 398 0505, arnie@aquatours.co.uk

THE BASICS

• Address book

Tourist Information

Information useful to your trip can be obtained from the offices of the **ONTT** (Office national du tourisme tunisien), the Tunisian National Tourist Office. Branches of the ONTT exist in most tourist resorts in the country. This organisation should not be confused with the **CRT** (Commissariat au tourisme), which deals with the inspection and regulation of hotels and restaurants, and with customer complaints in case of problems. In the absence of the ONTT, however, the CRT can give information to passing visitors. Certain towns also have a **syndicat d'initiative** (tourist office). *All these organisations are listed under Tourist Information in the "Making the most of" section of each town.*

Embassies and Consulates

United Kingdom – British Embassy, 5 Place de la Victoire, Tunis ☎ (01) 341 444 / 341 689 / 341 962, Fax (01) 354 877.
Consular and Visa Section, 141-143 ave de la Liberté, Tunis ☎ (01) 793 322 / 794 810, Fax (01) 792 644.
USA – Embassy of the United States of America, 144 ave de la Liberté, Belvédère, 1002 Tunis ☎ 01 782 566, Fax (01) 789 719.
Canada – Canadian Embassy, PO Box 31, 3 rue du Sénégal, Place d'Afrique, Belvédère, 1002 Tunis ☎ (01) 798 004 / 796 577, Fax (01) 792 371.

• Opening and closing times

Administrative organisations

From 1 September until 30 June, public offices are open from 8.30am-1.30pm and from 3pm-5.45pm, except Friday and Saturday afternoons and Sunday. From 1 July until 31 August, the majority of administrative offices take advantage of the hot weather and open only in the morning from 7am until 1pm.

Banks and Currency exchanges

Banks are open Monday to Thursday, 8am-12noon and 2pm-5pm. On Fridays, they are open 8am-12noon and 1.30pm-4.30pm. In July and August, they are only open 8am-11am, Monday to Friday. Currency exchanges are open at weekends in the majority of tourist cities. During Ramadan, banks close at 2pm. The hours may vary slightly from one bank to another.

Post offices

Post offices are open Monday to Friday, 8am-12noon and 3pm-6pm, and 7.30am-1pm on Saturdays. Hours change in the summer months: during the week they are open 7.30am-1pm. During Ramadan, the post office is open 8am-3pm. Some post offices offer limited services 5pm-7pm on weekdays and 9am-11am on Sundays.

Shops

In winter, stores are open 8.30am-12noon and 3pm-6pm except on Sundays and public holidays. In summer, stores often close later to cater for tourists. In the souks, shops are more likely to close on Fridays instead of Sundays, since they follow Islamic law.

Markets

Most of the weekly souks are held in the morning.

• Museums, monuments and archeological sites

Hours

In theory, museums are open from 9am-4pm from 1 April until 15 September and from 9am-12noon and 2pm-5.30pm the rest of the year. These hours are not always respected, as you will quickly learn. On the other hand, almost all museums are closed on Mondays. Open air sites are more often accessible from sunrise to sunset and mosques are open 8am-11am.

Entrance fees

The price of a ticket varies between TD1 and 2 (and up to TD5 for combined visits to several sites or monuments). It is generally necessary to pay a sum equivalent to the admission charge if you wish to take photos. When visiting certain cities, such as Kairouan or Tunis, it may be useful to hire an official guide, who will take you to the important sites and will protect you from being harassed by false guides and other hagglers. The price for a guide is approximately TD10. There are official guides at most archeological sites. Any gaps in their grasp of history is more than made up for by local knowledge. Their rates range from TD5 to 10 and can be negotiated.

• Postal service

Mail takes approximately a week to get to Europe and a few days more to the US, Canada and Australia. It costs 500 millimes for a 20 gram letter and 400 millimes for a postcard to the UK, 700 millimes for a letter and 600 millimes for a postcard to the US, Canada and Australia. For domestic mail, stamps cost 350 millimes.

The **"rapid poste"** express postal service accepts packages up to 20kg (44lbs). The Tunisian postal system guarantees a 2-day maximum delivery to Europe. Allow a few days longer for the US, Canada and Australia. Domestic deliveries take 24 hours. For European destinations, expect to pay TD14 per kilo and around TD7 for each additional kilo.

Each post office offers a **poste restante** service, **fax facilities**, as well as a **bureau de change**. Money orders can be cashed up to TD200 each. There is also a two-volume telephone book, one for Tunis and its environs, the other for the rest of the country. There is a disconcerting logic to the alphabetical order and several years may have passed since the last update.

• Telephone, fax and internet

There are little telephone offices called **"Taxiphones"** or **"Publitels"** everywhere. The touch-tone phones access all answering machines (note that the * button does not work) and all electronic information services. The phones take 100 and 500 millime coins or 1 dinar and are cheaper than calling from a hotel. Rooms in older hotels rarely have direct access to outside lines. The newer hotels are generally better equipped. Taxiphones sometimes have **fax** facilities.

International calls

To make an international call, dial **00 + country code + phone number**. Always omit the 0 before a city code. For reverse-charge calls, dial 17. (Reverse-charge calls cannot be made to Canada).

Local calls

To call within the same zone, dial the six-digit number directly. For long-distance calls, dial the complete area code (including the 0) followed by the usual six digits.

Dialling codes and rates

To other countries from Tunisia

United Kingdom: 00 + 44 + city code + phone number
USA / Canada: 00 + 1 + area code + phone number
Australia: 00 + 61 + city code + phone number

In Tunisia

Tunis	01	Gabès	05
Bizerte	02	Jerba	05
Nabeul	02	Tozeur	06
Hammamet	02	Kairouan	07
Sousse	03	Tabarka	08
Sfax	04	Le Kef	08

Rates

The rate to call home is approximately TD1 per minute for the UK and slightly more for the USA, Canada and Australia. Local calls cost 70 millimes every 6 minutes and long distance domestic calls (more than 100km) cost 175 millimes a minute. The lowest rates are from 8pm to 7am on weekdays and all day on Sunday. The first page of a **fax** sent in Tunisia costs TD1.50 and TD1.2 for each additional page. To send a fax to Europe, prices are TD3.5 and TD2.9 respectively.

Useful numbers

Information / wake-up	120
Reverse-charge calls	17
Telegrams by phone	14

(For emergency numbers, see the "Health" section on page 111)

● **Internet**

Since 1999 cyber-cafés, indicated by the sign **"Publinet"**, have sprung up in several Tunisian towns. The tariff varies according to region, but allow between TD2.5 and TD6 per hour of connection. The internet has proved extremely popular, particularly among the young. More and more cyber-cafés are expected to open in the future. Contact the Ministry of Communication to find out the addresses of the latest cafés to open, ☏ (01) 359 014.

● **Public holidays**

1 January – New Year's Day (Gregorian calendar)
20 March – Independence Day
21 March – Youth Day
9 April – Martyrs' Day. Commemoration of the demonstrations that took place on 9 April 1938 against French rule.
1 May – Labour Day
25 July – Republic Day. Anniversary of the proclamation of the Tunisian republic in 1957.
13 August – Women's Day. Commemoration of the personal Status Code declared once independence was attained.
15 October – Evacuation Day. Commemoration of the evacuation of the French military base in Bizerte.
7 November – Commemoration Day. Anniversary of President Ben Ali's inauguration in 1989.

There are also religious holidays to add to these public holidays. The dates of these vary from year to year and are determined by the lunar calendar. Among them is New Year's Day, the anniversary of the birth of the Prophet, the end of Ramadan and commemoration of the sacrifice of Abraham, etc. *(see the "Important Dates of Religious Events" section on page 56).*

GETTING AROUND

• By car

Car rentals

The major international car rental agencies are represented in the larger cities and at the airport in Tunis *(see the "Making the most of ..." section for each city)*. In the south, you can rent 4-wheel drives and a driver from local agencies (some international agencies like Hertz have recently started to rent 4-wheel drives without chauffeurs). Otherwise, ask for information at your hotel.

Rental rates in Tunisia are higher than in western countries *(see "Reservations" section on page 93)* and can be even higher if the rental period is increased, since this is regarded as a breach of the original contract. Count on spending between TD80 and 100 per day (unlimited mileage) for a bottom of the range vehicle. The conditions of your contract should be carefully checked beforehand. Often the rates indicated in the brochure do not include VAT, in which case 17 % needs to be added to the total. Note that car insurance does not cover theft, broken windows or damage to the tyres.

You must hold on to your contract carefully because it is the first document the police will request if they stop you.

An economy car is normally sufficient (Peugeot 205, Renault Clio, etc.). Most of the roads are surfaced *(see below and the chapter on "The South" on page 289)*. Since the summer months are very hot inland and in the south, the air-conditioning option is recommended.

Chauffeur-driven car

It will cost a further TD20 per day to employ the services of a chauffeur. You will also have to pay for his meals and accommodation, as well as petrol and the hire of the car.

Road network

Driving in Tunisia does not present any special problems as the country has a fairly dense road network which is surfaced for the most part, particularly in the north. The larger cities are connected by main roads called "GPs" or "Grands Parcours" (shown simply as "P" on some maps). The only toll road is the motorway between Tunis and Sousse (c 130km). In the south, the roads are well-maintained and more kilometres are being surfaced each year *(see chapter on "The South" on page 289)*.

Signs are almost always in Arabic and French, except on the Cap Bon road, where there is a distinct lack of signs in French, even though it is an area frequented by tourists. In some cities, too, such as Bizerte, many street names are shown only in Arabic. In the very unlikely event of getting lost, policemen and locals will be happy to point you in the right direction.

Driving

The **speed limit** is 50km/h in built-up areas, 90km/h elsewhere and 110km/h on the one motorway. Speeding can involve an on-the-spot fine or loss of licence. Traffic police are everywhere and can easily spot a foreign driver because of the blue licence plates which indicate a rented car. They are quite capable of stopping you and asking for a lift.

Wearing of **seatbelts** is compulsory and there is an on-the-spot fine of TD6, for not using them.

Getting around

Traffic lights have distinctive features in Tunisia. The green light flashes just before it turns red, while the amber light indicates that the red light is about to turn green. Inability to grasp this system will greeted by a chorus of car horns.

Tunisian roads are busy and dangerous. People often drive as if they have nine lives: motorcycles are often to be seen carrying an entire family as are old bumpy trucks. Be careful of the harnessed horses and donkeys that are rarely watched, as well as of the animals the peasants let graze along the roadside. It's the children, however, who present the greatest road risk. They literally throw themselves at tourist cars (with the special blue licence plates) to sell various local arts and crafts. **Drive with care** at all times.

Fuel

Many of the petrol stations are called "kiosks". Some of them are open very late at night, 7 days a week. A touch of the horn will wake up the attendant. A litre of ordinary petrol costs about 590 millimes; super and unleaded is about 670 millimes per litre.

Parking in town

Parking can be difficult in large cities, such as Tunis or Sfax, but drivers may still be asked for an additional fee by unofficial "parking attendants". The police are quick to clamp illegally parked vehicles. If this happens to you, go to the nearest police station. The fee for removal of the clamp is TD6.

In emergencies

In case of an accident involving a pedestrian, the driver is nearly always held responsible and may be taken for questioning. Contact your embassy immediately if you find yourself in this type of situation.

• By taxi

Taxis are very practical and **cheap**. There are several different types:

Small yellow taxis

These are only available inside the governorships and cost an initial fee of US$0.25 or 16 pence plus US$0.32 or 22 pence for each kilometre. They are equipped with a meter that indicates the rate in dinars. Between 9pm and 5am there is a 50% surcharge.

Big taxis

These taxis are either white or yellow and are generally Peugeots or Mercedes. They are not restricted to any particular area. They are considerably more expensive than the yellow taxis and have their own taxi stand.

Shared taxis or louages

A practical and less costly solution for visitors who are frequently on the move and interested in meeting local people. The cars generally have their own stand near the bus station. The driver waits until the car is full before leaving; each car can usually take up to 8 passengers according to the type of vehicle. Taxis that have a blue stripe on the bonnet operate locally, while those with a red stripe may go further afield. Only taxis with Arabic writing in red on the boot can drive throughout the country.

• By train

A cheap but terribly slow means of transportation, as the 2 200km of railway are single track and the engines are rather old. But the air-conditioned trains on the two main lines Tunis-Ghardimaou and Tunis-Gabès are very comfortable and represent the best way of travelling between these centres. To give an example, the trip from Tunis to Gabès costs TD11.550 and lasts 7 hours.

Heading north: Tunis-Mateur-Bizerte. The line that once connected Tunis to Tabarka has been removed and replaced with a train-bus connection with a transfer in Nefza.

Heading northwest: Tunis-Béja-Jendouba-Ghardimaou.

Heading west: Tunis-Gaafour-Dahmani. This is also the line that goes to Le Kef. However, it is better avoided because freight trains have priority and delays are common.

Heading south: Tunis-Nabeul-Sousse-Monastir-Mahdia-Sfax-Gabès-Melaoui. On the coast, a local train (the **"Sahel metro"**) connects Sousse, Monastir and Mahdia several times a day.

Tourist trains: The tourist train called the **Lézard rouge** (red lizard) departs from Metlaoui and runs through the gorges of Selja (*see the chapter "A Mountain Oasis" page 348*).

Tunis suburban: The TGM connects Tunis to La Marsa with stops in La Goulette, Carthage and Sidi Bou Saïd.

International: The railways traditionally provided cohesion and a popular means of exchange between the three countries of the Maghreb. Each year, 100 000 passengers used the line between Tunis and Casablanca. Morocco was the first to close its borders after the 1994 bombing in Marrakesh. The line between Tunisia and Algeria was interrupted soon after when fundamentalists blew up a bridge that connected the two countries.

Class of service
The SNCFT has three classes of service: Second, First and Comfort. First is 45% more expensive than Second. Only marginally more expensive than First, Comfort is the best option for night travel as it has reclining seats. There are no sleeping cars as such on Tunisian railways.

Train schedules
Photocopies of train schedules are available in all railway stations and in some tourist information offices. **Information** ☎ 01 244 440.

• By bus
The large cities are connected by the **SNTRI** – a national bus company with many air-conditioned buses – and by regional companies in each governorship. There are local bus service in most towns. The Tunis bus service connects with the metro and the TGM, but lack of route maps and the fact that signing is in Arabic makes it difficult to use for foreigners.
Information on bus schedules departing from Tunis ☎ 01 562 299. This is published daily in French in the paper "La Presse".

The bus is a **very cheap** means of getting around. For example, the trip between Tunis and Kairouan costs approximately US$5, Tunis to Gafsa is about US$12. There is little difference in the rates between national and regional companies.

Bus stations, usually at the cities' outskirts, are often difficult to find. Going by taxi is a far easier option if you have lots of luggage. Some cities have several bus stations according to the destinations and bus companies.

Getting around

• Renting two-wheel vehicles

It is possible to rent a scooter, motorbike or bike in Hammamet, Jerba, Monastir, Sousse, Tabarka and Tunis (*see the "Making the most of…" section for each of these cities or the local ONTT*). The ideal way to discover the island of Jerba is on two wheels.

• Hitchhiking

Hitchhiking is easy in the north and along the coast. Beyond Gabès it becomes progressively more difficult. It is not advisable for women travelling alone to hitchhike.

• Domestic flights

Domestic flights are provided by **Tuninter**, a 49% subsidiary of Tunis Air. The country has a total of 6 airports, with 8 departures daily from Tunis to Jerba, 5 departures to Sfax, Tabarka and Monastir and 3 to Tozeur. Even though the distances are not long, flying is a practical and inexpensive solution, especially for crossing the country from north to south. For example, a return ticket from Tunis to Jerba costs approximately US$85. Flights also exist between Jerba, Monastir and Tozeur.

Reservations can be made through travel agencies or directly via Tuninter at the airports in Tunis, Jerba, Tozeur and Sfax. Reservations can be made by phone and tickets picked up prior to departure ☎ 01 701 111.

• Organised tours and excursions

Most hotels organise excursions to the south of the country, as well as visits to the principal archeological sites.

BED AND BOARD

• Where to stay

The Sahel coast has a virtually uninterrupted beach running from Hammamet to Monastir. The two principal tourist centres of this Tunisian Riviera are Sousse and Hammamet. The main problem is deciding where to go in this area since there are hotels and resorts all along the coast. The other big tourist area is concentrated on the Isle of Jerba where there is also a wide selection of hotels.

The northern coast is less developed. Most beaches are practically deserted, not least because of the lack of places to stay. However, the existence of the newly-built airport at Tabarka, together with the trend towards eco-tourism means that many hotels are springing up in the area around the city, and it is here that the most recent developments in Tunisian tourism can be witnessed.

In the interior of the country there are few hotels, except in the larger cities and near tourist sites (eg the oases). It is still wise to reserve in advance if you wish to stay in Kairouan or Le kef. Since Tunisia is a small country, it is easy to explore inland while staying along the coast. Most of the excursions can easily be done in a day.

• Various categories of accommodation

Hotels

The big tourist boom in Tunisia started during the 1960s and has continued ever since, with constant additions to the stock of hotels. The majority are therefore new – the oldest hotels being only 30 years old – and offer excellent services, including swimming pools, tennis, golf and discos.

There is an old custom in Tunisia that no hotel must be built taller than the highest tree. There are also religious considerations added to this aesthetic rule. According to Islam, man is not permitted to build anything higher than God's creation. Much recent hotel construction has ignored these sensible precepts and only in Hammamet has building kept to the required scale.

At the beginning of the boom hotel accommodation was largely in the form of chalets and bungalows, but the current trend is towards single large buildings. Some of the most recent structures are inspired by Moroccan or Saharan architecture. From the outside, the most successful resemble cathedrals in the desert, or even cities taken straight from science-fiction. Inside, there is lavish use of marble floors and stuccoed ceilings.

Prices vary depending on whether you stay in town or on the beach. Hotels in the city maintain the same rates year round while beach accommodation varies in price according to the season (see the section "Planning your budget" page 92). In the coastal resort hotels, the rates are per person based on double occupancy. It is therefore more advantageous for a couple than for a person travelling alone who will pay a **single supplement**. Breakfast is generally included in the price of the room: half or full board arrangements are usually cheaper, but this carries with it a good chance of having mediocre international cuisine and missing out on traditional Tunisian meals like a méchouïa, a sheep barbecued whole over an open fire, a seafood couscous, or delicious grilled sea-bream.

The rates quoted are calculated on the basis of 2 people sharing, and include breakfast.

Small hotels or "gourbis"

Low budget travellers will find reasonably-priced lodgings in gourbis, as long as communal bathrooms and dubious bedding are acceptable. The "Making the most of…" sections in the guide include a number of well-kept gourbis that are located in the heart of the medina. Since they are surrounded by mosques, early wake-up calls should be expected as the morning prayer resounds throughout the area.

Camping

Camping is underdeveloped in Tunisia, as the State has never shown much interest in this type of tourism. In theory, the conditions are very basic: a dozen beds per tent and a communal portable toilet. "Camp sites" sometimes simply consist of the land in front of a hotel. In the low season, it is possible to negotiate the price to rent a tent for two people. Count on spending about US$10 per night for 2 people. This includes the camp site fee and the use of toilet facilities and electricity. Those tempted to camp on unauthorised sites are advised to request permission from the landowners as well as the local authorities.

The southern part of the country is the great exception. Spending the night in a Berber tent after an evening around the campfire is an almost compulsory part of every trek in the Sahara (see section "Package deals" page 95). By their very nature, conditions are basic: a dozen beds per tent and a communal portable toilet. This "encampment" is located within a camp site, sometimes even in front of a hotel. In the low season, it may be possible to negotiate the price of renting a tent for two people.

Apartment rental

Apartment rental is not widespread. Some tour operators nevertheless offer this option in tourist areas (*see the section "Package deals" on page 95*).

All-inclusive vacation resorts

Resorts offer a wide range of entertainment and activities, with guests able to find everything they could possibly want without ever having to leave the resort village. Typical pastimes include camel excursions, water aerobic classes, scuba diving, bridge, horseback riding and skydiving. This type of holiday is organised and is rarely available to individual travellers. However, if occupancy is disappointing, resorts tend to open the doors to individuals who are sometimes able to stay on without paying full-board prices.

Youth hostels

Youth hostels are a good choice, especially since many are located in interesting or attractive settings. The rules are almost always the same: girls on one side, boys on the other and no alcohol. For information, contact the **Association tunisienne des auberges de jeunesse** (Tunisian Youth Hostel Association), ave Mohammed V, Tunis. ☎ (01) 831 332.

Marhalas

You will only find these holiday cabins in the south of Tunisia. Often these are very basic shelters – communal dormitories with doors that don't have locks – managed by the Touring Club de Tunisie. Some are found in typical homes, such as in Matmata where you can spend a night in a former cave dwelling. The one in Nefta is the most luxurious.

Bed and breakfast

In a country where most tourism is carried out on a highly organised basis, this is an interesting alternative. It's also the best way to experience first-hand the legendary hospitality of the Tunisians. You should nonetheless be prepared for a basic level of comfort. Tourist offices will usually supply a list of addresses.

• Eating out

In hotels

Most hotels have full-board arrangements. Unfortunately, the cuisine is usually adapted to guests' normal tastes instead of introducing local specialities (*see the section "Hotels" above*). It is therefore often better to eat outside the hotel. Buffet breakfasts – the "all you can eat" type – are often German-style and include sausage, cheese and eggs.

In restaurants

Most restaurants offer good value for money, particularly considering the freshness of the products used. Unfortunately, they lack originality and often give a minimalist image of Tunisian cuisine. In most restaurants the menu only lists four or five appetisers (always the same ones), a couscous, some grilled meats and perhaps bean stew. As for the dessert menu, there is rarely much choice (*see the section "Food and Drink" on page 84*).

In seafood restaurants, tradition prescribes that the customer should always be shown the catch of the day. The choice of the mullet with the brightest eyes, the reddest gills, and curves untouched by ice, is then yours. If you are not shown the selection straightaway – which is very rare – ask to see the catch since some restaurants will serve a one pound monster without warning, and the

J.-F. Galmiche

price is calculated on the weight. The most expensive restaurants rarely cost more than US$20 per person, but you should easily be able to eat for approximately US$5 in decent cheap restaurants.

Alcohol

Tunisia is a tolerant Islamic country. Tunisians have vineyards and produce wine and some spirits *(see the section "Food and Drink" on page 84)*. Some even drink occasionally, though only in a limited number of places. Select your restaurant carefully if you wish to drink with your meal. There is little probability that you will be served alcohol in the modest kind of restaurant that caters essentially for Tunisian diners. Beer is usually available in tourist restaurants or your hotel's bar, but the majority of cafés serve only tea, coffee and soda.

SPORTS AND PASTIMES

A number of hotels compete in providing the widest possible range of activities for their guests: skydiving, tennis, horseback riding, etc. Tunisia has good facilities for certain sports, such as golf, which makes it a desirable destination for sports enthusiasts.

• Sport

Golf

With no fewer than 7 golf courses, Tunisia will satisfy even the most demanding golfers. Tunisia is good golfing country, with 18-hole golf courses at Tabarka, Carthage, Hammamet, Port el Kantaoui, Monastir or Jerba. Some of these courses were designed by the American architect, Ronald Fream and are in attractive settings of olive and orange groves or eucalyptus and cork-oak forests. The sun is always bright and the sea is never too far away. For information, contact the Tunisian National Tourist Office.

Hunting

Hunting is a very popular sport, particularly in the northwest of the country in the vicinity of Tabarka and Aïn Draham. There are approximately 1 500 foreign hunters among the total of 12 000 registered in Tunisia. The last wild cats were wiped out at the beginning of the century, and today's usual prey is wild boar, hare, partridge and geese. Hunting is strictly regulated, particularly for tourists. Hunters from abroad must apply for a hunting licence and pay a tax calculated according to the size of the bag.

Hunting is regulated by the **Ministry of Agriculture**. For information, contact the Ministry at 30 rue Alain Savary, 1002 Tunis, ☎ (01) 786 833. Hunting information is also available in the Hotel les Chênes in Aïn Draham (a small town in the Kroumirie province, 25km from Tabarka), ☎ 08 655 211 / 315.

Hiking

Tunisia lacks facilities for walkers and trekkers, except in the south (*see the section "Camel riding" below*). However, things are beginning to develop in the north where the well-shaded forests of the **Kroumiria** mountains are ideal for walking or riding holidays. Some travel agencies even offer mountain bike tours. **Tabarka Voyages** organises a number of hiking tours in Kroumiria (*see "Making the most of Tabarka" on page 219*).

• The sea

Scuba diving

In the north, **Tabarka** is famous for some of the Mediterranean's finest marine flora and fauna. On the other hand, this "Coral coast" has become progressively less worthy of its name because of the long-standing and intensive exploitation of precious madrepores. Off Tabarka, the **Isle of Galite** offers another surprise, a colony of monk seals. This island is a designated nature reserve.

To the east and as far as **Cap Bon**, the relief of the sea bed is particularly uneven. Some of the depressions are more than 250m deep. Off Sidi Daoud, a small town on the Cap Bon peninsula, the **Isle of Zembra** has vertical cliffs more than 400m high. The island is surrounded by water more than 100m deep. Zembra is also a nature reserve, with very restricted access. For further information, contact the **Centre Nautique International de Tunisie** (Tunisian International Nautical Centre), 22 rue Médine, Tunis, ☎ 01 282 209.

Sailing

In spite of extensive coastline, sailing in Tunisia is very undeveloped. There are only 26 ports and moorings for the entire 1 300km of coastline. To overcome this lack of facilities, the country has built several marinas during the past few years, among them Port El Kantaoui (300 moorings), Sidi Bou Saïd (380 moorings) and Tabarka (60 moorings). Access by boat to the Kerkennah Isles is very difficult to access because of the shallow depth of the surrounding waters.

For further information, contact the **Centre Nautique International de Tunisie** (*see address above*) or the **Fédération Tunisienne des Sports Nautiques** (Tunisian Federation of Nautical Sports), Cité Sportive Bourguiba, Tunis.

• Other activities

Camel riding

Seeing the south of the country from the back of a camel appeals to many visitors, but is not recommended for anyone in a hurry. Most of the agencies specialising in this type of trip can be found in **Douz** (*see the section on "Package deals", page 95 and the chapter "Douz and the Sahara" page 352*).

Health spas

Tunisia possesses a number of thermal springs which have been known since Roman and Carthaginian times. In the north, they form the basis of a number of health spas, while in the south the spa resorts are more for ordinary tourists.

The main hot springs are in **Korbous**, on the Cap Bon peninsula, **Jebel Oust**, southwest of Tunis and **Hammam Bourguiba**, near the Algerian border, which owes its name to former president Habib Bourguiba, a great fan of health spas.

• Nightlife

Dance performances

Numerous hotels organise belly dance performances for their guests, though these are rarely of a high standard. A better bet is to go to restaurants frequented by Tunisians themselves to see the local stars that collect crowds – and not just men. Traditional dances can also been seen during certain festivals *(see below)*.

Theatres and cinemas

Film and theatre schedules are published in the papers, or you can obtain information at your hotel's reception desk. Outside Tunis, there are not very many cinemas – and those that do exist offer little in the way of comfort. Several festivals are also dedicated to theatre and to cinema *(see below)*.

Casinos

There are two casinos, one in Hammamet and the other in Gammarth.

Discos

Nearly all beachside hotels have their own disco.

• Festivals

April

NabTataouine / Festival of the ksour – Exhibits of local arts and crafts and folklore demonstrations: dance, Arab thoroughbred races, etc.

Nabeul / Oranges Festival – The occasion for a huge international fair to commemorate the end of the orange season.

May

Dougga / Theatre Festival – Production of classical plays in the ancient theatre at the Dougga archeological site.

June

El Haouaria / Falconry Festival – Falconry competition: training for falconry hunting.

Tabarka / Coralis Festival – Underwater photography.

Maknassi / Festival of Arab Thoroughbreds – The event takes place at the end of breeding when the baby mares are put up for sale.

Sidi Daoud / Matanza – The Matanza is a spectacular type of tuna fishing. As well as having obtained all the necessary permits, it is important to be there at the right moment when the tuna are running *(dates vary between May and June)*.

June-July

El Jem / International Music Festival – There are classical and chamber concerts and the occasional jazz performance in the impressive ancient coliseum.

Kelibia / Amateur Film Festival – The event was the training ground for a good number of contemporary Tunisian film-makers. The festival still takes place, despite ups and downs in the past.

June-August

Hammamet / International Festival – This festival aims at the highest possible standards in dance, song and theatre and considers itself one of the most prestigious events of its kind in the whole of the Mediterranean area. Most performances are in Arabic.

July

Testour / International Festival of Malouf and Traditional Arab Music – The organisers invite Spanish and Tunisian musicians to play together. Flamenco finds its Arabic roots, while malouf is influenced by Western music.

Hammam-Lif / Festival of Bou Kornine – Shows featuring rap, rai and even techno.

La Goulette / Festival of Karaka – A more or less successful attempt to restore the La Goulette myth of the 1950s.

July-August

Carthage / International Festival – Arab and sometimes European stars perform in musical, theatre or popular dance events. The quality of the contributors varies considerably.

Jerba / Ulysses Festival – Outdoor screenings of mythological and historical films.

Kerkennah / Mermaid Festival – Marine folklore festival.

Monastir / Cultural Festival – Theatre, poetry and comedy.

Sousse / Aoussou Festival – Concerts, folklore and dance performances.

Tabarka / International Festival – This event, which has boasted stars such as Juliette Greco, Ravi Shankar and Joan Baez in the past, has little by little transformed into a not very distinguished variety show.

Sfax / Music Festival – Music and popular arts.

October-November

Carthage / Film Festival – This festival was originally dedicated to Arab-African cinema but has since incorporated films from other Mediterranean countries. The event takes place every other year on even-numbered years. The screenings take place in cinemas in Tunis.

Carthage / Theatre Festival – This festival takes place every other year during odd-numbered years.

November

Jerba / Puppet Festival – Art and puppet shows.

Tozeur / International Oases Festival – Camel races and popular traditions.

December

Kebili / Date Harvest Festival – Dates are a winter fruit harvested at the end of autumn. The harvest is the occasion for popular festivities.

Douz / International Festival of the Sahara – This is without a doubt one of the most spectacular events in Tunisia, with traditional weddings, camel parades and sand hockey among the array of shows and activities.

SHOPPING

Carpets, copperware, pottery. The souks overflow with a thousand and one riches, including Moroccan pottery and wood boxes from as far away as Syria. But then again, Tunisian arts and crafts have always been fed by foreign influences. Copper was imported from the Orient, and the splendid earthenware that can be admired in the old palaces originated in Andalusia, although nowadays it is considered typically Tunisian.

• What's on offer

See the "Crafts" section on page 75

Pottery and ceramics

Nabeul, which is the main centre of production, literally inundates the country with its pottery. Its success is due to growing mechanisation. Only twenty years ago, it was impossible to find two pieces of pottery to match. It was made by hand, decorated with a camel-hair paintbrush and covered by a primitive enamel. Today, such "handmade" pottery can only be found in dusty nooks of some stalls while the rare craft workshops in town centres are usually tourist traps. In the factories on the outskirts of Nabuel, goods are mass-produced. Clay is kneaded in machines, then moulded and graded prior to being dried for the first time. Each piece is then finished off on the potter's wheel. Only the largest pieces, particularly jars, are still entirely worked by hand.

Nabeul pottery is traditionally glazed and decorated with green and yellow patterns. Those that have blue designs on a white background, which are often presented as typical, are made using more recent techniques. On the latest work, the blue is enriched by touches of pink and green. There are also products on the market that are influenced by Moroccan and Sicilian designs. The former are characterised by enamelled geometric designs in emerald greens and bright reds, while the latter are decorated with fruits and leaves.

Carpets

Buying a Tunisian carpet can be a good investment. Price guidelines have been set by the National Association of Carpet Merchants as follows:

10 000 knots / sqm is TD69-78
40 000 knots / sqm is TD119
90 000 knots / sqm is TD219-236
160 000 knots / sqm is TD337-345

Silk carpets with 250 000 knots / sqm are TD835-850.
The price for a *mergoum* or woven *carpet* is about TD75 / sqm; a *killim* is between TD53 and 86.

The sealed label from the ONAT (National Office for Tunisian Artisans) is a **guarantee of quality**. The label gives a control number and lists the technical characteristics of the carpet (length, width, surface area, material, texture and date). Colour resistance is also stated. A second, optional, label gives the weaver's name.

Copper

Copperware and the art of copper craftsmanship are enjoying a revival. The craftsmen, who have often abandoned the copper souks to work in tourist areas nowadays spend their time adapting old objects to new functions, transforming a large pastry tray into a tabletop, a mortar into an ashtray and cauldrons into decorative flower pots.

Mats

In the past few years, cane weaving has become more varied. Traditional mats are often cumbersome, but place mats, lampshades, baskets, or even handbags make good souvenirs.

Jewellery

It is very difficult to find antique jewellery in the souks. The South at one time produced beautiful Berber jewellery, most often in silver, but today Tunis has the largest selection.

Shopping

Gold is less expensive than in many countries, but the quality is not as good. Each item is stamped differently according to its value: a horse's head (symbol of Carthaginian coins) or a ram for 18-carat gold; a scorpion for 9-carat gold; a grape for sterling silver. Since 1958 all jewellery must also have the gold or silversmith's stamp.

Leather goods

Master saddlers have mostly abandoned their traditional calling to produce belts, pouffes, office furniture or wallets. An improbably low price is very likely to indicate poor quality.

• Where to shop

What to buy where

Each city and town is famous for its crafts or culinary production:

Dar Chaâbane	stone sculpture;
Gabès	henna;
Ghomrassen	cornes de gazelle (a pastry filled with almonds and sesame);
Guellala (Isle of Jerba)	pottery;
Kairouan	carpets and makhrouds (small cakes dipped in honey and filled with dates);
Nabeul	pottery and orange flowers;
Sejnane	Berber pottery;
Sidi Bou Saïd	birdcages;
Tabarka	coral.

Shops

Before plunging into the bazaars, it is a good idea to have a quick look in the **SOCOPA** stores, managed by the Office National de l'Artisanat Tunisien (National Office of Tunisian Arts and Crafts) **(ONAT)** to get a taste of the variety of products and their prices. ONAT's main purpose is to maintain traditions, but it is also involved with the development of new products (eg colourful enamel dishes).

• Bartering

Being in an Arab country does not mean bargaining everywhere for everything. It's useless to challenge ticketed prices in the stores. On the other hand, everything can be negotiated in the souks where prices vary considerably. Again, to get an idea of the going prices, it is worthwhile visiting the SOCOPA stores, bearing in mind that their prices will be approximately 20 % higher than average.

• Regulations on certain items

The export of antiques is strictly forbidden by Tunisian law. Authorisation is only given in extremely rare circumstances.

• Dispatching your purchases

There are a number of reliable alternatives. Packages of less than 20kg can be sent by **post**. The shop or trader may also offer this service for larger consignments. A credit notice or receipt is required by Tunisian customs. For large consignments of more than 45kg, contact the various shipping companies. Plan on spending at least 2 hours to complete all aspects of the operation.

HEALTH AND SAFETY

• Precautions

Tunisia enjoys a healthy climate and there are no particular health risks. There have been some rare cases of **typhoid** in the south. Bear in mind that inoculations are not a 100% guarantee of immunity and that basic hygiene precautions are essential. It is more useful to be vaccinated against **hepatitis A** (spread by water or contaminated people and food) and **hepatitis B** (which is contracted through blood and sexual contact). **Jerbian**, more commonly called "turista", is the most frequent illness and usually afflicts its victims with diarrhoea. Watching what you eat usually leads to a cure within a few days.

Some basics – Avoid eating raw vegetables and unpeeled fruit. Wash hard-boiled eggs once you remove the shell. Only drink mineral water from a bottle that has been opened in front of you. Avoid ice cubes that have most likely been made from tap water.

Protect yourself from the sun, especially if you are travelling by boat. Glasses are better than contact lenses in a hot and dry climate. Take care when walking in desert dunes in the south and always wear closed shoes, as scorpions are very fond of bare feet.

• Medical kit

Bring a well-stocked first-aid kit with plasters and sterile bandages, antiseptic, mosquito repellent, cream for itches. Above all, don't forget to bring anti-diarrhoea pills as well as any regular medication.

• Health services

Pharmacies
Most standard medicines are available in pharmacies.

Doctors
Many Tunisian doctors received their training in France. Their addresses, as well as the address of local emergency clinics, called **SOS Médecins**, are given in the practical information section for each city.

Emergency numbers
Ambulance ☎ 190   **Police** ☎ 197   **Emergency services** ☎ 198

FROM A TO Z

• Electricity
Electricity is 220 volts in modern hotels and 110 elsewhere. Wall plugs have two round pins.

• Laundry Service
Many hotels offer laundry service but dry cleaners in town are cheaper. In some cases, they can return laundry within the day.

• Newspapers
There is a weekly newspaper in English called *Tunisian News* (price: TD1) which can be purchased at kiosks in major cities. British newspapers are usually available at such kiosks (the day after publication), as are the *International Herald Tribune*, *Time* and *Newsweek*.

• Photography

Almost all brands of film are sold in shops or hotels but it is best to bring several rolls with you. Film displayed in shop windows may be damaged because of the heat. Always ask permission before taking a photo of someone and don't insist if you feel they are uncomfortable.

• Smoking

Cigarettes and tobacco may be purchased everywhere in town and in hotel shops. All the top international brands are available, but it is cheaper to buy them tax free at the airport or on the ship. Tunisians are great smokers, and the country produces several brands of cigarettes.

• Theft

Tunisians are a law-abiding people and only the normal precautions are necessary, though special care should be taken at tourist sites and in the alleyways of the bazaars.

• Tipping / gratuities

Tipping is not compulsory, but it is customary to give 500 millimes to the parking attendant or TD1 to the hotel porter for carrying your bags. Don't forget that you are in a country where the minimum wage is less than TD150 a month and anything extravagant will be misunderstood. It is therefore sometimes wiser to smile or show your appreciation rather than leaving a large tip. In restaurants and cafés, it is customary to leave a tip equal to 10 or 15% of the bill.

• Units of Measurement

Tunisia follows the metric system.

Distances in this guide are given in kilometres. As a rule of thumb, one kilometre is five-eighths of a mile: 5 miles is therefore about 8 kilometres, 10 miles is about 16 kilometres and 20 miles is about 32 kilometres.

Consult the table below for other useful metric equivalents:

Degrees Celsius	35°	30°	25°	20°	15°	10°	5°	0°	-5°	-10°
Degrees Fahrenheit	95°	86°	77°	68°	59°	50°	41°	32°	23°	15°

1 centimetre (cm) = 0.4 inch
1 metre (m) = 3.3 feet
1 metre (m) = 1.09 yards
1 litre = 1.06 quart
1 litre = 0.22 gallon
1 kilogram (kg) = 2.2 pounds

LOOK AND LEARN

• General

GRANT, Michael, **The Ancient Mediterranean**, New American Library Trade, 1990.
KELLY, Robert C. et al, Country Review, **Tunisia 1998/1999**, Commercial Data International, Inc. 1998

Literature

FLAUBERT, Gustave, **Salammbô**.

MAUPASSANT, Guy de, **Letters from Africa**.

LECKIE, Ross, Hannibal, **The Novel**, Regnery Publishing, Inc., 1998

MEMMI, Albert, **Pillar of Salt**, Beacon Press, 1992

MEMMI, Albert, **The Scorpion; Or, the Imaginary Confession**, J. Philip O'Hara, 1975.

THEROUX, Paul, **The Pillars of Hercules**, Fawcett Books, 1996.

History

AUBET, Maria Eugenia, **The Phoenicians and the West, Politics, Colonies and Trade**, Cambridge University Press, 1996.

BAKER, G.P., **Hannibal**, Cooper Square Publishing, 1999.

COTTRELL, Leonard, **Hannibal: Enemy of Rome**, Da Capo Press, 1992.

DODGE, Theodore Ayrault, **Hannibal, A History of the Art of War**, Da Capo Press, 1995.

HOPWOOD, Derek, **Habib Bourguiba of Tunisia: The Tragedy of Longevity**, St. Martins Press, 1992.

HUMPRHEY, J.H., **Circus and a Byzantine Cemetery at Carthage**, University of Michigan Press, 1989.

LANCEL, Serge, **Hannibal**, Blackwell Publishers, 1998.

LAZREG, N. Ben and Mattingly, D.J., **Leptiminus, Journal of Roman Archaeology**, 1992.

MURPHY, Emma C., **Economic and Political Change in Tunisia: From Bourguiba to Ben Ali**, St. Martins Press, 1999.

RAVEN, Susan, **Rome in Africa**, Routledge, 1993.

SALISBURY, Joyce E., **Perpetua's Passion**, Routledge, 1997.

Art and Architecture

BLANCHARD-LEMEE, Michele, **Mosaics of Roman Africa: Floor Mosaics from Tunisia**, 1996.

BLOOM, Jonathan, **Islamic Arts**, Phaidon Press, Inc., 1997.

CARVER, Norman, **North African Villages: Morocco, Algeria & Tunisia**, Documan Press Ltd., 1992.

REVAULT, Jacques, **Designs and Patterns from North African Carpets and Textiles**, Dover Publishing, 1973.

SPRING, Christopher and HUDSON, Julie, **North African Textiles**, Smithsonian Institution Press, 1996.

Religion

ESPOSITO, John, **Islam, The Straight Path**, Oxford University Press, 1998.

FLUEHR-LOBBAN, Carolyn, **Islamic Society in Practice**, University Press of Florida, 1994.

LASKIER, Michael M., **North African Jewry in the Twentieth Century: The Jews of Morocco, Tunisia and Algeria**, New York University Press, 1997.

UDOVITCH, Abraham and VALENSI, Lucette, **Last Arab Jews: The Communities of Jerba, Tunisia**, Harwood Academic Publishing, 1984.

People and Culture

BRETT, Michael, **The Berbers**, Blackwell Publishing, 1997.

BROOKS, Geraldine, **Nine Parts of Desire, The Hidden World of Islamic Women**, Anchor Books, 1996.

HEJAIEJ, Monia, **Behind Closed Doors: Women's Oral Narratives in Tunis**, Rutgers University Press, 1996.
HOURANI, Albert, **A History of the Arab Peoples**, Warner Books, 1992.
VARGHESE BROWN, Roslind, **Tunisia (Cultures of the World)**, Benchmark Books, 1998.

● **Films**
BOUGHEDIR, Farid, **Halfaouine**, 1990.
GILLESPIE, Dizzy, **A Night in Tunisia**, 1990.
MINGHELLA, Anthony, **The English Patient**, 1996.
TLATLI, Moufida, **The Silence of the Palace**, 1994.

(See the "Cinema" section on page 72)

● **Music**
Art Blakey and the Jazz Messengers, **A Night in Tunisia**, Emd / Blue Note, 1989.
Dizzy Gillespie's Big Band, **Night in Tunisia**, Laserlight, 1996.
North Africa and the Middle East, Various Artists, Playasound, 1998.
The Secret Museum of Mankind: Music of North Africa, Yazoo, 1997.

● **Maps**
MICHELIN, **Tunisia** (Map 956), 1 / 8 000 000.

GLOSSARY

The majority of Tunisians speak Arabic and French fluently. They enjoy the company of foreigners and are delighted with any visitor who tries to speak a little Arabic. This little dictionary is therefore more useful for conversation than getting practical information.

Common expressions

Goodbye	Besslâma	How are you?	Chnoua halek?
Good day	Sebah el kheir	How are you doing?	Labes?
Good evening	Msa el kheir	Thank you	choukhran
Good night	Lila mebrouka		

Basic conversation

How do you say in Arabic?	Kîf'ach tqoûl b-el-'arbi?	Thank you	Choukhran – Barak allaou fik
I don't understand	Ma nefhemech	No	Lâ
I don't know	Mâ nârafch	Yes	N'am
Madam	Saïdati	Please	Min fadlak
Sir	Si		

Time

Day after tomorrow	Baad ghedoua	Morning	Sbah
Today	El yoûm	Afternoon	Nous ahar
Tomorrow	Ghedoua	Night	Lil
Yesterday	El-bareh	Evening	Achiya

Arabic words

Aïn	Spring, fountain
Bab	Door
Bey	Title given to sovereigns and to the Sultan's vassals

Glossary

Bir	Well
Bled	Town, country, countryside
Borj	Fortress, bastion
Cherif (pl. chorfa)	Descendant of the prophet Mohammed
Chott	Salt-water lake that is almost always dried out
Dar	Palace, a classical Tunisian home
Erg	Region where dunes are located
Fellah	Poor peasant
Fondouk	Former inn or caravanserai where travelling foreigners would stay
Ghorfa	Covered loft
Habous	Legal term referring to land or real estate dedicated to religious orders or public usage
Hadith	Collection of Mohammed's acts and words that complete the Koran
Haj	Pilgrim who goes to Mecca
Haïk	Long veil worn by women
Hanna	Henna
Imam	Religious leader
Jamâa	Mosque
Jebba	Loose-fitting clothing, similar to a Jellaba
Jebel	Mountain
Jellaba	Large cotton or wool tunic that is slipped over the head
Kantara	Bridge
Kef	Rock
Kasba	Fortified wall of an ancient city
Koubba	Mausoleum with a dome of a saint
Ksar (pl. Ksour)	Fortified palace
Malouf	Traditional music of Andalusian origin
Marabout	Saint or the sepulture of a saint
Medersa	Former residence for students at Koranic universities
Oued	River
Rass	Cape
Ribat	Fortified convent
Sahel	Coast
Sebkhet	Marshy area more or less dried up (or sebkha)
Tourbet	Mausoleum
Zaouïa	Place of cult located near the tomb of a saint

JF Galmiche

The Medina, Tunis

Exploring Tunisia

The magnificent
Roman remains
at Dougga

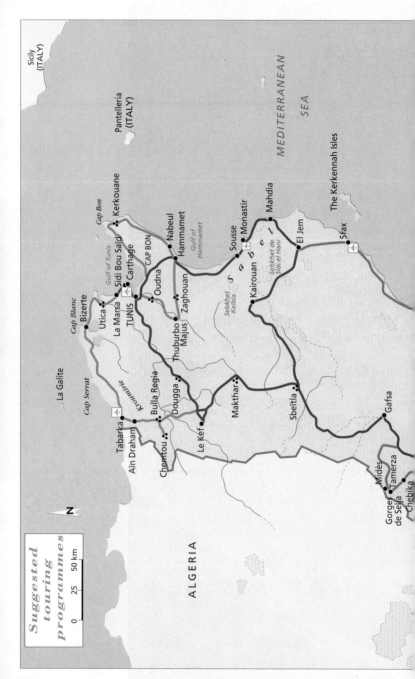

Suggested touring programmes

| 0 | 25 | 50 km |

118

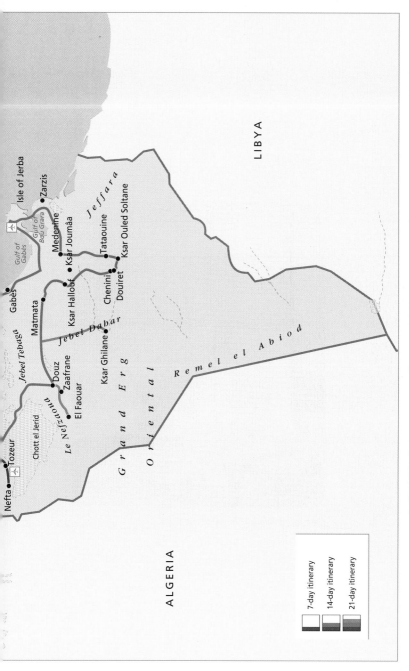

LIBYA

ALGERIA

Isle of Jerba
Zarzis
Gulf of
Bou Grara
Gulf of Gabès
Gabès
Medenine
Ksar Joumâa
Tataouine
Ksar Ouled Soltane
Ksar Hallouf
Chenini
Douiret
Matmata
Jebel Dahar
Jeffara
Jebel Tebaga
Douz
Zaafrane
El Faouar
Ksar Ghilane
Grand Erg Oriental
Remel el Abiod
Le Nefzaoua
Chott el Jerid
Tozeur
Nefta

7-day itinerary
14-day itinerary
21-day itinerary

Carthage: columns of the Antonine Baths

TUNIS AND THE SURROUNDING AREA

Although it lies in the north, away from the centre of the country, the region around the Gulf of Tunis always seems to have been destined to rule Tunisia. It was here that the Phœnicians built Carthage, capital city of their new empire, and when Carthage was destroyed the Romans rebuilt it to preside over the fate of their African province. Built with stones taken from the ruins of the ancient city, Tunis had to wait for several centuries, but it was inevitable that it should eventually become the capital of Ifriqiya, to which it gave its name. The city and its surrounding conurbation, which is now home to one-sixth of the population, is the focus of all the nation's activities and a magnet for investors. The source of employment and wealth, it has created a prosperous class of professionals, entrepreneurs, engineers and managers who now live in the luxurious villas of Carthage, Sidi Bou Said and La Marsa to the north of Tunis. This smart suburban district, where Punic and Roman ruins cluster round the fine sandy beaches, is the setting for most tourist hotels. The city of Tunis itself has no sea-front.

Within easy reach of the city are some of the country's major attractions, Cap Bon, Carthage itself, and, at Dougga, a hundred kilometres southwest of the city, in a landscape of hills and valleys, wheatfields and centuries-old olive trees Tunisia's most magnificent archeological site.

TUNIS ★★★

Capital city, seat of government
Pop c 1 500 000 including the outlying areas
Comfortable climate throughout the year.

Not to be missed
A stroll through the souks; the mosaics in the Musée du Bardo;
dinner in the Dar el Jeld restaurant.

And remember...
The best place to stay is La Marsa. The city has no sea-front,
but there are beaches at La Goulette, La Marsa,
Carthage or Sidi Bou Saïd.

Tunisia does not yield its secrets in a single day, and time is needed to discover all its charms. The city can be easier to define, not by what it is, but by what it is not. It is not a pretentious capital of grandiose monuments, nor is it particularly mysterious or exotic, certainly not something from the pages of *A Thousand and One Nights*. In some ways it is a straightforward kind of place, a thousand-year old Arab city certainly, but also a relatively modern French colonial town. There are all sorts of interesting juxtapositions; white domes and lanterned minarets stand next to Art Nouveau buildings and ultra-modern banks. Roads filled with ageing Citroëns and Peugeots evoke something of the atmosphere of 1950s France.

Sometimes Tunis has less of the feeling of a capital city than of a big provincial town, with its backgammon players in their dark brown *burnous*, its constant buzz of conversation in the streets, its idlers in the Belvedere Park... Tunis likes to take its time, its visitors should do the same.

History in Mosaics

Carthaginian suburb – Perched on a gentle hill a mere 44m high and protected from the sea and sea-borne invasion by its lake, Tunes was probably founded in the 4C BC, although some historians prefer to place its origins some five or six centuries earlier. The Tunes mentioned in a 4C chronicle was a Phœnician trading post. Later it was to be wholly identified with Carthage, and was finally invaded by Scipio before being completely destroyed in 146AD, suffering the same misfortune as its greater neighbour. The future Tunis then suffered a period of foreign invasions and influence which left it with a distinctly cosmopolitan character. Like much of the rest of the Maghreb, its fate was determined from outside. The Romans ruled it for nearly 400 years, followed by the Vandals in 429 and the Byzantines in 533.

Arrival of the Arabs – The Arab conquest of the Maghreb began in the 7C, when Uqba Ibn Nafi founded Kairouan in 670. Tunis itself fell to Hassan Ben Nomane, who demolished Byzantine Carthage in 698 along with its port and fortifications: he preferred to settle at Tunis, because of its easily defended sight. A canal built on Hassan's orders literally brought the sea to the gates of Tunis, at La Goulette, so that a war fleet could shelter there and be kept in readiness for operations in the Mediterranean. This combination of Tunis and La Goulette made Carthage redundant, while the Ez Zitouna Mosque built in the heart of the city (around 732) added a powerful spiritual and intellectual dimension.

Nevertheless, under the **Aghlabids** (800-909), Kairouan remained the capital. The 8C was a period of brilliance, marked by the arrival at Ez Zitouna of a doctor in theology, Sidi Ali Ben Ziad, who taught the doctrine of a great Imam of Mecca, Malik Ibn Anas. **Malekism** proclaimed a tolerant, sober and unadorned Islam, and it can be said without exaggeration that for eleven hundred years Tunis retained the marks of modesty and near self-abnegation that it inherited from Malekism; this included its architecture. For this reason, from 800 Tunis took a resolute stand against the brutal rule of the Aghlabids. The city's stubbornness cost it dear, for each of its many revolts was put down in fire and blood.

When the **Fatimids** (909-1171) came to power, they chose the coastal town of Mahdia as their capital. Tunis lost its status as the political centre of the kingdom, but enjoyed a great period of commercial expansion. Despite the Shiism that now became dominant, Malekism endured in Tunis and Jews were allowed to settle in the medina.

In the 11C the new dynasty of the **Khorassanids** ruled Tunis. They encouraged trade with the west, at the same time protecting the city with a formidable set of fortifications. But Tunis was still only the capital of a principality, not of a state. It was only under the Moroccan **Almohads** (1159) that the city came to control the entire territory of the future Tunisia. The Almohad princes were famous for their austerity, which was well suited to the Malekite temperament of the Tunisians. Skilled craftsmen were encouraged. The kasbah was built above the medina to house the political and military authorities.

A **golden age** was to begin with the rise in power of the **Hafsid** dynasty (1230-1574). For three centuries the city enjoyed great political stability, and unprecedented commercial expansion. Moroccans, Andalusians and Jews, expelled from Spain after the Reconquest settled in Tunis and enriched it with their contributions. A district of luxury craftsmen developed around Ez Zitouna. This was also a time of cultural renewal, marked by the birth in Tunis in 1332 of the great historian and philosopher Ibn Khaldoun. In 1534 the Turkish corsair Barbarossa managed to overthrow the Hafsid sultan, who was replaced on his throne the following year by the Emperor Charles V after the Spanish fleet's siege of Tunis – an episode which ended with three days of pillage, massacre and destruction. From then on, the Hafsid dynasty began to decline; despite the Spanish presence, the Turks were about to take over.

In the shadow of the Sublime Porte – Tunis fell into the hands of the Turks in 1569, Don John of Austria recaptured the city. It was only a temporary victory: in 1574 Sinan Pasha's Turks seized Tunis for the second time, "liberating it from the infidel". The Ottomans erected their own palaces, mosques (beneath an octagonal minaret finished with a lantern tower), mausoleums and souks. The Malekite rites had to adapt to the Hanefit rites of the occupying power – yet Tunis gained in status, importance and prestige, as can still be seen from the many Turkish monuments in the medina. After the dreary days of rule by the **Mouradite** dynasty (1612-1702) came the long **Husseinite** period: 29 princes (or Beys) succeeded each other, from 1705 (Hussein I) to the proclamation of the Tunisian republic on 25 July 1957. Beginning in the 18C, people of various nationalities settled in the capital, among them Maltese, Sicilians, Neapolitans, Sardinians and Jews from Leghorn. Then there were the corsair's captives, sold as slaves in the souk, employed as craftsmen or doomed to penal servitude. A clamorous mixture of different languages filled the souks and quaysides – Arabic, Turkish, Spanish, Italian, Judeo-Arabic and even French.

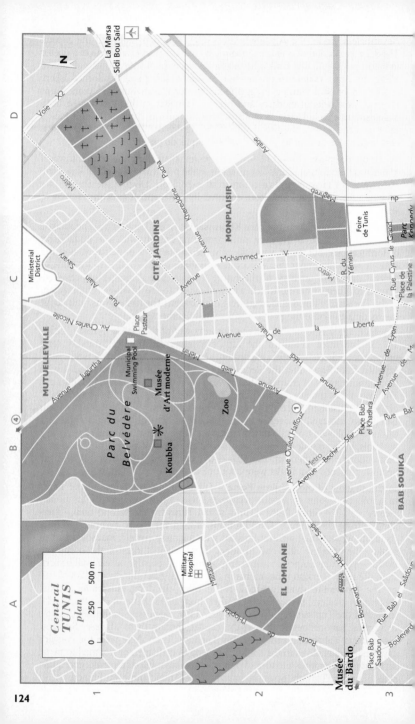

Central TUNIS plan 1

0 250 500 m

N

124

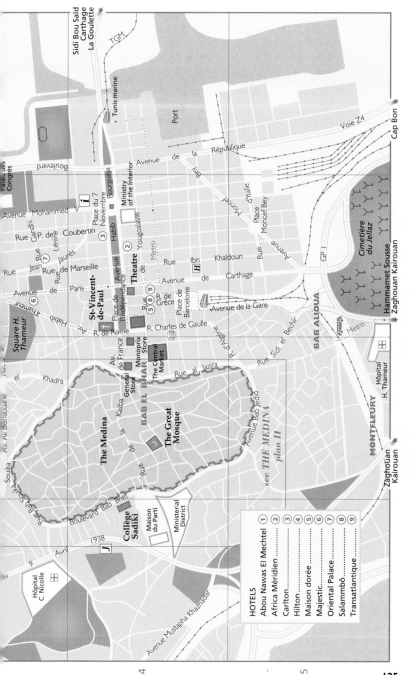

HOTELS

1. Abou Nawas El Mechtel
2. Africa Méridien
3. Carlton
4. Hilton
5. Maison dorée
6. Majestic
7. Oriental Palace
8. Salammbô
9. Transatlantique

125

The French Protectorate – At the end of the 19C, the beginnings of a colonial and maritime city appeared, a settlement outside the main city inhabited by Christians who were not made welcome in the medina. This necessitated the filling in of the lagoon between the lake and Bab el Bahr (the "gate to the sea") in the medina walls. This new, European-style city was seen as the antithesis of the Arab city. Over the years it played a major role in the reduction of the importance of the old city, which was abandoned by many of its inhabitants and left to degenerate. As a final insult before winning independence, Tunis suffered German occupation in 1942 before its liberation by Montgomery's 8th Army the following year.

It is easy to find one's way around the city, and most of the attractions are within walking distance. The modern town is bisected by two great avenues: the east-west ave Habib Bouguiba, which becomes the ave de France, is 1.5km long and runs from the lake of Tunis to the medina, and the north-south ave de Paris which later becomes the ave de Carthage.

The modern city
Allow an hour

The modern city began to develop when the Protectorate was signed in 1881. A typical example of colonial town planning, it consists of a network of parallel streets cut across by broad avenues, lined with hotels, banks, cafés and western-style shops – all the ingredients of a somewhat impersonal cosmopolitanism, apart from a few fine remnants of an eclectic selection of buildings dating from the late 19-early 20C, in Beaux-Arts, Art Nouveau or neo-Arabian styles.

Avenue Habib Bourguiba and Avenue de France (Plan 1)
The ave Habib Bourguiba, and its extension, the ave de France have become the capital's true centre. As such, they contain several of the modern city's most important buildings and monuments. The 1911 **Théatre municipal** (municipal théatre) is a rare example of a theatre in Art Nouveau style. To the west, the avenue ends in the Place de l'Indépendance, with its two symbols of the French presence: the **Résidence générale** (now the French Embassy), built in 1861, and the **Cathedral of St Vincent de Paul** (1882) in Romano-Byzantine style. To the east, towards the port, the former Place d'Afrique has been renamed **Place du 7 Novembre**, and the equestrian statue of President Bourguiba which once stood here has been replaced by a rectangular clock. This "alarm clock", as it is known to the people of Tunis, is supposed to proclaim the new era, that of President Ben Ali who came to power on 7 November 1987. It is probably the only clock in the world on which the figure 7 is engraved in place of the 6, in rather obvious symbolism. Since the ave Habib Bourguiba has to some extent been disfigured by modern buildings – such as the Hotel Africa which intrudes into the vista – handsome old-style façades are now to be found in the streets behind like ave de Carthage and ave de Paris, ave Habib Thameur, rue de Yougoslavie and rue de Rome.

Although the prestigious avenue has lost some of its glamour, it is still the place where Tunisians like to stroll. It is at its liveliest and most crowded in the evening, the hubbub reinforced by the shrill chatterings of thousands of sparrows sheltering in the fig trees in the central avenue. The moment when the offices close is the time to mingle in the crowd strolling beneath the trees: civil servants and white-collar workers, jasmine sellers and

Ch. Sappa/RAPHO

Place de la Porte de France

students, or idlers simply looking out for the lonely tourist. There is a tremendous din, a symphony of car horns, the whistles of the very elegant policewomen, and music blasting out of the neighbouring shops. It is a good place for people-watching. There are old men in three-piece suits and *chéchia*, noses deep in *La Presse*; teenagers in T-shirts hanging around in front of kiosks with their posters of film stars and pop groups; elegant ladies leafing through copies of *Elle* and *Paris Match* on display in the news-stand. But the quasi-European atmosphere comes abruptly to an end beyond the Porte de France at the entrance to the medina.

Continue along the ave de France towards the medina, and turn left into the rue Charles de Gaulle which runs beside the market.

The **Central Market** (*Open 6am-2pm*) is where the capital's pulse beats most strongly. The streets full of shops which approach it are a prelude to the tumult which fills the hall, with its abundance of fish and mountains of carrots, strawberries, beans and peas. There are French and Italian cheeses, as well as *robstabounes*, beautifully soft and fresh little bread rolls. In the butchery section, the oriental touch lies less in the display than in the signs with their picturesque names: "The King of Lamb" or "Meat of Delight". As may be imagined, merguez sausages and lamb dominate, but there is a small area devoted to horse-meat. In the spring, the aromas of spices and dried fruit are overladen with the heavy fragrance of dried geraniums, which housewives buy in bulk to extract the essence; it is used as perfume or, more oddly, in pastries.

The Medina★★

Allow 2-3hr. Avoid Fridays, when some of the shops in the souk are closed all day.
Morning visits are best.

The medina (Plan II) is such a contrast with the modern city that Tunis has been spoken of as a "double city" or even a "mirror-image city". Added to the UNESCO list of World Heritage sites in 1979, the Tunis medina is a true city within the city, dark and shimmering, secret and full of sales talk: noisy souks devoted to trade; quiet residential districts with houses and palaces; dead-end streets and sharp-angled lanes with their seemingly impenetrable dwellings, shut away from the gaze of inquisitive eyes.

It is useful to keep a few key details in mind. The Arab city has two main routes running across it: the first, running east-west, links the Porte de France with the Place du Gouvernement, while the second, on a north-south axis, runs from Bab Souika to Bab el Jazira. For some people, these roads represent the famous *"cardo maximus"* and *"decomanus"* of Roman cities, but nothing at all remains to confirm this. On the other hand, these two routes meet and cross at the Ez Zitouna mosque "towards which everything flows in and from which everything flows out again as if it were a heart" (J Berque). The whole medina is laid out round the Great Mosque, held as if in a spider's web by the souks which group together the skilled trades (weaving, perfumery, jewellery, books and bindings). The noisy or dirty trades (blacksmiths, tanners) are confined to the outer edge of the medina, while fruit and vegetable traders are located at the gates of the city, near the former **fondouk** (establishments used as lodgings and for storing merchandise, reserved for nomads and foreigners). Commercial activity is separated from housing, and some souks are closed at night by heavy padlocked gates. Residential districts are identifiable by their narrow alleys without shops, and by their blank walls without windows or doors. Unlike European houses and office buildings with their grand and impressive façades designed to be seen and admired from the street, all the decoration and wealth of the Tunis house is kept for the interior space. From the outside, there is nothing to indicate the social standing of the owner of such a house, apart from the ornamentation at the entrance, fine doors with iron studs and knockers which are often in the form of a Hand of Fatima.

The **Porte de France** marks the entrance to the medina. The former Bab el Bahr, the little "Arc de Triomphe" on the vast Place de la Victoire, was built in 1948; it is one of the gates of the city wall that once surrounded the medina. When he stayed in Tunisia, Garibaldi lived in the **rue de la Commission** (*immediately on your left*). In the square, on the right, is the British Embassy with its superb pale blue studded doorway.

From here, the **rue Jamaa ez Zitouna** slopes gently up towards the Great Mosque. You should not be discouraged by the first 300m of this very narrow lane, which opens out a little further on, and which is full of souvenir shops: plastic *narghilas*, copper dishes or bulbous bird-cages. Sometimes there are genuine Nabeul ceramic tiles amongst all this bric-à-brac, ancient marionnettes or beautiful jewellery in the form of a Hand of Fatima. The rue Jamaa ez Zitouna opens out into the little **souk el Fekka** (where dried fruit is sold), located at the foot of the great stairway into the mosque's inner courtyard.

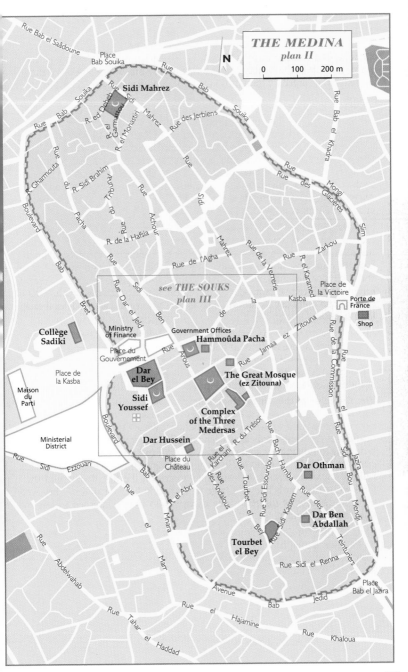

THE MEDINA
plan II

0   100   200 m

Rue Bab el Saâdoune

Place
Bab Souika

Sidi Mahrez

Rue des Jerbiens

Collège
Sadiki

Ministry
of Finance

Government Offices
Hammoûda Pacha

see THE SOUKS
plan III

Place de
la Victoire

Porte de
France

Shop

Place de
la Kasba

Place du
Gouvernement

Dar
el Bey

The Great Mosque
(ez Zitouna)

Maison
du
Parti

Sidi
Youssef

Complex
of the Three
Medersas

Ministerial
District

Dar Hussein

Place du
Château

Dar Othman

Dar Ben
Abdallah

Tourbet
el Bey

Place
Bab el Jazira

The Great Mosque** (La Grande Mosquée) – *8am-12noon, closed to non-Moslems on Fridays. Entrance charge. Visitors are not allowed to enter the courtyard.*

Nothing remains of the mosque built by the Ummayad around 732; **Jamaa ez Zitouna** (the mosque of the Olive Tree) was in fact completely reconstructed under the rule of the Aghlabid emir Ibrahim Ibn Ahmed, in 856-863, then renovated and enlarged by the Zirids in the 10C, and finally by the Turks in 1637. The oldest mosque in Tunis is also its largest, and the second largest in the country (after Kairouan). Originally Ez Zitouna was not only a place of worship: it housed a university famous throughout Africa, in particular because of the philosophical teachings of the famous Ibn Khaldoun. The mosque was also a commercial centre where contracts and trading deals were negotiated. Its sacred element prevailed, however, and commercial activity was relocated into the neighbouring souks. After independence, Bourguiba's secular regime put an end to the university elements in Ez Zitouna; they revived in 1987, however, under the encouragement of President Ben Ali, who was concerned to respond to the claims of Islamists.

With its 184 pillars from classical sites (mostly from Carthage), its 15 aisles, its capitals reinforced beneath the arches by imposts, its rush matting rolled round the columns and its impressive Venetian glass chandeliers, the **pillared prayer hall***** is the most impressive part of the mosque. Despite its re-use of Roman and Byzantine materials, it is a pure reflection of Arab genius. (*Access for Moslems only*). The hall can accommodate 2 000 of the faithful, who answer the calls of the muezzin every day – only on Friday is the call a recording broadcast through loud speakers.

Above the entrance to the prayer hall the very fine **"bahou" dome**, in two-tone stone, is an example of Zirid art dating from the 11C. The **courtyard**, lined on three sides by a wide gallery built by the Turks in 1653, opens on to the souks through a 17C **portico**. The present-day **minaret**, a large square tower typical of the Spanish-Moorish style and 44m tall, dates from 1834.

The Complex of the Three Medersas* (Moslem colleges) – *Turn right out of the mosque, into the souk des Libraires (the Booksellers' souk).* Two of the *medersas* have been converted into apprentice training schools, while the third is now the headquarters of the Tunis medical associations. This is not a public place, but there is nothing to stop visitors going through the door (which is often open) to appreciate the intimacy of these ancient sites of religious instruction. There is the familiar square courtyard with students' rooms on the first floor round three sides while the fourth houses a large hall formerly kept for prayer. They were built by the Beys of the Husseinite dynasty who were concerned to improve teaching and training.

Coming from the Great Mosque (*no 11 in the Souk des Libraires*), is the **Médersa du Palmier**, dating back to 1714 and named after the palm tree which used to grow in its little garden. On weekdays, there is an atmosphere that is both studious and welcoming.

A little further on, the **Médersa Bachiya** (1752) can be recognised by the fountain in the centre of the courtyard. Black marble columns with white marble capitals add to the attractions of the setting, as do the pottery tiles on the walls.

At the corner between the Souk des Libraires and the Souk Kachachine is the entrance of the **Médersa Slimaniya** (1754), with a delicate pillared porch and cornice of green tiles.

A little way back, on the opposite side is the **Kachachine Hammam**, with access through a barber's shop. With its immensely high ceilings, and voices echoing through clouds of steam. Visitors can glance into the waiting room with its green wooden seats and steps covered in rush matting, or even decide to have a full session here.

The souks** (Plan III)
Return to the Great Mosque and turn right beyond the rue Jamaa ez Zitouna.

Inside the souks, the shopkeepers call out to visitors in several languages, trying to find out if they are French, German, Italian or British – but the atmosphere is good humoured, and bargaining is customary. Anyone arriving at opening time (around 9am), will soon become aware that traders are anxious not to lose their first customer of the day.

The **el Attarine souk**** (perfumers' souk) dates from the 13C, and is undoubtedly one of the most beautiful in the old city, with its deep and narrow shops which seem to hold all the mystery of the Orient. Every stall is a treat for the senses, for the sense of smell above all, for they are all full of the sweetest and headiest fragrances – rose, jasmine, orange, and also cactus and musk, amber and incense. There are visual treats too, in the form of the treasure chest of multicoloured little bottles which the trader will hasten to open for his customer. Each stall-holder presides over a counter of filigree wood with golden strips, the shelving burdened with green heaps of henna and scented herbs.

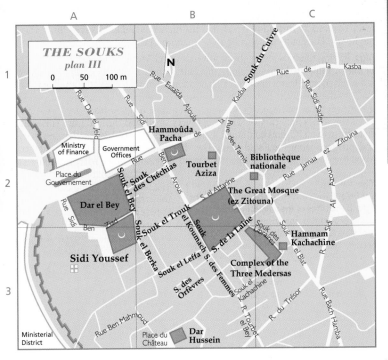

The **National Library** (Bibliothèque nationale) *(a little further along the Attarine souk)* is housed in barracks built by the Turks in 1814 and laid out round an oblong interior courtyard. The dormitories on the first floor where Turkish Janissaries once slept are now filled with thousands of books and Arab manuscripts from the great mosque and the *medersa*.

Go back the way you have come and continue beyond the Great Mosque.

The **el Trouk souk**** (Turkish souk) owes its name to the weavers and tailors who used to work there. Nowadays, as well as clothing, there are rugs, furniture, souvenirs, and above all leather articles. The street is completely covered in high brick vaulting which endows it with a certain elegance, and many of the shops have a terrace with interesting views over the medina and ez Zitouna. The finest panorama is undoubtedly the one from the **Ed-Dar house** *(no 7)*, literally at the foot of the minaret. The view down reveals the whole layout of the covered souks, with small openings piercing their barrel vaulting here and there. This ancient structure, which houses a famous antique shop, has managed to retain its elegance and style, with old-fashioned kitchens, crooked staircases covered with period tiles, and light-wells set into the roof (sadly some have been closed off for security reasons). Nearby is the terrace of the famous **M'rabet** restaurant, a good place to sit and sip a mint tea or smoke *chicha*.

The distinctly Turkish minaret of the **Sidi Youssef mosque*** marks the exit from the Turkish souk. Built in the 17C by the Ottomans who wanted to have their own *hanefite* rite mosque, it was the first mosque to be built with an octagonal minaret topped by a circular balcony and canopy. This enabled the muezzin to call the faithful to prayer without fear of getting wet. See also the **minbar**, made of masonry instead of wood, and the high dais *(sedda)* reserved for reading the *Koran*. The courtyard also houses the tomb of the founder, Youssef Dey.

After leaving the mosque, go back towards the el Trouk souk and then into the **El Berka souk*****. Half-way along this lane, which is entirely covered in, there is a small square. Here, under an arch supported on six columns painted red and black, is the site of the former **slave market**. The unfortunate captives were sold by auction on a platform. A bird singing in a cage hanging from one of the pillars is the souk's final captive. The cage is very small, and the bird tiny. This souk dates from the 17C, and continued its lucrative trade until 1841; today, jewellery and precious stones are sold here. The shops of carved and sky-blue painted wood are almost as beautiful as the myriad necklaces, rings, bracelets and earrings which sparkle everywhere.

The Amine

Just before you reach the slave market, on the right, is the office of the amine. In earlier times each corporation appointed an assessor responsible for setting a fair price for each transaction, to oversee trading and to settle disputes. The occupation itself no longer exists, but the Association for the Preservation of the Medina is promoting its revival. Every day the amine supervises a sale of jewellery around midday. If you arrive late in the morning, you may find yourself watching one of these strange auctions which take place in a hushed atmosphere, unheded by passers-by.

The shop-keepers sometimes wear the traditional costume of white trousers, white waistcoat and *chéchia* head-cloth – and not only to impress the tourist, for the clientele is largely Tunisian.

At right angles to the Berka souk is the **El Leffa souk*****, which specialises in woollen goods: carpets and rugs. The atmosphere here, as in the fascinating **Ed Dziria souk**, is more intimate than elsewhere. Everything is very old: the stalls and the traders, often dignified elderly gentleman in their best clothes. The floor of the shops is at waist level giving the passer-by intimate glimpses of craftsmen at work among their heaps of textiles.

At the far end of the Leffa souk, turn left into the **Koumach souk**** (textiles), dating from the 15C. It runs along the west side of the Great Mosque, and consists of three aisles divided by columns painted in red and green. Here too, the ancient stalls disappear under heaps of multicoloured fabrics and special clothing for feast days, like marriages and circumcision ceremonies. The draped fabrics and profusion of colours create an almost theatrical scene, with people playing roles which have not changed in a thousand years.

By going back the way you have come you will pass through several souks dedicated to trade in fabrics: the **souk des Femmes** (women's souk), specialising in second-hand clothes, then the **souk de la laine** (wool souk) and the **souk du coton** (cotton souk). Less spectacular, they are undoubtedly more genuine, more like traditional London street markets or the flea-markets of Paris suburbs than the delights of the Orient. It is fun to dig through the goods on offer, but the jewellery and clothes are in general designed for Arab women.

Beyond the wool and cotton souks is the maze of the **souk des Orfèvres**, or **jewellers' souk**, an Ali Baba's cave of oriental jewellery.

The southern quarters

It is not easy to suggest a specific route inside the souks, because part of the attraction of these busy labyrinths is the pleasure of getting lost in them. Some of the focal points of the medina which should not be missed are to be found to the south of Ez Zitouna.

Go down the rue Tourbet el Bey, the continuation of the Souk des Femmes.

The bustle of trade gradually gives way to the quiet atmosphere of the old city, with children playing, women holding their veils tight between their teeth and people just strolling along. It is difficult to get completely lost because at every street corner square tiles give directions to the main monuments along the "cultural" circuit.

The rue Tourbet el Bey ends with the monument of the same name, one of the most ornate structures in the medina. The **Tourbet el Bey*** *(open every day except Monday, 9.30am-4.30pm. Entrance charge)*, tomb of the Husseinite princes built in the reign of Ali Pacha II (1758-1782) is the largest funerary monument in Tunis, with domes which dominate the façade of yellow sandstone. The domes correspond to the various funeral chambers containing the tombs of sovereigns, their families and some of their ministers. Inside, the cool atmosphere is as striking as the apparent disarray in the arrangement of the tombstones, which interrupt the pathway. The walls are covered with ceramics in tones of orange and yellow, while the hall containing the tombs of those who actually ruled is richly decorated with Italianate polychrome marble. The men's sarcophagi are characterised by carved prismatic colonnettes, with a tarboosh or turban at the top. The women's tombs have marble plaques set at each end.

Go down the rue Sidi Zahmoul, along the left side of the mausoleum, then turn left again into an alleyway that runs under arches, the rue Sidi Kassem.

The Dar Ben Adballah ∗ – *Open 9.30am–4.30pm, except Mondays. Entrance charge.*
This sumptuous 18C palace, rich in panelling, plasterwork and ceramics, used
to house the **Musée des arts et traditions populaires** (Museum of Popular Arts
and Tradition). The entrance opens into a central court with access to four rooms
with displays evoking the daily life of Tunis' middle classes in the 19C and early
20C. The presentation is thematic and deals with "man", "the bride", "woman"
and "the child". Models in period costume, furniture, toys, jewellery and
domestic utensils make this a particularly vivid and effective exhibition. Apart
from the usual refinements like painted ceilings and a marble patio, the palace
still has its traditional **kitchen**. This is perhaps the most touching and attractive
feature (notwithstanding the heat) for modern visitors: it is functional, spacious,
and above all very bright, in contrast with the other very dark rooms which
open only onto the patio. There is a permanent exhibition of traditional crafts:
ironwork, weaving, shoe-making and so on.

Back to and turn right along the rue Sidi Kassem to the rue des Teinturiers. Turn left up
this street, then turn right into the rue El M'Bazaa, which has several vaulted stretches.
The Dar Othman is at 16b.

The Dar Othman ∗ – This little palace was built in the 16C
by Bey Othman, whose wealth was largely the
result of piracy *(see page 209)*. It consists
simply of a ground floor and four bedrooms; strange six-leaved doors open
from the bedrooms on to a patio garden, now somewhat neglected,
but still charming. The Dar Othman is now used as offices by the
Conservation de la medina (Medina
preservation), part of the Ministry of Culture
(not to be confused with the Association de
la sauveguard de la médina, situated at
Dar Lasram, rue du Tribunal): check
it out before it is restored.

If your feet are still up to it, go
back up the rue des Teinturiers,
then turn left into the rue du
Trésor and the

The souk des chéchias

rue el Karchani, peaceful streets with blind walls punctuated here and there with magnificent blue painted and studded doors. As you continue up the hill you will come to the **rue des Andalous★** *(turn right into it)* which is without doubt one of the most beautiful in the medina. The tall gateways under horseshoe arches are a reminder of the aristocratic past of this residential district, once the home of wealthy Andalusian refugees. After the noise and bustle of the rest of the medina, the street is a welcome haven of tranquillity.

From the rue des Andalous, turn up to the left to the Place du Château, leading to the Dar Hussein.

The **Dar Hussein★** (18C), one of the most beautiful palaces in Tunis, was bought and improved in the 19C by Youssef Sahib Et Tabaa, Hammouda Pacha's famous minister. The first municipal council met here in 1858, and in 1882, the palace was the headquarters of the invading French forces. The Place du Château, facing the entrance, dates from this period; it was laid out on the site of a former cemetery. Since independence the Dar Hussein has been the seat of the **Institut national d'Archéologie et d'Art** (National Institute of Archeology and Art). In theory, it is not open to the public, but there is usually no objection to a visitor bold enough to step inside: although there is no access to the various halls which are used as offices, it is possible to enter the enormous patio, with its white marble paving and columns, neo-Corinthian capitals, Kallaline pottery and plasterwork. A door in a corner of the patio opens into a small interior courtyard laid out as a pretty garden.

To the north of the Great Mosque
This route brings you back to the Porte de France. Go back to the corner of the souk el Koumach (fabrics) and the souk el Attarine by the Great Mosque – and go up the rue Sidi Ben Arous.

The first souk that you see on your left, selling the head-coverings known as **chéchias**, is easily identifiable by its gateway of brown stone forming a majestic archway into a kind of dark tunnel. The craft of making chéchias is an ancient one introduced into Tunis by Andalusian immigrants. It had its hour of glory when the *chéchias* of Tunis were exported throughout the East. Though the great days are long since gone, the shops with their tiled floors do not lack charm, with their pierced panelling, painted white, pale green and blue. The workshops are in the rooms over the stalls, and the offices lie at the back.

Beyond the souk of *chéchias* is the souk el Bey, striking in its plainness. Its high walls of dressed stone and its ochre tones make it a pleasant place to stroll through. It is located at the back of the **Dar el Bey★**, which stands at the top of the medina. The beys used to stay in this 18C palace, richly

All is lost...
Even though it has "lost some of its market share", the chéchia has survived the changing face of fashion better than some of its counterparts of the 1930s, such as the Basque beret in France. Tunisian chéchias are still exported to Libya, Tchad and Somalia, in a variety of styles. The Libyans, for example, wear black chéchias with a pompom. The hat has also kept up with modern taste: chéchias are now made in different colours for women, embroidered or decorated with pearls. Although the tradition continues, methods of manufacture have changed. The best chéchias are now made from wool imported from Australia, of the finest quality and impossible to crease. As for colours, the traditional procedures of the Orient have given way to German dyes which can be relied on never to run.

"I fell in love with Tunis when I saw it from the windows of the Salle du Divan in the Bey's palace. [...] It is two o'clock. Their Excellencies are having a siesta. [...] The guide opens the balcony window and sunshine floods on to the red armchairs, the green gold-braided rugs of the Administration, the curtains held back by sword-knot tassels, and the ceiling with its exquisite plasterwork... Tunis can be seen, all of it, against the background of the sea: the free zone, the consuls' houses, the old mosques with their minarets. Your gaze soars over terraces, and old tiled roofs, peers through plaster grilles and looks in vain on the walls for those terrible hooks where once were hung the heads of infidels and revolutionaries."

decorated in the flamboyant Andalusian style. During the Protectorate it was the seat of the Tunisian government, and important guests from Europe were lodged here. Today it is occupied by the prime minister and the minister for foreign affairs.

From the Place du Gouvernement (*in front of the Dar el Bey*), go down the rue de la Kasba. On the right is the elegant **Hammoûda Pacha mosque**, with its symmetrical layout, blind arches and superb octagonal minaret. The **Hammoûda Pacha mausoleum** (1655), next to the mosque, has the same graceful quality. This architectural ensemble was the model for Bourguiba's tomb at Monastir.

Further along the rue de la Kasba, turn right into the rue el Jelloud, then turn into the Impasse Echmmahia.

The **Grave of Princess Aziza** is at *no* 9 in this cul-de-sac, in a private house. This Ottoman princess was a charitable soul who enfranchised her slaves before her death in 1669. The mausoleum, which holds several tombs, is particularly interesting for its interior decoration: polychrome ceramics and plasterwork.

Continue down the rue de la Kasbah.

Before coming out of the medina into the Porte de France, you should first make a small detour through the **souk du cuivre** (copper souk) (*first turning on the left*). You cannot miss the hammering of the young craftsmen making the inevitable, somewhat shiny, carved dishes.

The outlying areas

To really get the feel of the "city within the city" which is the medina, it's best to move out from the centre with its crowds of tourists and wander through the outer areas. Although occasionally the temptation to restore houses and lanes in the "Sidi Bou Said" style has not been resisted, the medina still retains its essentially vernacular style which dates from the end of the 19C and early 20C. This was the time when the medina was opened up to the ordinary people, as wealthy Tunisians abandoned their ancestral palaces and houses and moved into the more prestigious surroundings of the European city. The medina still shows the after-effects of this radical transformation in the character of the area's population and, away from the areas frequented by tourists, it is not unusual to see children running down the alleys after a sheep, an old woman bent over a bucket as she pods peas, or scraggy cats picking over a pile of rubbish, while the menfolk read their papers in groups of two or three in the street.

The shared pleasure of the newspaper

The medina has undergone several more or less successful attempts to clean it up, as can be seen by visiting the district around the **place Bab Souika**. This project, one of the most extensive, dates from the 1980s, and involved the destruction of a large part of the existing urban fabric. The result is an eclectic group of buildings in Arab style, a group which also includes a pedestrian zone, a very large square and the somewhat inappropriate restoration of the **Sidi Mahrez mosque**. This 17C mosque, topped by several white domes, was directly inspired by the mosques of Istanbul. Most of the space in the relatively narrow L-shaped courtyard is occupied by the prayer hall of Sidi Mahrez, the patron saint of Tunis. On the other side of the street opposite the mosque is the **zawiya**. Deeply venerated sites such as this are not accessible to non-Moslems, nor is it really acceptable for them to try and snatch a quick look.

At the top of the medina, the **place du Gouvernement** opens on to the ministerial district with its plethora of flags, black limousines and Arab-style official buildings. With its marble paving, its fig-trees and its magnificent palaces, the square offers a modern and idealised interpretation of what it is to be Arab, in complete contrast to the shabby and dusty medina. These heights overlooking the city were the site of the old Kasbah. They are now crowned with a vast esplanade, open to the winds. At the top of the hill the enormous building, in Arab style, is the **Maison du Parti**. Slightly below it, on the right, in the rue Sinan Pacha, stands the prestigious **Sadiki College**, through which most members of the country's elite have passed at one time or another. The creation of the college in 1875 inaugurated a new era in Tunisia: the teaching of French and science enabled several generations of Tunisian students to have access to the vast field of European culture. The Sadiki college educated a profoundly westernised elite that was to lead Tunisia along the path of reform and independence.

Musée du Bardo★★★ (Bardo Museum)

Allow 2hr. Open 9.30am-4.30pm out of season,
9am-5pm in summer. Closed Monday. Entrance charge.

The museum is 4km from the city centre. From the ave Bourguiba, turn right along the ave de Paris then left into the ave de Madrid, level with the place de la République. Leave the city through Bab Saadoun and go along the bvd du 20 Mars 1956. Metro line 4.

The Museum once consisted of a vast group of buildings made up of several palaces. The oldest dated from the Hafsid period, the most recent from the Husseinite beys who made it their residence and the seat of government in the late 19C. A number of the buildings were destroyed in the 19C. Today the **National Assembly** occupies part of the site, with the remainder devoted to the museum that was established in 1888 in one of the 19C palaces. From the outside, the buildings look more like a barracks than a palace; only the sentinels in their uniform from the era of the Beys, who guard the entrance to the Assembly, recall the princely past. But its surprises are inside, and a visit to the museum gives a glimpse of the luxury which prevailed in the Beys' court. The collections are displayed in a series of splendid halls with magnificent ceilings of painted or gilded wood, including the airy space of a grand reception hall or a vast and elaborately decorated courtyard.

The museum contains a unique collection of mosaics, unmatched anywhere else in the world, recovered from the most famous sites of classical Tunisia: Carthage, Thuburbo Majus, Bulla Regia, Dougga, etc. The fifty halls and galleries of the Bardo are full of them; even Rome cannot match them.

The collections illustrate five great periods: prehistory, the Punic era, the Roman era, the Christian era and the Arab-Moslem period. A sixth section is devoted to Greek statuary discovered during the undersea investigations at Mahdia. The layout of the galleries is confusing. The exhibits are not in chronological order and the numbering of the rooms is far from systematic. In addition, some halls are closed for redevelopment. The following tour offers a selection of the most interesting Roman and early Christian mosaics.

Roman and Paleo-Christian Departments

Paleo-Christian Mosaics – *Ground floor rooms, to the left of the entrance corridor.* The mosaics displayed in these rooms come from Christian and Byzantine churches of the 4-7C. Many of them covered graves and are quite well preserved. One of them, taken from Tabarka and known as **"Ecclesia mater"** is very instructive, offering a fairly precise representation of a 4C church. Another, **"Victoria"** shows two people: a man seated behind a desk (a scribe, a clerk, or perhaps a banker), and a woman called Victoria who may be his wife or his daughter. The mosaics that illustrate martyrdom include a fine pavement showing **Daniel in the lions' den** (in the corridor leading to the collection of stelæ and sarcophagi).

Thuburbo Majus Room – The mosaics and sculptures from the site after which the hall is named (particularly from the 3 and 4C) include a magnificent marble figure of **Hercules.** The most interesting item is a small bas-relief in Hellenistic style, showing **mænads** (1C AD).

The **Bulla Regia Room** displays classical remains from Bulla Regia, including three statues from a temple dedicated to Apollo: **Apollo Citharoedus★**, **Æsculapius★** and **Ceres.**

Among several busts of emperors in a small room at the back is one of **Vespasian**, inventor of toilets with an entrance charge. Guides take pleasure in quoting the phrase attributed to him: "Money has no smell". Interestingly, his is the only bust that has not lost its nose.

Retrace your steps and go up the stairs to the first floor.

Carthage Room – This room occupies the former terrace of the Bey's palace. It is approached via a staircase laid with early Christian funerary mosaics (4-5C) and visitors are greeted on the way up by a 2C **Apollo** from the ruins of the theatre in Carthage. Most of the statues and busts in the room were also found in and around Carthage. Dominated on one side by the majestic silhouette (except for the broken nose) of the **Emperor Hadrian shown as the god Mars**, this vast and colonnaded room provides an excellent display area for superb mosaics spread about on the floor like rugs. **Ornamental tiling★** portrays scenes from rustic daily life. The two very large mosaics come from the house of the Laberii at Oudna. The first, of Greek inspiration (2-3C), depicts a scene from mythology, **Dionysios presenting the vine to Ikarios of Attica**. The second shows **scenes of rural life★**: work in the fields, and hunting. While hunting was a prestigious leisure pursuit for the wealthy who owned weapons and horses, it was a matter of survival for the poor, who made use of traps or tricks (such as goat skins used as camouflage) to catch birds.

The altar at the centre of the room is dedicated to the **gens August**, in other words the family of the Emperor Augustus (1C). Its four sides are decorated with allegorical or mythological bas-reliefs relating to the emperor: Aeneas (ancestor of Augustus in imperial mythology) fleeing from Troy; Rome represented as an Amazon: Augustus officiating at a scene of sacrifice; and finally Apollo as protector of Augustus.

Sousse Room (Hadrumetum) – Everything about this room is huge. As well as the head and the enormous foot from a **statue of Jupiter** (Thuburbo Majus), this former ceremonial hall of the palace houses the vast mosaic of the **Triumph of Neptune** (3C). The tiling measures 137sqm and formerly decorated a Sousse residence. In the centre, Neptune, on his chariot drawn by hippocampus, is sur-

rounded by 56 medallions portraying mermaids riding sea monsters. The most important piece in the room, however, is the mosaic known as the **Lord Julius★★★**. This work, which dates from the 4-5C, adorned a villa in Carthage, and is unique in its portrayal of the life of the great land-owners of North Africa under the late Byzantine empire. It can be read like a cartoon strip: at bottom right, Lord Julius, seated, receives a message; to the left, his wife attends to her toilette while a serving woman with a jewellery box hands her a necklace. The second layer shows the patrician villa and two hunting scenes. The top has been interpreted in various ways: the woman fanning herself at the centre may be the wife of the master, or the guardian spirit of the site.

Dougga Room – The room owes its name mainly to the two venerable models of the capitol and theatre in Dougga, the original location of some of the mosaics on show here, although the most interesting item, the 2C **God Neptune and the Four Seasons★★★ (La Chebba)**, was in fact discovered in the Sfax area. Some authorities see this mosaic as the finest piece in the museum. (*Sometimes also entitled the Triumph of Neptune, it should not be confused with the mosaic of the same name in the Sousse Room.*) There are two reasons for this: its excellent state of preservation, and the marked delicacy of its execution. The art of mosaic reached its peak in this work; its creators can no longer be considered mere craftsmen, they are true artists. The design, however, is less original: Neptune in triumph in his chariot, surrounded by four allegorical figures representing the seasons.

The God Neptune and the Four Seasons

Another item to be noted is a mosaic featuring three vast **Cyclops★** (slightly damaged), shown beating the metal in the fire of Vulcan's forge (Dougga thermal baths, 3-4C).

El Jem Room – Nothing remains of El Jem, the classical Thysdrus, except the coliseum. The city is thought to have been submerged, although archeologists have

Musée du Bardo/GIRAUDON

Tunis

recovered some mosaics shown in this room. One of these is the vast **pavement featuring still lifes** or *Xenia* (3C): ducks, fish, hares, fruit, vegetables, etc. There are also scenes from daily life, such as dice-players. On the ground is a **Triumph of Bacchus★★** (3C), with his chariot drawn by two tigresses and driven by the god Pan. As with all the realistic scenes, the mosaic known as the **hunting scene★** is particularly touching – the terrified hare can be seen crouching in a bush.

Go back through the Carthage room to the Althiburos room.

Althiburos Room – The orchestra balcony shows that this used to be the Bey's concert hall; the orchestra was hidden behind great curtains so that the sovereign's wives could not fall under the spell of any of the musicians. The 4C mosaic on the floor was taken from Medeina, the Althiburos of classical times. Entitled the **"catalogue of boats"★**, it is an outstanding textbook of techniques of fishing and navigation: 23 boats are shown with their names in Greek or Latin. The **banquet mosaic★★**, dating from the same period, offers a very valuable picture of patrician life in Carthage, and depicts the various elements of a feast: host and guests, servers, musicians and dancers. Unlike the popular image of Roman feasting, the guests are seated rather than lying on couches.

Oudna Room – This former dining hall with its ceiling of carved and gilded wood now has a beautiful mosaic with somewhat faded colours: **Orpheus charming the wild animals.**

Virgil room – This is without doubt one of the most beautiful rooms in the palace. Octagonal, richly decorated with plasterwork ceiling, it formed part of the Bey's private apartments. It contains the Tunisian "Mona Lisa" – a mosaic representing the great Latin poet **Virgil★★★**. This 3C work from Sousse shows the poet holding a papyrus roll on his knees on which can be read the eighth verse of the Aeneid. Virgil sits between Clio, the Muse of History, and Melpomene, the Muse of Tragedy. This mosaic, virtually complete, is now the only known portrait of Virgil.

Rooms containing items found beneath the sea at Mahdia – Unfortunately these rooms have been closed for a while, although they are due to reopen in 2000 .This is particularly regrettable because they contain treasures taken from a shipwreck 5km out to sea from Mahdia. The vessel was transporting a cargo of **works of art from the Hellenistic period** (3-2C BC): they include works in marble, and above all bronzes in a perfect state of preservation. The ship appears to have sunk with all its crew and cargo around 81 BC, and it was not until the early 20C that sponge-divers discovered the wreck lying in 39m of water.

Marine mosaic rooms – In this part of the palace the collection contains numerous **marine mosaics** depicting peasants on the sea-shore, Nereids, sea monsters, sea horses, dolphins, and so on. *(This section is currently undergoing renovation)*

Ulysses Room – Many visitors linger in front of the **Ulysses mosaic★★★** (Dougga, 4C), which recounts a famous episode from the Odyssey: Homer's hero is bound to the mast of his ship so that he cannot yield to the song of the Sirens, while his companions have blocked their ears with wax. According to Roman mythology, the Sirens were half-human and half-raptors, and are thus shown here with claws rather than a fish-tail, giving them an even more frightening appearance.

Musée du Bardo/GIRAUDON

Virgil and the muses

This room also contains more marine scenes, including a **Coronation of Venus** (Carthage, 4C), showing the semi-naked goddess crowning herself with a diadem. In the mosaic of the **Triumph of Neptune and Amphytrion★** (Utica, 3-4C), the head of the god Ocean is depicted in a style very often seen in North Africa, with lobster claws in his long hair.

Final rooms – The works on display in this part of the museum are variable in quality and state of preservation, but several of them are worth attention. The inscription on the **Venus crowned by two centauresses** (4C) no doubt refers to the names of the horses shown on each side: *Polystephanus* ("with many crowns") and *Archeus* ("the first"). The presence of horses in many of the mosaics is a reminder of the Roman's passion for racing. The design of **Theseus killing the Minotaur** is interesting for its geometric form symbolising the labyrinth. Finally, it is worth looking at a very fine **Diana the Huntress** (Thuburbo Majus, 3-4C). The goddess, mounted on a stag, is surrounded by medallions featuring a gladiator and various animals (not all wild) destined for the arena.

Parc du Belvédère (Belvedere Park)

Take the ave Mohammed V out of the city centre and follow it straight ahead for 2km to the place Pasteur.

A cool oasis in the heart of the city, the Parc du Belvédère is much larger than it initially appears to be. Although the shady entrance in the Place Pasteur seems to indicate an ordinary public garden, this is in reality an enormous space of more than a hundred hectares, criss-crossed with roads open to both cars and pedestrians. Laid out on a hillside, it is a pleasingly well-vegetated park planted with numerous specimen trees (pines, palms, figs, eucalyptus, olives, etc.) Shortly beyond the main entrance there is an artificial lake, surrounded by lawns. The tea house is a very popular meeting-place among the young people of Tunis, particularly for students and their professors. When the city is stifling in the heat, this concentration of greenery is a wonderful source of fresh air.

In the **Jardin zoologique** (Zoo) *(open 9am-6pm, closed on Mondays. Entrance charge)*, African fauna are the main attraction: pink flamingoes, elephants, lions, monkeys and jackals. Also worth noting is the 17C **midha** or ablutions room, and a Moorish café well screened from the sun. Nearby are attractions for children, and of course the inevitable sellers of ice-creams and sweets.

Anyone interested in seeing the work of contemporary Tunisian artists, should go to the **Museum of Modern Art** (Musée d'art moderne) housed in the former casino *(open every day, entrance free)*.

The top of the park is crowned by the 17C **Koubba,** an astonishing pavilion in Arab-Andalusian style. Formerly in the old Manouba district, it is enjoying a second lease of life in the Belvedere. Beneath its superb cupolas are magnificent galleries, arches of carved plaster, colonnades, stained glass and pierced panels of plaster-work. A haven of peace, the Koubba makes a good destination for a walk. The **view** from the terrace looks out over greenery to the Gulf of Tunis and the distant Bou Kornine. The atmosphere is particularly delightful as twilight falls.

The ministerial district

J.-F. Galmiche

Tunis

GETTING THERE

By air – Planes land at **Tunis-Carthage Airport**, ☎ (01) 754 000 / 755 000 / 848 000, mid-way between Tunis and Marsa (9km from each other). It has all the services necessary for your first contact with Tunisia, from travel agencies to a tourist office. Two banks are open daily for money exchange and there is also a cash dispenser. Be aware when leaving Tunisia that you must board the plane 40min before take-off.

The number 35 bus runs approximately every 30min between the airport and the centre of Tunis with stops at Habib Bourguiba, Tunis Marine, the Hôtel Africa and the Place de Palestine (behind the Republic metro station). The trip takes about 30min and costs 650 millimes. A bus company operated by the agency Transtours links the airport and the railway station, departing from Place de Barcelone, 6am-10pm (7am-9pm in the other direction).

By boat – There are regular crossings from Marseille and Toulon in France and Genoa and Naples in Italy. Ships arrive at the port in La Goulette, 10km from Tunis. A regular train service, the TGM (Tunis-La Goulette-La Marsa) connects with the centre of Tunis and with the different coastal resorts.

By train – **SNCFT**. The central railway station is located at Place de Barcelone, 5min walking distance from the ave Habib Bourguiba, ☎ (01) 345 511, schedule information ☎ (01) 254 440. It is only used for trains coming from the provinces since there are no longer services to Algeria and Morocco. Open daily 5am-12midnight.

Among the main lines, there are 5 slow trains daily to Bizerte (90min); one train daily to Hammamet (75min); 11 trains daily to Sousse, 2 to Mahdia, 7 to El Jem and Sfax, 3 to Gabès (7hr) and one night train to Gafsa (7hr 35min).

By TGM – The TGM (Tunis-la Goulette-La Marsa train) links the capital to the best-known seaside resorts and beaches. The train departs from the Tunis Marine railway station, near the ave Bourguiba (metro lines 1 and 4 and several bus routes), ☎ (01) 244 696. The trains depart approximately every 15min, from 3.30am-12midnight and take 35min to reach the terminus at Marsa beach. Single tickets cost 350 millimes for La Goulette and 560 millimes for La Marsa.

By bus – There are two bus stations, serving different destinations.

Gare routière Nord – 400m from Place Bab Saadoun heading towards Bizerte. For information call ☎ (01) 562 663. Three companies compete with each other:

SNTRI – Information available 4am - 9pm. ☎ (01) 562 299. This national company goes to all the northern cities. There are 8 services daily to Tabarka (3hr 15min), 5 services to Aïn Draham and 17 daily buses to Le Kef.

SRTB (Société régionale de transport de Bizerte / Bizerte Regional Transport Co) – For information contact ☎ (01) 563 653. This company operates buses to Bizerte (21 per day), Mateur and Menzel Bourguiba. It is worth paying a few extra millimes for the coaches with videos and air-conditioning (travel time, 1hr)

SRT Jendouba – ☎ (01) 246 053 goes to Jendouba, Beja and Menjez el bab.

Gare routière Sud – in Bab Alioua. For information, call ☎ (01) 399 255/ 399 548. Buses depart for every destination, including Libya and Algeria, from this station.

By shared taxi – Taxi stands are usually located near bus stations and serve the same destinations. Don't try to bargain as prices are fixed and are more or less the same as bus fares. You can always ask to see the price list.

Bab Saadoun – This station serves the north and east of the country. Le Kef, Tabarka and Bizerte.

Place Moncef Bey – Cars head south to Sousse, Monastir, Sfax, Gafsa and Kairouan.

Bab Alioua serves Cap Bon: Hammamet and Nabeul.

GETTING AROUND

It is easy to get around central Tunis on foot. Restaurants, hotels and embassies are concentrated around the ave Habib Bourguiba and are near to the medina, which can only be visited on foot.

By metro – SMLT (Société métro léger de Tunis / Tunis Light Railway Company) is enjoyable since it does not run underground. Since Tunis is at sea level, it was impossible to build an underground railway system. In 1985 the city adopted a tram system, called the "métro léger". There are 5 lines, all of which stop at the SNCFT station. Metro line 4 ends at the Bardo and line 3 stops near the Bab Saadoun bus station. Line 1 connects the TGM station with Tunis Marina. Pre-stamped tickets are available for 370 millimes. Weekly and monthly passes (valid for one return journey per day) can be purchased at the ticket counter in each station. On-the-spot fines of TD10 are payable for attempting to travel without a ticket (TD15 if paid within a week). For all fines, go to 60 ave J Jaurès, ☎ (01) 288 100.

By bus – Only the most adventurous visitors from abroad attempt to use the bus service, even though some lines operate round the clock. There are few maps, with the exception of those near the place de Barcelone, and all directions are in Arabic. Tickets cost between 250 and 750 millimes.

SNT (Société nationale des transports / National Transport Company), 1 ave Habib Bourguiba, ☎ (01) 259 422. For information, call ☎ (01) 571 11. For information at the Bab Saadoune depot, call ☎ (01) 801 216.

By taxi – There is a choice between the "big taxis" authorised by the city of Tunis to go beyond the boundaries of the Tunis governorship, or the "small taxis" which can be identified by their yellow colour. The latter are very reasonably priced and are only allowed to operate within the metropolitan area, which includes the nearby beaches. The pick-up charge is 310 millimes and rates are rarely more than TD2 within the city.

Count on spending approximately a dozen dinars for the beaches. The price of a taxi ride between the airport and the town centre should not exceed TD3; however, local taxi drivers are often unwilling to use the meter on this journey and instead charge a flat rate of TD5. All official taxis have meters. They are numerous and can be hailed on the street. **Allô Taxi**, ave Habib Bourguiba. ☎ 01 492 422/783 311.

By car – Avoid driving in the centre of Tunis. Parking is difficult, and one-way streets can be confusing. A car is useful only for the suburban areas or for the musée du Bardo. The parking meters may not work, however it is not uncommon for someone to ask for a parking fee. The only people authorised to do this are those who have a permit and can provide a receipt. As in the rest of Tunisia, be careful about getting clamped.

Car rental – In addition to the usual international companies, Tunisia has a dozen local rental companies. The majority of the rental agencies will levy a surcharge of TD5 if you drop the car at the airport.

Avis Hôtel Africa Méridien, ave Habib Bourguiba, ☎ (01) 341 249. Ave de la Liberté ☎ (01) 788 563. Hôtel Hilton Belvédère ☎ (01) 787 167. Airport ☎ (01) 750 299.

Europcar, 17 ave Habib Bourguiba ☎ (01) 340 303. 81 ave de la Liberté ☎ (01) 287 235. Airport ☎ (01) 233 411.

Hertz, 29 ave Habib Bourguiba ☎ (01) 248 559. Airport ☎ (01) 231 822. Port de la Goulette ☎ (01) 737 788. **Mattei (Ada)**, Airport ☎ (01) 767 0233.

Towing ☎ (01) 840 840 / 801 211.

ADDRESS BOOK

Emergencies

A list of emergency telephone numbers is published every day in the French newspaper "La Presse".
Pharmacie de nuit Khabthani Rached, 43 ave Habib Bourguiba ☎ (01) 252 507.

Pharmacie de nuit Karray, ave de la Liberté ☎ (01) 243 520.
SOS Médecins ☎ (01) 341 250.
Anti-poison centre ☎ (01) 245 075.
Hôpital Habib Thameur ☎ (01) 397 000.

Tourist information – ONTT (Tunisian National Tourist Office), 1 ave Mohammed V, ☎ (01) 341 077, Fax (01) 350 997. In summer, open daily, 8am-1pm, 4pm-7pm, 9am-12pm, Sundays; winter, open daily, 8am-6pm, 9am-12pm, Sundays. Free city plans, one of Tunis and a more detailed map of the medina are available, as well as a map showing the principal tourist attractions.

CRTT (Tunisian Regional Tourist Office), 31 rue Hasdrubal, 1002 Tunis Lafayette, ☎ (01) 845 618 / 840 622, Fax (01) 842 492.

Tourist Office at Tunis-Carthage airport, ☎ (01) 755 000, and at Tunis Railway Station, Place de Barcelone, ☎ (01) 334 444.

Banks / Currency exchange – There is a foreign exchange bureau in most large banks.

Amen Bank (formerly the Tunisian Land and Commercial Credit Bank), 13 ave de France.

Banque du Sud, 95 ave de la Liberté, 1002 Tunis Belvédère

STB (Société tunisienne de banque / Tunisian Bank Company), 52 ave Habib Bourguiba.

UIB (International Bank Union), 65 ave Habib Bourguiba. There are two **cash dispensers** which can automatically change foreign currency, on the ave Habib Bourguiba, near the rue de Hollande, and at the Amen Bank, 13 ave de France.

Cash Dispensers – There are numerous cash dispensers which accept credit cards on ave Mohammed V, 52 ave Habib Bourguiba, 57 rue Mokhtar Attia, the Dorra shopping mall, ave 1ᵉʳ Septembre 1969, Place de la Victoire and rue Hedi Nouira.

American Express – 59 ave Habib Bourguiba ☎ (01) 347 015 / 354 993.

Main post office – Open all year, daily, 8am-6pm, 9am-11am Sundays. In summer, 7.30am-1pm, 5pm-7pm, Monday-Thursday, 7.30am-1.30pm, Friday and Saturday. During Ramadan, 8am-3pm, Monday-Saturday.

Telephone / fax – There are public pay phones all over the city. The main office is at 8 rue Jemal Abdelnasser and is open 24 hours a day. The office at 5 rue de Marseille is open until 11pm, while the one at 6 rue de Carthage (on the corner of the Café de Paris) is open 24 hours a day. Some pay-phone offices are equipped with fax machines, for example at Publitel at the SNCFT train station at the place de Barcelone.

Internet – Publinet, Centre Aïda, Boutique 12, ave Tahar ben Ammar, El Menzah 9, ☎ (01) 881 061. Open every day 9am-midnight. Other cyber-cafés are set to open in the town centre. For information on new cafés, contact the Ministry of Communication, ☎ (01) 359 014.

Embassies and Consulates

United Kingdom, British Embassy, 5 Place de la Victoire, Tunis, ☎ (01) 341 444 / 341 689 / 341 962, Fax (01) 354 877.

Consular and Visa Section, 141-143 ave de la Liberté, Tunis ☎ (01) 793 322 / 794 810, Fax (01) 792 644.

USA, Embassy of the United States of America, 144 ave de la Liberté, Belvédère, 1002 Tunis ☎ (01) 782 566, Fax (01) 789 719.

Canada, Canadian Embassy, PO Box 31, 3 rue du Sénégal, Place d'Afrique, Belvédère, 1002 Tunis. ☎ (01) 798 004 / 796 577, Fax (01) 792 371.

Airline and Shipping Companies

Tunis Air, Reservations ☎ (01) 700 700, Fax (01) 700 009; main office, 113 ave de la Liberté ☎ (01) 841 967; El Mechtel office ☎ (01) 785 777; Hilton Hotel office ☎ (01) 782 800 / 282 000. Tunis-Carthage Airport ☎ (01) 754 000 / 755 000 / 848 000.

Tuninter, immeuble Maghrébia, bvd du 7 Novembre, ☎ (01) 701 717; airport ☎ (01) 754 000 / 755 000, extensions 3465 and 3466.

CTN (Compagnie Tunsienne de Navigation / Tunisian Navigation Company), 122 rue de Yougoslavie ☎ (01) 322 775 / 802, Fax (01) 354 855. La Goulette ☎ (01) 735 111 / 735 957, Fax (01) 736 506.

Miscellaneous – Left luggage at the SNCFT train station, place de Barcelone. Open 5.30am-9.30pm. Rates: TD2 for small lockers, TD3 for large ones.

WHERE TO STAY

Unlike the hotels at beach resorts where rates vary according to the season, hotel rates in Tunis remain the same throughout the year. For those on a low budget, staying in Tunis and using the TGM to go to the beach is the most economic solution. Hotels on the coast are nevertheless more pleasant and it is easy to do the journey in the other direction if you wish to visit Tunis (see Making the most of North Tunis, page 158).

Under US$20

Hôtel Transatlantique, 106 rue de Yougoslavie, ☎ (01) 340 680 / 334 319 – 45rm ✱ ✗ The building stands out because of the old tiling at the entrance. The rooms are spacious with wooden furniture dating from the 1950s. This would be an excellent address if the smell of disinfectant was not quite so strong.

Hôtel Salammbô, 6 rue de Grèce, ☎ (01) 334 252, Fax (01) 337 498 – 55rm ✱ A modest but clean and centrally-located hotel. Ask for a room with a private bathroom. A supplement of TD5 per day for air-conditioning and television is payable.

From US$18-42

🛏Hôtel Maison Dorée, 6 bis rue de Hollande (access by no 3 rue d'El Koufa), ☎ (01) 240 631 / 240 632, Fax (01) 332 401, majestic@gnet.tn – 48rm ✱ ℰ ✗ This is the best choice for someone looking for somewhere quiet and unpretentious to stay. Built in 1906, the hotel is one of the oldest in the city along with the Majestic. Even the staff seem happy – the same people work here year after year. Ask for a room with a private bath. Air-conditioning is optional.

Hôtel Majestic, 36 ave de Paris, ☎ (01) 332 848 / 332 666, Fax (01) 336 908 – 92rm ✱ ▤ ℰ TV ✗ This is the other veteran of the Tunis hotels. The elaborate façade is a reminder that until quite recently this was one of the most prestigious places to stay in Tunis. The rooms are comfortable and convenient and the terrace overlooking the city is a good place to enjoy an aperitif.

More than US$60

Hôtel Carlton, 31 ave Habib Bourguiba, ☎ (01) 330 644, Fax (01) 338 168 – 78rm ✱ ▤ ℰ TV ✗ CC Its central location makes this hotel convenient for business people. It was renovated in 1994 and has direct telephone and satellite television facilities in each room. Unfortunately, the reception staff are not particularly affable and the service in the restaurant is a bit slow.

More than US$75

Hôtel Africa Méridien, 50 ave Habib Bourguiba, ☎ (01) 347 477, Fax (01) 347 432 – 168rm ✱ ▤ TV ℰ ⌇ ✗ CC A big corporate hotel located in the centre of town. Part of the Meridien hotel chain, the Africa has a swimming pool on the 5th floor and a disco on the 20th. There is an excellent restaurant with panoramic views.

Hôtel Hilton, ave de la Ligue arabe, in the parc du Belvédère, ☎ (01) 782 100 / 782 800, Fax (01) 782 208 / 781 713 – 244rm ✱ ▤ ℰ TV ⌇ ✗ CC A new hotel overlooking the parc du Belvédère. Its guests are mostly business people who are prepared to pay up to half a million dinars for the presidential suite.

Hôtel Abou Nawas El Mechtel, 3 ave Ouled Haffouz, ☎ (01) 783 200, Fax (01) 784 758 / 785 564 – 486rm ✱ ▤ ℰ TV ⌇ ✗ CC Slightly away from the centre, this grand hotel is hardly affected by the capital's noise and congestion. To satisfy its exclusive clientele, it offers five restaurants as well as an Oriental dinner/show on the 9th floor. In the summer, avoid rooms overlooking the swimming pool as it can be rather noisy.

Hôtel Oriental Palace, 29 ave Jean Jaurès, ☎ (01) 348 846 / 342 500, Fax (01) 350 327 – 238rm 📶 🗎 🖉 📺 ✗ 📼 Despite its location in a run-down part of the city, this hotel caters mostly for government dignitaries. Security is correspondingly tight, and any visitors calling here will have to leave their papers at reception. But the classical antiquities which form part of the furnishings are authentic and have been chosen with great care.

EATING OUT

Restaurants in Tunis generally shut down during the month of August.

• In the modern city

Under US$6

Club Sandwich (Plan I, C4), 120 rue de Yougoslavie. This tiny establishment is always jam-packed. It serves the best sandwiches to take-away in Tunis. Open every day, except Sunday, until 9pm.

Carcassonne (Plan I, C4), 8 ave de Carthage. ☎ (01) 240 702. For those on a low budget, this restaurant offers a franco-tunisian set menu for US$3. Although unoriginal and basic, Carcassonne provides excellent value-for-money and very efficient service.

US$10-20

Chez Nous (Plan I, C4), 5 rue de Marseille, T (01) 723 992 / 243 043. 🍷 📼 Ever since its opening in 1935, this has been the most popular Tunis restaurant for night owls. The photos on the walls are evidence of how many stars have eaten here. The cuisine is irreproachable. Lovers of spicy food should order the harissa with its particularly delicious spicy sauce.

Chez Slah (Plan I, C4), 14 bis rue Pierre de Coubertin, ☎ (01) 258 588. 🍷 📼 This restaurant continues to maintain its reputation as the best seafood restaurant in Tunis. Although it is tucked away in a dubious neighbourhood, on the fringe of ave Habib Bourguiba , it is filled with businessmen at lunchtime and with families in the evening. Closed on Mondays.

L'Orient (Plan I, C4), 7 rue Ali Bach Hamba, ☎ (01) 242 058. 🍷 📼 Despite the heterogeneous decor (cross between the Orient and an alpine chalet), the Egyptian soap operas on the TV and the stained jackets on the waiters, this is a cheerful place, with excellent méchouïa, lamb cutlets and baked shrimps. Closed on Sundays.

Le Duc, (Plan I, C3), 7 bis rue Gandhi, ☎ (01) 350 020 / 337 979, Fax (01) 339 020. 🍷 📼 Specialises in Jewish cuisine. Closed on Friday evenings and for Saturday lunch. Take-away meals and banqueting service.

Margaritas (Plan I, C4), (this is the Hôtel Maison Dorée's restaurant), 6 bis rue de Hollande, ☎ (01) 240 631/240 632, Fax (01) 332 401. 🍷 This unpretentious restaurant, located in the centre of Tunis, serves Franco-Tunisian cuisine. Not the place for an exotic meal. The kitchen closes at 9.30pm.

More than US$20

L'Astragale (Plan I, C1), 17 rue Charles Nicolle (pass by the rue Khadi Iyad), ☎ (01) 890 455. 📼 Away from the centre in a villa with 1920s decor this restaurant caters mainly for business people and those who can afford the somewhat inflated prices. The menu is "nouvelle cuisine" with a Mediterranean touch.

• In the medina

Under US$10

Echikh (Plan III), 26 rue des Tamis, souk el Attarine, ☎ (01) 335 512. Lunch only, closed Sundays. There is a small terrace from which you can observe the comings and goings of the souk. Alternatively, dine on the first floor of the restaurant. This is an unpretentious restaurant where you can try Tunisian specialities at a reasonable price. Get there early, as only a limited quantity of the dish of the day is prepared.

Madhdaoui (Plan III, B2), rue Jamaa Zitouna, near the great mosque. This restaurant is ideal for some seafood or a quick bite while shopping at the souk. Open for lunch daily except on Sundays.

Tunis

From US$10-20

Le M'rabet (Plan III, B2), el Trouk souk, ☎ (01) 261 729 / 236 681. The food is nothing special, but at weekends, the evening meal is accompanied by a folklore show.

Dar Bel Hadj (Plan III, B2), rue des Tamis (on the left when heading toward the kasbah), ☎ (01) 336 910. ♈ In a typical medina dwelling, this formerly unpretentious restaurant has been elaborately restyled. There is malouf music at the weekend.

More than US$20

⊛ **Le Dar el Jeld** (Plan III, A1), 5 rue Dar el Jeld, ☎ (01) 260 916 / 567 129 / 567 130. ♈ ‖cc‖ A small bouquet of jasmine is served on a silver platter to each guest as they arrive in this 18C dwelling, built by a family of leather merchants (hence its Arabic name). It is furnished with antiques and fine old carpets. The menu has a good selection of specialities, such as spinach "m'batten" (veal meatballs with spinach), or tajines ("malsouka"), although the couscous is rather mediocre. The desserts are excellent. Bring a light sweater in the summer months when the air-conditioning is on full blast.

Essaraya (Plan III, A3), 6 rue Ben Mahmoud, ☎ (01) 560 310 / 260 703, Fax (01) 335 582 / 571 465 ♈ ‖cc‖ This is the most pretentious restaurant in the old city. It tries to be the centre of cultural and tourist activities in the medina. Like the Dar El Jeld or the less luxurious Dar Bel Hadj, it is a former residence that has been restored. The main room is dominated by a dome of engraved plexiglass. The service is obsequious. A security guard leads diners through the medina's maze if you come from the car park near the kasbah.

WHERE TO GO FOR A DRINK

Cafés – Sitting in cafés is a favourite pastime for Tunisians, along with the beach, and there are cafés everywhere. Those located on ave Habib Bourguiba are good places to people-watch.

• In the modern city

Café de Paris (Plan I, C4), 2 ave de Carthage (on the corner of ave Habib Bourguiba), ☎ (01) 240 583 ♈ 🍴 The terrace of this restaurant, a veritable institution, is one of the best places for people-watching in the capital. Even in the heat of Tunis, the waiters wear the uniform of a traditional French waiter.

Café de l'Hôtel Africa-Méridien, 50 ave Habib Bourguiba. Although the café is separated from the avenue by a low wall, this does not interfere with the view of the street life.

Hôtel Majestic, 36 ave de Paris, ☎ (01) 332 848 / 332 666, Fax (01) 336 908. A very pleasant terrace café on the first floor that overlooks a grove of trees across the street.

• In the medina

⊛ **Le M'rabet** (Plan III, B2), located in the el Trouk souk, is a good place to take a break and sip mint tea, either sitting on mats in the tearoom or under the trees in the small interior garden.

⊛ **Café M'naouar** (Plan III, B2), 31 rue Sidi Ben Arous. In this convivial café you can smoke chicha and drink mint tea. Fresh fruit juices and delicious cakes and pastries are also available. Closed on Sundays.

LEISURE

Festivals – Festival of the Medina. Numerous activities and concerts take place in the old city during the month of Ramadan.

Hammams – One of the most authentic for men is on the rue Kachachine. Open 5am-5pm. Entrance rate TD1. For women, the best hammam is the one on the rue de Marseille.

Cinema – The majority of cinemas are situated in the same area, between the ave Habib Bourguiba, rue de Yougoslavie and rue Ibn Khaldoun. Programmes are published in La Presse newspaper, published daily.

SHOPPING

Bakeries – For special occasions, Tunisians always order their cakes in advance at a private bakery. But cake fanciers have plenty of opportunities to satisfy their craving as and when it takes them.

Les Galets, 69 bis ave Taïeb Mhiri, ☎ (01) 796 359, Fax (01) 797 410 (in front of Belvédère, near the place Pasteur). Open until 7.30pm except on Sundays. Here you can find "baklaouas" or almond "caaks". These delicious pastries are easily transported and make good gifts. The owner will be happy to pack them in attractive boxes decorated with sugar "jewels".

Maison Dabari, 7 rue des Tanneurs. Open until 6pm except on Sundays. This bakery specialises in sugared doughnuts, "bombolonis" and "makhroud". There are also fricassees and savoury pastries stuffed with tuna, olives, hard-boiled eggs and harissa.

Ben Yedder, 7 rue Charles de Gaulle, 20 ave Charles Nicolle and 139 bvd du 20 Mars in the Bardo. This chain of bakeries has lost much of its former quality.

Pâtisserie, on the corner of Jamaa Zitouna and el Blat souk. Specialities of the house are "makhroud" and "caak".

Antiques and Handicrafts
• In the modern city

Antiquités Youssef Ayoub, 27 ave Habib Bourguiba, ☎ (01) 240 505. This is a real treasure house with genuine but very expensive antique enamel jewellery from Jerba, as well as more modestly-priced silverware and, above all, magnificent chandeliers. Some of these, such as the oil-lit chandeliers from mosques, may have new ironwork, but, as the proprietor will be keen to confirm, genuine old glass. However, this is not a place where bargaining is practised.

SOCOPA. The various state-operated stores offer a standard selection of Tunisian arts and crafts. In addition to the carpets and traditional pottery, some contemporary items are on offer.

Corner of ave H Bourguiba and ave de Carthage (ground floor of the Palmarium) ☎ (01) 348 860.

Ave de l'Indépendance, ☎ (01) 512 400.
Hôtel Abou Nawas, ☎ (01) 350 878.
Rue Kord Ali El Omrane, ☎ (01) 280 828.
Tunis-Carthage Airport, ☎ (01) 236 000, extension 3743. C
SOCOPA stores accept cash or credit cards.

• In the medina

El-Dar, on the corner of rue Sidi Ben Arous and El Trouk souk, ☎ (01) 261 732, Fax (01) 570 201. The prices may be high but this old house in the medina, which combines antiques with contemporary crafts, has a very good selection of Tunisian arts and crafts.

Hanout Arab, 52 bis rue Jamaa Zitouna, ☎ (01) 240 718. A refined shop amongst the stalls selling babouche slippers and ashtrays at rock-bottom prices. In what the owner calls his "secret garden of Tunisian crafts", there are a number of well-presented rare and unusual items.

Tapis Salem Ben Ghorbal, 11 El Leffa souk, ☎ (01) 261 049. Unlike the enormous carpet shops in the souks, this tiny shop offers an interesting selection of traditional "kilims".

Chez Mansouri Mouhani, 106 El Blat souk (go up the rue Jamaa ez Zitouna and turn left just before reaching the mosque). The proprietor is the king of gum arabic. He also offers good-quality henna and incense, as well as a specially-prepared love-potion.

Bookshops – Since French is a compulsory subject in schools, there are plenty of bookshops selling books in the French language. Almost all the kiosks along the ave Bourguiba carry international newspapers in English. The availability of French daily newspapers depends on the current political mood, while magazines, particularly those catering to women, can be found more easily. You can sometimes unearth old books on Tunisia, or paperbacks in French. As for novels, the classics can be found in bookshops along the ave de France.

Espace Diwan, 9 rue Sidi Ben Arous, opposite the El Dar Antique Shop, in the el Trouk souk, ☎ (01) 572 398. One of the best places to find old postcards as well as books dating from the time of the French protectorate.

Librairie du Carlton, in the gallery of the Carlton hotel, 31 ave Habib Bourguiba (enter on the rue Mustapha Kemal Ataturk), ☎ (01) 336 750. Open 9am-1pm / 3pm-7pm and until 9pm in the summer (though the owner is not always punctual). In addition to some paperback books or art books on Tunisia, this bookshop carries CDs of local music.

Second-hand bookstore, 10 rue de Marseille. The piles of books spilling out on to the pavement are the best advertisement for this establishment, which specialises in old textbooks, paperbacks and books on France. Unfortunately, there is nothing on Tunisia.

Bibliothèque de la Khaldounia (part of the National Library), Souk des Parfumeurs, ☎ (01) 245 338, Fax (01) 342 700. A good place to consult old reference books on Tunisia. Open 8am-2.30pm in winter, 7.30am-1.30pm in summer.

NORTH OF THE GULF OF TUNIS
FROM LA GOULETTE TO GAMMARTH
Governorship of Tunis
Gammarth is 27km from Tunis – a day's visit

Not to be missed
The palace of the Baron d'Erlanger
and mint tea in the Nattes café at Sidi Bou Saïd.
Dinner at La Goulette.

And remember...
Bring your swimming gear.
Sidi Bou Saïd is less crowded out of season.

Access by rail on the TGM line (Tunis-La Goulette-La Marsa): departures approximately every 15min (see Making the most of North Tunis). The train terminates at La Marsa, so another means of transport is necessary to reach Gammarth. By car, leave Tunis by the ave Bourguiba and cross the Lake of Tunis.

This tour close to the capital takes in a series of attractive small towns along the north coast of the Gulf of Tunis. After the enclosed atmosphere of the souks it is good to breathe in the open sea air in a green setting of scattered pines and mimosas. The names of Sidi Bou Saïd and La Marsa ring out like promises of luxurious idleness, blue skies and welcoming beaches. Salammbô and Carthage recall history and literature, in the works of Virgil, Flaubert and others down the centuries.

■ **La Goulette** – The trip across the Lake of Tunis to La Goulette is not particularly exciting: it passes through a no man's land of docks, pylons, electricity stations, cranes and oil depots. The square on the way into the town from the station does not bode well either lined as it is with shanty-town dwellings and with more than its fair share of rubbish blowing around. However, this is where it was decided to relocate the **equestrian statue of the "supreme combatant"**, which used to look haughtily down on the Place d'Afrique in Tunis. La Goulette was felt to deserve the honour just as much as Tunis, since it was here that Bourguiba received a rapturous welcome from the crowds on his return from France on 1 June 1955, where he had negotiated the first step towards independence at the Franco-Tunisian Conventions. Behind the statue is a far older monument, the gateway which once formed part of the line of the city walls built by Charles V of Spain. The Spaniards also built the now rather shabby-looking **Fortress of the Kasbah**, which fell to the Turks in 1574 despite being defended by, amongst others, Don Miguel de Cervantes, the creator of Don Quixote. The kasbah was subsequently used for many years as a prison.

Despite the less than attractive surroundings, the little town is not without charm. It has a cheerful atmosphere, particularly in the summer, when crowds of local people come here to enjoy the "complet-poisson", a dish that traditionally consists of freshly caught sea perch (loup de mer), served with tomatoes and chips. Evening is the liveliest time, when the jasmine sellers ply their trade and the restaurants are full of diners eating by the light of lanterns.

Leave La Goulette by the ave Franklin Roosevelt and go through the suburbs of Khereddine, Le Kram and Salammbô. Carthage comes into view, dominated on the left by Byrsa Hill above the vast ochre building of the cathedral of St Louis.

■ **Carthage**★★ – *(See page 162)*

Leave Carthage by going past the presidential palace (on your right) and continuing straight ahead to Sidi Bou Saïd.

■ Sidi Bou Saïd★
Allow 1hr

If you arrive on a TGM train, get out at the Sidi Bou Saïd station; the centre of the village is a 15min walk away. There is no access for cars, which must be left in the car-park (parking fee) below the village, near the old fountain.

Sidi Bou Saïd offers a stereotypical image of age-old Tunisia, with steep paved lanes and dazzling white houses with their blue shutters and studded doors. It is a kind of smart Montmartre, Hampstead or Greenwich Village, transported to a hillside overlooking Carthage and the Gulf of Tunis. The absence of cars helps create an attractive and peaceful atmosphere. Each of its proud dwellings hints at a mystery which, sadly for the outsider, remains mysterious: the only one of these luxurious houses that can be visited is the palace of the Baron d'Erlanger, though gateways opened from time to time to show sumptuous gardens, richly-planted and gloriously scented, full of bougainvillea, honeysuckle and wild vines. Ever since the time of Flaubert and Chateaubriand, writers and artists have been coming here, among them André Gide, Colette, Simone de Beauvoir and Paul Klee.

Strolling through Sidi Bou

The main street leads you to the impressive stone steps of the famous **Café des Nattes**★. Few visitors resist the ritual of sitting cross-legged among *chicha* smokers and drinking mint tea served with pine kernels. Towards the top of the village is a small **cemetery** with its white gravestones gently curving in at the top. These hollows which retain the rain are known as "bird-bowls". The **lighthouse** stands just below the cemetery; this is not a tourist attraction, but the

Doors which open onto magnificent gardens...

R. Renaudeau/HOA QUI

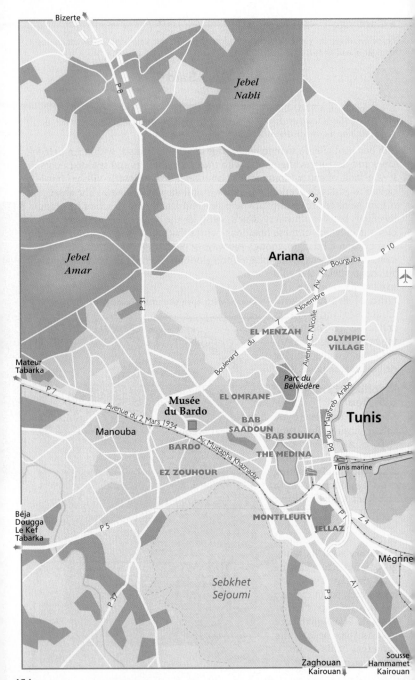

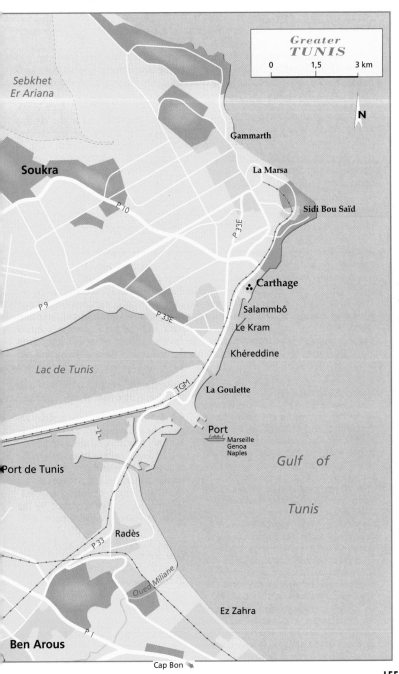

Greater **TUNIS**

0   1,5   3 km

Sebkhet Er Ariana

Gammarth

Soukra

La Marsa

P 10

Sidi Bou Saïd

P 33E

P 9

∴ **Carthage**

P 33E

Salammbô

Le Kram

Lac de Tunis

Khéreddine

TGM

La Goulette

Port

Marseille
Genoa
Naples

Gulf   of

Tunis

◀ **Port de Tunis**

Radès

P 33

Oued Miliane

Ez Zahra

P 1

Ben Arous

Cap Bon ◣

occasional interested caller is welcome. From the top of this little red tower there is a view over the blue bay to a distant majestic mountain often swathed in mist, the Mont Bou Kornine.

Otherwise, Sidi Bou Saïd is a place for relaxation rather than for sightseeing, and it is worthwhile leaving the centre to explore the lanes which have not been subjected to quite such a thoroughgoing restoration. On the way down the rue Taïeb Méhiri from the lighthouse, the domes of the zawiya are visible, the tomb of Abou Saïd, the village's patron saint. According to one legend, the saint was not Abou Saïd at all, but Saint Louis of France. Having succumbed to the charms of the country and a young Berber girl, the pious king is said to have adopted the identity of Abou Saïd, while a poor man, conveniently his double, died of the plague in his place. The truth is less exciting: Saint Louis genuinely died of the plague and Sidi Bou Saïd, a mystic of Moroccan origin, was a figure of Sufi belief. This place of calm and meditation is closed to non-Moslems.

The entrance to Baron d'Erlanger's palace is at the bottom of the village, close to the car-park, on the rue du 2 mars 1934.

Ennejma Ezzahra**, the palace built by Baron d'Erlanger between 1912 and 1922, is now the **Centre for Arab and Mediterranean Music** *(open 9am-1pm and 2pm-5pm, in winter, 9am-12.30pm and 3pm-6.30pm in summer, closed on Monday. Entrance charge.)*. It houses a varied range of activities concerned with preserving and developing the musical heritage particularly of the Arab world, and regularly puts on concerts. Overlooking the sea, approached along an avenue of aloes and orange trees and set in a large park with Andalusian and Persian gardens, the palace has superb rooms with a wealth of columns and wood panelling. The music salon, the library and the black marble fountain in the grand salon are truly amazing. The lavish interiors created by the Baron are at their most evocative when filled with the music which he loved and did so much to preserve.

Baron d'Erlanger (1872-1932)

Heir to wealthy French bankers of German origin, but brought up in London, Baron Rodolphe d'Erlanger settled in Sidi Bou Saïd in 1912. Hoping to improve his apparently fragile health in these enchanting surroundings, he was able to indulge his double passion for art and music. At the same time, he demonstrated an almost obsessional desire to impose his choice of a permanent blue and white colour-scheme on the village. In 1915, he succeeded in getting the colonial authorities to put a preservation order on the whole place. Initially an orientalist painter, the Baron was also highly enthusiastic about Arab music; he became a great expert on the subject, to the extent that between 1930 and 1959 a six-volume treatise entitled "La Musique arabe, ses règles, leur histoire" was published. In 1932 the Baron was even selected by King Fouad I of Egypt to organise the great Cairo congress of Arab music.

La Marsa, the terminus of the TGM railway line, is 3km from Sidi Bou Saïd.

■ **La Marsa –** This little holiday resort where the Beys used to have their summer residence is now a smart suburb of Tunis, with a beach extending as far as Gammarth. In season, sea-urchin fishermen offer vistors an on the spot tasting. Unfortunately, enjoyment is somewhat spoiled by the detritus (cans, yoghurt pots, etc.) which lie around along the shore-line. In the town itself, in a small square near the station, the sound of music emanates from the **Café Saf Saf** (Poplar Tree Café). This café is the great attraction of La Marsa, with a Hafsid period well and a camel which works the chain-pump, although the animal is most often seen at rest. By the café door, traders sell delicious fritters as well as fresh water in pretty coolers.

A few grand houses here and there are reminders of the aristocratic nature of the resort, among them **Abdalliya**, the **residence of the British consul** and the summer residence of the French ambassador *(on the Corniche road)*.

Leave La Marsa by the coast and turn left towards Gammarth.

The enormous 8.5ha **French cemetery** on the hillside facing the Spanish embassy contains the graves of 4 500 soldiers. Some of them were colonial troops who fought for France in the First World War. Others were members of the Free French forces who were killed in the Tunisia Campaign of 1942-43. An ancient Jewish necropolis has also been discovered here. From the cemetery there is a magnificent panoramic **view**★ over the sea.

■ **Gammarth** – Once prized for its long beach thickly lined with eucalyptus trees, Gammarth has changed considerably with the uncontrolled development of hotels and apartment blocks. There are many more attractive places for a Tunisian beach holiday than on this permanent building site.

Sidi Bou Saïd, a symphony in blue and white

M. Renaudeau/HOA QUI

North of the Gulf of Tunis

GETTING THERE

By car – Traffic flows easily between Tunis and the chic northern coastal suburbs. For car rentals, see "Making the most of Tunis", page 144.

By TGM – The trip takes approximately 35min from Tunis Marine. The line terminates at La Marsa, from where you will need to take a taxi or a car to continue to Gammarth.

By taxi – It is quite feasible and not expensive to get to the various beaches in Gammarth or Sidi Bou Saïd by taxi. Expect to pay not more than TD10.

By boat – See "Making the most of Tunis", page 144.

ADDRESS BOOK

• **La Goulette**
Emergency
Police Station, ☎ (01) 735 416.
National Guard, ☎ (01) 735 666.
Customs, ☎ (01) 735 064 / 736 856.

Tourist information – *Tourist Office*, port de la Goulette, ☎ (01) 735 300.

Banks
BNA, Port de la Goulette.
UIB, ave Habib Bourguiba.

• **Carthage**
Emergency
Police Station, ☎ (01) 730 780.

• **Sidi Bou Saïd**
Emergency
Police Station, rue de la République, ☎ (01) 741 487.
National Guard, Poste maritime, ☎ (01) 740 871.

Banks
UIB, ave Habib Bourguiba.

Post Office, ave de la République, ☎ (01) 270 795.

• **La Marsa**
Emergency
Police Station, beach, ☎ (01) 270 008.
National Guard, ☎ (01) 744 303.
Khalil Ben Salah Pharmacy, (open nights) 2 rue Tahar Ben Achour, ☎ (01) 775 770.

Banks / Currency Exchange – The majority of banks have a bureau de change.
CFCT, 44 ave Taïeb Méhiri.
UBCI, rue El Mekki.
UIB, ave Habib Bourguiba.

Airline and Shipping Companies
Tunis Air, 14 ave Habib Bourguiba, ☎ (01) 740 680 / 272 222.
Air France, 42 rue Abou Kacem Chabbi, ☎ (01) 746 247.

WHERE TO STAY

There are very few inexpensive hotels along the coast, and travellers on a budget are better off staying in Tunis. The majority of the establishments in the area were built 30 years ago and they still have a lot of charm. The enormous sandy beach in Raoued, north of Gammarth, is now lined with modern hotels catering mostly for package holidaymakers.

• **Carthage**
(See map on page 165)
From US$18-42
Hôtel Résidence Carthage, 16 rue Hannibal, adjoining le Tophet, ☎ 01 734 318 – 8rm This is a small hotel, well off the beaten track, but still close to the beach. There is an extra charge for a room with telephone.

• **Sidi Bou Saïd**
Less than US$25
🏠***Hôtel Sidi Bou Farès***, 15 rue Sidi Bou Farès, ☎ (01) 740 091 – 8rm ✗ If you come to Sidi Bou Saïd without having booked a hotel, this tiny family-run hotel near the café des Nattes offers 8 sparsely furnished rooms looking out over a central patio. The ninth room is actually the mausoleum of Saint Bou Farès, the village's patron saint. In July-August, the guesthouse also provides meals.

From US$40-80
Hôtel Amilcar, near the Port Sidi Bou Saïd, ☎ (01) 740 788, Fax (01) 743 139 – 243rm 📶 🍽 ✗ 🏊 📺 CC This large building was built during the 1960's and still belongs to UGTT, the main Tunisian trade union. One of the 4 restaurants serves kosher cuisine. Televisions in the rooms are an option.

From US$80-100

Hôtel Sidi Bou Saïd, rue de Sidi Drif, ☎ (01) 740 411, Fax (01) 745 129 – 32rm ⌐▢ ✎ TV ✗ ⌐ CC Even if the decor leaves much to be desired, the hotel's charm includes a fine location overlooking the bay.

• **La Marsa**

From US$40-80

Hôtel Plaza Corniche, 22 rue du Maroc (go left out of the TGM station), ☎ (01) 743 577 / 743 489, Fax (01) 742 554 – 14rm ⌐▢ ✗ ⌐ CC With each room decorated in a different style by the owner himself, this is a hotel unlike any other. The only disadvantage is that the rooms are quite small.

• **Gammarth**

From US$35-55

Hôtel Cap Carthage, Chott el Ghaba, on the road from Raoued, ☎ (01) 911 956 / 774 225, Fax (01) 911 980 – 348rm ⌐ ✎ ✗ ⌐ ✻ This new hotel is very popular with tennis players. There are at least 40 tennis courts, 11 of them hard courts.

Club Dar Naouar (Palace of Flowers), on the road from Raoued, ☎ (01) 741 000, Fax (01) 740 309 – 500rm ⌐ ✗ ⌐ ✎ CC This enormous complex of comfortable bungalows is equipped with an Olympic-sized pool. Bed and breakfast, half-board and full-board all catered for.

From US$42-75

Hôtel Mégara, avenue Taïeb Méhiri, ☎ (01) 740 366 / 741 052, Fax (01) 740 916 – 77rm ⌐ ✎ ✗ ⌐ ✎ CC Set in beautiful gardens, this hotel was constructed in the Twenties and harks back to the old colonial era. The beach of the hotel is not to be recommended. However, the beach at La Marsa is only a 5 minute walk away. Air-conditioning is optional.

More than US$75

Hôtel Abou Nawas, ave Taïeb Méhiri, Gammarth, ☎ (01) 741 444, Fax (01) 740 400 – 117rm ⌐▢ ✎ TV ✗ ⌐ ✎ CC This complex of deluxe chalets belongs to the Kuwaiti hotel chain which has several similar establishments throughout Tunisia. There are all the necessary services for business guests. Each room has a direct dial telephone and some even have kitchenettes.

Le Palace (Cleopatra World), Complexe Cap Gammarth, along the tourist route, ☎ (01) 728 000, Fax (01) 748 442 – 300rm ⌐▢ ✎ TV ✗ ⌐ ✎ CC This up-market establishment has a casino and suites costing up to a million dinars for lucky guests to spend their winnings on. The hotel's rates are not determined by the season, unusual for a seaside resort. However, as it only opened in 1996, the future of this hotel remains to be seen.

EATING OUT

There is one restaurant after another all the way along the beach, and probably the best plan is to choose the one with the finest view of the sea. Seafood is abundant and always fresh, although relatively expensive. Price is according to weight so you should be able to choose which fish you want to be cooked for you to avoid unpleasant surprises when you receive your bill.

• **La Goulette**

Less than US$8

Along ave Franklin Roosevelt, you can find stalls selling take-away doughnuts: very cheap and ideal for filling a gap.

From US$10-20

⊛ **Le Café Vert**, 68 ave Franklin Roosevelt, ☎ (01) 736 156 ⌐ ▼ CC This restaurant, which caters to hearty eaters, owes its reputation and popularity to the freshness of its fish and its generous portions. Try the menina, an assortment of small salads served as a starter. La Goulette is known for quality and quantity and this restaurant maintains the tradition. Sunday's dish of the day is a fish couscous. Closed Monday for lunch.

Le Chalet, 42 ave Franklin Roosevelt, ☎ (01) 735 138. ⌐ ▼ CC This restaurant still serves after 2.30pm which is exceptional in Tunisia. It closes only between 5 and 7pm, even in winter. The food is good with copious portions.

Le Grill, 52 ave Franklin Roosevelt, ☎ (01) 735 534 ⌐ CC The speciality is a whole fish served in typical La Goulette style. For a starter, try the snails cooked in a tomato and fennel sauce. The service does not quite match the quality of the food.

- **Carthage**

Less than US$10

Le Neptune (C3), at the bottom of the rue Hammarskjold, ☎ (01) 731 456 / 731 328 ⌂ This is the ideal place to tackle a whole grilled fish, while enjoying sea views. Informal and reasonably priced.

From US$10-20

Le Baal (C5), 16 rue Hannibal, Salammbô, ☎ (01) 731 072 ⌂ This hotel-restaurant is a good place to take a break from exploring the ruins.

- **Sidi Bou Saïd**

Less than US$10

Café Restaurant Chergui, to the right of the entrance of Café des Nattes, Sidi Bou Saïd, ☎ (01) 740 987 ⌂ CC What appears to be a Moorish open air café is, in fact, a restaurant serving tajine and couscous. It is very touristy during the high season but it is difficult to find an alternative in Sidi Bou Saïd.

L'Amphitrite, rue de l'Union, Amilcar Beach, ☎ (01) 747 591 ⌂ CC This unpretentious establishment serves good food at reasonable prices for a restaurant located on the beach.

From US$10-16

La Bagatelle, 9 ave Habib Bourguiba, ☎ (01) 741 116. CC A little less touristy than the other restaurants of Sidi Bou, this is situated 100m from the Place du 7 novembre. Here you can find good Tunisian cuisine at a reasonable price – set menus from US$6.

From US$20-45

Le Pirate, Port Sidi Bou Saïd, ☎ (01) 270 484 ⌂ ♈ CC A welcoming green oasis in the heat of summer, however, the standard of the cuisine does not live up to the location.

Au Bon Vieux Temps (Ayem Zamen), 56 rue Hedi Zarrouk, ☎ (01) 744 788 / 744 733 ⌂ ♈ CC The owners have a restaurant of the same name in La Marsa. Guests are made to feel at home in this traditional dwelling which has been tastefully restored and refurbished. Ask to select your own fish in order to avoid being served a one pound giant.

- **La Marsa**

From US$10-20

La Falaise (formerly L'Hippocampe), on the road from Sidi Dhrif

(go left out of the TGM station and pass through Corniche Plaza), ☎ (01) 747 806, Fax (01) 748 777 ♈ ⌂ CC One of the best establishments on the coast; the view overlooking the cliff is unrestricted. Meat and fish specialities. Warm reception.

Les Trois Perles, rue Mongi Slim, ☎ (01) 774 409, Fax (01) 748 666 ⌂ CC You can spot this restaurant from a distance. A curious-looking white house set on blocks, it was the former summer home of Bey Ahmed. The fish is always fresh and the bread tastes as good as cake. Some evenings there are belly dance performances.

Au Bon Vieux Temps, 1 rue Aboul Kacem Chebbi, ☎ (01) 744 322 / 749 060 ♈ CC Diplomats and the well-to-do from Tunis often dine in the comfortable ambiance of this typical French restaurant. Dinner and supper only.

- **Gammarth**

From US$10-20

Le Grand Bleu, ave Taïeb Méhiri, ☎ (01) 46 900, Fax (01) 746 504 ⌂ CC The hotspot for local jet-setters. The fish, however, could be more tender.

Les Ombrelles, 107 ave Taïeb Méhiri, ☎ (01) 742 964 ⌂ CC This is the place to go for anyone who enjoys dining in a nightclub atmosphere.

WHERE TO GO OUT FOR A DRINK

Cafés

- **La Goulette**

Café La Marina, 144 ave de la République, La Goulette Casino. This café is at the end of the beach, level with the canal. It has an enormous terrace facing the sea, with pizzas and other snacks available.

- **Sidi Bou Saïd**

Café des Nattes, on the top of the hill overlooking Sidi Bou Saïd, ☎ (01) 749 661. This simple Moorish café is probably the most famous place in Tunisia. The likes of authors André Gide and Simone de Beauvoir and painter Paul Klee amongst other celebrities have sat on its floor mats. The mint tea may not be outstanding, but there is a great view of one of the prettiest villages in Tunisia. Open from 7.30am-2am.

Café Sidi Chabaane, rue Sidi Chabaane (the street to the right of the Café des Nattes). The most beautiful view in Sidi Bou Saïd can be seen from the terrace of this café. Come early in the day to avoid the crowds of tourists.

• La Marsa
Café Saf Saf, opposite the Mosque, ☎ (01) 749 347. This café is almost an institution in La Marsa. Briks and mint tea are on the menu, while games of chess form part of the entertainment. Evening meals are also available. This establishment seems to have successfully retained its authentic atmosphere, despite the influx of tourists.

Nightclubs

• La Marsa
Plaza Corniche Hôtel, 22 rue du Maroc, ☎ (01) 743 577 / 743 489. On Sidi Dhrif's coastal road just after the Restaurant La Falaise. This nightclub is a honey pot for Tunisian high society.
La Baraka, the best-known club in La Marsa. Here you can dance under the stars until the sun rises over the sea.

LEISURE

Festivals

• La Goulette
Karaka Festival. Variety shows evoking the great days of La Goulette in the 1950's. Takes place in July.

• Carthage
Carthage International Festival, in July-August. Music, film, drama and dance, some of it of the highest quality. Many performance traditions include the restored Roman theatre. For information, contact the Maison de la Culture **Ibn Khaldoun**, 16 rue Ibn Khaldoun, ☎ (01) 242 356.
Carthage Film Festival. A Mediterranean film festival organised every two years in October-November. In odd numbered years, a drama festival takes place instead of films.

• Sidi Bou Saïd
Ennejma Ezzahra, ☎ (01) 740 102 / 746 051. Twice a year, in the autumn and spring, the Centre of Arab and Mediterranean Music organises musical events. Programme in the local newspapers.

• La Marsa
La Marsa at Night. Variety shows, theatre or films of variable quality in July and August.

Hammams
• La Marsa
Sfaxi, 13b rue Ali Belhaouane. Open for men, 6am-midday and for women, 2pm to 6pm.

SHOPPING

Bakeries
• La Marsa
Salem, in front of the TGM train station at Marsa Beach. When the sun is so strong the pavement begins to melt the crowds rush to the stands serving delicious ice cream, as well as European cakes and biscuits. You must pay at the cash desk before you are served.
La Petite Pâtisserie, ave Taïeb Méhiri, next to the supermarket on the road leading to the hotels. Sells delicious pastries.

Antiques
• La Goulette
SOCOPA, at the harbour station, ☎ (01) 275 000.

• Carthage
Carpets: Byrsa, 20 chiral Bourguiba, just after the rue des Phéniciens.
Berber pottery, on the corner of chiral Bourguiba. This is a warehouse filled with ochre-coloured pottery from Sejnane.

• La Marsa
Maison Abdel Majid, ave Fatima Bourguiba, 13km, route de la Soukra, ☎ (01) 764 725. Despite the less than hearty welcome, these two shops, located next to each other, house real treasures: from mosaic tables or consoles dating from Tunisia's colonial period to furniture inlaid with mother-of-pearl from the Middle East. The prices are quite high. Count on spending about TD700 for a set of shelves made of decorated wood or TD300 for a silver bracelet.

Bookshops
• La Marsa
Le Mille Feuilles, 1 rue de la Mosquée, ☎ (01) 744 229. Opposite the TGM station, a genuine Ali Baba's cave frequented by the intellectuals of La Marsa. A selection of books on Tunisia, essays, novels and art books.

CARTHAGE ★★

Governorship of Tunis
17km from Tunis via La Goulette
For practical information, see "Making the most of North Tunis", page 158

Not to be missed
The Salammbô Tophet.
The Antonine Baths.

And remember...
In summer, it's best to sight-see early
before lunching by the sea – perhaps at The Neptune.

Carthage can be reached by road from Tunis (30min via La Goulette) or by the little TGM train (20-25min from Tunis to Carthage). Get out at the Carthage-Salammbô station for the Tophet visit and the Punic ports, and at the Carthage-Hannibal station to visit Byrsa Hill and the Antonine baths.

For most people, it is love at first sight when they encounter the calm and beauty of this elegant suburb of Tunis, with its enormous villas and peaceful streets shaded with bougainvillea, palm-trees and giant eucalyptus. It is hardly surprising that the President of Tunisia and several embassies have settled here. But first and foremost this is the site of the proud city that made Rome tremble, a metropolis with more than 400 000 inhabitants at the height of its splendour, a place with a name that became legendary through the exploits of its greatest soldier, Hannibal.

Information panels scattered throughout the vast area will help revive whatever schoolroom memories remain of the long-vanished Punic civilisation. And a good dose of imagination will be helpful in bringing to life the remains of the ancient city: the twin ports and the evocative sanctuary of the "tophet", the Antonine Baths, the Roman Villas...

A picture will gradually emerge of the rich complex and often violent past – buried and painfully rediscovered – of a city that was in turn Punic, Roman, Vandal and Byzantinem. Each set of rulers set their stamp upon the place before being vanquished by their successors and disappearing from the stage of history. Not surprisingly, the figure of Hannibal looms large. The guides always speak with emotion of the great man, as if the general who was "equalled but never surpassed" had only just died. Sometimes they make you take a very cautious taste of the "salt earth", for according to tradition, once Carthage was destroyed the Romans spread salt on the ground to make it infertile.

Since 1973 UNESCO and the Tunisian government have continued the excavations and the conservation that began early in the 19C.

A long history

In the beginning was woman...
True history merges with myth in the story of Queen Dido and the foundation of Carthage by the Phoenicians in 814 BC.

The legend of Dido
After the assassination of her husband by her brother Pygmalion, Dido left the kingdom of Tyre and set off to found Carthage. In the lines of the Aeneid Virgil tells of the guile of this woman, who asked only to occupy the area covered by the skin of an ox ("birsa" in Greek). It was offered to her without misgivings; but she sliced the skin into such fine strips that she was able to extend her chosen territory over several hectares, thus covering the present-day hill of Byrsa.

Carthage

Carthage developed what was to be its own specific culture: the Punic civilisation, a blend of Phoenician and Berber influences. It soon took the lead as a trading power, and steadily extended its hold over the Mediterranean, controlling – apart from part of Tunisia and the coasts of North Africa – Sicily, Sardinia, Malta and the Balearics, and southern Spain.

In the 5C BC its navigators were the first to explore Black Africa as far as Mount Cameroon.

Against the Greeks (480-264 BC) – Carthaginian attempts at territorial expansion into Sicily sparked off hostilities with the Greeks. In 480 BC the Carthaginians were defeated at Himera and forced to leave Sicily. At the end of the 5C, a new conflict brought the Greeks and Carthaginians face to face in Sicily: the Carthaginians captured Selinonte but suffered a setback at Syracuse. In 339, still in Sicily, the Punic army was defeated at Crisimos. Agathoclus, who had seized power in Sicily, landed in Africa in 310, but was defeated by the Carthaginians. After the collapse of Alexander's empire the Greeks were no longer capable of defying Carthage, which now became the dominant Mediterranean power.

Against Rome (264-146 BC) – The **First Punic War** (264-241) was caused by Rome's imperialism, when she attacked Sicily after concluding the conquest of southern Italy. The struggle ended for Carthage with the loss of Sicily. More is known about the **Second Punic War** (218-201), when **Hannibal** and his elephants crossed the Alps and marched on Rome, though in the event, he was unable to besiege the city. **Scipio Africanus** counterattacked, conquered Spain, and landed in Africa. Hannibal was forced to abandon Italy and was crushed at Zama in 202. Despite the decline of the Punic city, the Romans feared its return to power: the slogan *Delenda est Carthago*, "Carthage must be destroyed" was repeated by Cato at the end of every speech he made in the Senate. The Romans eventually decided to finish with Carthage once and for all, and it was the **Third Punic War** (149-146) which ended with the complete destruction of Carthage by the legions of Scipio Emilius.

Roman Carthage – In 44 BC Julius Caesar decided to rebuild Carthage. Following the assassination of Caesar, it was Octavius, the future Emperor Augustus, who brought the project to fruition; capital of the Roman province of Africa and corn-basket for the Empire, Carthage gradually became the second largest city in the west, after Rome.

Christian Carthage and the last invasions – Christianity appeared in Africa at the end of the 2C, and saints and martyrs provide evidence of the courage of the first Christians in the African capital: Perpetua and Felicity were thrown to wild beasts in 203 and Cyprian suffered martyrdom in 258. With Tertullian (c 155-c 220), Cyprian, and above all **Saint Augustine** (350-430), Carthage could take pride in having given Christianity its first theologians.

In 439, the Vandals captured the city and made it their capital. Liberated by Belisarius in 534 during the Byzantine conquest, Carthage experienced a brief revival, but the empire, with serious internal problems, lost interest in the city; gradually abandoned by its inhabitants, it fell into Arab hands in 698. The former city was treated as a quarry, and used as a source of building materials for the construction of Tunis.

The Archeological Sites★★

Allow half a day

Open 8am-7pm in summer and 8.30am-5pm in winter

The ruins are scattered over a considerable area and there is an entrance charge to see them. An inclusive ticket available at a number of sites gives admission to all of them as well as to the museums.

The Punic Ports

It is difficult to believe that these great stretches of stagnant water, surrounded by luxurious villas facing the sea, were the home of the much-feared Punic fleet. They were laid out in the 4C BC to an ingenious design, and became the key to Carthaginian supremacy in the western Mediterranean. The first port, a rectangle, was used for **trade** while the second, circular with an island at the centre, was devoted to **military** purposes. The island and the port were surrounded by docks supposedly large enough to cope with up to 220 sixty-oar vessels, and beyond the central island a very narrow dry-dock is still visible. The two ports were surrounded by walls and linked to the sea by a canal which could be closed with a chain. Communication between the two was by means of a secret passage, and it seems that the Romans only discovered the existence of this arsenal after the end of the third Punic War. The Romans built their port on exactly the same site as the Punic ports. Coins with the head of Augustus have been found here, evidence of the lively export trade with Rome.

The Punic Tophet★

With its headstones emerging from the rough grass, the tophet has something of the atmosphere of a rural cemetery. It is one of the oldest Punic religious sites and is thought to have been the setting for barbaric rituals. Its Carthaginian name is unknown, and the expression "tophet" comes from the Old Testament, referring to the Ben Hinnon sanctuary where child sacrifice was practised. Archeologists use the name to refer to children's burial grounds which have been discovered in Phoenician and Punic towns.

This tophet was an open-air sanctuary inside a wall two metres thick, a little of which remains. It was dedicated to Baal Hammon and Tanit, two guardian divinities of the city. The votive headstones that marked the location of urns containing the ashes of sacrificial victims bore the symbols of the two gods: the solar disc beneath the upturned crescent of the moon. Often one can even make out the silhouette of a new-born child carved in the stone. Although many of the headstones have had to be replaced after the archeological excavations, some of them still lie in the place where they were found by the Carthaginians.

Several children's headstones are hidden in the greenery, in a ditch planted with palm trees at the lower end of the sanctuary. By plunging

Child sacrifice – legend or fact?

The theme of child sacrifice, which owes much to Roman anti-Carthaginian propaganda, has been the object of much bitter controversy. Nevertheless, analysis of the urns leaves no doubt that although there may have been substitution sacrifices of lambs or kid goats, the bones are indeed those of young children of a few days or a few months old. The excavations also show the persistence of the cult over nearly seven hundred years. It remains to be discovered whether these children were still-born or died soon after birth, or whether they were buried alive; today, archeologists and historians generally favour the latter theory. Expiatory sacrifices when the city was endangered, they could also have been part of a system of population control.

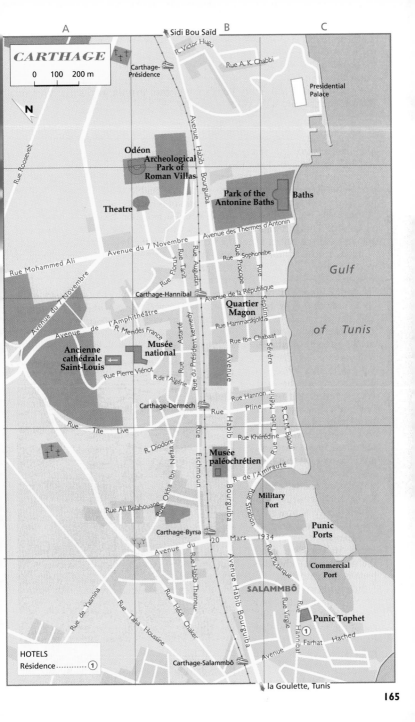

CARTHAGE

0   100   200 m

N

Sidi Bou Saïd

R. Victor Hugo

Rue A. K. Chabbi

Carthage-Présidence

Presidential Palace

Avenue Habib Bourguiba

Rue Roosevelt

Odéon

Archeological Park of Roman Villas

Park of the Antonine Baths

Baths

Theatre

Avenue des Thermes d'Antonin

Avenue du 7 Novembre

Rue Mohammed Ali

Avenue du 7 Novembre

Rue Tahit

Rue Plutarque

Rue Augustin

Rue Procope

Rue Sophonisbe

Rue Septime

Gulf

Carthage-Hannibal

Avenue de la République

of   Tunis

Quartier Magon

Avenue de l'Amphithéâtre

R. Mendès France

Avenue   de

Rue Astarté

Rue du Président Kennedy

Rue Hammarskjolde

Rue Ibn Chabaat

Avenue Sévère

Ancienne cathédrale Saint-Louis

Musée national

Rue Pierre Viénot

R. de l'Algérie

Rue Hannon

Carthage-Dermech

Rue   Pline

Rue   Tite   Live

R. Diodore

Rue Okba Ibn Nefaa

Rue Eschmoun

Rue Khérédine

R. Ct.M. Bijaoui

R. de Tanit Miloti

Musée paléochrétien

R. de l'Amirauté

Military Port

Punic Ports

Rue Ali Belahouane

Rue Strabon

Rue Habib Bourguiba

Carthage-Byrsa

Avenue   du   20   Mars   1934

Rue Plutarque

Commercial Port

SALAMMBÔ

Rue Habib Thameur

Rue Hédi Chaker

Avenue Habib Bourguiba

Rue Virgile

Punic Tophet

Rue de Yasmina

Rue Taha Houssine

Rue Hannibal

Farhat   Hached

①

Carthage-Salammbô

la Goulette, Tunis

further into this thick growth of pomegranates, caper plants, nasturtiums and papyrus, you will come to some small arched vaults where more headstones can be seen in the damp darkness. No one who has the good fortune to go in alone can fail to be moved by the atmosphere: the souls of young sacrificial victims seem to live there still. Even though it is known that the vaults date from the Roman era, they are still a place of mystery.

The Park of the Antonine Baths★★

This site includes the baths themselves and a 4ha archeological park next to the president's palace (*NB: photographs of the palace area are forbidden. Ignoring this ban can lead to confiscation of your film*).

The archeological park is criss-crossed with avenues which mostly follow the line of old Roman roadways across a veritable jumble of architecture and plant life. The avenue of vegetation (*on the left just beyond the entrance*) leads up to a **Roman villa** (4C AD) with a peristyle and a reception hall in the shape of a clover-leaf. Little remains of the villa apart from a fascinating mosaic in one of the apses of the hall: it shows four children dancing beneath a dome building supported on Corinthian columns. Its exact significance is unclear, though it may represent one of the ceremonies performed as part of the cult of the Emperor.

In the Byzantine era, two basilicas stood just above the villa (*at the intersection with Cardo XIV*). The basilica known as Dermech II, on the left, has almost completely vanished; but on the right, the vast open space with shafts of columns emerging out of it marks the site of the 4C **Dermech I**. The general lay-out of this five-aisled church can still be made out, together with some fine mosaic paving and the baptistery. The site of a third church has been identified inside the park, and it is thought that there may have been a fourth, proof positive that during these early centuries of Christianity a powerful faith took root among the inhabitants of North Africa. In Carthage alone, the names of 22 churches have been identified.

A little further up the park, behind the basilica, is a **Punic burial site**. The oldest of the tombs here date back to the 8C BC, but most are from the 7 and 6C. They consist either of caves dug into the ground

The Carthage Tophet

and constructed of large stone blocks – the small square entrance is visible – or trench graves in which the body was laid in a coffin or on a wooden platform in a ditch which might be as much as five metres deep. These trenches are scattered across various parts of the site, and some can be seen at the intersection of *cardo XVI* and *decumanus IV*. A number of these graves contained funerary furnishings: pottery, statuettes and grimacing masks, which are now mostly in the Bardo museum.

Decumanus IV, a handsome Roman road sloping gently down towards the sea, leads to a small promenade overlooking the **Antonine Baths★★**. The view from here has become one of the classic clichés of tourist Tunisia: the imposing column of the *frigidarium*, with the sea and Bou Kornine mountain as the backdrop. Here too there is a model which shows the lay-out of the very complex building (*see also the architectural plan, page 43, for a description of typical Roman baths*).

The construction of these baths, the most impressive remains of Roman Carthage, continued for 17 years, from 145 to 162 AD. Nothing remains today, except for the basements which were reserved for the staff and were used as stores, particularly for wood storage. A few columns have been set up again, including the pillar of the *frigidarium* which gives the viewer an idea of the colossal size (1 034sqm) of this hall. The granite column weighs around 50 tonnes and supports a four-tonne capital made of white marble. It is estimated that the vaults of the *frigidarium*, held up by eight similar columns, were as much as 30m high. The great size and luxuriousness of these baths made them amongst the most impressive in the empire.

Roman Villas★

Located on the side of the Odeon hill and surrounded by blue thistles, mimosas and the strange caper-plant flowers which retract in the sun, the Roman villas are outstanding particularly for the **view★** that they offer over Carthage, the Gulf of Tunis and the mountains of Cap Bon. This residential district of Roman times was built on a former Punic burial ground, from which the occasional stone sarcophagus has now been turned into a garden trough.

The villas have been overtaken by the passage of time. Many suffered greatly at the hands of various invaders. Yet here and there beautiful **mosaics** still survive, half-hidden in the dust, but ready to spring into life and vivid colour when they are sprinkled with water. There are animal designs to be seen, or hunting scenes: hunting with a lasso, for example – and the guides take pleasure in telling you that "the Americans were not the original inventors". One of the villas (3C), known as **"la volière"** ("the aviary") because of its very fine mosaic, has been turned into a display of antiquities: pillars have been set up alongside a collection of numerous stone fragments, including a magnificent torso of an ephebe, a handsome young man.

The current excavations are far from finished. Habitués of the site watch the showers that disturb and redistribute the surface soil, and reveal old coins or mosaic tesserae.

Further towards the top of the hill are remains of the 3C **Odeon**. Little remains of it now, although in the Roman era it was the largest building of this type anywhere. At the foot of the hill, the 2C **theatre** has had its splendour restored, and following substantial restoration it is now the setting for the **Carthage International Festival.**

Le Musée national★ (National Museum)

(Open 8am-7pm in summer, 8.30am-5.30pm in winter. Entrance charge.) As with all the higher sites in Carthage, the museum is immediately striking for its **panoramic view★**: the gulf, Carthage itself and a steep view down to the Punic ports below, the excavation site and Byrsa hill. Here, before your very eyes, is where the last of the Carthaginians put up a desperate house-to-house resistance to the furious attacks of the Romans. An orientation panel set on the base of a broken column helps to identify the various features. The museum gardens are like a stone-mason's yard, with Punic headstones, Corinthian columns, fragments of barley-sugar columns, and headless statues.

The collections of the museum itself, installed in the former Whitefriars monastery, illustrate various periods in the history of Carthage. The finest items relating to the Punic period are unquestionably two late 4C or early 3C BC **sarcophagi★**, discovered in 1902 in a cellar. Each is topped by a life-size reclining human figure. One is probably the final resting place of a priest, the other of a priestess. These creations are the fruit of a three-fold influence: Etruscan in the representation of the dead person on the sarcophagus, Greek in the style of the statuary and materials and Punic in the position of the two figures.

Grimacing masks, which the Carthaginians placed near their dead to protect them from evil spirits, are characteristic of the Punic civilisation. A large and particularly striking mask (3 or 2C BC) was discovered in the Salammbô tophet. Most of the **funerary steles** (or tombstones) also come from the tophet and are classified in chronological order. A **model** shows a section cut through the excavated area of the sanctuary, indicating that it was in use from the 9C BC, the date of the foundation of Carthage, until the destruction of the city in 146 BC. **Enamelled amulets** were another Carthaginian speciality: the glass-makers of Carthage were past-masters in the art of miniaturising, making little polychrome masks to accompany the dead in their final repose.

The Roman period is represented by various sculptures taken from the various Carthage sites. The immense figure of **Victory** which dominates the ground-floor hall and which was discovered in the amphitheatre is unmissable; such Victory figures were "mass produced" in Rome, and despatched throughout the empire to guard against the possibility of defeat. There are also several busts, including a fine **emperor's head with lion-skin head-dress**: with the great majority of such sculptures, particularly those which fell into the hands of the Vandals, the nose is missing.

The **mosaics** on display are mostly pavements taken from the surrounding villas.

The **amphora room** is a genuine curiosity. Phoenicians and Romans made all kinds of large storage jars: cylindrical, round-bellied, ovoid, with or without a neck, closed with a plaster stopper... some have an ear of wheat engraved on the shoulder, others a square stamp on the lip bearing the maker's name. The type and form of the amphora often indicates what it contained: sometimes they were used as a coffin for a child.

Phoenician mask

Musée de Carthage/GIRAUDON

Hucksters lie in wait for visitors leaving the museum with a less than convincing array of oil lamps and supposedly authentic coins.

The former cathedral of Saint Louis

At the side of the museum, open 9am-7pm, entrance fee (not included in the entrance to the ruins).

Built in 1890 in a rather uneasy mixture of Byzantine and Moorish styles, the cathedral was intended both to honour St Louis, the French king who died during the Crusaders' siege of Tunis in 1270, and to recall the early days of Christianity in Carthage (both St Cyprian and St Augustine are represented in the stained glass windows along the central aisle).

The moving spirit behind the construction of the Cathedral was the French Cardinal Lavigerie, whose statue caused so much trouble when it was erected at the entrance to the medina in 1930. His aims were far from identical with those of Tunisian nationalists, and no services have been held here since the country won its independence. The building is now used for cultural purposes.

In the **Magon quarter** *(entrance by the ave de la République)*, there are breakwaters and other features which were part of the original fortifications surrounding Carthage. The walls had two levels of internal galleries, one reserved for elephants, the other for soldiers and horses. Models in two halls recreate the fortifications and the residential districts.

The **Musée paléochrétien** (Paleo-Christian Museum) contains little of interest, apart from a pretty **statuette of Ganymede**: discovered in 17 pieces, it has been wonderfully restored. Otherwise there are some amphoræ, pottery and oil lamps which should really be in the musée national.

The archeological sites

SOUTH OF TUNIS
FROM TUNIS TO ZAGHOUAN
Governorship of Zaghouan
Approx. 57km from Tunis – allow a full day

Not to be missed
The Zaghouan temple in its mountain setting.
And remember...
Set out early in the morning
in order to visit Thuburbo Majus before the heat of the day.

This tour to the south of Tunis crosses a cereal-growing plain dominated by the majestic mass of the 1 300m high Jebel Zaghouan, one of Tunisia's most spectacular mountains. Some Roman sites and monuments of great interest can be seen along the route, beginning with the lace-like stonework of the Zaghouan aqueduct.

Leave Tunis on the P 3 road to El Fahs and Kairouan. After about 30km, take the left fork and turn left towards Zaghouan.

■ **Zaghouan Aqueduct★** – This impressive structure, which dates from the era of Hadrian (AD 120), was built to supply Carthage with water from the Zaghouan Temple of Springs, a distance of 123km. Restored at several periods in its history, the aqueduct appears to play hide-and-seek with the driver. Sometimes the arches are at ground level – when they have not disappeared altogether, where the conduit is carried underground – sometimes they stand out at their full height for several kilometres, particularly along the approaches to Oudna.

About 3km beyond the fork in the road, turn left again, following the line of the aqueduct towards Oudna. Beyond Oudna station continue straight on for 5km, 3km of which is dirt track.

■ **Oudna** – This site has been intensively excavated since 1993. Oudna, the classical Uthina, was one of the oldest Roman settlements in Africa; colonised by veterans of the 13th Legion, it reached its peak in the 2C AD, then declined from the time of the Vandal invasions. The site is still more of an archeologists' camp than a tourist attraction, still in the process of revealing its secrets; barely a month goes by without teams of archeologists uncovering columns, shards of pottery and slabs of marble.

These ruins are emerging from a landscape which has changed very little in nearly two thousand years. The first monument to be seen is a vast **amphitheatre** capable of holding 15 000 spectators. Large **public baths** have recently been uncovered, together with around twenty **villas**. The most substantial is the **Ikarios** house, named after a mosaic of Dionysus as a youth offering the vine to Ikarios of Attica (now in the Bardo museum). This vast residence with peristyle and more than 30 rooms lies next to a large baths complex. The rooms were decorated with numerous mosaics, which are now preserved in the Bardo museum. Other significant remains deserve attention: enormous **cisterns** the **capitol** and the still richly decorated **House of Industrius**.

Continue to Zaghouan and go through it without stopping to visit. Go straight on to the Temple of Springs (temple des Eaux), which is reached along the main street and take a small road leading up from it, climbing across a wooded hillside.

■ **The Temple of Springs at Zaghouan★** – Built in the reign of Hadrian, this **grotto** is like an open scallop shell embedded in the mountainside. The upper part forms a semicircle consisting of 12 niches which held statues of nymphs. At the centre, a larger thirteenth niche formed the temple itself, with the statue of the spring's protective divinity. From the terrace, steps lead down to a basin that received the waters. From the café at the foot of the site, there is a magnificent view over this theatrical setting.

Go back through Zaghouan, continue straight on for about 7km, then turn left towards El Fahs. Thuburbo Majus is about 4km from El Fahs, on the P 3 road to Tunis.

■ Thuburbo Majus★

Allow 90min
Open 8am-7pm in summer, 8am-5.30pm in winter. Entrance charge.

Lost in-among the wheat fields, Thuburbo Majus is one of the main archeological sites in the Tunis area. "Thuburbo" is probably a Berber name in origin, which would indicate an extremely ancient occupation of the site. But virtually nothing more is known of its beginnings, beyond the fact that the city paid very heavily for backing Carthage against Rome. The victorious Romans burdened it with taxes, and it was not until AD 128 that it won the status of municipality. This marked the beginning of a period of prosperity which lasted for 150 years, as can be seen in the superb mosaics preserved in the Bardo. Prestigious public monuments were erected and the wealthy land-owners built sumptuous villas. As with all the towns of Roman *Ifriqiya*, the arrival of the Vandals brought disaster: deserted by its inhabitants, what had been a fine city of around 10 000 residents in the days of its splendour found itself reduced to an insignificant backwater. It was finally abandoned with the arrival of the Arabs.

The site was only rediscovered in 1857 by the French archeologist Charles Tissot, but proper archeological excavations only began in 1912.

The archeological site

The 40ha site still has many treasures to reveal. The hillside with the amphitheatre has not yet been explored, nor the site of the cisterns – yet the ruins uncovered so far are very substantial, in particular those of the **capitol★**, with its fluted columns and great stairway. After the Roman period, when the temple must have fallen out of use, an olive-press was established in the vaulted basements. The remains of an enormous **statue of Jupiter** on display in the Bardo have also been found here.

Measuring 49m along its edges, the **forum** of Thuburbo Major is larger than those of Dougga and Bulla Reggia. It was built between 161 and 192 AD, and substantially reconstructed around 376, and was originally paved and surrounded on three sides by a Corinthian-style portico; a few of its columns are still upright. The site of the **altar** at the foot of the capitol is still visible. Apart from the capitol, the **forum** is flanked by several temples: including the **Temple of Peace** and the **Temple of Mercury**, both dating from the 2C AD. Traces of the former remain – a few steps, a marble pavement, and a bas-relief representing the winged horse Pegasus. The circular courtyard of the temple of Mercury, surrounded by columns, can still be made out.

Thuburbo Majus

At the southern corner of the forum, the site of the 2C **market** is visible, with one of its three courtyards opening on to the **Aurigian way**. Further along this way to the southeast are the **winter baths**, which still have large areas of white mosaic inlaid with tiny tesserae. On the other side of the track the little horse-shoe shaped **temple of Baalat** (2C) is visible. The ruins of a **Byzantine basilica** stand on the neighbouring hillside, surrounding a baptistery of the same era. The rue des Petronii diverges from the Aurigian way beside the winter baths and leads to the **Palæstra of the Petronii**∗ (AD 225), which has retrieved a little of its former glory with the reconstruction of the portico, twelve marble columns with Corinthian capitals. According to an inscription, the city owed this magnificent edifice to Petronius Felix. This was where the inhabitants of Thuburbo Majus practised gymnastics or wrestling before going to the baths. The Roman alphabet of 36 letters is carved on the ground in a corner of the courtyard. The palæstra also had a mosaic representing boxers – it has now been removed to the Bardo, like so many others.

This is no doubt justifiable in museological terms, but represents a net loss to the sites themselves, which are deprived of much.

Next to the palæstra, are the **summer baths** (2-3C). 2 400sqm in area, they are much larger than the winter baths. A vestibule leads to the two pools in the frigidarium, which is still covered with white mosaic. Two rooms, a splendid one for relaxation and another for massage, still offer the visitor a sense of well-being. The excavations have also brought to light several private houses with a hypocaust heating system supplying currents of warm air.

The capitol at Thuburbo Majus

DOUGGA ★★★
Governorship of Béja
Tunis 110km; Le Kef 60km
Archeological site. Alt 500m

Not to be missed
The theatre and the Capitol.
Spring is the best season when the countryside is a riot of flowers.
And remember...
Dougga deserves more than the lightning visit suggested by some guides.
Suitable for a picnic.

Dougga can be easily visited from both Tunis and Le Kef. Take the P 5 road between these two cities, then turn off for Dougga. If starting from Tunis, follow signs for Béja, since Le Kef is very rarely indicated.

Tunis to Dougga

The outskirts of Tunis are not impressive: shacks, waste ground, and a bare and scruffy landscape. After about 15km this is left behind, and the scene changes to the fertile (though somewhat flat and monotonous) plain of the River Méjerda. Beyond Mejez el Bab the road follows the course of the river through gently hilly countryside of fields, orchards and olive groves. In the spring the landscape even has a hint of Tuscany. It is no surprise that the Romans felt at home here!

Testour, on the road to Dougga, is worth a brief visit. This little town was built in the 17C by refugees from Andalusia: it has houses with tiled roofs, broad straight streets, a central square, and a rectangular **minaret** – the only minaret with a clock in the Islamic world. Beyond Testour the landscape becomes more rugged and the road more winding. Pines and eucalyptus alternate with luxuriant green fields which turn red and sandy brown once the harvest is over.

Set on a spur, the market town of **Téboursouk** has fine **views** over the surrounding area. As you leave the town, turn right for Dougga, 5km away. Dougga makes a dramatic appearance as the four pillars of the cliff top Temple of Saturn come into sight round a bend in the road. The whole site, spread out in all its splendour, can be seen as the road winds round the steep slope. The site, which at first was wild and desolate, now looks pleasantly pastoral: planted with olive trees, the harmonious landscape of the valley of Khalled Oued is preserved from modernisation and modern urban development.

Arriving from the south on the El Krib road, the **panorama**★★ is even more spectacular. In this field of ruins that blends so well into the countryside, visitors are struck by the Libyan-punic mausoleum in the forefront, whereas the majestic silhouette of the capitol can be distinguished in the distance.

The road ends at a car park almost next to the theatre. There is a bar overlooking the valley just below the car park, offering refreshments in the shade of centuries-old olive trees. New additions are designed with deliberate discretion and do not intrude on the pastoral atmosphere of the ruins.

A Little History, from Tukka to Dougga al Jadida

Libyo-Punic La Tukka – The favourable location, climate and soil led to this site being occupied since very remote times – the plateau and cliff provided strong defences, the near-mountainous surroundings helped to keep temperatures down. The Latin name of the town, "Thugga", is a form of "Tukka", seen in inscriptions in Libyan, and probably meaning "pointed rock". The name confirms the site's strategic significance, and is a reminder that the first people to live here were Numidians, or Berbers.

According to Diodora of Sicily, the town was already of "a fine size" in the 4C BC. Then, and for another two centuries, it was under the influence of Carthage. This double heritage of Libyan and Punic (Carthaginian) origins has left its mark in many remains: traces of an earlier sanctuary dedicated to Baal have been found beneath the Temple of Saturn, while the funeral mausoleum of the Numidian leader Ataban dates from the end of the 3C BC. After the demolition of Carthage in 146 BC and the outbreak of the Third Punic War, Tukka fell into the hands of the Numidian king Massinissa, an ally of Rome (*see page 224*). In 46 BC, after the defeat of Juba I who had the misfortune to support Pompey against Caesar, the Numidian kingdoms were absorbed into the Roman province of Africa.

Roman Thugga – To the existing Punico-Numidian population were added immigrants of Roman origin, although there was no intensive colonisation. The two communities coexisted, but were ruled under separate administrative systems: the original inhabitants retained the Punic city model of municipal assembly (*civitas*) under decurions, while the Romans were governed within the framework of the civic constituency known as the *pagus*. This double administration reflected a difference of status between Roman citizens and others, who were of a lower order. It was not until AD 205, in the reign of **Septimius Severus**, the first "African" emperor, that Thugga was elevated to the status of a municipality and all its inhabitants became Roman citizens.

When Septimus came to power, the race for honours and rewards intensified, and Thugga began to give itself the trappings of a fine city. The Roman patrician was expected to mark his elevation to a position of dignity, with a grandiose monument to commemorate his generosity and great deeds. Thugga benefited from competitive munificence and the city was endowed with ever grander and more handsome buildings. In the 2C, the wealthy Gabinii clan built the Temples of Concord, Frugifer and Liber Pater, and a few years later they opened their wallets again to present the Forum portico and the Temple of Minerva. The Maedii family did not intend to be left behind, and donated a temple to Fortuna Augusta, Venus and Mercury. Meaner or more modest, the Pompeii restricted their prodigality to the tiny temple of Pieta Augusta. It must have been pleasant to be one of the Marcii under Marcus Aurelius, for there was no shortage of gold: they threw themselves into an orgy of spending, financing in succession the Unnamed Temple, the Theatre, and the Capitol.

A Slow Death – In the case of Dougga, the breakdown of Roman civilisation owed nothing to the Vandals, as in the rest of North Africa; there is no trace of these great destroyers of life and prosperity in the little provincial town. Far away from the great communication routes, it seems that the people of Thugga were quite simply forgotten, by their official representatives who had departed to make their fortunes in Rome, as well as by the Vandals and other looters. By the 4C there was no more building, simply restoration. Although Dougga seems to have yielded to enthusiasm for the new Christian faith, traces of this period are rare. No doubt temples were simply transformed into churches. The Byzantines fortified the forum and the capitol, but the town no longer had a strategic importance compared to Téboursouk or Aïn Tounga.

At the time of the Arab advance, Dougga was already very dilapidated, the temples in a state of ruin, the inhabitants living rough or in shacks. The town gradually collapsed, undermined by water and subsidence, and it reverted to farmland. Nevertheless, community life of a sort survived on the site of the old city, and only a few decades ago the last local inhabitants were still living miserably in the old Roman water cisterns. When the site was restored, they were forced to move to the newly-built **Dougga al Jadida** (New Dougga) a few kilometres away.

"But mankind, indifferent to the dream of ancestors ..." – Faithful to these old stones which for so long gave them shelter, the original inhabitants continue to haunt the site. It is not unusual to meet a peasant on his mule, trotting briskly between the capitals and the chipped shafts of columns, or a small boy, guarding his family's two or three cows.

It is above all in the evening, though, when tourists are fewer, that the shepherds and their flocks filter silently into the ruins, like shadows.

Site Visit

Allow 3 hours. Open 8am-7pm in summer,
8.30am-5.30pm in winter. Entrance charge.

The layout of the city appears to have been defined by the steepness of the site and perhaps the outline of the earlier Numidian occupation, for it has little of the geometric logic of conventional Roman towns. The imposing monuments were built according to the lie of the land. In the days of its greatest splendour, Dougga consisted of an astonishing concentration of temples and public buildings, with no apparent concern for scale or harmony. Similarly, the often steep and twisting streets follow the contours of the land (*see illustration page 116*). The city's inhabitants must have had strong legs, and that is what the visitor needs too.

The normal starting point for a tour of the site is the theatre. This is the monument nearest to the car park, and the best preserved in Dougga. Its top tier offers a view over the whole site.

The **Theatre***** was built in AD 168-169, by the Roman citizen Publius Marcius Quadratus, a "flaminus" (priest) of the imperial religion: eighteen hundred years later the monument is admired by thousands of visitors, and classical plays are still performed here (*Dougga Festival, see page 107*).

Marcius was ambitious: the **cavea** could accommodate 3 500 spectators, even though Dougga had only 5 000 inhabitants in his day. It rose 15m above the orchestra with three tiers of seats separated by access galleries – unfortunately, cement has been used to restore the upper rows. The reconstruction of the **stage portico**, on the other hand, is very successful. The stage wall no longer exists, but the stage itself still has its mosaic paving. The two side stairways leading to the orchestra are separated by niches, which no doubt originally contained statues or fountains. The scene-changing machinery was hidden in an arched

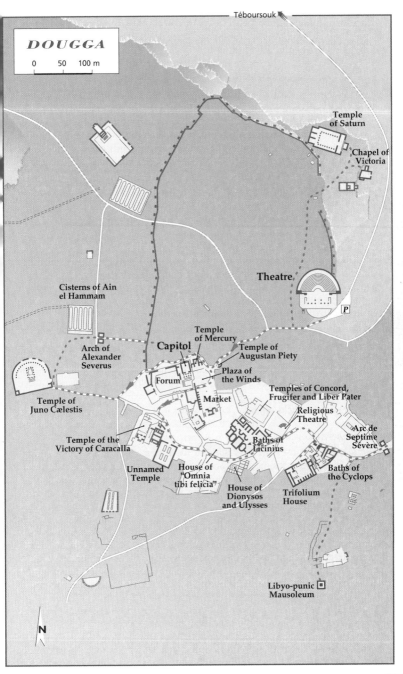

DOUGGA

0   50   100 m

Téboursouk

Temple
of Saturn

Chapel of
Victoria

Theatre

Cisterns of Ain
el Hammam

Temple
of Mercury

Capitol

Temple of
Augustan Piety

Arch of
Alexander
Severus

Forum

Plaza of
the Winds

Temples of Concord,
Frugifer and Liber Pater

Market

Religious
Theatre

Temple of
Juno Cælestis

Arc de
Septime
Sévère

Temple of the
Victory of Caracalla

Baths of
Licinius

Unnamed
Temple

House of
"Omnia
tibi felicia"

Baths of
the Cyclops

House of
Dionysos
and Ulysses

Trifolium
House

Libyo-punic
Mausoleum

N

P

177

space beneath the stage. When the sun was too strong an awning was stretched across *(see architectural plan, page 43)* and sprinkled with fresh water – no doubt from the tanks beneath the seating.

If time or energy is short, go straight to the Capitol; otherwise, climb up above the theatre to the Temple of Saturn and Chapel of Victoria.

Built on the edge of the cliff which dominates the valley to the northeast, the **Temple of Saturn** (AD 196) occupies the former site of a sanctuary dedicated to **Baal**. The temple consisted of a vestibule and courtyard surrounded by a portico leading to three halls, the central one housing the statue of Baal. The Romans had an unusual capacity for integrating the gods of conquered lands into their own pantheon: Saturn is the Romanised version of Baal.

The **Chapel of Victoria** (late 4C – early 5C), a little below the temple, is the only Christian monument in Dougga. An inscription in the crypt evokes the dead Victoria, perhaps a nun or early martyr.

From the theatre, make your way towards the Capitol along the Roman road which winds through thistles and buttercups.

The **Temple of Augustan Piety** (2C) is remarkable above all for its small size, the result of the meanness of the inheritors of one Caius Pompeius Nahanius, whose will insisted on its construction. The tiny apse is set beyond a vestibule with two columns and four of its remaining sturdy pillars. A little further back to the right is the former **mosque** of the Arab village, a small square building erected on the remains of the **Temple of Fortune**.

The **Plaza of the Winds** owes its distinctive semi-circular design to the concern to correct a street scene that had been disturbed by uncoordinated building. Its name comes from the great circle carved into the tiles showing the twelve winds. From the square, the **Temple of Mercury** is reached up a stairway with four steps. The building consists of a vast portico, with ten columns, and three assembly halls.

The **market** was held opposite, on the other side of the square; with ten stalls set out round an open courtyard. It was no doubt the patrons of the temple and the market who laid out the square at their own expense.

The **Capitol**, the site's most magnificent monument, is striking in its beautiful golden sheen. Its grace, elegance and grandeur make it one of the most beautiful Roman buildings of North Africa. The climb up the impressive stairs to the portico leaves few vistors unmoved. The six 8m high columns (five of them monoliths) support an **architrave** with an engraved dedication to the capitoline triad together with the names of the two donors, a prominently-placed reminder that *Sua pecunia fecerunt* – their money created the building. The bas-relief of a man carried off by an eagle which is still just visible on the **pediment** represents the apotheosis of the Emperor Antoninus the Pious. The **cella** has three niches which held statues of the gods, the centre one a colossal statue of Jupiter of which the head has been discovered, while the two others held figures of Juno and Minerva.

The small paved space at the foot of the steps no doubt served as an **area**, but no trace has been found of the altar used for sacrifices.

From the *area* a flight of steps leads to the **forum**. Modest in size (38.5m x 24m), it must have been well-filled with statues, if we can judge by the number of pedestals. The family of the Gabinii donated the 2C arcade which surrounded it on three sides and which gave access to various public and religious buildings.

The forum was wrecked in the 6C when the Byzantines fortified the whole of the Capitol district, demolishing the temples and buildings around the forum as well as the market. The **Temple of Juno Cælestis** stands among olive groves to the west of the capitol. This elegant edifice is unique of its kind. The **cella**, surrounded by a **portico**, stands on a platform at the centre of a semi-circular courtyard which was originally completely walled in. An arcade runs along the curving section of the wall, creating a gallery which was probably used for processions. Since the temple was built around AD 222-235 on a site of worship formerly

Eurasia Press/DIAF

The Capitol

dedicated to Tanit, some authorities think that the design represents the Punic goddess's famous crescent moon.

The **Cisterns of Ain el Hammam**, which can be seen not far from the temple, under the olive trees, were fed by an aqueduct which brought water from a spring 12km away. The nearby **Arch of Alexander Severus** straddles an avenue of Barbary fig trees leading to the forum. It was built between AD 222 and AD 235, probably to commemorate the granting of certain privileges to the city.

From the forum, a charming roadway leads down to the right to the **Temple of the Victory of Caracalla** (AD 214) and the **Unnamed Temple** (AD 164-166). As its name indicates, the exact function of the latter building is not known; it is sometimes known as **Dar Lachheb**. It was probably a temple, to judge by the enormous courtyard set inside an arcade, at the back of which would have been the cella. The doorway, in an excellent state of preservation and with a stylish fluted column in front, makes an ideal frame for the Capitol in the background. A little further down, the road leads to two Roman houses where mosaics were discovered which are now displayed in the Bardo. The **House of "Omnia tibi felicia"** derives its name from the formula for good luck carved on the mosaic in the vestibule: "May everything bring you happiness". As for the **House of Dionysos and Ulysses**, it has supplied the Bardo with one of its finest items.

179

Despite the sloping ground, the **Baths of Licinius**∗ (3C AD) are laid out according to the classical plan *(see the architectural plan, page 43)*, although substantial earth-moving was obviously carried out. Originally, the visitor to these winter baths entered through a vestibule on its north side; the room still has some columns and a section of its mosaic paving. From the main street, two underground passages led into the baths. Deep and dark, they require the visitor to plunge in as if into water: the reward for such boldness is to come out into a vestibule next to the frigidarium. At one end of this cold room, the view out is framed between the two beautiful columns of one of the doors: to the side, three great arcades provide a little freshness.

Construction of the **temples of Concord, Frugifer** and **Liber Pater** lasted from AD 128 to AD 138 on land belonging to the Gabinii, father and son, who also financed the work. This group is interesting particularly for a small religious **theatre** (sometimes called the "auditorium"), whose purpose is not well understood. It may have been used to celebrate the mysteries linked to the cult of Liber Pater. It is true that the site forms an attractive viewpoint, and that its layout is very suitable for rites of initiation. It is also a good spot to rest and take in the surroundings.

A small lane below leads down to the **Trifolium House**. The entrance is indicated by the two pillars of the entrance gate which survive and encroach somewhat onto the paving. This 3C house is the largest in Dougga, with two levels accessible from the street. The ground floor is laid out round a large courtyard bounded by an arcade. The centre of the courtyard was once laid out as a garden.

The **Baths of the Cyclops** take their name from a mosaic which shows these giants hard at work manufacturing Jupiter's thunderbolts. This beautifully made mosaic, sadly much damaged, is now in the Bardo museum. Because of their small size, the baths must have been reserved for private use by residents of the Trifolium House close by. The latrines, in an excellent state of preservation, consist of a semi-circular stone bench with twelve holes. A basin faces the bench, fed by water from a cistern and provided for handwashing.

The **Arch of Septimus Severus**, in very poor condition, was built in AD 205 to commemorate the town's accession to full municipal status. The arch marked the beginning of a roadway leading to the main route between Carthage and Thevesta (Tebessa, in Algeria).

Turn back. Half-way between the Arch and the Baths of Cyclops, take the road on your left.

The only vandal to have left his mark on Dougga was Sir Thomas Read, the British consul in Tunis. In 1842 he was responsible for the demolition of the **Libyo-Punic Mausoleum**, a rare example of royal Numidian architecture to have survived virtually intact until the 19C. It appears that under the burden of his name Thomas Read was obsessed with written material; in order to gain possession of the bilingual inscription (in Libyan and Punic), he did not hesitate to dismantle the monument stone by stone. This "Rosetta Stone", now held in the British Museum, tells us that the tomb was the burial site of the Numidian leader Ataban.

The mausoleum was restored between 1908 and 1910. Built on these three levels and 21m high, it dates from the 3C BC, and its design is a blend of various influences: Greek, oriental and Egyptian. An opening in the lowest level, closed with a paving stone, gave access to the funeral chamber *(see also pages 30 and 47).*

Mosaic of Ulysses, detail (Musée du Bardo)

A. Reffet/EXPLORER

The spa baths at Korbous

B.Brillon/MICHELIN

CAP BON

The peninsula of Cap Bon thrusts out into the Mediterranean at the extreme north of the country, between the Gulf of Tunis and the Gulf of Hammamet. A fertile land blessed by providence, it is a pleasing mosaic of orchards and gardens with a fertile and generous soil famous for its sunshine. Abundant springs mean that vines flourish, lemon and orange trees bend beneath the weight of their fruit, and roses compete with jasmine for supremacy. It is hardly surprising that this African bridgehead so close to Europe – Sicily is only 140km away – should have stirred up envy in all the invading forces of the Mediterranean basin. Now, however, the invasion is a benign one, made up of the armies of tourists heading for the seaside resorts of Nabeul and Hammamet – leaving the rest of the peninsula in peace. In this tranquil land it is not unusual to pass a valiant little donkey on the road, hauling a tottering cart loaded with straw, citrus fruit or Barbary figs – which, despite the precepts of Islam, produce an agreeable white brandy and dry muscat wine. The local people have a relaxed life-style and have kept many traditions: there are festivals celebrating the orange harvest, falconry and tuna fishing.

At the base of the Cap is the market town of Nabuel, Tunisia's pottery capital, and Hammamet, the country's premier resort.

THE CAP BON PENINSULA★★

Governorship of Nabeul
230km from Tunis to Hammamet – allow a day

Not to be missed
The coastal landscape round Korbous.
The Carthaginian site at Kerkouane.

And remember...
Bring your swimming gear.

Leave Tunis by Bab Alioua, passing the Jellaz cemetery. Avoid the motorway to your right and instead turn left towards Megrine; further on, take the Hamman Lif road. 8km further, at Borj Cedria you reach the border of Ben Avors governorship. Follow the signposts to Soliman and Kelibia, on the left. You enter Nabeul governorship after passing the railway.

■ **Soliman** – The first stop on the tour round Cap Bon is at this market-garden village founded by the Andalusians, fleeing from Spain, in the 17C. These immigrants prospered and were responsible for Soliman's **mosque★** with green tiled roof, an architectural feature rare in Tunisia.

About 8km beyond Soliman, turn left towards Korbous.

The route soon becomes a corniche road. Ochre cliffs covered with aloes and Barbary figs drop directly into the sea with its shifting tones of blue and green. The **view★★** takes in the whole of the Gulf of Tunis. Then, as a bend is rounded, the tiny white village of Korbous appears, nestling in a rocky valley running down to the sea.

■ **Korbous** – Known since classical times for its warm springs, Korbous was relaunched in the 19C by the beys, who built a pavilion here which now houses the spa offices **(Office du thermalisme)**. Nowadays the baths at Korbous are used by beneficiaries of the Tunisian social security system; many of the springs with their evocative names – *Al Kebira* ("the great"), *Es Sbia* ("health"), etc. – are considered effective in treating arthritic conditions and high blood-pressure, in addition to obesity, cellulite or rheumatism. However, there is no need to be out of sorts to come here and appreciate a magnificent panoramic view over the sea, and to swim, a little further on *(about 2km away)*, at Aïn el Atrous, where a spring pours warm (50° C) water straight into the sea.

Beyond Korbous the road runs along the coast and then crosses the jebel before descending once more through a valley full of olive and fig trees.

10km beyond Korbous, the road forks. Turn right towards El Haouaria and, 3km further on, take the C 26 road to the left. Continue for about 45km, then turn left for the port of Sidi Daoud.

■ **Sidi Daoud** – There is no way in which the residents of Sidi Daoud can be identified as different from other local people; they have the same friendly air, the same casual style that is a characteristic feature of an area where the living is easy. Yet this little port owes its fame to an extremely violent form of tuna-fishing: the **matanza**. Late May and early June is the period for this blood-stained ritual dating back to the most distant classical times. The shoals of tuna that

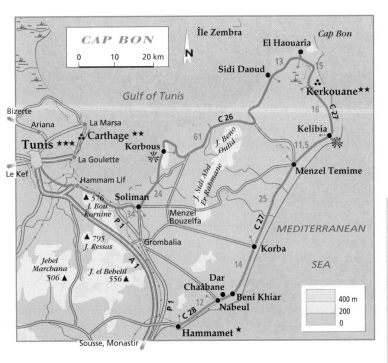

come to spawn in the Mediterranean are directed by a system of vast nets into madragues. Once trapped, the great fish are put to death in their thousands: bludgeoned, harpooned or knifed at close quarters in a foaming flood of crimson. If this brief marine episode has not conclusively put you off the idea of tuna, it is worth knowing that Sidi Daouad's preserved foods are famous throughout Tunisia; they are considered the first choice of food items for the preparation of a méchouis and egg fritter dishes.

On leaving Sidi Daoued, join the main C 26 road once more. Continue along it for about 11km, then turn left at the crossroads for El Houaria.

■ **El Haouaria** – Cap Bon is the final stopover for migrating birds before they fly over the Mediterranean. Among these flocks, large numbers of birds of prey take shelter in the cliffs that form the farthest tip of the cape. In El Haouaria, the most northerly village in the peninsula, young falcons are captured in March and then trained for several weeks. Next comes the hunting season, which ends in June with the **Sparrow-hawk festival** (festival de l'epervier). This is the moment for the falconers to give spectacular demonstrations of hunting, as their birds of prey swoop down on partridge, quail and other small game birds. It seems that the falcons are released when the season ends.

Go up the main street from the central square dominated by the imposing figure of a bird of prey and then carry on along a dirt track for 3km in the direction of the Cap, to reach the **Roman quarries**, or **Ghar el Kébir caves★** (*open 8am-7pm in summer, 8am-5pm in winter, entrance charge*). The cliff is inhospitable, but access to the site is straightforward. Slaves extracted enormous blocks of stone from the three great excavations in the rock, which were then taken by sea to neighbouring cities. It was used for the construction of Punic Carthage, among other places, and the quarry continued in use under the Romans. Look upwards, and you will see the narrow openings through which the stone blocks were raised to the surface. Holes hollowed out along the sides enabled the men to get in and out of the caves. One particular rock on the way into the main cave looks exactly like a dromedary lying down, but, contrary to legend, it is the result of human labour and not the effect of erosion.

At the very tip of the peninsula **Cap Bon** itself can only be visited by following a stony track in bad condition and walking several kilometres along the cliffs from the site of the Ghar El Kébir caves. *(Boat trips can be arranged from the Daurade restaurant in El Haouaria.)*

Go back through El Haouaria and take the C 27 to Kerkouane, 15km away. Go through Dar Allouche then, 6km further on, turn left for Kerkouane. 2km outside Kerkouane a minor road to the left leads to the Punic ruins.

■ **Kerkouane ruins**★★ — *8am-7pm in summer, 9.30am-4.30pm in winter. Entrance charge.* The finest Punic ruins in Tunisia are fascinating as much for their archeological interest as for their lay-out and appearance. The old city stands in luxuriant gardens on its promontory site a few metres above the crystal-clear sea. It was discovered in 1952 and partly excavated in the 1960s, but little is known of its history, except that it was probably founded in the 6C BC. The date of its destruction, however, is less easy to establish. It may have been sacked during the First Punic War (3C BC) or it may have shared the sad fate of Carthage in 146 BC. Whatever the truth, the city was abandoned completely, with the advantage that it therefore offers archeologists a virgin site with no trace of any other civilisation, whether Roman, Byzantine or Arab. In the streets of Kerkouane it is possible to explore a fortified town of 2 000 inhabitants as it must have been in Hannibal's day. Although the remains barely reach knee-height, the general lay-out remains clearly visible: fine paved streets, enormous open squares, shops, flights of steps, great columns here and there. From one house to the next the plan scarcely changes: the entrance leads into a court with a well serving the various rooms. The most astonishing feature is undoubtedly the **bathroom**, complete with slipper bath with a red lining. This coating was extracted from murex, a mollusc used by Phoenicians, Greeks and Romans alike to manufacture purple. The city appears to have lived mainly off this activity, to judge by the amount of murex shells found here. The indoor pavements consist of somewhat plain mosaics: pottery fragments with the occasional piece of white marble or murex shell. The only motif appearing with any frequency is the symbol of the goddess Tanit.

The town's immediate surroundings included a sanctuary, and above all a necropolis where a large number of objects has been discovered. These are now on display in the **museum** built near the site. The finest item among them is a **sarcophagus** made of cypress wood, its lid carved to represent a goddess watching over the sleep of the dead. The show-cases also hold a rich collection of jewels, ceramics, perfume-burners and black enamelled pottery, or buttons made of bone and feeding cups shaped like a hedgehog.

Continue along the C 27. Kelibia lies on the left after about 15km.

Aerial view of the Kerkouane ruins

■ **Kelibia** – This little town is strategically located, looking out over the straits separating Tunis and Sicily. Almost surrounded by water on its peninsula, Kelibia's location was no doubt the cause of its ruin: occupied by Agathocles in 310 BC and then by Regulus in 256, it finally suffered the same fate as Carthage at the end of the Third Punic War. Later it suffered from attack by a series of invaders, undergoing a particularly destructive onslaught by the Spanish (1535-47). In fact very little of the Carthaginian city remains, and of the classical Roman site of Clupea, only a few ruined **villas** remain *(near the fishing school)*.

The **fortress*** is really the only monument worth looking at *(open 8am-7pm in summer and 8am-5.30pm in winter. Entrance charge)*. Built in the 6C by the Byzantines, it was restored and redeveloped over the centuries by the Spanish and the Turks. Today it contains a lighthouse and a meteorological station behind its crenellated walls. The ramparts give a **panoramic view** over the beaches of white sand and the fishermen's harbour. It is the fishing port which is the best-known feature of Kelibia nowadays, along with its light dry muscat wines. The town can also be proud of its very beautiful beach *(1.5km away)* as well as of its **international amateur film festival**, which creates a lively atmosphere in summer.

Continue along the C 27 towards Hammamet.

Y Traverd/DIAF

Go through **Menzel Temime**, famous for the peppers that can be seen drying in colourful garlands in summer, then **Korba**, a little garden town, blessed with one of the most beautiful beaches of the region and where a lively drama festival takes place every year. At **Beni Khiar** visitors can watch craftsmen making the famous striped Tunisian blankets, as well as **woven and black-point rugs**. **Dar Chaâbane**, a little further on, is a centre for stone quarrying and **stone carving** (*see under "crafts", page 75*).

Beyond Dar Chaâbane continue on the C 27. Nabeul is 2km away.

The port and the castle, Kelibia

Making the most of Cap Bon

GETTING THERE

By car – Travelling by car is the best way to discover Cap Bon.

WHERE TO STAY

The small number of hotels protect this beautiful coast from becoming a destination for mass tourism. It remains one of the rare secret spots of Tunisia.

• El Haouaria

From US$18-42

Hôtel l'Epervier, 3 ave Habib Bourguiba, ☎ (02) 297 017 / 297 044, Fax (02) 297 258 – 11rm ⌂ 目 TV ✗ CC Avoid the rooms overlooking the street in this modest hotel, located in the centre of the village. This is the best place to stay if you come during the Falconry Festival in June.

• Kelibia

From US$18-42

Pension Anis, ave Erriadh (take the road on the right across from the fish market), ☎ (02) 295 777, Fax (02) 273 128 – 12rm This well-kept pension is excellent value for money. The shared showers and WCs on the landing are kept as clean as the rest of the establishment.

From US$42-75

Hôtel Mamounia, Kelibia Beach (turn at the sign indicating the hotel and continue straight on for 1.5km),

☎ (02) 296 088 / 296 219, Fax (02) 296 858 – 117rm 🛏 ✕ ⚊ ♨ ⒸⒸ This somewhat run-down resort nonetheless offers good value for your money. It is located on a superb and relatively unused beach.

Hôtel Palmarina, Kelibia Beach, ☎ (02) 274 062 to 065, Fax (02) 274 055 – 36rm 🛏 🖃 ♫ ⓉⓋ ✕ ⚊ ♨ ❦ ⒸⒸ This is Kelibia's only hotel of any pretension. It is nevertheless within this price range. The rooms have wrought-iron furniture.

EATING OUT

• El Haouaria
From US$18-42
La Daurade, near the Roman caves, ☎ (02) 269 080, Fax (02) 269 090. 🕌 ⒸⒸ The restaurant has a spectacular setting overlooking the tumultuous waters of Cap Bon. Delicious grilled fish are a must. Book in advance for dinner (several choices of menu) and the evening entertainment programme.

• Kelibia
Less than US$10
Restaurant Anis, ave Erriadh, ☎ (02) 295 777, Fax (02) 273 128. The decor is as simple as the pension of the same name. The chef offers a choice of fish or grilled meat.
Sidi el Bahri, port de Kelibia, ☎ (02) 273 925. ♟ 🕌 This café-cum-pizzeria nestling in front of a small private beach is open 24 hours a day.

From US$10-22
El Mansourah, Kelibia, ☎ (02) 295 169, Fax (02) 273 206. 🕌 There is a sign to this restaurant just beyond the harbour. About 1.6km further on there is a bend. Take the road that continues straight. Follow it for another 600m. The service

is less than brilliant, which is a shame because the fish is very good and the restaurant is on a floodlit beach. Take advantage of this occasion to try the delicious dry muscatel from Kelibia.

WHERE TO GO OUT FOR A DRINK

Cafés

• El Haouaria
La Buvette, below the restaurant La Daurade. Situated on a cliff looking out to sea. It is a pity that the deafening music spoils the tranquillity of the site.

• Kelibia
Sidi el Bahri, port de Kelibia ♟ 🕌 A pleasant place for a beer or some mint tea.

FESTIVALS

• El Haouaria
Falconry Festival, ☎ (02) 297 066. Falconry competitions (see El Haouaria section). The event takes place in June when the birds have reached adulthood.

• Sidi Daoud
La Matanza takes place from May to the end of June. Traditional tuna fishing, using rituals similar to those practised in Sicily. Authorisation to attend this event is difficult and time-consuming, and can only be obtained by contacting a number of ministries and official organisations.

• Menzel Bou Zelfa
Orange Festival. Events centred on the orange harvest in March.

• Hammam Lif
Bou Kornine Variety Festival. Rap, Rai or techno music in July-August.

• Kelibia
Amateur Film Festival. This is a long-standing event which served as a crucible for Tunisian cinema today. June-July.

NABEUL
Centre of Governorship
Pop c 40 000
67km from Tunis

Not to be missed
The Friday market.
And remember...
If you want to buy Tunisian pottery, this is the best place for it.
The town is very spread out; use a means of transport.

Founded by the Phoenicians in the 5C BC, this former hub of Carthaginian trade is now the capital of Cap Bon and the centre of a governorship. The reputation of the little city of 40 000 inhabitants is based on an ancient craft tradition of lead-glazed pottery and ceramics, an activity that dates back to at least the Roman era when the city was called *Colonia Julia Neapolis*. Today, the pavements of the shopping streets are always full of brightly coloured jars and vases of all sizes. Trinkets, two-toned crockery (generally green and yellow), wide-bellied jars and tiles of glazed ceramic, superbly decorated with traditional or modern designs, are piled up in the shops and workshops: Nabeul has managed to retain its traditions of craft and workmanship despite its beautiful beaches and the nearness of Hammamet *(see under "Crafts", page 75, and "Shopping", page 108)*.

Visits and shopping

Nabeul is less fashionable than Hammamet, its rival in this part of the coast which accounts for nearly one-third of Tunisia's tourist activity. But it manages to make the most of its advantages – its craftsmanship, of course, but also its commercial dynamism. Its weekly market is one of the largest in the country.

The orange flower miracle
"Zehar" (orange-flower water) combines utility and pleasure, curative properties and edible delight. Zehar is supposed to cure everything, or nearly everything – the heart, migraines, gastric problems, insomnia, and above all, it flavours confectionery, fruit salads, coffee, even the feeding-bottle for a feverish baby. The Tunisian housewife always has a supply in store, and Cap Bon produces no less than 2 000 tonnes of orange flowers each year. Their distillation represents a major part of local economic activity, and half of it is undertaken as a craft activity in family stills. Each tonne of flowers produces 500kg of water. This miraculous flower is celebrated in the spring, in Nabeul's orange flower festival.

The **Friday market*** *(mornings only)* gives a good idea of the local products with plenty of pottery, as well as very beautiful embroidery and essential oils; Nabeul is a great centre for the distillation of orange, geranium and jasmine flowers. The riches of the Orient are piled up higgledy-piggledy with heaps of sheep skins and an astonishingly varied mixture of objects "Made in Europe" or "Made in Taiwan". Nabeul also takes pride in its importance in the camel trade, which may seem surprising if one considers the rare and unhappy specimens to be seen in the town.

To appreciate the skill of Tunisian craftsmen it is best to visit the ONAT – the **Tunisian National Craft Bureau**

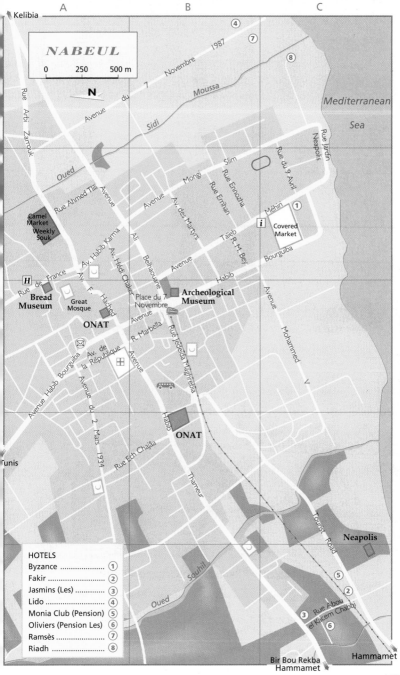

NABEUL

0 — 250 — 500 m

N

Kelibia

Mediterranean Sea

Tunis

HOTELS

Byzance .... ①
Fakir .... ②
Jasmins (Les) .... ③
Lido .... ④
Monia Club (Pension) ⑤
Oliviers (Pension Les) ⑥
Ramsès .... ⑦
Riadh .... ⑧

Camel Market Weekly Souk

Bread Museum

Great Mosque

ONAT

Archeological Museum

Covered Market

Place du 7 Novembre

ONAT

Neapolis

Bir Bou Rekba Hammamet

Hammamet

Rue Arbi Zarrouk

Avenue du 7 Novembre 1987

Sidi

Moussa

Oued

Rue Ahmed Tlili

Avenue

Av. Habib Karma

Av. Hédi Chaker

Ali

Belhaouane

Mongi Slim

Av. des Martyrs

Rue Ennozha

Rue Emhan

Rue du 9 Avril

Rue Jardin Neapolis

Méhiri

Taïeb R. M. Bey

Avenue Habib Bourguiba

Habib

Rue de France

Av. F. Hached

R. Marbella

Avenue

Av. de la République

Avenue du 2 Mars 1934

Avenue Habib Bourguiba

Rue Jedeida Magrrebia

Habib

Rue Ech Chajãa

Thameur

Souhil

Oued

Avenue Mohammed V

Tourist Road

Rue Abou el Kacem Chabbi

(Office National d'Artisanat Tunisien) – in the ave Habib Thameur. Here it is possible to see plenty of work in individual crafts: ironwork, stone sculpture, rush matting being made by young workmen sitting cross-legged, rugs being knotted, pottery being painted. The quality is outstanding, but the goods are priced to match.

In April 1999, a new museum opened in the rue Mongi Slim (running perpendicular to the rue de France). The **Bread Museum** (Musée du pain) *(open 10am-6pm, closed Mondays, entrance charge)* was founded by Dr Farouk Chaabouni, who travelled the length and breadth of Tunisia for 6 years in his search for tools and utensils, anecdotes and proverbs relating to bread-making. Brought together in a beautiful house dating from the 18C, these objects and documents, together with explanatory notes and photos, explain the whole bread-making process in detail. *(Guided visits only by arrangement,* ☎ *(02) 272 664, entrance charge about TD70 for a group of 10 people.)*

The **archeological museum** (musée archéologique) *(open 8.30am-5.30pm in winter, 8am-7pm in summer; entrance charge)* is dedicated to archeological remains from Cap Bon. The collections are somewhat sparse, although there are some interesting terracotta statues, Carthaginian ceramics, cult objects and above all mosaics from the site at Neapolis. *(The museum is currently being renovated. It is expected to re-open in 2000 after a year of work.)*

Take the tourist route towards Hammamet. Neapolis lies opposite the Monia Club, in open ground beside the sea.

Excavations at **Neapolis** have uncovered a Roman villa from the 4C AD. The house of some twenty rooms was, as expected, paved with mosaics now preserved in the Nabeul archeological museum. More unusually, a *garum* production unit has been discovered on this site: *garum*, a sauce highly prized by the Romans, was made from a base of assorted small fish and fish intestines dried in the sun.

Excavations will continue for the foreseeable future; consequently the site is currently closed to visitors.

Pottery on display in Nabeul

Nabeul

GETTING THERE

By train – SNCFT, ave Habib Bourguiba, ☎ (02) 285 054. There is only one train to Tunis per day. It makes more sense to go to Bir Bou Rekba where there are 11 trains daily to Tunis (from 50-70min), 6 to Sousse (1 hour 20min), 2 to Monastir (1 hour 50min) and Mahdia (2hr 40min), 6 to El Jem (3hr) and Sfax (3hr 50min), 2 to Gabès – including a night train (6hr) – and 1 night train to Gafsa (9hr).

By bus – Bus terminal, ave Habib Thameur, ☎ (02) 285 273 / 285 043, Fax (02) 285 929. **SRTG** and **SRTN** coaches put Nabeul within range of Tunisia's main cities. There are 12 connections daily to Tunis in air-conditioned coaches and 5 departures on Sundays (55min). There are 4 coaches going to El Haouaria (1 hr 45min), 3 departures to Kairouan (5hr), 8 to Zaghouan, 2 to Sousse (4hr 15min), 1 to Monastir and 1 to Mahdia. Finally, there are 9 shuttle buses daily between Nabeul and the station in Bir Bou Rekba, via Hammamet.

By shared taxi – Station, ave Habib Thameur, next to the bus terminal. Nabeul is a much visited artisan centre. Shared taxis are everywhere and there is never a long wait.

By car – Nabeul is one hour from Tunis if you plan to drive. Avoid getting stuck in Hammamet by leaving the motorway at the Grombalin exit and taking the C 27 towards Dar Chaâbanne.

GETTING AROUND

By car – A car is very useful to visit beaches outside the city.

By taxi – Allo Taxi, ☎ (02) 222 444. The yellow taxis that dash across the city are a good way of getting to the hotels on the outskirts of town.

Car hire – Hertz, ave Habib Thameur, ☎ (02) 285 327.

Motorbike hire – Several companies located in the larger hotels rent motorcycles. Try **Rollers Rent**, at the Khéops Club, ave du 7 Novembre, ☎ (02) 226 990 / 282 723.
There is a larger selection of rental companies in Hammamet.

ADDRESS BOOK

Emergency – Police station, ave Habib Bourguiba, ☎ (02) 285 474.
National Guard, ave Taïeb Méhiri, ☎ (02) 286 153.
Dialysis Centre, on the road from Nabeul, ☎ (02) 280 677.

Tourist information – Regional Tourist Office, ave Taïeb Méhiri, ☎ (02) 286 800 / 286 737, Fax (02) 224 262. Open daily 8.30am-1pm / 2pm-5.45pm in winter, except Sundays, and 7.30am-1.30pm / 5-8pm in summer. Sundays 9am-12pm / 5-8pm. Ask to look at the file containing information on train and bus schedules as well as on different activities and events in the area. Town plans of Nabeul and Hammamet are also available.
Tourist Information Centre, Place du 7 Novembre (facing the railway station), ☎ 02 280 423. Open daily 9am-12.30pm / 4-9pm, except Mondays. There is slightly less information here than at the ONTT, however, this centre is more centrally located.

Banks / Currency Exchange – The numerous banks often provide money exchange services. Open 7.15am-12pm in summer.
Cash dispenser – STB Bank, 60 ave Habib Bourguiba.

Post office – ave Habib Bourguiba, ☎ (02) 287 000. In winter the post office is open daily but only from 8am-6pm on Sundays. In summer, it is only open from 7am-1pm.

Airline and Shipping Companies – Tunis Air, ave Habib Bourguiba, (02) 285 193. Reservations ☎ (02) 286 200.

WHERE TO STAY

Less than US$8
Camping les Jasmins, rue Abou el Kacem Chabbi, ☎ (02) 285 343 / 285 699, Fax (02) 285 073. This camping site is situated next to the hotel of the same name (see below). Campers must pay for use of the pool.

From US$18-42

Pension les Oliviers, in the street which runs opposite the Les Jasmins camp site, ☎ (02) 286 865 – 30rm ⌂
Peace and quiet in a family-run pension in olive groves (however the beach is not far off). All of the rooms are beautifully clean and open on to their own balcony. There is no swimming pool or restaurant but guests can use amenities at the Hôtel les Jasmins for a fairly moderate price.

Hôtel Les Jasmins, rue Abou el Kacem Chabbi, ☎ (02) 285 343 / 285 699, Fax (02) 285 073 – 45rm ⌂
✆ ✗ ☴ Realising they were sitting on a gold mine, this Tunisian family decided to transform their home into a hotel. Amenities include a bar and a swimming pool set amongst the olive groves and a restaurant serving not only Tunisian cuisine, but also, surprisingly, specialities from far-off Slovenia.

Hôtel Fakir, on the tourist route, ☎ (02) 285 477, Fax (02) 287 616 – 50rm ⌂ ✗ ☲ This small, simple hotel located near the former site of the Neapolis is a good solution if you want to take advantage of the beach without spending a fortune. The sea is only 100m away. Unfortunately, the railway tracks are nearby.

Pension Monia Club, tourist route, opposite the entrance to the Neapolis site, ☎ (02) 285 713 – 20rm ⌂ ✗ ☲ This simple hotel is sandwiched between the railway station and the beach. It has a pleasant restaurant which serves meals on the terrace in the summer.

Hôtel Club Ramsès, ave du 7 Novembre, ☎ (02) 362 777 / 773, Fax (02) 362 663, 307rm ⌂ ✗ ☴ ☲ Situated next to the beach, this holiday club has a friendly atmosphere despite its size. At the time of writing, air-conditioning is soon to be installed.

More than US$42

Hôtel Byzance, located on a small road running perpendicular to ave Taïeb Méhiri and Bourguiba, right next to the fairgrounds, ☎ (02) 271 000 / 271 299, Fax (02) 287 164 – 70rm ⌂ TV ✗ ☴ ☲ CC One of Nabeul's most recent hotels located 50m from the beach.

Hôtel Iberostar Lido, ave du 7 Novembre, ☎ (02) 362 988, Fax (02) 361 487 – 370rm. Large parties tend to favour this hotel. If you prefer, you can hire one of the bungalows in the grounds of the hotel (supplement for a TV). A varied programme of sporting activities is on offer.

Hôtel Riadh, ☎ (02) 285 744 / 285 645, Fax (02) 285 057 – 95rm ⌂
✆ ✗ ☴ ☲ CC This establishment has all the comfort and conveniences of a modern hotel situated on the beach.

EATING OUT

Less than US$10

La Rotonde (C2), Nabeul Beach. Take the coastal road via ave Taïeb Méhiri. ☎ (02) 285 782. ☲ Indifferent service, but good food. The restaurant has the advantage of being on the beach, a rare occurrence in Nabeul.

From US$10-20

L'Olivier (B3), ave Hédi Chaker (near the corner of the ave Habib Bourguiba), ☎ (02) 286 613 ☲ CC Shaded by trees, l'Olivier is a haven when Nabuel is burning hot. Service is attentive; good quality European dishes are on offer.

Le Flamboyant (Monia Club) (C5), on the tourist road, ☎ (02) 285 713. ☲ This restaurant allows you the opportunity to sample grilled fish in a lush setting near the beach and archeological site at Neapolis.

WHERE TO GO FOR A DRINK

Café – Errachidia (A3), ave Habib Thameur (next to the ave Habib Bourguiba). For all the locals, including the jasmin sellers, and tourists, this is the place to go for some mint tea and Tunisian cakes, served in a typically Tunisian setting (it's worth having a peek into the kitchen). Note: the nibbles served with the mint tea will be added on to the bill.

LEISURE

Festivals – Orange Festival, place de la Foire, ave Habib Bourguiba, ☎ (02) 285 374. The end of the orange harvest is marked by this large international-scale fair with folk entertainment. End March and April.

Nabeul Summer Festival, open air theatre, ave Taïeb Méhiri, ☎ (02) 286 683. From mid-July to mid-August. Performances by Tunisian variety singers and plays from the whole of the Mediterranean area. But note that all performances are in Arabic.

Hammams – Bains Sidi Maaouia, ave Habib Thameur in front of the orange fountain.

SHOPPING

While the capital of Cap Bon is renowned for its pottery, the neighbouring village of Beni Khiar, is known for its striped carpets, blankets and traditional clothing. Dar Chaâbanne, near Nabeul, is an important quarrying centre with stone sculptures. The factories outside the centre have a larger choice at warehouse prices.

Weekly souk. Open Friday mornings. This bazaar caters exclusively to tourists. Don't forget that prices are set individually for each customer and you should barter. Offer 70% less than the asking price. Avoid going to the camel market which is a veritable tourist trap.

Antiques and handicrafts – SOCOPA, shop located at the Tunisian National Artisans Office **(ONAT)**, ave Farhat Hached, ☎ (02) 285 177 and ave Habib Thameur, ☎ (02) 285 007.

Centre des traditions et des métiers d'arts (ONAT) (Centre of Art Traditions and Trades), ave Habib Thameur, right behind SOCOPA.

Open 8.30am-1pm / 3-6pm in winter and 8am-12pm / 3-6pm in summer. Closed Sundays.

Pottery – Boutique Ben Harriz, rue Arbi Zarrouk, ☎ (02) 285 563. One of the last workshops where old honey-coloured pottery can still be found, examples of Berber pottery from Sejnane.

Poterie Gastli. This pottery has outlets at 117 ave Farhat Hached, ☎ (02) 272 008 and at 190 ave Habib Thameur, ☎ (02) 271 516. It is also possible to make purchases directly at the factory, located in the industrial zone on the road from Tunis, ☎ (02) 222 247, Fax (02) 285 553. This is one of the largest factories in Nabeul and produces large quantities of ceramics that are distributed throughout the country. There are the typical blue and white Tunisian models as well as items inspired by Moroccan and even French designs.

Khedidi, located 1.5km on the road from Tunis, ☎ (02) 287 576, Fax (02) 287 955. This factory has a varied selection of tiles. The most beautiful tiles are handmade but these are also the most expensive (TD45/sqm as opposed to TD15-25/sqm for machine-made tiles). Panels with a tree of life design cost between TD180 and TD400. Open 8am-12pm / 1-5pm in winter and 7am-2pm in summer. Closed Sundays. Visa and MasterCard are accepted.

Bookshops – Librairie Mon Plaisir, 25 ave Hédi Chaker, ☎ (02) 285 094, Fax (02) 272 988.

Librairie, 80 ave Habib Thameur.

Hammamet, a little corner of paradise

HAMMAMET★

Nabeul Governorship
Pop c 40 000
Pleasant climate throughout the year

Not to be missed
The vast beach of fine sand and fine bathing.
Mint tea at the café Sidi Bou Hedid.
And remember…
If you prefer peace and quiet, avoid July and August.

From Nabeul, continue along the main road (here numbered C 28) for about 12km.

Despite the proliferation of hotels along the sea-front, Hammamet is still the little earthly paradise which became a focus for the intelligentsia of Europe during the 1920s and 1930s. André Gide, Georges Bernanos, Paul Klee, Man Ray, and Frank Lloyd Wright were all guests of the Romanian multi-millionaire Georges Sebastian, who built a highly original house here which is now home to the **Centre culturel international** (International Cultural Centre) *(see page 200)*. With the Second World War, General Rommel and the Afrika Korps moved in, though before very long they were succeeded by Montgomery's Desert rats, and the massive profile of Churchill could be seen puffing at his inevitable cigar. After the war various film stars were attracted to Hammamet, and Sophia Loren could be seen stepping daintily across the vast beach of fine sand. But the expansion of this modest fishing village did not truly begin until the 1960s: gradually hotels appeared amongst the sumptuous villas, laying the first stones of what would become the "Tunisian Riviera". Yet these recent buildings have managed to blend into the landscape due to developmental regulations which state that no building may be taller than a cypress tree.

The Villa Sebastian
Nothing could be better than this villa to demonstrate how perfectly the Arab style can be integrated into contemporary architecture. Inspired by the traditional Tunisian house, the Villa can be seen as an interlocking set of parallelepipeds, lime washed with white, of a rigour and simplicity that are wholly modern. This minimalism is softened by the arcarding with its squat columns, particularly round the swimming pool. On the beach side, stepped terraces lead into a garden of rare luxuriance. Seduced by this architectural success, Europeans and wealthy Tunisians had their holiday houses built on the same lines. The hotels also copied the Sebastian style, and Hammamet perhaps owes part of its charm to the good taste of the Romanian multi-millionaire.

After the beach…

The numerous beach activities offered by the hotels should not be allowed to displace the enduring spectacle of the old port and its lantern fishermen setting out at night in the shadow of the **Kasbah**★. From the top of this 15C building *(8.30am-6pm out of season, 8am-7pm in summer; entrance charge)* there is a **magnificent view** over the **medina** and Hammamet Bay. The old town, enclosed within its ramparts, retains all its colourful charm. You can stroll here peacefully along the quiet, winding alleyways which even in midsummer do not give the impression of being overwhelmed by crowds of visitors. The **souk** occupies a single narrow street, with heaps of fabrics and perfumes, ceramics and rugs.

HAMMAMET

0   200   400 m

N

Nabeul

R. Zayane

Avenue de la Liberation

Avenue Assad Ibn el Fourat

R. Sidi Bou Ali

Sfar

Avenue Tahar

Avenue Hedi Chaker

Av. Taïeb Azzabi

Rue du Stade

Av. Habib Thameur

Av. de la République

Rue des Ben Jasmines

R. S. Ben Youssef

R. M.Bachrou

Behaouane

Avenue 7 Novembre 1987

Avenue Hedi Ouali

Oued el Kaïd

Avenue Mongi   Slim

⑦

i

①

R. el Irmam   Salmour

Avenue   Habib   Bourguiba

R. Ibn Khaldoun

R. du 20 Mars 1956

Rue   Ali

Medina

⑥

i

Kasbah

Av. Taïeb Méhiri

Plantation

Av. du 3 Août 1903

Av. du Roi Fayçal Ibn Abdelaziz

Av. du Koweit

Rue de la Corniche

Rue   Patrice   Lumumba

Avenue des Nations Unies

M e d i t e r r a n e a n

S e a

ir Bou Rekba

Oued Faouara

⑧

Villa Sebastian
(International
Cultural Centre)

T

Tourist Road
② ③ ④ ⑤ ⑨   Tunis, Sousse

HOTELS

Alya....................................	①
Bennila................................	②
Citronniers (Les)................	③
Fourati.................................	④
Orangers (Les)....................	⑤
Résidence Hammamet....	⑥
Sahbi...................................	⑦
Sinbad.................................	⑧
Camping Les Samaris........	⑨

Wandering souls will find material for meditation on the far side of the medina. Here, between the ramparts and the sea, the **naval cemetery** has a few Christian graves which stand out at the foot of the wall, and the white mass of Moslem graves. The cemetery is a popular meeting place: women chat in groups of four or five, sitting on the ground or on the edge of a tomb.

Continue to the hotel district by the ave des Nations-Unies, in the direction of Sousse.

Since 1959, the **villa Sebastian*** *(see sidebar page 198)* has been the property of the Tunisian state. It has now been transformed into a **Centre culturel international** (International Cultural Centre) *(8.30am-6pm, entrance charge)*. To this day, visiting VIPs are received in the dining room of this luxurious house. The villa is surrounded with beautiful **botanic gardens*** which cover 14ha and stretch to the sea. It is pleasant to stroll through the gardens, a million miles from the hubbub of Hammamet. In 1964, an open-air theatre was built in the grounds. This is where Hammamet's international festival takes place in July and August. *(see Making the most of Hammamet)*

As you continue towards Sousse you will discover the old Roman city of **Puppet** *(open 8.30am-4.30pm)*, where there is little to see and virtually nothing to comment on, the major part of the site being under excavation or beneath a hotel.

From Hammamet several trips are available within a 100km radius: Tunis, 60km to the north; Zaghouan and Thuburbo Majus, 50km and 80km respectively to the west; Takrouna, about 45km to the south.

Making the most of Hammamet

GETTING THERE

By train – For once, travelling by rail is not the best means of success. The railway station is located at the end of ave Habib Bourguiba and is far from the centre of town. Moreover, there is only one direct train for Tunis per day. For all other trains, you will need to change in Bir Bou Rekba (see Making the most of Nabeul, page 194).

By bus – Most of the buses run from Nabeul, which has a much better service. Buses to Nabeul arrive from Sousse, Monastir and Mahdia.
SRTG: There are 9 buses daily to Nabeul and Bir Bou Rekba, 3 buses per day to Kairouan, 8 to Zaghouan and 8 to Grombalia.
SRTN: 16 buses daily to Tunis (2hr).

By shared taxis – Shared taxis are a very quick way of getting between Tunis and Hammamet, and there is very rarely any need to wait long.

By car – Hammamet is only 60km from Tunis and takes only 50min on the motorway.

GETTING AROUND

Although the centre of town is quite compact, the tourist areas extend from the north to the south of the city.

By car – Cars are not recommended in the town centre because of congestion and the lack of parking spaces. A car is nevertheless useful as many of the hotels are situated far from the centre. Moreover, Hammamet is an excellent starting point if you plan to make excursions throughout the country, particularly to Cap Bon.

By tourist train – 3 such trains are available starting and finishing at the kasbah. They provide a service to the different hotels on the tourist route to the north and south of Hammamet.

By taxi – *Allô taxis*, ☎ (02) 222 444. The taxi rank is located at the entrance of the kasbah.

Car hire – **Avis**, rue de la Gare, ☎ (02) 280 164 and on the road (Route des Hôtels), ☎ (02) 280 303.
Hertz, on the hotel road, ☎ (02) 280 187.
Intercar, ave Dag Hammarskjöld, ☎ (02) 281 423.
Europcar, on the hotel road, ☎ (02) 280 146 and ave Dag Hammarskjöld, ☎ (02) 280 084.
Mattei (Ada), on the northern hotel road, ☎ (02) 278 705.

Moped hire – **Société de Tourisme et Loisirs Plus (STLP)** (Tourism and Leisure Society), ave Dag Hammarskjöld (next to the Hotel Fourati), ☎ (02) 279 087. Price: TD10/hour, TD50/day and TD200/week.
Locamob, bike hire, rue Dag Hammarskjöld, ☎ (02) 280 339.

ADDRESS BOOK

Emergency – An all-night **pharmacy** is located on ave de la République.

Police – ave Habib Bourguiba, ☎ (02) 280 079.

Tourist office (ONATT) – ave Habib Bourguiba, ☎ (02) 280 423. Open in winter 8.30am-1pm / 3-5.45pm Mondays-Thursdays; 8.30am-1.30pm Fridays-Saturdays. In summer 7.30am-1pm / 4-11pm daily.

Banks / Currency Exchange – There are numerous banks, many of which offer money exchange facilities.
American Express, hotel route, ☎ (02) 282 880.
Cash dispensers: STB, Shopping Centre.

Post office – ave de la République, ☎ (02) 280 598. Open 8am-12pm / 3pm-6pm Mondays-Thursdays; 8am-12.30pm Fridays. 7am-1pm / 5pm-7pm in summer, 7.30am-1.30pm on Fridays and Saturdays. Closed on Sundays.

Telephone – Numerous public pay phones are scattered throughout the city and are often open until 11pm.

WHERE TO STAY

The summer heat can turn this tourist paradise into an inferno. The best time to visit is in spring or autumn, when hotel rates are more reasonable too.

Less than US$8

Camping les Samaris, ☎ (02) 226 353. About 5km to the south of Hammamet on the P 1 road to Sousse, behind the Elf petrol station. Although a bit scruffy and next to a busy roundabout, this is your only option if you want to camp in the Hammamet area.

From US$18-42

Hôtel Sahbi, ave de la République, ☎ (02) 280 807, Fax (02) 280 134 – 120rm ⁞ ✖ This hotel offers excellent value for money, since it is located only a step away from the medina and very close to the beach. The rooms are decorated in an original style with furniture made from carved wood. On the other hand, the red and green carpets are not in the best taste. The restaurant does not serve alcohol.

Hôtel Alya, 30 rue Ali Belhaouane, ☎ (02) 280 218, Fax (02) 282 365 – 35rm ⁞ ✖ A modest establishment half-way between the town and the beach. Certain rooms open onto little balconies; all are well-kept. The hotel is situated on a busy street – the rooms at the back of the hotel are quieter.

Hôtel Bennila, rue de Nevers (near the Hôtel des Citronniers), ☎ (02) 261 894 – 74rm ⁞ ✖ ⌣ ⌗ This reasonably-priced hotel has a swimming pool and is located close to the beach.

Hôtel Les Citronniers, rue de Nevers, ☎ (02) 281 650 / 282 088, Fax (02) 282 601 – 60rm ⁞ ✎ ✖ ⌣ ⌗ cc This unpretentious hotel offers reasonably-priced rooms away from the hordes of tourists. The beach is across the street. On the other hand, it is rather noisy: you can hear the TV from the restaurant. Closed November to February.

From US$42-75

Résidence Hammamet, 72 ave Habib Bourguiba, ☎ (02) 280 733 / 406, Fax (02) 280 396 – 184rm ⁞ ▤ ✖ ⌣ cc This establishment is situated in the centre of Hammamet and has a small pool on the third floor, although the beach is only 300m away. Rooms have kitchenettes.

Hôtel Fourati, rue de Nevers, ☎ (02) 280 388, Fax (02) 280 508 – 400rm ⁞ ▤ ✎ ✖ ⌣ ⌗ ✖ cc Go here if only to visit a delightful colonial residence decorated in typical Tunisian style. Unfortunately, the service is comparable to the worst of the tourist traps with music playing until 1am. For a modest supplement there are rooms with a sea view.

More than US$75

Hôtel Les Orangers, rue de Nevers, ☎ (02) 280 144, Fax (02) 281 077 – 239rm 🏠 📖 ✐ TV ✕ ⚒ 🐾 🍴 🐫 CC This tourist hotel is set in a beautiful garden. To reach the beach, you need to cross the Orangers Beach, the hotel's latest and fanciest addition.

Sinbad, ave des Nations-Unies, ☎ (02) 280 122, Fax (02) 280 004 – 145rm 🏠 📖 ✐ TV ✕ ⚒ 🐾 CC This is the hotel to visit off-season when you can take advantage of luxurious surroundings at affordable rates. On the other hand, prices are sky high in the summer. Guests have access to Hammamet's golf course at discounted prices.

EATING OUT

Less than US$10

Le Pêcheur (C2), opposite the taxi rank to the right of the Post office, ☎ (02) 226 353 🏠 This tiny café is hidden from view by a tree. Daily specials and grilled fish are on offer at unbeatable prices – no wonder the place is often packed.

L'angolo vert (C2), corner of rue du Stade and rue Ali Belhaouane, ☎ (02) 262 641 🏠 The pretty terrace shaded by trees and parasoles attract a trendy Tunisian and cosmopolitan crowd. A varied menu of pizza and pasta, as well as ice-creams are available.

Restaurant de la Poste ("Chez le Chef") (C2), ☎ (02) 280 023 🏠 When you are at the taxi station with the medina behind you, look up. This was the first restaurant to open a "hanging" terrace overlooking one of the most beautiful bays in Tunisia. While you are enjoying the delicious homemade couscous (minimum 4 people sharing) or

tajine, the owner will tell you stories of famous visitors during Hammamet's golden years.

Le Barberousse (C2), ☎ (02) 280 037 🍷 🏠 CC This establishment has occupied the best site in Hammamet for 20 years at the top of the ramparts. Uninspired French-Tunisian cuisine is on offer on a superb terrace overlooking the sea and the medina.

From US$10-20

Chez Achour (C2), 55 rue Ali Belhaouane, ☎ (02) 280 140 🍷 🏠 CC This little shaded retreat is a bit outside Hammamet's commotion. If you reserve ahead of time, you can order the delicious lamb dish. The chef puts a little too much mayonnaise in his salad dressings. The restaurant has music at the weekend.

WHERE TO GO FOR A DRINK

Café – Sidi Bou Hedid, ☎ (02) 280 040 🏠 Squeezed between the ramparts of the medina and the wall of the Kasbah, this open-air café is one of the most beautiful in Tunisia. The smell of chichi, the carpets and cushions evoke a traditional Tunisian ambiance. Outside the ramparts, a second terrace gives an unrivalled view of the gulf of Hammamet.

Nightclubs – The nightclubs in several hotels are open to the public, in particular, **Les Orangers**, the **Hammamet Hôtel,** the **Miramar** and the **Hôtel Venus** situated on the tourist road. Other nightclubs include: **Manhattan**, 4km south of Hammamet, ☎ (02) 226 226; the **Tropicana** across from the Manhattan, ☎ (02) 281 200; the **Nirvana**, North Hammamet, ☎ (02) 278 408.

LEISURE

Sports – Golf Citrus, ☎ (02) 226 500, Fax (02) 226 400. 2 golf courses with 18 holes each on 420 acres of ground surrounded by olive groves and 6 lakes. 6 hotels are shareholders and can therefore offer preferential conditions to their guests. Abou Nawas, ☎ (02) 281 344, Fax (02) 281 089; Aziza, ☎ (02) 283 666, Fax (02) 283 099; Manar, ☎ (02) 281 333, Fax (02) 281 772; Méditerranée, ☎ (02) 280 932, Fax (02) 281 476; Phénicia, ☎ (02) 226 533, Fax (02) 226 337 and Sinbad, ☎ (02) 280 122, Fax (02) 226 337.

Golf Yasmine, 18-hole course, ☎ (02) 227 001 / 665.

Scuba-diving: a diving school located at the Hôtel Le Sultan offers beginner's classes as well as day and night dives for licenced divers.

Club Hippique Phénicia, ☎ (02) 226 533, Fax (02) 226 337.

Festivals – International Festival, International Cultural Centre, ave des Nations-Unies, ☎ (02) 280 410, Fax (02) 280 722. The festival takes place from June to mid-August in the open air theatre at the Villa Sebastian. The programme includes Maghreb and Middle-Eastern variety shows, in particular. Performances begin at 9.30pm.

Casinos – Grand Casino, Hôtel Sol Azur Beach, on the tourist route, Hammamet, ☎ (02) 261 777, Fax (02) 261 138. The different games (blackjack, poker, roulette, slot machines, etc.) are exclusively in foreign currency. Card games open 5pm-4am and all other games open 8pm-4am. There is also an American-style bar and a restaurant on the premises. Entrance to the casino is limited to over-18s.

SHOPPING

Weekly souk, Thursdays.

Bakeries – La Reine (B2), ave Mongi Slim (on the corner with ave de la République), ☎ (02) 283 444. Café with terrace. Fresh fruit juice and pastries are available. Specialises in millefeuilles, a multi-layered pastry with cream filling. **Larabi** (C2), 14 rue Ali Belhaouane, ☎ (02) 283 061.

Antiques and handicrafts

Village ken, Sidi Khalifa (Bouficha), 20km on the road from Sousse, ☎ (02) 252 110, Fax (02) 252 112. This live artisans' and Tunisian folklore museum is the first of its kind in Tunisia. **Centre d'artisanat tunisien Kochach** (Kochach Tunisian Handicrafts Centre), ave de la Libération, ☎ (02) 278 397. **Maison de l'artisanat** (House of Handicrafts), located in the Hotel Pyramide on the hotel route.

Making the most of Hammamet

Under the cork oaks in Khroumiria

THE NORTH

This route, which runs along the north coast before turning inland, is an opportunity to explore. The highway
heading north out of Tunis runs in a straight line. As far
as Pont-de-Bizerte; it is a beautiful road, typical of the
north, lined with eucalyptus trees. As always in Tunisia,
the peasants take their livestock out to browse along the
verges, while others enjoy their siesta curled up at the
roadside, unconcerned by passing traffic. The main roads
are also a kind of market, selling plastic furniture, or fruit
and vegetables, small boys offer tea or little bread rolls.
About 18km out of Tunis, beyond the bare hill of the
Ariana, is the plain of La Mejerda. These alluvial levels
have little to offer the eye – but they are laden with
history: the port of Utica was dug here, and ever since
classical times they have been an important cereal-
growing area. Rather than heading directly to Bizerte
along the P 8 beyond Utica, it is more enjoyable to take
a detour along the coast to the little towns of Ghar el Melh
and Raf Raf with their vast beaches of fine sand, with
fewer people than the beaches in the south.

The coast becomes more dramatic beyond Bizerte, a
centre of heavy industry and the third largest city in the
country. There are dunes, cliffs and tumbled rocks on
which the sea breaks and foams all the way to the
Algerian frontier. But the beaches are still beautiful.
Tunisia's finest shrimps and lobsters come from these
waters. The country inland is also richer than elsewhere.
There are lakes, the rich pasture-lands of the Mogods and
the oak forests of Khroumiria. With their generous rainfall, Khroumiria and the Mogods are the only regions in
Tunisia able to indulge in the luxury of intensive dairy-
cow rearing. From Tabarka inland to Le Kef, the road
runs right across Khroumiria, where "green" tourism has
recently been developed. This is a different Tunisia, not
only in its climate and vegetation, but also its housing,
for here the houses have pitched roofs.

FROM TUNIS TO BIZERTE

Governorship of Bizerte
Tour c 140km - allow a whole day

Not to be missed
Ghar el Mehl lake at sunrise.

And remember...
The beach at Sidi Ali el Mekki is better for swimming
than the one at Raf Raf.

Leave Tunis on the P 8, towards Bizerte. About 5km beyond Pont-de-Bizerte (shown as Protville on some maps), take the slip road to the right which crosses back over the main road. Continue for about 3km past the little Utica museum. The ruins are signposted 1km further on, on your left. Follow the track for 500m to the site entrance.

■ Utica

Archeological site. Open 8.30am-5.30pm in winter and 8am-7pm in summer. Entrance charge; the ticket also includes access to the museum. Allow 45min.

Perfidious Utica

A dedicated individual has done his best to embellish the ruins of the ancient city of Utica by planting quantities of geraniums and hollyhocks. But his efforts cannot conceal the shabby state of the site.

Was it the Arab conquest or the silting of the port that sounded Utica's death-knell? The town lies buried beneath the alluvial deposits of the Méjerda, and even the sea itself, more than 12km away, appears to have turned its back on the town.

Could this sorry fate be retribution for Utica's crime against Carthage? The town, which took pride in being older than its cousin, was (according to Pling the Elder) founded by the Phoenicians in 1101 BC, some three hundred years before Carthage. In the 5C BC, however, it was no longer capable of matching Carthaginian power, and came under its domination. Carthage nevertheless considered its rival more of an ally than a vassal, and enjoyed the older city's support in its conflict with the Greeks. In the second Punic War, Utica assisted Carthage again, but in 146 BC delivered itself body and soul to Scipio's troops, who used it as a rear base. With Carthage obliterated, Rome rewarded Utica for its disloyalty by awarding it the title of free city. Yet it seemed fated to play only secondary roles, and lost its status as African capital as soon as Carthage rose again from its ruins. But it prospered again under the Vandals and the Byzantines, and its total disappearance, coinciding with the Arab conquest, has not been fully explained. A mysterious, not to say inglorious, fate.

Visit

In view of its historical importance, the site itself is somewhat disappointing, but it is consoling to think that there are still 80 hectares to be excavated: a good excuse to return.

The Punic Era – The remains of the pre-Roman city are barely visible, having been buried under later layers. From this early period it is the **necropolis** that offers the greatest interest, with the oldest tombs dating from the 7C BC and

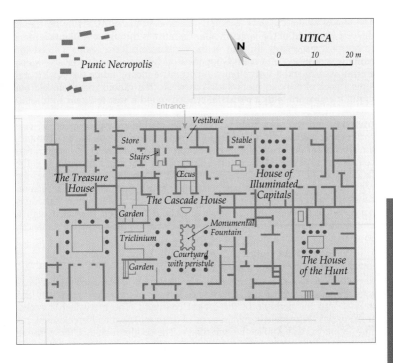

the most recent from the 4C BC. No traces have been found from before the 8C BC, which raises the question of Pliny the Elder's belief that the city was founded in 1101 BC. The burial places are of several kinds: simple ditches dug into the tufa rock, monolithic sarcophagi, or tombs consisting of blocks of shell sandstone or sun-dried bricks. At the bottom of very deep trenches, little chalk cremation caskets have also been found: the practice of cremation dates back to the 3C and 2C BC. A small fortification built on the necropolis encloses the tomb – and the skeleton – of a young girl who died in the 4C BC (*ask the warden-gardener to open it for you*). According to a custom whose significance has been lost, the skull was covered with a funeral mask made from the shell of an ostrich egg. Human features were painted on to the shell, no doubt those of the dead girl. A fragment of the mask is on display in the little local museum, as well as part of the burial furnishings discovered in the tombs (*see below*).

The Roman Era – Since most of the public buildings have vanished, only the Roman villas are worth a brief visit; of the twenty or so houses uncovered, only four are really interesting. Some mosaics have remained in place, but they are protected by wooden shuttering. It is better to arrange to be accompanied by the warden, for apart from the fact that it is always agreeable to enliven ruins with some local commentary, he will be able to uncover the mosaics and brighten the colours by sprinkling them with fresh water hauled up from an ancient Roman cistern. The edge of the cistern is heavily worn from centuries of use, and the rope of the bucket runs in this ancient groove.

The **House of the Cascade** (maison de la cascade) (4C-5C AD) is by no means the best preserved or the largest house. Entrance is through a **vestibule** leading to several passages. At the end of the central corridor a fountain faced the entrance, consisting of a basin (supported on two small marble pillars, which are still visible) and a square bowl. A decorative mosaic inside the bowl represents a mass of octopus, morays and other fish. The various rooms are laid out round a **courtyard with a peristyle**, centred round a **vast fountain** with semicircular niches. One side of the peristyle opens into the dining room or **triclinium**, recognisable from its handsome marble paving designed in *opus sectile*: circle motifs set inside squares. The yellow marble comes from Chemtou, the green from the island of Euboea in Greece. The *triclinium* is set between two courtyards, each embellished with a little garden area and a fountain. It is the fountain in the northern courtyard which has given the house its name: the water flows down a sloping base, creating a small waterfall effect. Decoration consists of a mosaic featuring a fishing scene. The north side of the peristyle is partly taken up with another small semicircular fountain decorated with a mosaic showing a boy fishing. At one of the corners of the house, the stable can be recognised from its stone feeding troughs.

The **Treasure House** (maison du Trésor) owes its name to some coins that were found there during excavations in 1957.

The **House of Illuminated Capitals** (maison des chapiteaux historiés) (1C AD) has a somewhat unusual layout. The entrance consists of three great gates that lead directly into the peristyle of the central courtyard. The peristyle has twelve columns with illuminated capitals, some of them representing Hercules with his club, Minerva, and Apollo the lyre-player. The southern side of the peristyle opens into a room which extends the full width of the house and leads into three more small rooms.

The **House of the Hunt** (la maison de la chasse) contained a mosaic representing several hunting scenes *(now preserved in the museum)*.

The **museum** *(about 1km away. Open 8.30am-5.30pm in winter, 8am-7pm in summer)* may look uninteresting, but it nonetheless houses some fine pieces.

In the **Punic Room** are the funeral furnishings discovered on site. There is plenty of commonplace Punic and Greek pottery, as well as the oil lamps which can be seen in every antique store in Tunisia, but the jewellery is truly outstanding and worth attention among it is a gold ring representing the god Baal Hammon, carnelian or rock crystal scarabs, pearl necklaces and amulets. As well as a very fine terracotta mask, there is a fragment of ostrich egg shell which was used for a funeral mask *(see above)*, on which it is still possible to make out the image of an eye and a fringe of hair.

The **Roman room**★ displays some Roman statues excavated on the site which, very unusually, have not been transferred to the Bardo: there are marble figures representing Æsculapius, a toga-clad child, Ariadne asleep, and above all a very handsome Hercules.

In the garden is an enormous marine mosaic representing the god Ocean, surrounded by a whole assortment of aquatic fauna, boats and fishermen.

Beyond Utica, continue on the same road across the Méjerda plain.

Gradually the wheat fields give way to market gardens, which appear with increasing frequency as the coast is neared. They are little plots of land marked out by cypress trees, with the occasional hut set here and there among the neatly-planted rows.

About 2km beyond Aousja, turn right for Ghar el Melh.

■ **Ghar el Melh** – This fishing village is built along the foot of the Jebel Nadour, on the banks of Lake Ghar el Melh. This vast stretch of water, which is linked to the sea, is lined with luxuriant vegetation: palms, cypresses, Barbary figs and aloes, a treat for the eyes in the morning light. Unfortunately the lake is silting up, and the murky water along the shore is not exactly inviting for a swim. Two old **Turkish forts** are reminders that Ghar el Melh was once a strategic location: and yet, looking at the sleepy old port, its colourful boats and the stagnant water, it is difficult to imagine that this was once Porto Farina, one of the most feared pirate haunts of the whole Mediterranean. At the end of the 18C, when the pirate wars had run their course, the beys intended to transform Gahr el Melh into a naval port, but the silting up of the lake defeated the project.

To reach the **new fishing port**, continue along the road beyond Ghar el Melh for about 3km, then turn right on to a narrow track between the sea and the lake. Rather than turning off towards the not particularly picturesque port, it is more rewarding to continue along the track to the **Sidi Ali el Mekki beach**: white sand and turquoise sea, a striking contrast to the pinkish water of the lake. *(6km from the old port to the beach, including 3km along a stony track. The beach is virtually deserted, but it does have a restaurant).*

Piracy
The Moslem corsairs, or "raïs", were very often former European slaves who had converted to Islam. Under cover of waging a "holy war", Christians and Moslems engaged in what was effectively true economic warfare. The trophies – from which the rulers took their share – were reintroduced into the commercial world through unofficial networks. The merchandise would next be seen in the souks of Tunis or Algiers. This predominance of economic factors raises questions over several legends: the captive was primarily a piece of merchandise to be looked after if he was to be ransomed or sold as a slave, and his circumstances were therefore probably not as terrible as has been described. Similarly, and according to a fairly widespread understanding, the pirates did not venture to engage battle or massacre crews except in cases of absolute necessity or clear superiority.

Go back the way you came for about 14km from the old port of Ghar el Mehl, and turn right towards Raf Raf.

■ **Raf Raf** – The road to this famous seaside resort winds through pretty hills covered with orchards, vines, olive groves and clumps of pines. But the bay of Raf Raf is a disappointment: the beach area has been invaded and spoiled by holiday houses, which the better-off citizens of Tunis have built in recent years. Those who love the place talk about a "shanty-town": unfinished brick houses, crude, box-like structures or pseudo-Arab buildings in the worst possible taste. Some of the buildings have invaded the beach itself. Fortunately, **Pilao island** has been spared such despoilation. Facing the beach, it is a constant reproach to the vandals of the local building industry.

Perhaps it is best to turn round and go through **Metline**. From this high-perched village there is a **panoramic view** of the coast and Raf Raf which at this distance seems almost beautiful.

About 10km beyond Metline, turn right at the crossroads towards Bizerte, about 20km away.

BIZERTE ★

Centre of Governorship
Pop c 100 000
65km from Tunis on the P 8 road,
or 150km via Raf Raf

Not to be missed
A drink in the old port.
And remember...
Hire a bike or moped to visit the outskirts.
In winter, there are more birds in Ichkeul Natural Park.

Bizerte is not a city designed for tourists, even though most visitors find its streets, its port and its medina attractive enough. It could be said that because it does not set out to attract, it is never a disappointment.

Yet Bizerte is finding it difficult to decide on what its image should be. Although it has become a leading steel and oil centre since independence, it still seems to hesitate over its real identity. The surrounding countryside is profoundly rural, but because of its geographical setting and its history the city, called *Hyppo Diarrhytus* in ancient times, looks outwards towards the open sea.

Bizerte is the key to a system of waterways linking Lake Ichkeul and Lake Bizerte to the Mediterannean. *Diarrhytus*, in Greek, means "with water flowing through". Its outstanding strategic location gave the city control of the access to Lake Bizerte, which has always been an ideal harbour for war-ships of foreign powers; Roman, Spanish, Turkish and more recently, German, and above all, French. The French naval base closed in 1963, but Bizerte continued to be a garrison city. The authorities, who would like to eliminate this double industrial and military identity, have embarked on projects designed to emphasise the historical heritage, for example in the efforts to restore and renovate the medina – which is much in need of it.

Dying for Bizerte
Together with Toulon and Mers el Kebir, Bizerte was the spearhead for the French presence in the Mediterranean, and therefore a significant factor at the time of decolonisation. Bourguiba, who was concerned to preserve good Franco-Tunisian relations, left the air and naval base under French control, but in the midst of the Algerian war, this French enclave was seen as a symbol of imperialism. The people of Bizerte mobilised on 18 July 1961 to demand the evacuation of the French forces, and demonstrators forced their way into the base. French troops opened fire and caused at least a thousand civilian deaths. Negotiations began under the aegis of the United Nations, and the French finally withdrew in 1963. The Martyrs' Cemetery, lying above the city, is a reminder of this painful episode.

Bizerte can also take pride in all the advantages of a modern seaside resort: beach, pine woods, comfortable hotels and golf-course, but to enjoy all this, visitors must leave the city and take the corniche road to the north. In addition, Bizerte and **Cap Blanc** *(20km away)*, the northernmost point in Africa, do not enjoy a long summer season. Except in July and August the sea may be thought too cold, and the air a little cool.

Bizerte

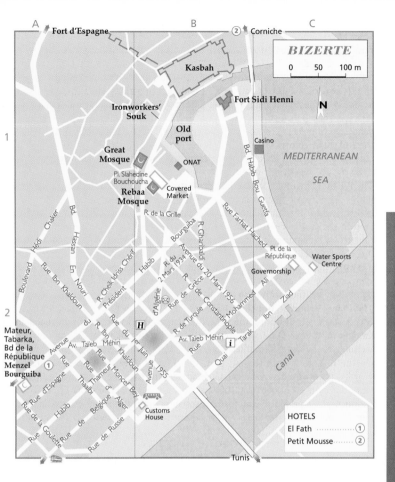

Exploring Bizerte on foot
Allow 2hr

Cradled between the kasbah and Sidi Henni fort, the **old port*** is the most attractive part of Bizerte. The quay stretches out in a curve bounded by little white buildings and the ochre-coloured walls of the Kasbah. All the familiar sights of a Greek or Spanish fishing village are here: gaily coloured fishing boats buzzing about or riding at anchor, the catch being unloaded at the quayside, but instead of a church tower in the background there is a minaret.

The way into the **Kasbah*** with its proud crenellated walls is through a very low and crooked gateway, originally designed in order to make access to the medina as difficult as possible. Women in white robes, but with their faces entirely veiled in black (including the eyes), hold out their hands and beg for

211

alms. A strange and exotic vision, very rare in this country where, since Bourguiba's day, women are accustomed to wearing what they wish. The narrowest of lanes make up a mysterious maze populated with children and scrawny cats. There are no shops, just simple, unmodernised houses.

In this part of the city the absence of commercial activity has helped to retain a certain authenticity: here you will find no souvenirs or other gaudy knick-knacks. There is a real impression of meeting people in their own homes, of venturing into their private lives, even if the visitor's eye catches nothing more than sneaked glimpses of dark interiors, terraces and winding passages. Every voice and every step re-echo like the hammer-blows from the ironworkers' souk close by, on the far side of the wall.

The life of the harbour, whose fortunes were very much tied to piracy, together with the influx of Andalusians, led to the development of skilled trades and craftsmanship. Bizerte established its own speciality, ironwork, which can be seen in the **Ironworkers' souk** (souk des forgerons). The souk exists essentially to meet local demand. Picturesque elements are not lacking, as blacksmiths bash metal and joiners chisel wood, chickens cackle and customers bargain. But it is a scene which has nothing to do with tourism and everything to do with everyday life as lived here for hundreds of years, watched by the octagonal minaret of the **Great Mosque** nearby.

The **Place Siahedine Bouchoucha** marks the line of a former stretch of canal which was filled in during the 19C. Markets are held here, at their liveliest in the late mornings. The square minaret of the green and white **Rebaa mosque** looms over the covered market.

On the hillside next to the old port, the **Spanish Fort** (Fort d'Espagne) stands guard; it is now used as a theatre. Contrary to what its name implies, this fortress was built by the Turks in the 16C. Facing the Kasbah and closing the harbour entrance, the little **Sidi Henni fort** houses an oceanographic museum of limited interest *(open daily, entrance charge, terrace bar with attractive view over the harbour)*.

Around Bizerte

Leave Bizerte along the Boulevard de la République and take the direction of Mateur.

Menzel Bourguiba

25km from Bizerte. The former Ferryville – named in honour of Jules Ferry, the architect of France's African colonial policy – used to be called "little Paris". The comparison was no doubt overstated, but older residents say that 20 years ago the town did indeed resemble some areas of Paris. Today, following uncontrolled building, it no longer looks like anything in particular, and only the plane trees in some of the streets recall the French presence, but even these reminders are not in good condition.

Menzel Bourguiba is now situated near Ichkeul Lake.

Ichkeul Natural Park ★

On leaving Menzel Bourguiba, follow the signs to Mateur. 3km further on, take the P 11 for another 4km. A sign behind the railway line indicates the park's entrance. The car park is 6km away, at the foot of the stairs leading up to the Ecomusée.

7am-7pm all year round (museum, 8am-6pm), small entrance fee. No photographs.

Ferryville used to be called "little Paris"

This natural park comprises a lake, marshlands and Ichkeul jebel (511m). In 1997, Unesco added it to the list of world heritage sites. It is one of the most beautiful bird reserves in the world, home to whistling ducks, grey geese and coots. In winter, some 200 000 birds inhabit the reserve, providing a fascinating display. With a little luck, wild buffalo can even be seen roaming the park.

Making the most of Bizerte

GETTING THERE

By train – SNCFT, rue de Russie, ☎ (02) 431 222. 4 local trains a day link Bizerte with Tunis on the TA line (former Tunis-Algiers line). The trip lasts 1hr30min and the fare is TD2.750.

By bus – SNTRI, rue d'Alger, ☎ (02) 431 222. Service to Menzel Bourguiba, Ras Jebel, Raf Raf, Ghar el Melh and Tabarka.

Société Régionale de Transport de Bizerte (SRTB) (Bizerte Regional Transportation Co.), quai Tarak Ibn Ziad, ☎ (02) 431 371 / 431 736. Services to the tourist area along the Corniche as well as to Tunis.

By shared taxi – The station by the canal, near the pont de Tunis. Since Bizerte is a cul-de-sac, it often makes sense to go via Tunis (TD6.7) to the other large cities in the country.

By yacht – Port de Plaisance (100 moorings), ☎ (02) 431 688 / 431 412.

GETTING AROUND

By bus – *Société Régionale de Transport de Bizerte (SRTB)* (Bizerte Regional Transportation Co.), quai Tarak Ibn Ziad, ☎ (02) 431 371 / 431 736. Serves the tourist areas on the Corniche.

By taxi – Can be hailed throughout the city.

By car – It is much better to walk around the centre of town. A car is nonetheless useful to reach the various beaches on the coast.

Car hire – Avis, 7 rue d'Alger, ☎ (02) 431 076.

Europcar, 19 rue Mohammed Rejiba, Place des Martyrs, ☎ (02) 431 455 and 52 ave d'Algérie, ☎ (02) 439 018, Fax (02) 431 455.

Euro Rent, rue d'Algérie, ☎ (02) 435 189, Fax (02) 431 455.

Hertz, place des Martyrs, ☎ (02) 433 679.

Inter Rent Europe Car, rue Ahmed Tilli, ☎ (02) 431 455.
Mattei, rue d'Alger, ☎ (02) 431 508.

Scooter hire – Palais du cycle, 50 ave Habib Bourguiba, ☎ (02)431 622. Around TD30 per day.

ADDRESS BOOK

Emergency – Police, rue du 20 Mars 1956, ☎ (02) 431 200 / 431 065.
National Guard, ☎ (02) 431 663.
Night pharmacy Mahmoud Srarfi, 28 rue Ali Belhaouane, ☎ (02) 432 461 / 439 545.

Tourist information – Regional Tourism Commission (houses the local Tourist Information Centre), 1 rue de Constantinople (on the corner of ave Taïeb Méhiri and quai Tarak Ibn Ziad), ☎ (02) 432 897 / 432 703, Fax (02) 438 600. 8.30am-1pm / 3pm-5.45pm; 8.30am-1.30pm Fridays and Saturdays, closed Sundays.

Banks / Currency Exchange – BIAT, rue Moncef Bey, ☎ (02) 433 109.
BNA, rue du 1ᵉʳ Juin, ☎ (02) 439 708.
STB, 1 rue de Belgique, ☎ (02) 432 256.
UBCI, 25 rue Ibn Khaldoun, ☎ (02) 433 689.
UIB, ave Taïeb Méhiri, ☎ (02) 432 532.
Post office – ave d'Algérie, ☎ (02) 431 190.

Airline and shipping companies – Tunis Air, 76 ave Habib Bourguiba, ☎ (02) 432 201 / 432 202, Fax (02) 442 033.

WHERE TO STAY

• In the modern city
From US$18-42
Hôtel El Fath, ave du Président Habib Bourguiba, ☎ (02) 430 596 – 30rm 🛉 A clean and centrally-located establishment. Rooms have en-suite showers, but the toilet is on the landing. Ask for a room overlooking the courtyard to avoid the noise. You will still be awakened by the muezzin, however, because the mosque is nearby. The hotel has 2 restaurants, one of which does not serve alcohol.

• Along the Corniche
More than US$42-80
Hôtel Petit Mousse, Corniche, ☎ (02) 432 185 / 438 871, Fax (02) 437 595 – 10rm 🛉 🖥 ☞ ✗

☼ The price to pay for being by the seaside is a noisy location on the Corniche road.

EATING OUT
There are few restaurants in town, with the exception of pizzerias. You'll need to go outside the centre to find chic restaurants that serve fish and seafood.

• In the modern city
Less than US$10
Eddalia (A2), 106 ave du Président Habib Bourguiba. ☎ (02) 436 490. This simple restaurant serves Franco-Tunisian specialities as well as very good pizza in the evenings. Alcohol is not served.

Eddouali (A2), ave du Président Habib Bourguiba (near the Eddalia Restaurant), ☎ (02) 439 490. 🍷 The service is attentive in this restaurant that specialises in Italian-Tunisian cuisine. Pizza is served in the evenings.

La Mammina (A2), 1 rue d'Espagne. This pizzeria has a rustic setting despite being in the centre of Bizerte. Spaghetti is served at noon and pizza in the evenings. Alcohol is not served on the premises. Closed Sundays.

From US$10-20
Restaurant du Bonheur (A2), 31 rue Thaalbi, ☎ (02) 431 047. 🍷 CC The centrally-located restaurant serves Franco-Tunisian specialties. Ask to sit in the back room which has air-conditioning. High quality food and service.

Le Sport Nautique (C2), quai Tarak Ibn Ziad, ☎ (02) 432 262 / 432 362 ☂ 🍷 CC This restaurant has a large room with picture windows overlooking the marina. The house specialities are international seafood dishes, such as fish couscous, paella (to order only) or seafood risotto.

• Along the Corniche
From US$10-20
L'Eden (not on the city plan), on the Corniche, ☎ (02) 439 023 / 421 148 ☂ 🍷 CC This restaurant has an international menu, from the seafood plate to Lebanese-style lamb to Chinese fondue.

Le Petit Mousse (not on the city plan), on the Corniche, ☎ (02) 432 185 / 438 871, Fax (02) 437 595 ☂ This is Bizerte's trendy restaurant. Besides the fresh fish and shellfish, the restaurant serves Franco-Tunisian specialities. There is a snack bar in the summer that faces the sea.

WHERE TO GO FOR A DRINK

Cafés – **Café Manhattan**, several tables located on the pavement. Ave Taïeb Méhiri, across from the Monoprix supermarket.

Café Le Pacha, old port, to the right of SOCOPA. This spacious terrace with shady parasols overlooks the fishing boats. If you come for a drink in the early evening, you can admire the golden rays of the sunset on the opposite bank

Nightclubs – **Hôtel Jalta**, ☎ (02) 431 169, Fax (02) 434 277.

Hôtel Corniche, ☎ (02) 431 844 / 431 831, Fax (02) 431 830.

LEISURE

Sports – **Centre équestre Mohammed Hajji** (Mohammed Hajji Equestrian Centre), Hôtel Corniche, ☎ (02) 431 844 / 431 831, Fax (02) 431 830.

Festivals – **International Festival**. Primarily Mediterranean music and variety shows.

SHOPPING

Markets

• **In the city**
On Saturdays (and Tuesdays for agricultural products), Place du Marché, across from the casbah.

• **In the surrounding area**
Sejnane: on Thursdays
Ras Jebel: on Fridays
Mateur: on Fridays and Saturdays.

Bakeries – **La Délicieuse,** 52 ave du Président Habib Bourguiba, ☎ (02) 432 152.

Bertfouma, ave du Président Habib Bourguiba, ☎ (02) 431 283.

Makhlouka, rue Ibn Khaldoun.

Antiques and handicrafts – **Au Palais d'Orient**, ave du Président Habib Bourguiba (on the corner of rue d'Alger). All types of handicrafts, from terracotta mosques to copper trays, all types of handicrafts piled into one shop. Credit cards are accepted.

SOCOPA, quai Khémais Ternane (in the old port), ☎ (02) 431 091 / 439 684. Closed Sundays.

Bookshops – **Librairie Sciences et culture**, ave Taïeb Méhiri (on the corner of rue Moncef Bey).

The Old Port at Bizerte

H. Choimet

TABARKA ★
Governorship of Jendouba
Pop c 10 000
180km from Tunis via the P 7; 150km from Bizerte

Not to be missed
The view from above the Genoese Fort.
The fresh fish and sea-food.
The rock formation known as "Les Aiguilles".

And remember...
Tabarka is in the north and rain is not uncommon.
Tabarka is an excellent starting point to visit
Aïn Draham, Bulla Regia and Chemtou.

The road to the old Phoenician harbour town of Thabraca ("shady place") is a fine introduction to this favoured part of Tunisia. It runs through a beautiful game-rich forest of cork oak cladding hills and valleys. Woodland aromas mingle with breezes blowing from the Mediterranean, which yields its own abundant harvest of coral and seafood.

Basically a little port and market town, Tabarka itself is still coming to terms with its ever-increasing popularity with visitors from abroad.

Coveted riches

Marble and games – Having become a Roman colony in the 3C, Thabraca owed its prosperity to trade in wild animals (destined for the circus), building timber, iron and lead ore, and the yellow marble of Chemtou which clad so many patrician dwellings and was used in Rome. Since then, supply and demand have evolved somewhat, and anyone expecting to come across African wild animals is liable to be disappointed. If local records are to be believed, the last lion of Tabarka was killed towards the end of the 19C, although panthers were slightly more fortunate: the last one died in 1932 in Babouch, a neighbouring village.

The Coral War – Later, foreign powers fought over another natural resource, coral. In 1542 the Genoese won the monopoly for dealing in coral, an advantage that they managed to retain for two hundred years. They settled on the island of Tabarka and built the fort, the town itself having been virtually abandoned since the Arab conquest. The French, who had a trading post at Cap Negro and had long coveted the precious coral, managed to evict the Genoese in 1781. Coral is still extracted nowadays but on a much smaller scale than before, because of the invasive and damaging fishing system – heavy metal bars, in the form of a St Andrew's cross, rake across the sea-bottom and tear up everything in their way. Local craftsmen still find supplies of coral, however, as can be seen in the town's shops.

The Poor Khroumirs – With the establishment of the French Protectorate, what had been merely a trading post on the island of Tabarka was to become a town. The French who had occupied Algeria more than thirty years earlier seized on the pretext of alleged frontier disturbances – with the turbulent Khroumirs as the supposed instigators – as an excuse to invade Tunisia. The invasion began from the west, in 1881, when a French fleet arrived off Tabarka

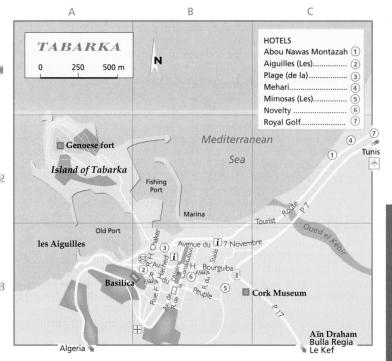

and briefly bombarded the port. Once installed, the French, unconcerned at the fate of the Roman antiquities, razed the site and rebuilt the town from scratch – hence the current appearance of Tabarka with its ruler-straight streets and its red tile roofs.

Don't overdo the suntan – Apart from activity linked to coral, Tabarka lives off a few local industries, but it would not be accurate to speak of a true economic expansion. The cork factory is the region's main industry; then there is pottery-making and a small amount of food-processing. In the craft sector, Tabarka has developed a speciality in olive-wood carving and briar pipes.

In essence, however, Tabarka now earns its living from a well-planned and effective tourist industry, which successfully combines seaside enjoyment with the pleasures of hillwalking. Exploring on foot or on horseback, diving and undersea photography figure amongst its leading activities. The coast, exposed to the wind and studded with rocks, has a large number of wrecks which are a delight for divers. The region is also a paradise for boar-hunting, and increasing numbers of foreigners take part in the organised autumn drives. The wildlife of the surrounding woods is also an important feature for "green" tourism.

For a long time now, Tabarka has offered a different kind of tourism. The little seaside resort had already launched its **festival** in the 1970s (*see Making the most of Tabarka*) with a famous slogan invented by Lotfi Belhassine, the founder of Air Liberté: "Ne bronzez pas idiot" – "Don't overdo the suntan". A different kind of tourism, but for how long? For the time being, the town is still small and very peaceful. The residents are simultaneously welcoming and discreet. They appear to go about their daily business without much concern for tourists, who soon fade into the background. This tranquillity is under threat, to judge by the new international airport and the hotels which are shooting up like mushrooms.

The Town
Allow 1hr

The town is small and has few sites of interest. It's better, therefore, just to absorb the atmosphere of the place and people-watch on a bench in the little square round the statue of Bourguiba. The scene is one of quiet animation, and the Supreme Combatant, stick in hand and seated on his rock, looks like an ordinary man in retirement. The air brings a pleasant smell of warm bread, on the terrace of the nearby cafés the menfolk of Tabarka drink mint tea while others, a little higher up towards the mosque, chat in front of the barber's while they wait their turn for a shave.

If you fancy a stroll, it is a good idea to follow the causeway which links the town with an island topped by a **Genoese fort**. The summit of the island offers a magnificent **panorama★**, although the fort cannot be visited.

Les Aiguilles *(on the promenade, the continuation of the ave Bourguiba)*, are immense monolithic blocks of rock, like the dorsal of a sea monster. One of the rocks, pierced by a natural hole, offers a way through to a seaside walk. The water is transparent and turquoise-blue, but it is a pity that the little creek behind the rocks is full of rubbish.

The **Basilica** *(rue de l'Indleus, at the end of rue Hédi Chaker)* is in fact an old Roman cistern transformed into a church. In front of the building, on a little sandy stretch of ground with a few trees, some stone fragments, capitals and columns, are arranged in a curving line *(closed to the public, but the keeper will open the gate if he's around)*.

By the entrance to the cork factory is a **Cork Museum** *(on the Aïn Draham road, on the edge of the town)*. In a very simple and attractive way it shows the many stages of transforming the ultra-light bark of the cork oak. *(During the summer, 7am-12noon / 4pm-7pm; 9am-12noon / 4pm-7pm, weekends. Out of season, 7.30am-12noon / 1.30pm-5pm; 9am-12noon / 3pm-5pm weekends. No charge.)*

Around Tabarka

La Galite

This volcanic archipelago *(about 60km out to sea from Tabarka)* consists of seven rocky islands, with a few families living off lobster fishing on the largest, La Galite (5.3km x 2km). There is no hotel, or even an official way of getting there, but diving enthusiasts should be able to overcome this obstacle by asking the hotels and the fishermen in Tabarka, or the local diving club. The wildlife is very abundant and is well worth the effort: grouper, sea perch, lobster, langoustines and above all a **colony of monk seals**, the last in the Mediterranean.

Aïn Draham★

25km from Tabarka. This mountain village, at 800m, is overwhelmed with greenery, for the heavy rainfall makes the region into a different sort of Tunisia from the conventional image. There is moss, heather, mastic, evergreen oaks, chestnuts and maritime pines and the beds of the wadis overflow with oleander. The climate is stimulating, and older people come here for the sake of their health. There are winter visitors too, for this is one of the rare places in Tunisia where snow can be seen.

The houses here are equally unusual. The village was built by the army and colonial settlers after Tunisia was taken into the French empire: large square white houses, red tiled roofs, chimneys and shutters. Although there is nothing much worthy of interest in Aïn Draham itself, it is an ideal starting point for a hunting or walking trip in the mountains (*see Making the most of Aïn Draham*). Around 2km outside the village on the way from Tabarka, the road leading up to the **col des Ruines** (Pass of Ruins) provides an excellent viewpoint of neighbouring Algeria, especially at sunset.

Making the most of Tabarka

GETTING THERE

By air – 7 Novembre Airport, ☎ (08) 680 005 / 113 / 127 / 130. During the high season, the airport is mostly used by charter flights.
Tunisair, ☎ (08) 680 082 / 092.

By train – There is no railway station in Tabarka, but the town in linked by a bus service to the station at Béja (4 trips daily; change in Jendouba for Aïn Draham). The buses are air-conditioned (3hr30min).

By bus – SNTRI, 18 rue du Peuple, ☎ (08) 670 404. Buses arrive from Tunis. The better route is via Béja. There are 5 departures a day via Mateur and 3 departures via Béja (3hr15min). Choose one of the green buses which are more likely to have air-conditioning.

By shared taxi – The taxi rank is located on ave Habib Bourguiba, near the petrol station (at the foot of the road leading up to Hotel Mimosas). Taxis are regularly available for Jendouba, Aïn Draham and Tunis and less frequently for Bizerte.

By car – Although the road via Mateur and Nefza is shorter, the road that passes by Béja and Aïn Draham is a bit quicker. Count on a 3hr drive from Tunis.

By boat – Tabarka's small marina hosts sailing regattas coming from France and Italy. To contact the Harbour Master, ☎ (08) 670 599, ☎ and Fax (08) 673 595. A mooring costs TD135 a month for a small sailboat no more than 10m.

GETTING AROUND

By bus – This is the cheapest way of getting to the hotels in the tourist area: **SRT Jendouba** (Regional Transportation Co.), 84 ave Habib Bourguiba, ☎ (08) 670 087. Buses operate from 7am-11.45pm in summer and until 12.45am on Thursdays and Saturdays with hourly departures. Price: TD250. The bus stop is in front of the BNA, 69 ave Bourguiba.

By taxi – Allô Taxi, ☎ (08) 643 636. The taxi stand is on the rue de la Constitution near the statue of Bourguiba.

By car – Since the town is so small, it is quite easy to explore it on foot. A car is however very useful for exploring the Kroumirie mountains.

Car hire – Hertz, Résidence Corallo, Port de Plaisance, ☎ and Fax (08) 670 670.
Europcar, Résidence Corallo, Port de Plaisance, ☎ (08) 670 834.
Liberty Rent Car, bvd du 7 Novembre, ☎ (08) 673 423.

ADDRESS BOOK

Emergency – Ambulance, ☎ (08) 673 661 / 665.
Emergency Road Help, ☎ (08) 670 021.
Sidi Moussa General Hospital, ave Bourguiba across from the Hôtel Les Aiguilles, ☎ (08) 671 200. Health centre for artificial kidneys and dialysis.

Bessassi Nourreddine Night Pharmacy, opposite l'Hôtel Novelty, 19 rue Ali Zouaoui, ☎ (08) 673 314.

Tourist information – The **Regional Tourist Office** is situated in the former railway station, 65 bvd du 7 Novembre (entrance 3 rue de Bizerte), ☎ (08) 671 491 and 673 496 / 555, Fax (08) 673 428. 8.30am-1pm/3pm-5.45pm, Fridays and Saturdays 8.30am-1.30pm, closed Sundays

Tourist Office, 32 ave Habib Bourguiba. Summer, 9am-1pm / 3pm-7pm, closed Mondays. Out of season, 8am-12noon / 2pm-6pm, closed Sundays. Call CRT for telephone enquiries.

Bank / Currency Exchange – Most of the banks provide money exchange facilities every Saturday and Sunday from 9am to 11pm.

UIB, 48 ave Habib Bourguiba. Open 8-11.30am / 2-5pm.

BNA, 69 ave Habib Bourguiba. Open 8am-12pm / 2-5pm Mondays to Thursdays; 8am-12pm / 1.30-4.30pm Fridays.

STB, 54 rue du Peuple (on the corner of rue de la Constitution).

Banque du Sud, Résidence Corallo, Port de Plaisance. Open 8-11.30am / 2-5pm Mondays to Fridays. In summer, 7.15-11.45am.

Post office – 12 ave Hédi Chaker. Open in winter from 8am-12pm / 3-6pm. In summer, 7.30am-1pm / 5-7pm with limited facilities available. Open 7.30am-1pm on Saturdays.

WHERE TO STAY

● **In the city**

Less than US$8

Hôtel de la Plage, ave. du 7 novembre, ☎ (08) 670 039 – 20rm. This is undoubtedly the best value-for-money in the town. Simple, somewhat basic facilities, (shared shower and toilet for some rooms), but totally spotless and the staff are friendly. A new building with around 20 rooms of a higher standard (air-conditioning, telephone and TV) should be finished by the end of 2000.

From US$18-42

Hôtel Les Aiguilles, 18 ave Habib Bourguiba, ☎ (08) 673 789, Fax (08) 673 604 – 19rm ⁂ ✗ This is a modest

but clean hotel. Ask for one of the rooms overlooking the garden and the harbour which are quieter than those facing the street. Breakfast served on the third floor terrace.

Hôtel Novelty, 68 ave Habib Bourguiba, (enter by the rue Ali Zouaoui) ☎ (08) 670 176 / 673 178, Fax (08) 673 008 – 26rm ⁂ ♪ TV ✗ CC This is an exceptionally clean hotel. Unfortunately the rooms are either facing the noisy street or have balconies a bit too close to the neighbours. Only the double rooms have bathrooms. Reduced rates are available in low season.

Hôtel les Mimosas, enter by the ave Habib Bourguiba next to the service station, ☎ (08) 673 018, Fax (08) 673 276 – 77 rm ⁂ ✗ ⌕ CC This is a beautiful hotel built at the turn of the century on a hill overlooking Tabarka. The bathrooms look their age, but the seaview makes up for it. Bear in mind that this old residence (and its modern annexes) is built on several floors and there is no lift. Guests who have problems with stairs should ask for a room on the 1st floor.

● **At the beach**

From US$42-80

Hôtel Royal Golf, tourist area, ☎ (08) 673 899 / 625, Fax (08) 673 838 – 160rm ⁂ ▤ ♪ ✗ ⌕ ◐ ⁑ CC Only 300m from the beach, this hotel's rooms are comfortable if somewhat lacking in charm. A wide range of sports are available to guests and the UCPA sports centre is located in the establishment from May to October.

Abou Nawas Montazah, along the tourist route, ☎ (08) 673 514 / 532 / 554, Fax (08) 673 530 – 306rm ✗ ⌕ ⁑ CC The hotel is separated from the sea only by some sand dunes. Although this is one of the most modest hotels belonging to this chain, it maintains the organisation's tradition of quality.

Around US$80

Mehari, on the new tourist route, ☎ (08) 670 001 / 440 / 441, Fax (08) 673 943 – 200rm ⁂ ♪ ✗ ⌕ ⁑ CC This establishment consists of a hotel (half-board only) and 57 self-catering chalets. Chalet residents can use the hotel facilities, which include dance and exercise classes.

EATING OUT

Less than US$10

Le Corail (B3), ave Habib Bourguiba (near Hôtel Novelty) 🛋 CC Although this isn't the liveliest part of the avenue, the hotel's terrace is very pleasant. The owner of this little restaurant can be relied upon to supply the freshest fish or shellfish (don't miss his delicious shrimp briks).

La Perle du Nord-Ouest (B3), 53 ave Habib Bourguiba, ☎ (08) 670 164. 🍷 🛋 In addition to a reasonably priced menu where you can eat for less than US$8, you will also find Tunisian home cooking here, such as "kamounia" (a lamb stew seasoned with cumin), "mermez" (a chickpea stew) and a shrimp "oja" (omelette). The large terrace is always lively.

From US$10-20

Le Panorama (B3) (this restaurant is located in the Hôtel Les Mimosas). Enter from the ave Habib Bourguiba, ☎ (08) 673 018 / 028. 🍷 🛋 CC The panoramic view of Tabarka's coastline is perhaps more of a draw than the food itself. The ham comes from wild boar hunted by the owners themselves, but unfortunately it is a bit on the salty side. Another local speciality is lamb cutlets cooked in butter. During the hunting season, game is the house speciality.

Le Novelty (B3), 68 ave Habib Bourguiba, ☎ (08) 670 176 / 673 178. 🍷 🛋 CC This restaurant belongs to the hotel of the same ·name and serves fairly decent food. There is Tunisian home cooking, particularly the chorba, a slightly lemony soup, for less than US$10. On summer evenings, the terrace is a good spot to observe this lively scene.

Les Aiguilles (B3), 14 ave Hédi Chaker (on the corner of ave Habib Bourguiba), ☎ (08) 673 789, Fax (08) 673 604. 🍷 🛋 Another hotel restaurant that offers a large assortment of fish and shellfish. It is possible to eat well here for less than US$10.

Khemiri (B3), ave Habib Bourguiba (opposite Hôtel de France), ☎ (08) 671 586 🍷 🛋 CC As is the case in many of Tabarka's restaurants, the menu here is almost entirely composed of fish and shellfish. However, the meat dishes are excellent and couscous is prepared on request. Pleasant staff.

Touta (B2), Port de Plaisance, ☎ (08) 671 018. 🛋 One of Tabarka's main attractions is its port where boats from all over Europe are moored. Enjoy the scene over a seafood platter, one of the house specialities.

Le Pirate (B2), marina, ☎ (08) 670 061 🍷 🛋 CC The terrace set on a small lawn opposite the sea is quite irresistible. Excellent fish, shellfish and crayfish specialities.

WHERE TO GO FOR A DRINK

Cafés – 🏛 **Café Andalou** (B3) at the top of rue Hédi Chaker (on the corner of rue du Peuple), ☎ (08) 671 032. This is Tabarka's best place for a glass of mint tea. Although this is a fairly new café, the beautiful Andalusian tiles give the impression that it is centuries old. This is also the place to find card players and other local characters, from the harbour captain to the regional tourism representative.

Nightclubs – Most of the hotels in the tourist area have a night-club. In the summer, the beach cafés also turn into lively discos-cum-bars in the evening, among which, only the **Blue Lagoon**, opposite the Golf Beach Hotel, is open all year round.

LEISURE

Sports – Tabarka Golf, at the end of the tourist road, turn immediate left and continue for 700m, ☎ (08) 670 028 / 038, Fax (08) 670 057. The 18-hole course costs TD40 a day and TD255 a week. The club also organises hour-long classes for TD20 per person as well as training courses (beginners: TD315 a week; advanced: TD425 a week). Credit cards are accepted.

Fishing – NTH (Nautic Tunisian Holidays), Résidence Tabarka, 8110 Tabarka, ☎ (08) 670 050, ☎ and Fax (08) 670 057. This company was started by a Frenchman and organises fishing parties from June to October.

Scuba-diving – Le Crabe, Hôtel Mehari, ☎ (08) 673 136, Fax (08) 673 868. This club also organises classes for beginners or licenced divers. All credit cards and Eurocheques are accepted.

*Hiking – **Tabarka Voyages**, 13 route Aïn Draham, ☎ (08) 673 740, Fax (08) 673 726.*

Festivals – *Tabarka's International Festival* is held in July-August but the famous "Don't overdo the suntan" celebrations of the 1970s have lost some of their glitter.

Tabarka Jazz Festival. The co-ordinators have attempted to recreate the past by inviting well-known players to this festival, held during the last two weeks of August. The concerts are held at the small theatre in the basilica.

Coralis Festival. Underwater photography competition held in June.

Hammams – *Saïd*, 52 Farhat Hached (on the corner of the rue de Tunis). Open 5am-11.30am / 5am-6.30pm for men; 11.30am-5pm for women. The hammam is reserved for men only on Sundays. Amenities are basic. Price: 800 millimes.

Coral – Coral remains one of Tabarka's specialities even though it has almost entirely disappeared from the local area. You can still find it however in the stores that line the ave Habib Bourguiba. In view of the increasing rarity of coral, however, it is perhaps best not to buy at all.

Carpets and olive wood products – Rather than purchasing these in Tabarka, go instead to Aïn Draham, a former popular tourist spot in the mountains. There is a preview of the local products along the way where children try to sell you bowls and small statues but it is better to buy in the village where there is a greater selection.

Foreign newspapers – *Tabac*, at the end of the marina near the harbourmaster's station.

Kiosque, in the square with the statue of Bourguiba.

Making the most of Aïn Draham

GETTING THERE

By bus –SRT Jendouba, ☎ (08) 655 022, on the ave du 7 novembre, in the heart of the village, runs daily services between Jendouba and Tabarka via Aïn Draham.

By shared taxi – The best way of getting to or from Aïn Draham. However, very few group taxis leave for Tabarka in the afternoon.

By car – The P 17, which runs from Tabarka to Jendouba (see Making the most of Jendouba), cuts through Aïn Draham.

USEFUL ADDRESSES

Tourist information – The **syndicat d'initiative (Tourist office)** (the only sign which is in Arabic) is wedged in between a Taxiphone and the "Salon des Amis" hairdressers on ave Habib Bourguiba. Opening times are irregular because it is staffed entirely by unpaid volunteers. When open, everyone will do their utmost to help, but means are limited.

L'association des chasseurs (Hunters' Association) might be able to provide information about hunting excursions. The manager, Abdelhafidh Alfaoui, runs the grocery store opposite the school on ave Habib Bourguiba.

WHERE TO STAY AND EAT

Most of the hotels are located outside the village, making personal transport preferable. A new establishment with some 15 rooms intended primarily for families, is due to open on ave Habib Bourguiba in early 2000. The central location of this future hotel will make it ideal for those who prefer to stay in the centre of Aïn Draham (prices should be around US$20 for a double room).

From US$15-US$32

Hôtel Les Chênes, 7km south of Aïn Draham, ☎ (08)655 211 / 315, Fax (08) 655 578 – 34rm ⌂ ♗ ✗ ⌘ ☞ cc Set in the heart of a forest of oak and cork trees, this establishment, with

its open fire and hunting trophies, has an inn feel to it. Reasonably-priced, but a few signs of wear and tear.

Hôtel Rihana, 2km south of the village, ☎ (08) 655 391 / 392 / 697, Fax (08) 655 396 / 578 – 74rm ⌂ ⩱ ✗ ☞ cc On the same road as the above establishment. Hunting is also the star attraction in this hotel. Reasonable rooms, some of which overlook the valley.

From US$32-US$60

Hôtel Nour El Aïn, Col des Ruines, 2km to the north of Aïn Draham, ☎ (08) 655 000, Fax (08)655 185 – 61rm ⌂ ♗ ✗ ⌘ cc Set in the Pass of Ruins, the spacious rooms of this hotel overlook the forest. Guests can also use the establishment's hammam, gym room and large covered swimming pool.

Around US$70

Hôtel La Forêt, 4km to the south of Aïn Draham, ☎ (08) 655 302, Fax (08) 655 335 – 60rm ⌂ ▤ ♗ TV ✗ cc The region's most luxurious establishment opened in 1998. All the rooms are immaculate and extremely comfortable, although not quite as opulent as those of the seaside resorts. A swimming pool and activity centre are planned for the end of 2000.

SPORTS AND PASTIMES

Hunting – Wild boar hunts are organised by Rihana and Les Chênes Hotels from mid-October to the end of January.

Riding – Les Chênes Hotel organises hiking excursions in the forest, which can last from 1hr to several days.

Walking – Paths are marked and maintained, but tourists would do better to set out with a local guide. Les Chênes and Rihana hotels (yet again!) can find guides to accompany walkers.

Mountain biking – Despite the nationwide campaign to promote this sport in Kroumirie, facilities have yet to be properly organised. However the situation should improve rapidly because the owner of Les Chênes Hotel intends to set up this activity very shortly.

BULLA REGIA★

Jendouba Governorship
64km from Tabarka, 69km from Le Kef
Archeological site at the foot of Jebel R'Bia (Alt 649m)

Not to be missed
The House of the Hunt.
And remember...
For visits to Bulla Regia and Chemtou,
personal transport is the best option.

Take the P 17 road from either Tabarka or Le Kef. At its junction with the C 59 road a sign indicates the site 3km away. The road opposite leads to Chemtou.

The little community and its few modern buildings around the site should not discourage the purists, for these buildings remain discreet and do not intrude on the profoundly rural atmosphere of the surroundings. The first feature to be noticed is the R'bia, a bare hillside which overwhelms the ancient settlement with its austere and almost hostile presence. Bulla, built on a gently sloping site, looks across its former possessions: a rich plain planted with cereal crops and olive trees.

Bulla Royal

Rich alluvial soil (Mejerda), a damp climate, a wealth of springs – which still supply Jendouba – all help explain why this site was occupied at a very early date by the Numidians.

On the death of Massinissa his inheritance was dismantled by the Romans and shared out as several small kingdoms, with Bulla as one of the capitals – hence its name of *Regia*, meaning "royal". Integrated later into the Roman province of Africa, Bulla was a link in the vast road network linking Hippone (Annaba, in Algeria) with Carthage, via Thuburnica, Chemtou and Dougga. The town was promoted to the rank of municipality under Vespasian (AD 69-79) and became a colony under Hadrian (AD 117-138). Bulla enjoyed its greatest political and cultural influence between the 2C and 4C, and was one of the provinces of Africa which gave the empire the greatest number of senators. The little city was full of public monuments, and most of the remains date from this period. But there is always a mean spirit to interfere with the peaceful enjoy-

The Numidians

They were Berbers, nomads, and the Greeks called them "The shepherd people". Their territory stretched from Carthage in the east to the Moulouya wadi in Algeria, in the west. Two Numidian tribes shared the territory in the 3C, the Massyles and the Masaesyles. Massinissa, King of the Massyles, was a man of outstanding drive. In the midst of the Punic Wars he took the side of Scipio Africanus against Carthage and its Masaesyle allies, and with the backing of Rome he annexed the Berbers in the west to create a powerful Numidian state. He encouraged his people to settle and to farm their land. Uniquely in the history of Africa, the original native people were finally masters in their own land. The Numidians were no doubt aware of the originality of their culture even though it borrowed heavily from Carthage. According to Livy, Massinissa promoted the idea of "Africa for the Africans" – a formula that was to have a certain amount of success, but the Romans made great efforts to break up this legacy.

ment of prosperity: in AD 339, St Augustine visited Bulla and preached to the inhabitants, criticising their morals and their excessive pleasure in theatre-going.

Very little is known of the Vandal period, although the presence of a bishop in the 7C has been confirmed. The discovery of a cache of 260 pieces of silver dating from the 12C probably indicates that the site was occupied until the Middle Ages. However, this is no more than a theory at this stage; excavations focusing on the Islamic period may reveal more.

E. Boucher/MICHELIN

The peristyle of a underground house

The mystery of the underground houses

Without a doubt, Bulla Regia's most fascinating feature is its underground houses, both a sight for tourists as well as being an enigma for many archeologists and historians. The layout of the basement of these dwellings is effectively the same as that of the upper floors: a courtyard and peristyle, a *triclinium* and two bedrooms for the grandest residents. They consisted of luxurious rooms which were ventilated and lit naturally, although extending several metres under ground level – a type of dwelling unique in the history of classical times.

In an area where it is not unusual to see the thermometer reach 40°C in the shade, with occasional peaks to 50°C, the most obvious and no doubt the most probable explanation is that this was an early form of air-conditioning. It provided an ideal temperature for the nobility during the hottest period of the year.

However, no trace of such buildings has been found in any other African and Eastern regions of the empire, although they suffer equally high, if not higher, temperatures. Some specialists have therefore come up with an alternative theory: thwarted by town planning restrictions and a lack of space, the wealthiest patricians who wanted to extend their living area had to wait until land was available, or until they were able to buy up houses in the same block.

Where a town was able to grow and develop naturally, the privileged few could satisfy their aspiration by building luxurious houses in new suburbs, or on the site of former town walls. But Bulla, despite its dynamism, never expanded beyond its ring of fortifications.

Underground Visits

Allow 1hr. 8am-7pm in the summer,
8.30am-5.30pm out of season. Entrance charge.

In view of the shabbiness of the site and the unfinished state of excavation, a comprehensive visit is not available. It is better to confine oneself to the underground houses, the real jewels of the site. As you go down the steps which lead into the privacy of these aristocratic dwellings, bear in mind that they are between 1600 and 1800 years old, and that they are extraordinarily well-preserved.

The **House of the Hunt***** (La maison de la chasse) has earned its name from a mosaic of which very little remains. This paving, which evokes the mosaics from the New Hunt, tells us about the site's immediate surroundings: the Jebel R'bia, so bare today, was once rich in game (hare, boar, panther) but the forests which sheltered it were burned down in the 11C by the Beni Hilal. The **underground apartments**, 5.15m below ground level, still retain their beautiful paving almost intact. In the bedrooms, the location of the **beds** is indicated by a small platform decorated with monocolour mosaic. The **peristyle** consists of eight columns with Corinthian capitals, which no doubt extended into the upper storey. The **vaulting** is particularly notable, built in a very unusual style with interlocking terracotta pipes.

The **New House of the Hunt** (La maison de la Nouvelle Chasse) displays magnificent paving, particularly a **hunting scene** in the *triclinium* of the **ground floor**. These mosaics were unfortunately damaged by graves dug out in the Byzantine era.

The **Villa with the Fishing Scene*** (La maison de la Pêche) is one of the largest in Bulla. The **underground** mosaics have been damaged by saltpetre, for these rooms are quite dark and damp (4.40m below ground level). This is the coolest house in summer, and tourists enjoy lingering here before going up and out into the furnace-like heat once more. The pavement of the *triclinium*, which shows **cherubs fishing**, has here again given its name to the house.

At The **House of Amphitrite**** (La maison d'Amphitrite) the **ground floor** is in a ruinous state and the mosaic in the *triclinium*, **Perseus rescuing Andromeda**, is now kept in the Bardo. The **underground** area, on the other hand, has some splendid surprises in store for the visitor. The lay-out is quite distinctive: three rooms opening at right-angles off a vast gallery vestibule, with two other smaller rooms on the

Apollo Citharœdus

other side of the vestibule. The pavements are in excellent condition and the *triclinium* is embellished with a particularly effective composition depicting the **triumph of Venus**. The goddess, naked and bejewelled, is borne in triumph by two sea monsters. The name of the house can be explained by the frequent confusion between Amphitrite, wife of Neptune, and Venus. In the vestibule a mosaic features a half-length female figure set in a handsome frame of plants. This design faced a fountain set into the wall, and here and there traces of the plasterwork can still be seen on the walls. Guides often describe this house as a temple; it is full of a semi-mystical light, but there is nothing to confirm the assertion. Since the finest statues – of Æsculapius, Apollo, Saturn and a priestess of the imperial cult – have been moved to the Bardo, the need to visit the **antiquarium** is no longer quite as pressing.

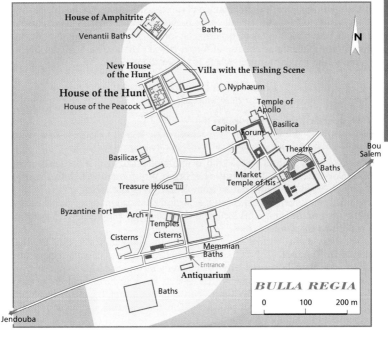

CHEMTOU

Governorship of Jendouba
76km from Tabarka and 81km from Le Kef

Not to be missed
Archeological museum.
Marble quarries.

And remember...
Museum visits are best with a guide.
Stay at Le Kef, Aïn Draham or Tabarka.

Same access route as for Bulla Regia on the P 17, from Tabarka or Le Kef. At the intersection with the C 59, turn west (away from Bulla Regia). After 15km, turn left until you reach the museum car park, some 2km further on.

Overlooking the fertile valley of Mejerda, although similar in appearance to all the other hills in the region, actually withhold a variety of treasures. The site of Chemtou in fact owes its reputation to its famous pink, mauve and yellow marble which adorned so many monuments of the Roman Empire, and later, of the Byzantine era. Given the current state of the excavations, the scant remains of former Simitthus are of little interest to the layman, but the quarries and recently opened archeological museum are more than worth the detour.

The sacred rock

The Numidians were the first to inhabit what was then known as **Simitthus**, the Numidian name for Chemtou. The remains of a sanctuary (2C BC) discovered at the summit of the "sacred mountain" substantiate the use of marble at this time, even though the site actually dates back to an earlier period – a monument dated 5C BC was discovered beneath the forum. The quarry's heyday was in Roman times, thanks to the use of forced labour. The marble was then transported to the port of Tabarka, where it left for Rome by sea.

The "Marble Mountain"
Start with the museum

The archeological museum★
8am-7pm in the summer, 8am-5.30pm out of season. Entrance charge. Guided visits available. The rooms are organised clockwise, in chronological order.

The museum is built of marble and is of a modern design. It has been open since November 1997. Its construction began very promisingly, with the discovery of 1 648 gold coins dating from 4C BC, weighing 7.2kg.

The first room provides background geological information, as a suitable introduction to the museum. This section is devoted to the Numidians and features a handsome collection of coins.

In the next room, visitors discover one of the museum's star exhibits, the **Numidian Temple★** (130 BC), engraved with Hellenistic designs. Fragments which have been discovered have been cleverly incorporated into a reconstruction of the magnificent sanctuary that used to stand at the summit of the hill. Room 3 takes us to Roman times with numerous samples of marble from Chemtou and other imperial provinces. This room focuses on the extraction, transport and cutting of marble.

The museum's last section presents different works of the Roman period, including a series of original **votive headstones**★ devoted to Saturn, dating from the 2C and 3C AD.

A global view of Simitthus

A map of the site is available from the museum.

About one kilometre from the museum *(accessible by car from the road that takes you back to the C 59)*, the **quarries**★ nestle in the hillside, home to a few stray goats who can sometimes be found grazing among the sheer gold and pink rock faces.

The summit reveals a variety of overlaying constructions which illustrate the successive waves of occupation endured by Chemtou. A Roman sanctuary devoted to Saturn, followed by a Christian basilica, were built on the ruins of the former Numidian temple *(reconstructed in the museum)*. Nearby, motifs engraved in the rock, also in honour of Saturn, are barely visible.

A **workers' camp**, which lies to the north of the hill, housed the cells of the prisoners condemned to forced labour, as well the marble manufacture workshops.

The site also comprises a theatre (not yet excavated), the remains of thermal baths and an aqueduct.

Chemtou

LE KEF★

Centre of Governorship
Pop c 30 000
Alt 850m

Not to be missed
The panoramic view from the top of the Kasbah.
A mint tea at the Café Bou Makhlouf.

And remember...
Visitors not in search of luxury should stay at Le Kef,
an excellent starting point for excursions to Dougga (60km) and Maktar (69km).

The town with two faces

Le Kef has two faces, depending on mood or season. At first sight this town clinging on to the mountainside (*kef* means "rock") can appear austere and forbidding. In summer the citadel dominates a vast burning plain which vibrates in the evening dust like a remote desert. It is like gazing into empty space. Yet the town can offer a far more agreeable and welcoming appearance: in the spring it is the capital of a fertile and productive countryside, and although the rocks break through the hillsides around, the water of the springs is all the more pure and the pine trees more vigorous. Despite heavy unemployment the town seems prosperous and well-maintained: perhaps this well-cared for appearance is due to the presence of a **presidential residence** on the heights, or perhaps it reflects the character of the inhabitants. The people of Le Kef have a reputation for hard work, and for their love of the soil. Other Tunisians are inclined to call them the "08s" (from the region's telephone code), to indicate a somewhat rough-mannered and parochial outlook.

Until very recently the absence of tourist information, the lack of hotels and the poor quality of the restaurants gave little encouragement to stay long. The construction of Les Pins hotel is an improvement, but Le Kef still lies off the main tourist routes – not the least of its attractions.

The Mercenaries' War

After their defeat in Sicily during the First Punic War, the Carthaginians had to cope with their troublesome army of mercenaries. These Numidian, Libyan, Iberian and Celtic soldiers wanted their pay, but the demands of the war and the tribute paid to Rome had ruined Carthage. The Punic city paid out money in tiny amounts and removed these unwanted subjects by billetting them at Sicca (Le Kef). It was this concentration of tough soldiers that lay behind the revolt. Aware of their strength, they rose up, besieged Utica and Bizerte, and, under their captains Spendius, Autolicus, and Matho even managed to paralyse Carthage. Hamilcar Barca managed to retrieve the situation, however, and the revolutionaries' leaders were crucified outside Tunis, which was held by Matho. In his famous novel, Gustave Flaubert extends the story with Matho suffering a hopeless love for Hamilcar's daughter Salammbô.

Mercenaries and soldiers

Le Kef was a Numidian city under Carthaginian protection. At the end of the First Punic War the Carthaginians chose to send their mercenaries there when they were chased out of Sicily. It was a fatal error which led to the Mercenaries' War. Under the reign of Augustus, Le Kef became a Roman colony and then, in St Augustine's time, a centre of Christianity. After the Arab conquest the town was used as a stronghold to repel the attacks of the Algerian Ottoman chiefs.

During the Second World War, when the town escaped occupation by the armies of the Axis, it was chosen by the French to be the country's administrative centre. Marshal Juin, Commander in Chief for the whole of North Africa, based his headquarters here for a time.

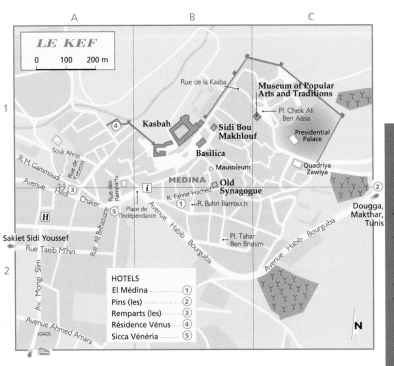

Up and down the lanes
Allow 2hr

Begin your walk at the Tourist Office – it is unlikely you will find any useful information – and go up the rue Fahrat Hached.

Le Kef has not yet been invaded by tourists, and the old town has not had to suffer the vagaries of modern town planning. You are in a genuine Arab town, without excessive outbreaks of picturesqueness. The old town has a network of lanes and steep alleys, interconnected by stairways. No cars are allowed, and rubbish is collected by mule.

The **Old Synagogue** (ghriba) is established in a little house no different from all the others. Left abandoned for several decades, it has recently been given a fresh start. No worship takes place there, but it is open to the public. The building, which has no historical or architectural claim to attention, is touching in its intimate style and unexpected simplicity: it could be an old-fashioned classroom. Time stopped here with Tunisian independence: religious objects and ex-votos were left in place and have simply been dusted off.

Turn into the first street on the left beyond the synagogue, and go up it to the kasbah at the end.

As you look at the powerful walls and strategic location of the kasbah* it is easy to imagine the importance of this 17C Ottoman citadel. Reconstructed in 1813 to ward off Turkish attacks from Algeria, it was still in use until recently. During the Second World War the threat came from the east and the south, as the Axis forces seized Bizerte and Tunis, and Rommel's Afrika Korps was pushed back by Montgomery and retreated from Libya. French troops were billetted in the kasbah under **Marshal Juin**. The smaller of the fortress's two sections was used as a **prison**. During this difficult period the French used it indiscriminately to intern German prisoners, collaborators and independently-inclined political prisoners suspected of passing intelligence to the enemy. The tiny cells where the detained men were kept at night still exist; Bourguiba spent a week in one of them. Inside the prison walls you can still see the somewhat dilapidated house used by Marshal Juin as his headquarters.

The largest section of the citadel is now used as a site for festivals and cultural events. The east side of the courtyard leads into an enormous vaulted hall, known as the **Turkish mosque**, partly constructed with columns and capitals from classical times. The **east bastion**, the highest in the kasbah, overlooks the whole of the surrounding region: there is a very fine **view**★ over Le Kef, the plain, the wooded hillsides, and the blue line of the Algerian frontier some forty kilometres away.

Just a few steps below the fortress you will find a Christian basilica (4C-5C), also known as the Great Mosque or "the building with troughs". No one is yet sure of the original purpose of this ancient building. Low and rectangular, it consists of an enormous square courtyard surrounded by a portico and a vaulted cruciform hall. This hall is lined with a series of stone basins, and niches like hatches. What were they for, and what was the purpose of the whole building? Perhaps it was a covered market, a tax office, or a bank. The building, which was turned into a mosque in the 8C, now hosts part of the Bou Makhlouf festival. (*See Making the most of Le Kef*).

On the left as you come out of the basilica, a street with several steps leads to the Sidi Bou Makhlouf mosque★ (17C), identifiable by its octagonal minaret and its two enchanting ribbed domes. The dazzling white mosque owes its fame to its interior decoration: finely carved plaster-work and ornamentation consisting of crescents and green stars. A very narrow staircase leads to the top of the minaret, with a splendid view of the town's roofs and the distant plain on the horizon.

Go up to the town ramparts and walk along them to the Rue de la Kasba, on the right. The Museum of Art and Popular Traditions stands a little lower down the street, in a small square with a roundabout (Place Cheïk Ali Ben Aïssa, but the street sign is in Arabic).

Museum of Popular Art and Traditions (Musée des Arts et Traditions populaires) (*9.30am-4.30pm out of season, 9am-1pm; 4pm-7pm in summer; closed on Mondays. Entrance charge*) has been laid out in the **Sidi Ali Ben Aïssa zawiya**. This very well thought-out and charming museum is mainly concerned with the nomadic way of life. A Bedouin tent is set up in the middle of a large hall, presented with many evocative tools and objects: carpets, goatskin water-

The Sidi Bou Makhlouf mosque

bottles, blankets, including the rugs used to cover the camel's hump and its pack. A wall-map indicates the number of nomads counted by tribe, another shows their movements. A document reproduces a verbal contract between a land-owner and a shepherd: ten young lambs as payment for guarding 100 sheep, clothing costs, supplying a sack of wheat or barley, and so on. A neighbouring hall devoted to jewellery displays a rich sample of elaborate necklaces, bracelets and anklets.

Le Kef *(vertical side text)*

GETTING THERE

By train – The nearest railway station is in Dahmani, 24km from Le Kef on the Tunis-Kalaa Kasba line. There are three local trains per day and the trip lasts 4hr. You can take a taxi to Le Kef.

By bus – **Bus station**, rue Mongi Slim, ☎ (08) 223 168 / 224 366. Le Kef is linked with Tunisia's main cities by companies such as SNTRI, STK (Le Kef Transport Co.) and other regional bus companies. There are departures for Tunis every hour (3hr) and 3 departures daily for Sousse (4hr30min).
SNRTI, ☎ (08) 226 205.
STK, ☎ (08) 224 336.

By shared taxi – **Station**, rue Mongi Slim. The trip to Tunis lasts about 2hr15min, 90min for Tabarka, 2hr30min for Kairouan and 3hr for Bizerta. To get to Dougga, take a taxi to Tunis. The driver will drop you off on the way.

By car – Le Kef is 168km from Tunis by the P 5 and 2hr from Tabarka via the Kroumiria Mountains. Be wary of children – in the Tabarka and Aïn Draham region they practically throw themselves at cars to sell their handicrafts. Also watch out for the cows near Tabarka as they cross the road regardless of traffic.

ADDRESS BOOK

Emergency – National Guard, ☎ (08) 223 690 /674.
Police, ☎ (08) 201 386.
Jeljeli Night Pharmacy, 21 rue Omar Khiam, ☎ (08) 200 804.
Mohamed Bourguiba Hospital, ☎ (08) 228 815 / 923 / 900.
Regional Hospital, ☎ (08) 228 900.
Hosni Hospital, rue du 8 juillet, ☎ (08) 203 573.
Jugurtha General Hospital, rue Salah Majed, ☎ (08) 204 214 / 202 611 / 200 620.

Tourist information – Le Kef makes no effort to attract tourists: there is no **ONTT** (National Tourist Office) and the local tourist office has unpredictable opening hours and a lack of brochures and maps.

L'Association de sauvegarde de la medina (Association for the Protection of the Medina), 7 Place de l'Indépendence, ☎ (08) 221 148 shares premises with the tourist office and suffers from the same lack of information.

Bank / Currency Exchange – BH, rue Mongi Slim.
BNA, 2 rue Ali Belhaouane.
BNDA, 2 rue Ali Belhaouane.
Banque du Sud, Ctama building.
BT, 2 rue d'Alger.
STB, rue Salah Ayach.
There is a cash dispenser opposite Hôtel Sicca Véneria.

Post office – rue Hédi Chaker.

WHERE TO STAY

Le Kef has lost much of its former character, from the days when the city was a genuine multicultural crossroads with its mix of Muslims, Jews, Tunisians, Italians and Maltese. The hotels suffer the effects of this.

Less than US$18
Hôtel el Médina, 18 rue Farhat Hached, ☎ (08) 204 183 – 12rm This hotel is reasonably priced and relatively clean, although basic: showers are off the landing and the water is cold.

From US$18-42
Résidence Vénus, rue Mouldi Khamessi, ☎ (08) 204 695 – 14rm ⚐ ╳ A good hotel although with a modest level of comfort. The rooms are very clean.

Hôtel Les Remparts, 5 rue des Remparts ☎ and Fax (08) 202 100 – 12rm ⚐ This is slightly less appealing than the Résidence Vénus but is just as clean and more centrally-located. Upon request the hotel serves meals and alcoholic drinks for its guests.

⚐ **Hôtel Les Pins**, ave de l'Environnement, on the way in to Le Kef from the north, on a bend in the road leading up to the town centre. ☎ (08) 204 300 / 204 021, Fax (08) 202 411 – 30rm ⚐ ✆ ╳ This hotel opened in 1997 and is the best in town. The rooms are spacious and well-furnished. There is a beautiful view of the valley and the hotel is peaceful despite its proximity to the road.

Hôtel Sicca Vénéria, ave Habib Bourguiba, ☎ (08) 202 388 – 34rm ⚐ A modern hotel set right in the heart of the town. Extremely comfortable, pristine rooms, which however are a little lacking in charm.

EATING OUT

The lack of tourists is especially apparent in the restaurants. You will find authentic cuisine in Le Kef.

• **In the modern district**

Less than US$10

Vénus (B2), rue Farhat Hached, on the corner of Place de l'Indépendance (the restaurant is not in the same place as the hotel). ☎ (08) 200 355. 🍷 Near the Kasbah, a relatively comfortable and extremely clean hotel.

WHERE TO GO FOR A DRINK

Cafés – *Café Barbouch and Café du Dinar* (A2), Place de l'Indépendance. Each café has its own little terrace where local people gather at midday in the offseason to make the most of the sun.

Café des Vitres (B2), ave Habib Bourguiba (on the corner of rue Farhat Hached). This new establishment overlooking the ave Bourguiba is a meeting place for the young.

⚐ Café Bou Makhlouf (B1), on the steps leading to the mosque, a few tables under a mulberry tree provide one of the nicest spots in town to stop for a mint tea.

Café Edir (Not located on the city map), rue Edir. Leave the town centre and follow the ave Bourguiba in the direction of Hôtel Les Pins to find this café. Air-conditioned interior and terrace. Alcohol is not served.

LEISURE

Festivals – *Sidi Bou Makhlouf Festival*, where theatrical groups perform as well as local and foreign musicians. In July-August.

SHOPPING

Cakes – *Beignets*, 42 rue Hédi Chaker, open every day until 1pm.

Antiques and handicrafts – You will find several jewellers in the medina.

Bookshops – *Journaux-tabac*, rue de Tebessa (on the corner of rue Hédi Chaker).

Librairie Numidia, 3 rue d'Alger, ☎ and Fax (08) 225 803. Some books in French. Book lovers should try to meet the owner who is a specialist in archeology.

MAKTHAR★

Not to be missed
Thermal baths in the southeast.
The schola of Juvenes.

And remember...
Bring water and protection from heat of the summer sun.
Accommodation at Makthar is not all it could be;
visitors should stay at Le Kef or Kairouan.

Makthar is reached via the P 12, which runs from Le Kef to Kairouan. The archeological site is at the entrance to the town.

Makthar, formerly known as Mactaris, is perched on a plateau subject to scorching arid heat in the summer, but often covered in snow during the winter. Whether arriving from Le Kef or Kairouan, the picturesque road into the city winds through a beautiful cereal region. Its position, in the heart of northern Tunisia, takes it off the beaten track of classic tourist routes. Makthar is nonetheless more than worth a detour, not just because of its enchanting pastoral landscapes, but more significantly because of its remarkable ruins, among the few remaining tributes to Tunisia's historic past.

Ramparts protect against nomads

From 200 to 46 BC, the region was in the hands of **Massyli Numidians**, a Libyan-Berber tribe with strong agricultural roots. Its strategic position, on a plateau between Kairouan and Le Kef, made it an ideal stronghold to withstand nomadic life. The harsh task of settling the nomads fell to **King Massinissa** *(see page 224)*. A large number of megalithic monuments dating back to the Numidian era, from simple dolmens to vast funeral chambers overflowing with offerings, still remain today.

At the fall of Carthage (146 BC), a sizable colony of Punics emigrated to Makthar. This civilisation of Phoenician influence, left in their wake a large number of inscriptions, sculptures, tombstones and a very damaged tophet – discovered in the ravine dominated by the Bab el Aïn Ark.

Peaceful Roman conquest

Makthar was finally annexed to the Roman Empire by Julius Caesar in 46 BC. Although situated in the heart of this bustling centre with over 60 agricultural outlying villages, the Punic civilisation was to retain its very particular character within the Roman empire. At the request of the people of Makthar, **Emperor Trajan**, keen to develop improved integration, granted the city's elite Roman citizenship, a foretaste of the status of Roman colony that the city reached in 180 AD.

Within this important agricultural and industrial centre, the concept of social advancement is perfectly illustrated by the harvester's inscription (3C AD), now in the Louvre Museum but not exhibited. Makthar was also the birthplace of surprisingly large numbers of Imperial senior civil-servants, a fact which didn't fail to have repercussions on the city itself. Around 200 AD, a whole series of major building works were undertaken, including an aqueduct and large thermal baths.

Makthar

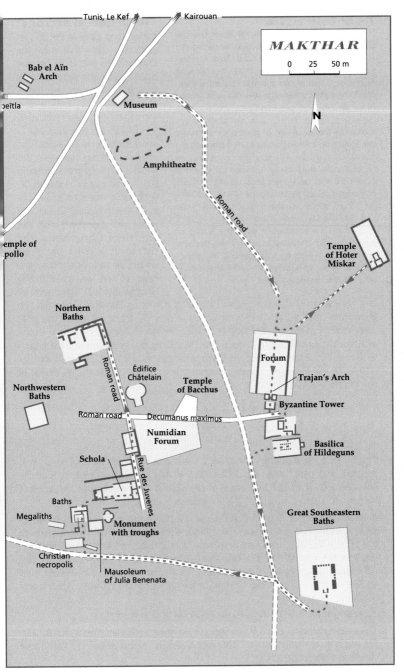

MAKTHAR

0   25   50 m

N

Tunis, Le Kef — Kairouan

Bab el Aïn
Arch

beïtla

Museum

Amphitheatre

Roman road

Temple of
Apollo

Temple
of Hoter
Miskar

Northern
Baths

Roman road

Édifice
Châtelain

Temple
of Bacchus

Forum

Trajan's Arch

Northwestern
Baths

Roman road

Decumanus maximus

Byzantine Tower

Numidian
Forum

Basilica
of Hildeguns

Schola

Rue des Juvenes

Baths

Megaliths

Monument
with troughs

Great Southeastern
Baths

Christian
necropolis

Mausoleum
of Julia Benenata

The harvester's epitaph

"I was born into a poor family; my father had neither work nor a house of his own. Since the day of my birth, I worked in my fields. Both my land and myself toiled ceaselessly. When the harvests were ripe, I was always the first to cut my stubble. When the countryside was rife with groups of harvesters, who came to Cirta, the Numidian capital, to find hired work in the plains, overlooked by the mountain of Jupiter, I was always the first out harvesting in the fields. I then left my native home and for 12 years hired myself out to harvest under the burning sun, then for 11 years, I led a team of harvesters and cut wheat in the Numidians' fields. By stint of hard work and frugal living, I was at last able to buy my own house and land. Today I live in ease and have gained recognition. I was called to sit in the Senate of my city, and from modest peasant, I have become censor. I have seen my children and my grandchildren grow up around me and I have had a peaceful life, respected by all."

The decline of Makthar

However as early as the 3C, an economic crisis was to hit the Empire hard and taxes became heavier. The first signs of "class struggle" between the lower classes and the landowners were to emerge. The revolt of El Jem in 238 *(see page 276)* was to affect Makthar in its wake. The schola of Juvenes *(see below)*, destroyed by Emperor Maximin's troops, was only restored 50 years later when order was finally re-established at the end of the 3C. However with the growth of Christianity, the threat of a split between Catholics and Donatists soon emerged and was to leave the Church divided. The arrival of the **Vandals** in 430 was to herald troubled times for Makthar. Although the **Byzantine** conquest saw the construction of new churches, the peace was only comparative, as the construction of a defensive tower during this period to the south of the Ark of Trajan reveals. The Byzantines finally abandoned the region to the Arab invasion. The site remained inhabited until the 11C, when it was destroyed by the **Hilalians**. The city was not rebuilt until 1890, to the northwest of the former Makthar.

Visit to the archeological site

8.30am-5.30pm in the summer, 9am-7pm in winter.
Charge. Allow 90min.

The ruins at Makthar cover a vast area, flanked to the north by the bed of oued Saboun, over which rises the **arch of Bab el Aïn**. On the roadside, outside the site, the arch marks the entrance to the city. It now constitutes an excellent marker for visitors, because it's a few metres from the museum.

Before setting off on foot to visit the site, go round the museum, which houses funeral and votive tombstones from the tophet (dating for the most part from the 1C and 2C AD), a few statues, some Roman relics, oil lamps, ceramics and two mosaics. One of the showcases has a bronze statue of the god Mercury (1C AD) which is a particularly fine example of craftsmanship. Other headstones and ancient capitals from the site can also be found scattered around the garden surrounding the museum.

From the garden, take the Roman road to the left of the map of the site.

The **amphitheatre**, which you will leave on your right, dates from the 2C AD. Although quite well-preserved, this monument is far less impressive than those visible at Dougga or El Jem.

Before you reach the forum, take a short 10m detour through the fields to the **Temple of Hoter Miskar**, regretfully in ruins. Erected by the Carthaginians in honour of the divinity Hoter Miskar, it was rebuilt at the end of the 2C or 3C of our era.

Continue on your way, heading towards the ark, until you reach a vast Roman **forum**, with exceedingly-well conserved tiles. The **Arch of Trajan***, built in 116 AD, lies to the southern side of this rectangular plaza. Visible from all over the site, it was later to be integrated into a **Byzantine tower**, whose foundations are still visible.

To the south lie some rather nondescript ruins of Roman villas and of the **Basilica of Hildeguns**, built in the 5C, in memory of the Vandal chief who is buried there.

Return to the Roman road and continue southwards.

The **large southeastern thermal baths***, built around 200 AD, are an impressive ramble of ruins. Some of the 10m-high walls are still well-conserved and tower above a maze of rooms that the Byzantines turned into a fortress in the 6C.

East of the thermal baths, a jumble of Corinthian columns stands on the former site of the **schola of juvenes*** – subsequently transformed into a Christian basilica. The seat of a young people's association, founded around 1C AD, it used to house a variety of rooms for games, swimming pools and offices. The likely-function of this paramilitary association was city militia, but it was probably also in charge of collecting taxes in kind. The small building, known as the **quadrilobe of troughs** (4-5C AD) was probably used to store dues such as wheat or oil.

A few hundred metres to the northeast of this complex, the **temple of Bacchus**, one of the city's patrons, formerly dominated the **Numidian forum**, on the other side of the Roman road.

This road leads to the **northwestern thermal baths**, built during the second half of the 2C AD. A **Christian basilica** was erected in the frigidarium around the 5-6C. Nearby, the more recent **northern thermal baths** date back to the Byzantine era.

Return to the museum and turn left for around 500m, until you reach the **temple of Apollo**, of which only the foundations remain. This temple, from the Roman era, was erected on the site of a Carthaginian sanctuary, most probably devoted to Baal Hammon. Nearby, remains of the **aqueduct** are still visible.

Visit to the archeological site

The Sahel: an olive tree every 20 metres

THE SAHEL

Between the Gulf of Hammamet and the Gulf of Gabes, from Sousse to Sfax, the Sahel and its coastline form the extension of the lower plains with the inland town of Kairouan at their heart. These two regions form a geographical continuity and correspond approximately to the Romans' Byazacena. Sbeïtla on the southern border of the former province, and above all El Jem, drew their wealth from the olive oil which was exported to Rome from Hadrumetus (Sousse). After the Arab conquerors founded Kairouan, the country's centre of gravity shifted to the interior, but Sousse very quickly revived as a substantial port.

The Sahel is now Tunisia's leading economic zone, and Sfax is its second city. Its prosperity is based on olive oil production, industries like textiles, construction and, electromechanics and above all tourism. The Sousse-Monastir conurbation, with its international airport, is the country's main focus of tourism, with Hammamet next in size. In the seasonal bustle, Mahdia and the Kerkenna Islands still provide a haven of peace, but for how long? The most characteristic feature of the landscape in this region is undoubtedly its olive plantations: a strictly geometric pattern with a tree every twenty metres, stretching away apparently into infinity. According to Latin texts, olive trees once provided shade all the way from Sfax to El Jem. Having suffered during the first Arab invasions, Hadrian's fine olive groves were comprehensively ruined during the second invasion by the Beni Hilal: the countryside returned to its original condition of dusty plain. Olive cultivation did not reappear here until the end of the 19C, under the French Protectorate, when Tunisia became the world's fourth largest olive oil producer, after Spain, Italy and Greece.

SOUSSE★★
Centre of Governorship
Pop c 200 000
Pleasant climate throughout the year

Not to be missed
The museum and the ribat.

And remember...
This is the capital city of Tunisian tourism:
despite a few cultural diversions, everything is geared towards leisure,
swimming and sunbathing.

The third largest city in the country, after Tunis and Sfax, the Mecca of Tunisian tourism has nevertheless preserved its medina and fishing harbour. But Sousse is also an industrious town with nearly 800 companies in fields as varied as machinery, car assembly, textiles, building materials and food processing. Surrounded by 250 000 hectares of olive trees, Sousse also remains an important oil producing centre. The commercial harbour is steadily growing more active, with fishing not far behind: 5 000 tonnes of fish are handled each year. Sousse is also a university centre, with nearly 10 000 students.

And yet the image that sticks in the mind is above all that of an immense seaside resort, under assault from 700 000 holiday-makers every year. The "Pearl of the Sahel" manages its tourist potential skilfully: feet in the water, with just the right touch of local colour. After a day of sun and sea, tourists stroll about in the evening along the promenade lined with palms, where the scent of orange flower petals and *chicha* float in the air. Although heavily restored, the old fortified city still has many picturesque scenes: red mullet coming into the market, fresh from the sea and neatly arranged in wooden boxes; dates or spices being sorted; children dancing spontaneously to the latest local pop song.

Visitors attracted to Sousse and the Sahel are not only foreigners, for this "California of the Maghreb" exercises an irresistible appeal over young unemployed Tunisians, fascinated by the rarely fulfilled vision of a Western way of life.

The city with four names
Founded by the Phoenicians in the 9C BC, Sousse, like Utica, can take pride in being older than Carthage. The little trading post soon became a flourishing city under the name of **Hadrumetum**, but in the 6C BC it had to come to terms with the powerful city of Carthage. In the first two Punic wars, the people of Hadrumetum were ranged alongside their Carthaginian cousins, and the town served as a rear base for Hamilcar. The city barely survived each of these interminable struggles and turned to treason: during the Third Punic War it took the side of Rome. It was a well-rewarded betrayal, for Carthage was wiped off the map and the Romans granted Hadrumetum the status of free city.

In the 1C BC Hadrumetum was once more drawn into struggles which overwhelmed it. This time it backed the wrong side, taking the side of Pompey against Caesar, and lost its privileges. Roman domination was still useful, however, and from the reign of Augustus the town became an important commercial centre once again. Trajan (AD 98-117) granted it the status of colony, and Diocletian (AD 284-305) made it the capital of Byzacena, a vast province which included the whole of the centre of Tunisia.

Sousse

The medina ramparts, Sousse

A worthy capital of a Roman province, the city was equipped with all the infrastructure necessary for the Roman way of life: baths, theatres and temples, of which virtually nothing remains. The Christian era left more traces, like the catacombs or the splendid mosaics on display in Sousse museum. This luxury did not pass unnoticed by the Vandal soldiery who arrived in Africa in the 5C. Huneric, one of the barbarian chiefs, seized Hadrumetus for himself, and the town found itself designated with the grandiose name of **Hunericopolis**. Recaptured by the Byzantines around 535, the old city was renamed once more, and was known as **Justianopolis** until the arrival of the Arabs.

It was a shattering arrival, for the horsemen of Uqba Ibn Nafi were not patient people. Irritated by a delay caused by two months of siege, they were determined to make these "Justiniapolitans" pay dearly for their arrogance. Barely a stone was left standing in the city, which nevertheless acquired the charming nickname of **Siussa** – hence Sousse.

50km inland, Kairouan, the new capital, needed access to the sea. This was provided by Sousse, which enjoyed fresh prosperity, but when the Fatimids came to power and the capital moved to Mahdia, it was eclipsed for a time. Under Turkish domination Sousse lived off piracy, like so many other coastal towns (*see page 209*). In the 18C this led to reprisals from the European nations, including bombardments by the Venetians and the French. Following an apparently irreversible decline in the 19C, Sousse came to life again under the French Protectorate. The construction of a railway line and a commercial port confirmed it in its former role of regional centre. Only the names are different: no longer "capital of Byzacena" but "chief town of the Sahel".

Sousse inside and outside the walls

Allow half a day, including 2hr for the museum

In the old city

Enter the medina through the Place des Martyrs. This square follows the line of the former **town wall**, which has disappeared here, destroyed in the Second World War. The area lined with cafés forms a link between the medina and the European town. A sculpture with eight figures similar to Rodin's "Burghers of Calais" commemorates the martyrs of Sousse. Behind them, set into the ramparts, is the copy of a famous mosaic uncovered at Sousse *(now in the Bardo museum)*: it shows Virgil surrounded by the Muses of poetry and history. Seen from outside the walls, the medina offers an enchanting vision, with palm trees and the dazzlingly new-looking walls which appear to come straight from a film set. It is difficult to believe that they date from 859, despite the confirmation in an inscription in Cufic lettering on the southern rampart. The walls should be imagined facing the sea, as they were before the commercial harbour and the modern city were built.

The kiosk at the entrance to the medina, opposite the mosque, sells entrance tickets for the Great Mosque and the ribat.

The **Great Mosque**⋆ *(immediately on your left; 8am-2pm, Fridays, 8am-1pm; entrance charge)* looks more like a fortress than a place of prayer, and this appearance is further accentuated by the lack of a minaret. Built on the site of the old Kasbah around 850, its role was originally defensive. Together, with the neighbouring *ribat* (fortified monastic building), it protected access to the port. The **courtyard** dates back to the 9C, but the arcaded **portico** is a 17C construction. Non-Moslems are not allowed into the Holy of Holies, but when the gates are open it is possible to admire the **prayer hall**: it has 13 bays, their vaulting resting on a forest of columns and ancient capitals. The central section which leads to the *mihrab* is topped with two cupolas.

Ribats and soldier-monks

Ribats are veritable fortresses of faith, fortified monasteries which were designed for both military and religious purposes, and which make their first appearance in the 8C. Having seized Ifriqiya, the Arabs felt the need to maintain their conquests from Christian incursions. Over a long period the threat came from the sea, and in order to deal with it the Moslems studded their coasts with fortresses, from Alexandria all the way along to Ceuta in Morocco. Ribats were part of this defensive system, but were also centres for the propagation of the word of the Prophet. They were kept by soldier-monks, who handled the scimitar and the Koran equally well. For the faithful it was a place for teaching the Koran, a stop along the way on the pilgrimage to Mecca, and a shelter in case of enemy attack. As pressure from Christians diminished, the role of the ribats became more spiritual than military.

The fortified monastic building stands quite near the Great Mosque, a little higher up inside the medina, on the right.

Like other monuments in the medina, the **ribat**⋆ *(8am-7pm in summer; 8.30am-5.30pm in winter, entrance charge)* has been subjected to a thorough-going restoration. Without the ancient columns of the **entrance porch**, stripped bare and heavily damaged, one might doubt its authenticity. Yet the monastery dates from the 8C and, together with the similar building in Monastir, it is one of the largest in the Maghreb.

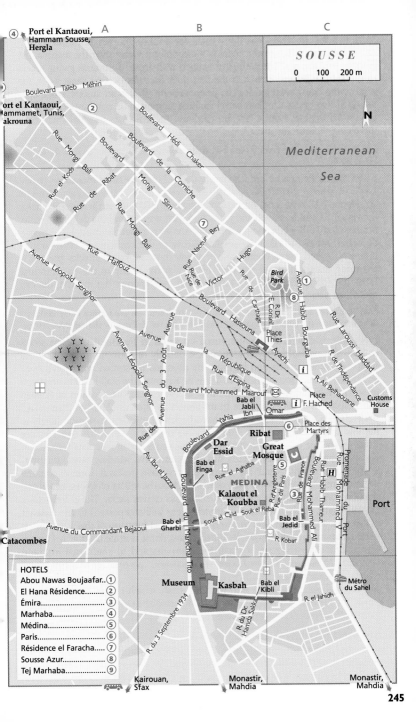

SOUSSE

0   100   200 m

N

Mediterranean

Sea

HOTELS

Abou Nawas Boujaafar.. ①
El Hana Résidence......... ②
Émira............................ ③
Marhaba........................ ④
Médina.......................... ⑤
Paris............................. ⑥
Résidence el Faracha..... ⑦
Sousse Azur.................. ⑧
Tej Marhaba.................. ⑨

④ Port el Kantaoui,
Hammam Sousse,
Hergla

Port el Kantaoui,
Hammamet, Tunis,
Akrouna

Boulevard Taïeb Méhiri

②

Boulevard Hédi Chaker

Boulevard de la Corniche

Rue Mongi Bali

Rue el Kods

Rue de Ribat

Boulevard

Rue Mongi Bali

Mongi Slim

Rue Haffouz

Avenue Léopold Senghor

⑦

Rue Naceur Bey

Rue de Nice

Hugo

Victor

Rue de Carthage

Bird
Park

⑧

Avenue Habib Bourguiba

①

Rue Laroussi Haddad

Boulevard Hassouna Ayachi

R. Dr.
E. Conseil

Place
Thies

R. de Thédépendance

i

R. Ali Belhaouane

Customs
House

Avenue de la République

Rue d'Espina

Boulevard Mohammed Maarouf

✉

Bab el
Jabli
Ibn

🚌 **i** F. Hached

Omar

Place

Place des
Martyrs

Promenade du Port

Rue Mohammed V

Port

Avenue Léopold Senghor

Avenue du 3 Août

Avenue de la

Rue des

Rue Ibn Yahia

Boulevard

**Dar
Essid**

Ribat

⑥

**Great
Mosque**

⑤

Rue Habib Thameur

H

Bab el
Finga

Rue el Aghalba

MEDINA

Rue d'Angleterre

Rue de Paris

Rue de France

③

**Kalaout el
Koubba**

Bab el
Gharbi

Souk el Caïd Souk el Reba

Bab el
Jedid

Rue Habib Thameur / Rue Mohammed Ali

R. Kobar

Catacombes

Avenue du Commandant Bejaoui

Av. Ibn el Jazzar

Boulevard du Maréchal Tito

Museum

Kasbah

Bab el
Kibli

Métro
du Sahel

R. du 3 Septembre 1934

R. Dr.
Hamda Sakka

R. el Jahidh

Kairouan,
Sfax

Monastir,
Mahdia

Monastir,
Mahdia

245

Small in scale the ribat looks like a castle for dolls or gnomes, but from the top of the *nador*, or watch-tower, there is a magnificent **view**★ over the medina, the harbour and the sea. The courtyard is lined with arcaded porticos giving access to the **soldier-priests' cells**. On the first floor the cells occupy three sides, the south wing being reserved for the **prayer room**. This is an austere space consisting of two bays with plain barrel vaulting supported on substantial cruciform pillars; light comes from a few slit windows. Archeologists consider that this is the oldest mosque in Africa.

Return to the ramparts behind the ribat, and follow the surrounding wall to the left for about 300m.

At 65 rue du Rempart Nord, the heavy door of the **Dar Essid Museum**★ (*10am-7pm in the summer, 10am-1pm / 3pm-6pm out of season; entrance charge*) opens to reveal an elegant 10C residence. An explanation sheet given out at the entrance helps the visitor to wander at will and easily find their way around the delightful patio, ornamented with a ceramic patchwork. As visitors progress through the richly-decorated rooms, whether the smallest alcove or the kitchen, the Essid family's intimacy is laid bare. Photos and a whole host of knick-knacks provide a charming insight into the everyday life of a noble family in the past century. From the top of the 65m-high tower which overshadows the medina, the city sprawls at your feet.

Plans are afoot to install a little bar selling refreshments on the terrace early 2000.
Return towards the Great Mosque and take either the rue de Paris or the rue d'Angleterre.

From here you enter the most spruced-up **souks** in Tunisia. Unlike the souks in Sfax, for example, they consist almost entirely of souvenir shops: fake old puppets, leather jackets and luggage, toy dromedaries stuffed with polystyrene and other "exotic" souvenirs. As in Tunis or Kairouan the stall-holders greet you in several languages, but here the range is wider, with the addition of Russian and Polish. "*Dzien dobry*" can be heard almost as often as "*hello*" or "*Guten Tag*" since charter-loads of Slav visitors have begun to invade the seaside hotels in the low and medium seasons. Like the city's medina – which has figured since 1986 on the list of world heritage sites – the souks are immaculately clean but also well preserved. They stretch out along attractive winding lanes, intermittently covered with vaulting. Some traders have resisted tourist-tempting presentation more effectively than others, such as the sellers of spices, beans and semolina who display their goods in enormous canvas sacks. The el Reba souk on your right, leads you into a courtyard (very well-signposted) to the **Kalaout el Koubba**. Experts have yet to determine the exact function of this 11C edifice: palace, hammam or otherwise. Its fluted-zigzag dome is quite unique in Tunisia. The building now houses a small **museum** devoted to traditional arts and customs (*10am-1pm / 4.30pm-7.30pm in the summer, 3pm-6pm out of season, closed Fridays, entrance charge*).

The souk el Reba continues into the Caïd souk, which climbs up steps to the top of the medina. There is a more authentic atmosphere in this part of the old town with ironworkers' forges, baths and forgotten old houses.

Sousse Museum★★ (Le Musée de Sousse)

9am-noon; 3pm-6pm in summer, 9am-noon; 2pm-5.30pm in winter, closed Mondays; entrance charge. The layout is not in chronological order, so the rooms of the museum need not be explored in any particular order. Only the most important rooms are men-

tioned here. Tunisia's second most important museum occupies part of the former Kasbah at the top of the medina. For anyone unable to see the mosaics in the Bardo museum, this is an excellent alternative. The mosaics are superb, and the setting in which they are displayed is calm and welcoming.

The visit begins with a very pretty terrace with white arcading round a small garden. Among other fragments of sculptures and mosaics, the south gallery of the patio displays a fine **tragic mask in marble***. The east gallery contains various Roman epitaphs. You will also see here the **tomb** of a young boy – "Cæcilius Silvanus, dead at the age of 6 years" – on which are depicted bowls and cooking utensils as a reminder that funeral meals at the tomb of the deceased were a common practice until the 4C. The north and west galleries are more particularly devoted to mosaics and epitaphs from the early Christian and Byzantine period. The most handsome items come from the city's catacombs. The stele of the **Good Shepherd**, which has given its name to one of the catacombs, represents a shepherd bearing a ewe on his shoulders. This Christian image was already present in Græco-Roman statuary in the form of Hermes Criophorus ("bearing a ram") holding a lamb on his shoulders. The 4C **funeral mosaic of Hermes** has also given its name to one of the catacombs. It embellished the floor of a funeral hall and probably illustrated the words of St Paul: "like an anchor sure and firm for the soul". At the corner of the two galleries is a monumental **mosaic of the god Ocean*****. This 2C work once graced the pool of a villa in Hadrumetus.

From the terrace there is access to Rooms A and H. The first displays various sculptures and inscriptions, with the most memorable being a mosaic with a central medallion showing a **Medusa's head****, it was part of a 2C or 3C pavement from the private baths of a local Roman villa. The most beautiful mosaics, most of which were discovered in Sousse and El Jem, are grouped together in Room H. The **Triumph of Bacchus***** (3C) is one of the finest pieces in this group, showing the young god in a chariot drawn by four tigresses with a satyr holding the reins. He is accompanied by Victory and a tambourine-playing mænad. Another masterpiece, **Neptune's chariot*****, which has remained in a remarkable state of preservation, is a very finely worked mosaic dating from the 3C. **Zeus carrying off Ganymede**** (3C) illustrates an episode in classical mythology: Zeus, in love with Ganymede, changes himself into an eagle and carries off the young shepherd-prince to Mount Olympus. The scene, which fills the centre of the mosaic, is surrounded by eight medallions depicting various circus animals. Another mosaic of lesser quality illustrates the same topic. The room is also worth visiting for a marine mosaic showing **fishing scenes*** and a great variety of sea creatures. The vast mosaic known as the **Nile landscape** is in very poor condition, but it is perhaps this one which most keenly engages the imagination. As a picture which probably depicts the fauna and flora of the Nile it is a fascinating achievement.

Corridor B leads to Rooms D, E and F which display funeral furnishings discovered in Carthaginian and Roman burial grounds and in the catacombs.

This passage leads to a large garden at the foot of the surrounding walls. It is a good place to pause for a while, surrounded by sections of columns and fragments of stone. From the garden there is access to three rooms in sequence (I, J, K), with the first and last containing three fine works. The **Mosaic of the Tragic Poet**** (3C) depicts the world of the theatre: standing next to a seated person (perhaps the playwright), the actor holds in his hand the mask of his role. Papyrus rolls at their feet perhaps indicate that they contain the text of the play. In the last room, the **Smirat mosaic**★★ depicts a battle between gladiators and wild animals. Apart from the gladiators' names, there are the commentaries and acclamations of the spectators. From the other side of the room, a headless marble represents a **Priapus**★ (badly damaged). As the protective deity of gardens he bears a basket of fruit and vegetables on his monstrous phallus.

As you come out of the museum you will see on your left the **tower of Khalef**, a lighthouse built in 859, which forms the highest point of the medina.

The catacombs

8am-noon, 3pm-7pm in summer; 9am-noon, 2pm-6pm in winter, closed Mondays; entrance charge. The site is really only accessible by car, and it is advisable to seek directions from the museum staff, as the route is only very roughly indicated. These catacombs, which were discovered at the end of the 19C, are among the most important in the classical world, matching those of Rome, Naples and Syracuse. They have 240 galleries extending over nearly 5km and containing some 15 000 burial places. Only the **Catacomb of the Good Shepherd** is open to the public. It owes its name to the marble memorial representing a shepherd bearing a ewe *(see museum, above)*. A winding passageway leads to some of the tombs and to rooms equipped with benches, for it was to here, faithful to an old pagan custom, that the first Christians in Africa came for their funeral feasts.

North of Sousse

Port el Kantaoui

Just under 10km north of Sousse. Leave by the corniche road and head towards Tunis. To-

E. Boucher/MICHELIN

The two "old ladies" of Takrouna

day, Port el Kantaoui is the leading holiday complex in Tunisia. Built by the eminent Tunisian architect Cacoub (who also designed the new station in Tunis), this large-scale tourist development took its shape and colours from the famous village of Sidi Bou Saïd: arcading, domes, traditional moucharabias (iron grilles over windows, allowing fresh air into the house but concealing the interior), floral courtyards. A haven for pleasure craft, it has mooring space for more than 300 boats. Swimming, sailing, waterskiing, horseriding, golf – it is all available at Port el Kantaoui, in a relaxed and exclusive atmosphere where pedestrians and the red-wheeled wooden carriages have priority. Luxury hotels, discos, restaurants and casinos are on the look-out for tourists, as are the traders in the "genuine" souk and organisers of sea trips aboard mock galleons and glass-bottomed boats. The overall effect gives a very falsified image of Tunisia: an artificial paradise which has nothing at all to do with its surroundings.

Hergla

27 km to the north of Sousse. After Port el Kantaoui, follow the signs straight on to Hergla. From Sousse, catch the 18 bus.

The way in which this charming little village only a few kilometres from Port el Kantaoui has resisted the onslaughts of invading tourists is almost miraculous. The little fishing port built on the edge of a cliff still evokes an appealing picture of innocence to the delight of morning walkers. Start from the main square, where the mosque stands, and walk past the hundreds of tombs in the cemetery which almost seem to fall down the hill into the sea. As you make your way round the tiny winding streets, you will meet a few inhabitants busy weaving alfa on their doorsteps, while the muezzin calls out towards the sea. Perhaps the calm before the storm of tourists?

Takrouna

About 50km along the A 1 road. Be careful! This road is often very crowded. At Enfida, turn left towards Zaghouan at the roundabout with a clock. Takrouna is 6km away. You can park at the top if it is not too crowded. The tiny village can be seen in 15 minutes, but if you want to enjoy the viewpoint and visit a house, allow 30.

There is nothing very much to see at Takrouna, but in a brief visit this may be your opportunity to explore a small picturesque village, the opposite of Port el Kantaoui and the other coastal resorts. Takrouna clings to a rocky peak which looks across the Enfida plain. A steep road with hairpin bends climbs up to the height, with goats browsing at the road-side among the rocks and Barbary figs. According to local people, the old village has no water supply and no more than three families in permanent residence. Most of the inhabitants have moved down to the plain, into the new houses at the foot of the hill. Even though the village has been abandoned, you will be greeted by a rabble of little boys – you can take your pick as to who will guard your car or act as your guide. The two old ladies of Takrouna, who can be seen in traditional costume in some of the tourist guides, are never far away either. They will allow themselves to be photographed in return for a few coins.

Making the most of Sousse

GETTING THERE

By train – SNCFT railway station, bvd Hassouna Ayachi, ☎ 03 224 955. There are 11 trains daily arriving from Tunis. With the exception of local trains, all have air-conditioning and "comfort" class. (3hr). There are a dozen connections to Bir Bou Rekba, the station that serves Nabeul and Hammamet (1hr20min). There are 7 trains daily to El Jem (55min), 6 to Sfax (1hr45min), 3 to Gabès (5hr) and 1 night train to Gafsa (5hr30min).

Sahel Metro, Place Bab Jedid, ☎ 03 225 321. This is the name of the local railway that stops at nearly every station on the way to Monastir (18 trains daily, 30min) and Mahdia (11 trains, 90min). Trains are less frequent at the weekend and the fare is slightly more expensive.

By bus – Buses are ideal not only for travel but also for day trips. Only the SNTRI coaches (that go longer distances) are air-conditioned.

Departures from Place Sidi Yahi (near Place Farhat Hached), ☎ 03 224 382. **STS** has connections to Hergla (bus number 18, 4 departures daily, 45min), Chot Mariem (bus number 16, 6 departures daily, 30min), Monastir (bus number 52, 12 departures, 45min), Mahdia (14 departures, 90min).

Departure from Souk Lahed – The new railway station is next to the Sunday market place, 1km south of the medina on avenue du 3 septembre 1934, ☎ (03) 237 978. Six coaches departing to Sfax via El Jem (2hr 30min); 7 to Gabès (5hr); 1 to Jerba via Jorf and a night coach via Zarzis (6hr); 1 night coach to Matmata (7hr); 1 night coach to Tataouine (9hr); 2 coaches to Zarzis via Medenine, of which one is a night coach (5hr); 11 coaches to Kairouan (90min); 1 to Le Kef (4hr).

6 departures daily to Tunis (2hr 30min); 1 to Bizerta (13hr 30min) 5 to Nabeul via Hammamet (2hr); 1 to Zaghouan with a return trip during the same day (2hr).

10 buses daily to Enfidaville (1 hour); 2 to Le Kef via Fahs and Dougga (4hr 30min); 2 to Béja via Mejez el Bab (4hr).

By car – A toll motorway connects Tunis with Sousse.

By shared taxi – The rental station is opposite the bus station. Serves all of Tunisia's large cities: Tunis (TD6.350), Jerba (4hr), Gafsa (3hr), Tozeur (4hr).

By boat – The marina at Port el Kantaoui has 340 moorings, ☎ 03 241 799.

GETTING AROUND

By car – A car brings Monastir or Kairouan within easy reach.

By bus – **STS** (Sahel Transportation Company). Bus number 12 connects the city centre with Port el Kantaoui. Departures approximately every 20min from 7.30am to 8.15pm.

By taxi – The taxi stand is at Place Farhat Hached on the corner of bvd Hassouna Ayachi (formerly bvd René Millet), as well as Port el Kantaoui.

By tourist train – **The Happy Noddy Train**, ☎ 03 240 353 / 227 014. Departures every hour between Sousse Boujaffar and Port el Kantaoui from 9am-7pm. Fare: TD3.5.

Car hire – **Avis**, on the tourist road, Port el Kantaoui, ☎ 03 270 091.

Budget, 65 ave Habib Bourguiba, ☎ 03 227 611. Open daily 8am to 8pm including Sundays.

Europcar, on the Corniche, ☎ 03 227 562.

Hertz, ave Habib Bourguiba, ☎ 03 225 428 / 226 827.

Mattei (Ada), 13 rue Ahmed Zaatir, ☎ 03 219 704.

ADDRESS BOOK

• Sousse

Tourist information – (ONTT) 1 ave Habib Bourguiba, ☎ 03 225 157 / 225 158. Open in winter from 8.30am-1pm / 3pm-5.45pm from Monday to Thursday, 8.30am-1.30pm Fridays and Saturdays. Summer hours are 8.30am-7.30pm daily and 9am-12pm / 4pm-7.30pm on Sundays. The welcome is warm and useful information is available.

Tourist Information Kiosk, located in the small kiosk on Place Farhat Hached. Winter hours are 9am to 12pm and 2-5pm. Summer hours are 8am to 6pm and 8am to 12pm / 2-8pm on Sundays. This tiny office doesn't even have pamphlets to hand out and is therefore not particularly useful.

Regional Tourism Board, 1 ave Habib Bourguiba, ☎ 03 225 157, Fax 03 224 262.

• Port el Kantaoui

Emergency – Police Station, rue Pasteur, ☎ 03 225 566.

National Guard, ave Léopold Senghor, ☎ 03 225 588.

Neji Khelifa Night Pharmacy, 38 ave de la République, ☎ 03 224 795. Located 800m from Place Farhat Hached.

Abdelhamid Meddeb Night Pharmacy, 10 route de Tunis (on the tourist road coming from Sousse, turn left 1.5km beyond the Casa del Gelato on the ave de la Plage. At the clock, turn left and continue for 300m Hammam Sousse, ☎ 03 240 157.

Night doctors, bvd Mohammed el Karaoui, ☎ 03 224 444.

Dialysis Centre, bvd du 7 Novembre, ☎ 03 241 868.

Tourist information – Tourist office, ☎ (03) 246 540. **Regional Tourist Office**, ☎ (03) 241 799.

Banks / Currency Exchange – During the summer, the banks offer an exchange service even on bank holidays. **BNA**, ave Habib Bourguiba. Open in summer from 7am-1pm / 9.30am-3pm Saturdays and Sundays. Exchange service and Visa transactions available with a minimum withdrawal of 100 dinars. Not a particularly friendly reception, however this is the only bank open at the weekend.

DAB Visa, **Banque STB**, ave Habib Bourguiba.

American Express, ave Habib Bourguiba.

Foreign Money Exchange, Centre Soula, Place Sidi Yahia, ☎ 03 229 612, Fax 03 229 617. This small office is open nearly every day and changes cash and traveller's cheques.

Post office – On the corner of bvd Mohammed Maarouf and ave de la République, ☎ 03 224 518 / 231 622. Winter, open 8am-12pm and 3-6pm Fridays and Saturdays, closed on Sundays. Summer hours are 7.30am-1pm.

Internet – Publinet, in the Gloulou building, ave Mohammed Maarouf, behind the boy's secondary school, ☎ (03) 212 780. Every day 8am-8pm (Sundays from 3pm). TD3 per hour of connection.

Airline and shipping companies – Tunis Air, 5 ave Habib Bourguiba, ☎ 03 227 955 / 223 952, Fax 03 225 233.

CTN, rue Abdallah Ibn Zoubeir, ☎ 03 224 861, Fax 03 224 844.

WHERE TO STAY

Sousse has the largest selection of hotels, from the decent hotels in the medina to those on the edge of the water, a 5 minute walk from the city centre. The hotels all have a common factor: the noise, whether it's loud music or roaring traffic.

• In the modern city
From US$18-42

Hôtel Sousse Azur, 5 rue Amilcar, between the bird park and ave Habib Bourguiba, ☎ (03) 226 960 / 227 760, Fax (03) 228 145 – 22rm This establishment has everything to make it worth a stay: impeccable rooms, some of which have a balcony overlooking the sea, a friendly welcome and reasonable rates. Air-conditioning is planned for the summer 2000.

Résidence el Faracha (Butterfly), rue el Faracha (in a cul-de-sac, some 200m from the beach, at right angles to rue Naceur Bey near La Mama restaurant).

• In the Medina
Less than US$10-25

Hôtel de Paris, rue du Rempart Nord, ☎ 03 220 564, Fax 03 219 038 – 42rm Although this hotel dates from before the war, there is no sign of decay. It is remarkably well-maintained and extremely clean. It will charm anyone who accepts a basic level of comfort and shared showers on the landing in exchange for a low room rate. Breakfast is not served but can be taken for a small price at the Restaurant du Peuple below.

Hôtel Médina, 15 rue Othman, behind the Mosque, ☎ 03 221 722, Fax 03 221 794 – 55rm This hotel is a bit more expensive, but is nonetheless more comfortable. Only showers are available. Very pleasantly-decorated, contrary to the welcome given to clients.

Hôtel Emira, 52 rue de France, ☎ and Fax 03 226 325 – 16rm With a more or less equivalent level of comfort, plus a lovely view of the medina from the hotel's terrace on the third floor. Friendly service.

• At the beach
From US$42-75

Hôtel Marhaba, on the tourist road, ☎ 03 242 170 / 242 180 / 242 019 / 240 091, Fax 03 243 867 / 241 666 – 210rm This is one of the less costly options for anyone wanting a sea view. The rooms are spacious with balconies overlooking luxuriant gardens. An upmarket package holiday establishment with the ubiquitous sound of blaring music.

El Hana Résidence, on the Corniche, ☎ 03 225 818, Fax 03 226 076 – 129rm This is the most intimate of the three establishments along this section of the shore which belong to the same hotel chain. The others are Chems el Hana and El Hana Beach. Residents in any of the hotels can use the facilities in the other two. Supplement for a room with sea view.

More than US$75

Abou Nawas Boujaafar, at the end of ave Habib Bourguiba (heading towards the city centre), ☎ 03 226 030, Fax 03 226 574 – 234rm With the normal standard of comfort provided by this chain, this establishment has a beachside location in the middle of town plus a spa. Supplement for sea views.

Hôtel Tej Marhaba, bvd Taïeb Méhiri, ☎ 03 229 800, Fax 03 229 815 – 352rm ⏚ ✆ 📺 ✕ ⌇ ⌇ 💳 The foyer is decorated in marble in Oriental style. This hotel is typical of second generation properties (the sea is across the road). It's a shame that Tunisia's tradition of hospitality does not extend to the staff.

EATING OUT

• In the modern city

Less than US$10

Les Jasmins (C3), 22 ave Habib Bourguiba, ☎ (03) 225 884 ⏚ ⌇ Simple, clean establishment with a menu that features every variety of couscous imaginable. Set menu at about US$5.

Paradise Pizza (C2), in the Boujaafar commercial centre, ☎ 03 229 787. ⌇ The only advantage to eating here is the sea view and the peaceful atmosphere a stone's throw from the medina. This is so rare in Sousse that it's easy to forget about the food you are served.

From US$10-20

Le Bonheur (C3), Place Farhat Hached, ☎ 03 225 742. ⌇ Located on Sousse's main square between the medina and the beach, this restaurant serves classical Franco-Tunisian food.

L'Escargot (A1), 87 route de la Corniche (across from Hôtel Hana), ☎ 03 224 779, Fax 03 243 513. ⌇ 💳 This restaurant provides a varied menu for snail lovers and for anyone interested in French-style cooking. Try the snails cooked with bacon or the monkfish with tarragon.

⊛ **Le Lido** (C4), ave Mohammed V, ☎ 03 225 329. ⏚ ⌇ 💳 Across from the commercial port, separated from the sea by the railway line cutting across the city. This restaurant with its handful of tables on the pavement is a typical example of a Sousse restaurant. The grilled fish is cooked Sfax-style, lightly marinated in cumin.

La Marmite (C3), 15 rue de Rémada, ☎ 03 226 728. ⏚ This restaurant has made an effort even though the result is rather odd, with old Tunisian sideboards casually placed next to mock Roman frescoes. There is an à la carte menu featuring moules marinieres, "oja" with merguez sausage, couscous and steak with a Bearnaise sauce. The food is good, although the "méchouia" (barbecue of a whole roasted sheep) may be a bit spicy for some people.

La Calèche (C3), 6 rue de Rémada, ☎ (03) 226 489 ⏚ 💳 The sophisticated ambiance of this restaurant would be more reminiscent of a French inn if it weren't for the Roman mosaics that add a little local colour. The Franco-Tunisian menu is presented according to themes: children, vegetarian, tourist, Tunisian, hunting, fishing and royalty. Music on Saturday nights.

More than US$20

Le Gourmet (C2), 3 rue Amilcar (across from Hôtel Abou Nawas), ☎ 03 224 751. ⏚ The house specialties are lamb and fish cooked in an earthenware pot, that you must throw on the ground (outside) after being served because it brings good luck! Taïeb, the owner, is a veritable jack of all trades – a sculptor, painter, restaurateur and an entrepreneur.

L'Orange Bleue (not on the city map), ave Taïeb Méhiri, towards the Tej Marhaba, ☎ and Fax 03 227 682. ⏚ ⌇ 💳 This French-owned restaurant is decorated with lovely Tunisian handicrafts. A Tunisian chef has recently joined the staff to add diversity to the menu. They have even maintained the French tradition of serving a measure of spirits between the first and second courses.

• In the médina

Less than US$10

Restaurant du Peuple (C3), rue du Rempart Nord (to the right of the hôtel de Paris). This tiny eating-house brings its tables onto the pavement, improvising a little terrace in the shade of the ramparts, where there is always a light breeze, even in the height of summer. Decent, but not unforgettable, cooking.

Restaurant at the Hôtel Médina (C4), 15 rue Othman Osman, ☎ 03 221 772, Fax 03 221 794. Under the stone archways, the restaurant belonging to the hotel of the same name also offers tajines and "kamounia" as well as spaghetti and steak with Bearnaise sauce.

• Port el Kantaoui

From US$10-20

Neptune V, at the far end of the port, ☎ 03 246 730. ⏚ ⌇ 💳 A restaurant aboard a rather strange galleon. Considering the touristy location, the prices are reasonable.

More than US$20
Le Méditerranée, Port el Kantaoui, ☎ 03 240 788, Fax 03 246 972. ♈ 🏠 This establishment has the freshest fish in the harbour area. There is also a pleasant terrace overlooking the marina in summer. Closed Tuesdays.

Lau Daurade, Port el Kantaoui, ☎ 03 244 893. ♈ 🏠 CC Good quality fish at this overpriced restaurant. Closed Wednesdays.

WHERE TO GO FOR A DRINK

Cafés – Café Central (C4), Place des Martyrs, ☎ 03 221 547. Open 4am to 11pm. This café serves fresh orange juice on its terrace which is ideally located at the entrance to the medina.

Nightclubs – Maracana, Hôtel Tej Marhaba, on the tourist road, ☎ 03 229 800.

Samara King, Hôtel Samarha, on the tourist road 2.6km from Place Farhat Hached, ☎ 03 226 699. There is a piano bar and laser show.

LEISURE

Festivals – Sousse's International Festival, music and open-air theatre, rue Abou Kacem Chabbi from 1 July to 15 August. Performances primarily in Arabic.
Baba Aoussou Festival (in Arabic, August), concerts, folklore shows, parades with majorettes. In July and August.

Sports – El Kantaoui Golf Course, Port el Kantaoui, Hammam Sousse ☎ 03 241 756, Fax 03 241 755. An 18 and a 9-hole course on 103 acres close to the beach.
Centre de Plongée sous-marine (Underwater Diving Centre), ☎ 03 247 155 / 246 722.

Hammams – Hammam Shifa, 21 rue de la Victoire. Take the ave Zama Balaoui from the post office and continue in the direction of Tunis and Sousse. The hammam is at the end of the second cul-de-sac on the left, after the Renault garage. Open 6am-2pm for men and 2-8pm for women. Entrance is 900 millimes and massages are TD1. You need to bring your own towel and soap.

Hammam Sabra, rue Ali Belhaouane, in front of the Porte des Martyrs. Open mornings for men and afternoons for women.

SHOPPING

• **Sousse**
Weekly souk on Sundays.

Bakeries – Shérif, ave Habib Bourguiba, on the right next to the Restaurant des Jasmins. Specialises in ice cream and pastries.
Cherif, 83 ave de la République Trocadéro (near the night pharmacy). Soussians come from all over the city to buy their cakes here.

Ice-cream parlour – Casa del Gelato, bvd du 7 Novembre, 4.1km from the city centre, heading towards Hammam Sousse, ☎ 03 244 996, 244 997, Fax 03 244 998. Open 7am to midnight and until 1am in the summer.

Bookshop – Cité du Livre (Librairie Taïeb Kacem), 5 ave Habib Bourguiba, ☎ 03 225 097. Winter, open 8am to 8pm. In summer, open 8am to 2pm and 4-10pm. This shop has an impressive selection of French books.
Librairie el Maaref, rue de France, in front of Centre Soula, ☎ 03 221 734. In winter, open 8am to 7.30pm. In summer, hours are 8am to 1pm and 4-7.30pm.

Antiques – SOCOPA, ave Habib Bourguiba, Sousse, located on the first floor of the shopping mall at the Hôtel Abou Nawas Boujaafar (outside the hotel on the left), ☎ 03 229 900, Fax 03 229 904. Off season hours are 9am to 6pm and summer hours are 9am to 8pm. Open Sundays 10am to 6pm.
SOCOPA, rue des Jasmins, ☎ 03 241 066.
Centre commercial d'artisanat (Handicrafts shopping mall), Centre Soula, Place Sidi Yahia, ☎ 03 229 612, Fax 03 229 617. Open in winter, from 8am to 5pm. Summer hours are 8.30am to 9pm. Tunisian arts and crafts of every imaginable kind (including some items imported from India) are available at a price.

MONASTIR★

Pop c 36 000
Centre of governorship
20km from Sousse

Not to be missed
The ribat and the Bourguiba mosque.
A feast of fish at Le Pirate restaurant.

And remember...
The best hotels are in the tourist area.

Monastir seems to have an exaggerated idea of its own importance, for every-thing in it is out of proportion and slightly pretentious: broad avenues, vast palaces, alarmingly empty promenades and views, lawns worthy of rain-soaked Europe. The birthplace of the former president seems to have adopted his mod-ernist visions as "Supreme Combatant": Habib Bourguiba wanted to make a fresh start and this is what he achieved. The medina has vanished, torn apart by arte-rial roads driven straight through it. One-third of the old city was destroyed in the 1960s, and with it some of its 37 mosques, 20 *zawiyas* and its 5 *ribats*. New monumental buildings have appeared, elegant but without ornamentation, and rather cold. The result is a clean, artificial and somewhat soulless city.

Nevertheless, Monastir can boast several advantages: a superb, almost turquoise sea and a beach right in the middle of the town, at the foot of a venerable *ribat*. Its airs and graces notwithstanding, the city is really not much more than a seaside resort with a bigger than usual range of facilities, including a leisure harbour, a hotel area extending as far as Skanès, an 18-hole golf course and an international airport.

Exploring Monastir
Allow 2hr

Defying the open sea, imposing in its power and dignity, the **ribat**** *(see sidebar, page 244)* has been scrubbed like a new penny until it looks almost like a repro-duction. It is regularly used for filming, and it is almost impossible to make out which is genuine stone and which is the designer's work. Yet the oldest part of the building dates from 796, when it was the first Arab fortress built on the coast. Following successive alterations, the original *ribat* became "a fortress inside a fortress". The way in which the monastery has evolved over time reflects history and change in the town. In the 11C, following the sack of Kairouan by the Beni Hilal *(see page 20)*, many intellectuals and members of the religious community settled in Monastir, which became Tunisia's holy city and large numbers of the faithful flocked to it. No doubt they were attracted as much by the teachings of the imams as by the promise of a place in Paradise. According to tradition, the Prophet said: "In the west, in *Ifriqia*, is one of the gates of Paradise. Its name is Monastir. Whoever lives within its *ribat*, even for a single day, can be certain of enjoying eternal bliss". This spiritual dynamism continued until the 14C. After this period all was quiet in Monastir until the arrival of the Turks in the 16C, who turned it into a stronghold and altered the monastery buildings once more.

A **museum** *(8am-7pm in summer; 8.30am-5.30pm out of season)* has been established in the prayer hall, with beautiful illuminated versions of the *Koran* and manuscripts. No-one should leave the *ribat* without climbing up the nador, the

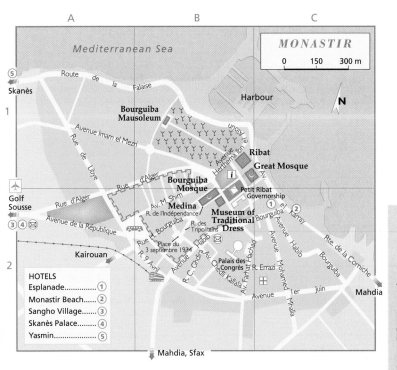

watchtower which offers an **overall view** of the building, the town and the bay. What looks like a modest fort below the *ribat* is in fact the **Great Mosque**. Built in the 9C, it was enlarged by the Zirids. A small **ribat** behind the mosque consists of a modest rampart and small round towers.

At the entrance to the **cemetery**, two octagonal pavilions flank the promenade leading to the Bourguiba family mausoleum. One is the Martyrs' Memorial (the equivalent of a European war memorial). At one time the cemetery stretched down to the sea. The modern coastal road and alterations to the tomb have taken away much of its provincial charm, but it still looks attractive. The **mausoleum** makes an interesting terminal feature at the end of the enormous promenade. Built in 1963, it has a gilded dome and a green-domed building on each side, one of them the tomb of Bourguiba's parents and his first wife. Two tall marble-clad minarets provide a solemn entrance to the funeral monument.

The **Bourguiba mosque** (1963), traditional in design, is remarkable for the richness of its décor. It has 19 carved teak entrance doors, the work of Kairouan craftsmen. The **prayer hall**, with its vaulting supported on 86 pink marble pillars, can hold a thousand of the faithful. The **mihrab**, indicating the direction of Mecca, is framed within onyx colonnettes. The **minaret** has all the features of the Ottoman style: octagonal in form, slender and delicate, topped with a small gallery.

On ave de l'Indépendance, to the left of the mosque, the **Museum of Traditional Dress** (Musée de costume traditionnel) *(9am-1pm / 3pm-6pm (7pm in the summer), closed Mondays; entrance charge)* owns a fine collection of wedding dresses in a dazzling array of velvet, silk, gold and silver.

Monastir

GETTING THERE

By air – Skanès Airport, on the road from Sousse, Skanès, ☎ (03) 521 300, on the tourist road between Monastir (5km) and Sousse(15km).

This international airport has direct flights to Paris, Lyon, Marseille, Nice and Strasbourg. There are Saturday flights to Munich, Frankfurt, Dusseldorf, Amsterdam, Vienna and Geneva. Sunday flights to Munich, Dusseldorf, Rome and Palermo. There are twice-weekly flights to Brussels and Luxemburg on Tuesdays and Saturdays. An STS bus departs hourly between the airport and Monastir.

Civil aviation, ☎ (03) 521 375.
Customs, ☎ (03) 521 300.

By train – SNCFT Station, ☎ (03) 460 755. There are two air-conditioned trains between Monastir and Tunis (2hr50min). Six other trains run along the same route with a stop in Sousse.

The **Métro du Sahel** is a local train with 18 daily trains to Sousse (25min), 12 to Moknin (30min) and 11 to Mahdia (1hr).

By bus – Bus station, located on the square on the corner of ave de la République and rue de Libye, ☎ (03) 461 059. Only **STS** (Sahel Transportation Company) provides service to Monastir, ☎ (03) 460 926 / 461 059. Coaches are not air-conditioned. Hourly departures to Sousse from 5.15am to 8.15pm (40min). There are three departures daily to Kairouan (TD3.4), as well as to Nabeul and Hammamet. The service to El Jem has been discontinued.

By car – Monastir is 160km from Tunis and approximately 20km from Sousse.

By shared taxi – The station is next to the bus station on ave de la République, ☎ (03) 520 059. The main destinations served by shared taxis are Tunis (TD6.5), Kairouan, (TD3.850), El Jem (TD2.9) and Mahdia (TD2).

By boat – Moorings at Cap Marina, ☎ (03) 462 305.

GETTING AROUND

By taxi – The main taxi stand is on the corner of the rue de Libye and the ave de la République, but you can also hail the yellow taxis in the city. Three stands have telephones: at the airport, ☎ (03) 464 003, across from Sahara Beach, ☎ (03) 464 002 and in front of Hôtel Abou Nawas, ☎ (03) 466 000.

By tourist train – The trip between the city centre and the hotels in the tourist area can be made by two small tourist trains:

La Flèche bleue, ☎ (03) 467 143. Departures from the Hotel Les Palmier in Skanès to Ribat Square in Monastir. Rates: TD2.5 adults, TD2 children. The train stops at the Dkhila Jockey Club, Ruspina and Festival hotels. There are three trips a day in the summer and two in the winter.

The Noddy Train goes from the city centre (on the corner of ave du Combattant Suprême) to the Hôtel Sahara Beach.

Car hire – A number of car rental agencies are located behind the Hôtel Esplanade as well as at the airport.

Avis, Skanès Airport, ☎ (03) 521 031.
Hertz, ☎ (03) 460 300. Open off season 8am-2pm and 2.30-6pm. Summer hours are 8am-12pm and 4-7pm.
Europcar, Skanès Airport, ☎ (03) 521 314.

Scooter rentals – Behind hôtel El Habib, ave Habib Bourguiba. TD40 a day for a scooter and TD12 for a bicycle.

ADDRESS BOOK

Emergency – Police Station, rue d'Algérie, ☎ (03) 461 431.
National Guard, rue Chedly Khallala, ☎ (03) 461 022.
Civil Protection, route du Port, ☎ (03) 198, 461 455.
Emergency assistance, ☎ (03) 190, 241 919.
Rida Chaouch Night Pharmacy, rue Chedly Khallala, ☎ (03) 463 311. Open 8pm-8am.

Airline Companies – Air Liberté, Skanès Airport, ☎ (03) 467 101, Chaouch building, on the road from Sousse, ☎ (03) 467 102.

Tunis Air, at the airport, ☎ (03) 462 550 / 462 566, Fax (03) 464 210. Freight: ☎ (03) 462 943.

Tourist information – ONTT, rue de l'Indépendance, near the Mosque. Open 7.30am-7pm, Sundays until 12pm. The office also has a stand at the airport.

Regional Tourism Board, in the tourist area near the Hôtel Skanès Palace, Skanès, (03) 520 205 / 520 089 / 520 894, Fax (03) 520 219.

Banks / Currency Exchange – There are banks, money exchange offices and cash dispensers all along the ave Bourguiba.

STB, ave Habib Bourguiba.

Banque du Sud, ave Habib Bourguiba.

UIB, ave Habib Bourguiba.

Post office – There are two post offices in the city, one on the ave Habib Bourguiba, the other on the ave de la République. In winter, open 8am-6pm and 9-11am on Sundays. In summer, the post office is only open Monday to Friday, 7.30am-1pm and evenings 5-7pm with fewer services available. Open Saturday 7.30am-1pm and Sundays 9-11am. The post office also has a currency exchange service. A third office that also provides a changing service is located at the Skanès Airport. Open 7am-7pm except Sundays when the opening hours depend on the flight arrivals.

Telephone / fax – Public telephones are available throughout the city, particularly near the Ribat. The public phones in the SNCFT train station also have fax facilities.

Internet – Monde Internet, in the railway SNCFT station, ☎ (03) 461 368. Around TD3-4 per hour. **Publinet Monastir**, Stambouli building, rue Mohammed M'halla, behind the city hall, ☎ (03) 467 136.

WHERE TO STAY

Monastir's distinctive geography means that some hotels combine the advantages of a beachside and city centre location. But the best beaches are in the tourist zone with its hotel complexes patronised mostly by package deal holiday-makers. The swimming is fine, but watch out for the jellyfish.

• **In the modern city**

From US$18-42

Hôtel Monastir Beach, on the Corniche, ☎ (03) 464 766 / 464 767, Fax (03) 463 594 – 45rm ⁋ ✗ ⚘ It's difficult to get any closer to the beach than this hotel which is located in the arcades under the road bordering the sea. It can be reached by going down a set of stairs leading to the beach. The rooms, although somewhat rustic, are not without charm. Air-conditioning should be available soon.

From US$42-75

Hôtel Club Esplanade, ave Habib Bourguiba, ☎ (03) 461 146 / 461 147, Fax (03) 460 050 – 130rm ⁋ ▮ ℱ ✗ ⚘ ⚘ ⚘ Right next to the Ribat, this hotel benefits from a central location facing the sea. The level of comfort has improved considerably since the hotel was renovated in 1996 despite the plastic plants and flowered wallpaper in the foyer.

• **At the beach (towards Skanès)**

From US$18-42

Hôtel Yasmin, on the cliff road (heading towards Skanès), ☎ (03) 501 456 – 15rm ⁋ ✗ ⚘ An architectural fantasy from A Thousand and One Nights. Its main attraction is its location right across the road from the beach. The grim interior decor and the plumbing in the showers (don't even hope for a bathtub) is showing its age. In summer, the restaurant is in the garden, which means that the rooms suffer from noise.

• **In the tourist zone**

From US$42-75

Skanès Palace, Dkila beach, ☎ (03) 461 350 – 232rm ⁋ ▤ ℱ TV ✗ ⚘ ⚘ ◖ ⚘ ⛭ CC Out of all the region's grand hotels, this one actually has the most atmosphere. Indeed this was where President Bourguiba used to receive foreign delegations when they came to Monastir.

Sangho village, tourist route, ☎ (03) 521 790, Fax (03) 520 788 – 150rm ⁋ ✗ ⚘ ⚘ CC Somewhere for those who prefer little bungalows to the massive concrete blocks on the beach. A holiday club with a good range of leisure facilities. During the summer, breakfast is served outside. Closed from October to April.

EATING OUT

Monastir is known for its tuna fishing. In the summer, the catch also includes "liche", a large white fish that the fishermen catch at the same time as the tuna.

• On the road from Mahdia

From US$10-20

El Farik (not on the town plan), on the Corniche heading towards Mahdia, ☎ (03) 468 555. ⚲ This restaurant with its triangular windows stands high above the ground, and eating here is a bit like being aboard a ferry. The chef offers a range of seafood, from octopus "kamounia" (a cumin stew) and seafood cooked in an earthenware pot (steamed with tomatoes).

Le Pirate (not on the town plan) (located at El Ghèdir fishing port, 2km from Monastir on the road to Mahdia), ☎ (03) 468 126. One of the best restaurants in Tunisia, but bird-like appetites would do well to abstain. Three set-menus with a full range of starters, grilled fish, desert and mint tea, for between US$10-20. In the summer however, there's only one menu available, dishes are served direct without ordering. As most of the clientele is Tunisian, the restaurant does not serve alcohol. Closed on Mondays and during Ramadan. Reservations are recommended.

• The harbour
(Cap Monastir)

From US$10-20

Le Chandelier (B1), ☎ (03) 462 232. ⚲ 🍴 CC You can sample a large selection of Franco-Tunisian specialities while watching the boats.

The Captain (B1), ☎ (03) 461 449, Fax (03) 473 820. ⚲ 🍴 CC This café-restaurant that caters to tourists made an effort with its decor. As far as the food goes, there is good grilled fish or sample the "koucha" (lamb stew).

WHERE TO GO FOR A DRINK

Cafés – Café-restaurant les Remparts, ave Habib Bourguiba, near the entrance to the medina.

LEISURE

Sports – Golf course, on the road from Ouardanine, BP 168, 5000 Monastir,

☎ (03) 461 095 / 461 148, Fax (03) 461 145. Turn left beyond the level crossing 4km from the town centre and continue for just over 2km through the olive groves.

The 18-hole course is TD30 per day (TD33 in summer) and TD170 per week (TD190 in summer).

Golf Palm Links, Dkhila, ☎ (03) 466 910 / 466 911.

Monastir Plongée et Loisirs (Monastir Diving and Leisure), Cap Marina, ☎ (03) 462 509.

Tunisie Yachting et Loisirs (Tunisia Sailing and Leisure), ☎ (03) 463 831.

Festivals – Cultural Festival, a medley of theatre, poetry, comedy and variety shows from the Arab countries and the Mediterranean basin. Mostly in Arabic. July-August.

Olive Tree Festival, in November-December. A variety of events organised around the olive harvest.

Hammams – Founa, ave Ali Ibn Abi Taleb, lot R4. Turn right after the post office on the ave de la République at the roundabout and continue for 100m. With its studded wooden door and blue and white dome, the hamman is easy to find.

SHOPPING

Markets – Weekly souks take place every Saturday. In the surrounding area there are markets in Ksibet el Mediouni (10km) on Thursdays, in Jemmel (18km) on Fridays, in Ksar Hellal (18km) on Tuesdays and in Moknine (20km) on Wednesdays.

Bookshops – Kiosque, ave Habib Bourguiba, near the post office.

Poly service, Place de l'Indépendance, ☎ (03) 463 054. Also has several public phones and fax facilities.

Librairie Le Phénix, rue Chedley Khallala, ☎ (03) 462 701.

Antiques – SOCOPA, rue Abdessalem Trimch. To the left of the Habib Bourguiba Mosque. ☎ (03) 462 190. Winter hours, 8.30am-7pm. Summer hours, 8.30am-8pm Monday to Saturday and 9am-1pm Sundays. Credit cards are accepted.

The Bourguiba mausoleum from the ribat

MAHDIA
Centre of Governorship
Pop c 37 000
6km from Sousse

Not to be missed
The sight of trawlers unloading their catch.
The boats fitted out with lanterns for fishing at night.
Tea at the Café Gamra.

And remember...
This is Tunisia's leading fishing port,
so enjoy the fresh fish.

The fishermen of Mahdia

Mahdia lies on the Sicilian Channel, one of the richest areas in fish of the whole Mediterranean. "Lamparo" fishing is traditional here, a technique inherited from the Sicilians: at night, the fish are attracted by electrically-lit navigation lights on the small boats, and trapped in nets. According to legend, the women of Mahdia sold their jewellery so that their husbands could buy the Sicilians' fishing fleet.

Mahdia is a little fishing port of classic Mediterranean charm, with its old fort (the borj el Kebir) and its vividly coloured fishing boats swinging at anchor. Life here is regulated by the sea and its offerings, and the squid, octopus and fish fresh from the sea attract plenty of idlers to the quayside. Until very recently Mahdia, Tunisia's leading fishing port, had escaped mass tourism, but this is less and less true; more and more hotels are being built in the "zone touristique" and souvenir shops are proliferating.

A dagger in a fist

Mahdia lies on a rocky peninsula which ends at Cap Afrique. Ibn Khaldoun saw in this proud promontory "a dagger held in a fist" and it was undoubtedly this factor that decided Obaïd Allah, known as *"El Mahdi"*, (The Saviour), to set the first stone of his future capital here. The strategic significance of the site was not lost on his successors either, from Roger of Sicily and Charles V to the Ottomans. The foundation of the town in 916 came at the end of seven years of violence and religious intolerance. Having overthrown the Aghlabids and proclaimed himself Imam, Obaïd Allah needed to consolidate his position in *Ifriqiya* against the Sunni majority. However, for the new Fatimid dynasty *Ifriqiya* was merely a stage in their conquest of the Islamic world, and when the *Mahdi's* successors conquered Egypt they abandoned Mahdia and settled in Cairo. The regency of *Ifriqiya* was entrusted to one of their lieutenants, the Berber Belogin Ibn Ziri and the Zirid dynasty was born. In the 11C the Zirids broke away from their Fatimid overlords to take revenge, in cowardly fashion, on the bloodthirsty hordes of the Beni Hilal *(see page 20)*. *Ifriqiya* was destroyed. Mahdia, isolated, resisted and turned to the sea; the town has lived off fishing ever since. In 1148 Mahdia was occupied by the Normans of Roger of Sicily. Later, the fortress was to suffer the assaults of the Genoese and the French, but it was the Spanish who caused the greatest suffering. The troops of Charles V, who captured the town in 1550, blew up the ramparts and the Great Mosque before departing. Prosperity did not return until the 16C, with Ottoman domination.

Strolling through Mahdia
Allow 2hr

Mahdia is above all a place to stroll, along the little lanes and beside the sea. Approach the town by the "dark gate", or **Skifa el Kahla**, a monumental gate built immediately after the Spanish period on the foundations of the 10C gateway. This was in fact a true fortified entrance with two bastions, used as gun emplacements. From the bastion terrace there is a **fine view★** over the town and the coast. The Ottomans altered the **vaulted passageway** which dates from the town's foundation. Originally it passed through a wall that was more than 10m thick, closing off the isthmus, and seven gates decorated with bronze lions guarded the entrance.

Beyond the gate is the **souk**, consisting of little more than a central street which is quickly explored. Traders come here regularly to sell jewellery and traditional clothing, including the marriage garments, silk ribbons and fabrics on which Mahdia's fame is built. The street runs past the little **Place du Caire★**, which is not without charm with its old arcaded cafés and its domino players dressed in chéchia and burnous.

The street opens out a little further on at the **Great Mosque** *(on the right)*, a low and compact building without a minaret. The current building is a copy built in the 1960s based on the design of the Fatimid mosque of 916, the Spanish having blown up the original building in 1554. The mosque is entered through an imposing **porch**. Only the *Mahdi* and his suite were permitted to pass through this porch, with more ordinary mortals using the side doors. The very large **prayer hall** was designed on the lines of the Kairouan prayer hall with a central aisle larger than the other bays. Further along the cliff road behind the mosque is the **borg el Kebir** *(9.30am-4.30pm in winter; 9am-noon, 2pm-6pm in summer; entrance charge)*. This 16C Turkish fortress dominates the cape; from the top of its ramparts there is a fine **view** of the **sailors' cemetery**, where the women of Mahdia gather on Thursdays in the late afternoon. Still visible is the water-gate, the **Bab el Bahr**, an arch which guarded the entrance to the harbour.

The sailors' cemetery and the old port

J. Guillard/SCOPE

Mahdia

GETTING THERE

By car – Mahdia is 62km from Sousse if you follow the coastal road.

By train – *SNCFT Train Station*, ☎ (03) 680 177. There are 2 trains daily to Tunis. There is also the *Sahel Metro*, a local train that stops at all the stations on the way to Sousse (11 trains daily, 90min).

By bus – Bus station, Place du 1ᵉʳ Mai, ☎ (03) 680 372. Both the STS and SO-RATRAS buses use this station as a base. There is hourly service to Sousse during the day (90min, TD2.4), 3 buses to Sfax (2hr) and 1 to Nabeul.
Mahdia has no *SNTRI* service, and to get to Tunis it is necessary to take the bus from Ksour Essaf, 10km south of Mahdia on the road from Sfax. The bus stops in front of the Hajer Café opposite the Esso petrol station.

By shared taxi – Place de la Gare. Shared taxis to different destinations throughout the country, particularly to Sousse (1hr, TD2.5), Jerba (5hr, TD15), Gabès (3hr, TD9) and Sfax (1hr15min, TD4.150).

GETTING AROUND

By car – With a car it is easy to visit Monastir, Sousse, or visit the El Jem Festival in the summer.

Taxis – ☎ (03) 605 900.

Tourist train – *Bel Azur*, ☎ (03) 681 241. This little train tours the city and returns to the hotels. On Fridays, Bel Azur organises a shuttle between the tourist area and the hotels. Fare: TD3.

Car hire – *Avis*, ave Habib Bourguiba, ☎ (03) 696 342.
Hertz, ave Habib Bourguiba, ☎ (03) 671 255.
Mattei (Ada), 77 rue du 7 Novembre, ☎ and Fax (03) 696 716.

ADDRESS BOOK

Emergency – *Police Station*, ave Taïeb Méhiri, ☎ (03) 681 099 / 681 419. Hiboun, ☎ (03) 681 303.

Tourist Police, ave Habib Bourguiba, ☎ (03) 681 221.
National Guard, ave Bechir Sfar, ☎ (03) 680 381.
Customs, ave Farhat Hached, ☎ (03) 680 588.
Khalfallah Moncef Night Pharmacy, Place du 1ᵉʳ Mai, ☎ (03) 681 490.

Tourist Information – *ONTT*, rue el Moéz, at the entrance to the medina, ☎ and Fax (03) 681 098. The office, located in a former "marabout", is open from 7.30am-6pm in summer, 8.30am-5.45pm in winter. Closed on Sunday.

Banks / Currency Exchange – Banks are open from 8am to 4pm Mondays to Fridays in the off-season and 7.10am-12.20pm during the summer. They alternate in providing a permanent money exchange office open 4-7pm during the week and 9am-12pm on Sundays and holidays.
STB, ave Habib Bourguiba.
BIAT, ave Habib Bourguiba.
Banque du Sud, ave Farhat Hached.

Post office – ave Habib Bourguiba, ☎ (03) 681 714 / 681 388

WHERE TO STAY

Mahdia is yet another city that has succumbed to mass tourism. Its fabulous beach is now lined with the usual concrete structures.

From US$18-42
Hôtel Corniche – ave du 7 Novembre, ☎ (03) 694 201 / 692 196– 7rm 🛁 While this is the most economic place to stay, it is certainly not the most romantic. The bathrooms are old. There is a supplement for rooms with a view of the sea and for rooms with en-suite shower.

From US$42-75
Hôtel Dynastie, on the tourist road, ☎ (03) 694 889, Fax (03) 694 300 – 76rm 🛄 📺 ✕ 🍴 🐾 cc This is an unpretentious and well-kept hotel.
Sirocco Beach, ave du 7 Novembre, ☎ (03) 671 655, Fax (03) 671 920 – 70rm 🍽 🍷 ✕ 🍴 🐾 cc Among the hotels recently built in Mahdia, this one is closest to the city centre. Satellite television is optional.

Cap Sérail, on the tourist road, ☎ (03) 672 300, Fax (03) 671 532 – 75rm ⚑ 🖾 🖉 ✗ 🕮 🐾 CC With only 75 rooms, this hotel has a more human scale. The Moorish style decor is very attractive though perhaps not to everyone's fancy.

El Mehdi, on the tourist road, ☎ (03) 672 300 / 301, Fax (03) 671 309 – 280rm ⚑ 🍷 🖾 🖉 ✗ 🕮 🐾 ✗ 🐾 CC Part of this enormous establishment consists of chalets. The 30-year-old hotel boasts luxurious gardens. Televisions are available for a supplement. Full board is compulsory from March 2000.

More than US$75

Cap Mahdia (belonging to the Abou Nawas chain), on the tourist road, ☎ (03) 680 300, Fax (03) 696 632 – 263rm ⚑ 🖉 ✗ 🕮 🐾 CC This Arab-Moorish style hotel with its Moroccan influence is set amidst lush vegetation. The establishment also has 35 bungalows, pompously named "Summer Pavilions". Rates start with half board.

El Borj (belonging to the Abou Nawas chain), on the tourist road, ☎ (03) 694 602 / 694 677, Fax (03) 696 632 – 228rm ⚑ ✗ 🕮 🐾 CC Stay in a "Summer Pavilion" (comprising 4-6 rooms), where you will not be deafened by the constant music many of the hotels blare. The music is played softly. Rates start with half board.

EATING OUT

Less than US$10

Médina, Place du 1ᵉʳ Mai, next to the market, ☎ (03) 680 607. Local people and tourists alike come here to sample the fish couscous or the "kamounia", which are both under US$8 but are served without alcohol. Only the freshest ingredients go into the food here, but as they tend to run out during the course of the evening it is best to get here early.

From US$10-20

🍴 **Le Lido**, ave Farhat Hached, ☎ (03) 681 339 🍷 �café The terrace is full every evening, and although many Mahdians will give up their seat to a foreigner this kindness should not be relied upon. The fish is extremely

fresh. The chef's only fault is his tendency to drown the seafood salad in mayonnaise.

L'Espadon, on the Corniche (next to the Hôtel des Sables), ☎ (03) 681 476. 🍷 �café Come here to eat on the terrace that overlooks one of the most beautiful beaches in all of Tunisia.

Neptune, ave du 7 Novembre (which eventually becomes the Corniche), ☎ (03) 681 27. 🍷 �café CC Grotto – not to say grotty – style decor, but excellent fish dishes. Who cares, though, when the fish is good.

WHERE TO GO FOR A DRINK

Cafés – 🍴 **Café Sidi Salem**, located just beyond the Mosque on the road heading towards the fort. This is a romantic spot much favoured by the Mahdians after a quiet walk through the cemetery.

🍴 **Café Gamra**, place du Caire. Reminiscent of France's Provence, with little tables set in the heart of a delightful square under the shade of four large trees.

Café de Tunis, Place du 1ᵉʳ Mai, behind the harbour.

Café de Mahdia, Place du 1ᵉʳ Mai, across from the Café de Tunis.

L'Espadon, on the Corniche, ☎ (03) 681 476. Lovely beachside terrace (see the above section on restaurants).

Festivals

Fishing Days in June. A variety of events organised around sardine fishing.

Mahdia Nights, in July. Variety shows of local or Mediterranean music.

SHOPPING

Markets – Weekly souk every Wednesday. Also at Ksour Essaf (12km) on Mondays, Moknine (23km) on Wednesdays and Ksar Hellal (21km) on Tuesdays.

Bookshops – Maison de la Presse, Place du 1ᵉʳ Mai. Open 7am-1pm / 3.30-7.30pm. Closed Sundays and Monday afternoons.

KAIROUAN ★★★
Centre of Governorship
Pop c 140 000
Climate: dry and very hot in summer
The mausoleum of the Barbier

Not to be missed
The Great Mosque.
And remember...
Avoid Mondays, because of tourist crowds.
Practically all the guides, official or otherwise
will take you to a carpet factory at some point or other.

The first sight of Kairouan is of a city made up of white low-lying buildings, an essentially horizontal silhouette broken only by the spikes of innumerable minarets. The minarets express Kairouan's celestial aspirations, and the city is of course the fourth holy place of Islam, after Mecca, Medina and Jerusalem. But it is a place that is firmly attached to the earth as well. Fields stretch to the horizon, and every morning the central market is full of their produce: vivid red peppers, tomatoes and fat pumpkins, grain and apricots.

Inside the great town walls is the large open-air souk, with its striking air of abundance and energy. It is full of traders busying themselves with their displays and of craftsmen attending to their work or enjoying a glass of tea. Gleaming daggers, jewels and piles of henna are displayed next to flat round loaves of bread or the heaps of *makhrouds* (little cakes soaked with honey and stuffed with dates) that are Kairouan's speciality. Outside the walls, once past the various "palaces" dedicated to crafts or carpets, there are streets and tiny shaded squares, richly-planted gardens full of birds and open-air cafés where conversation runs as naturally as the looms of the *mergoum*. Although the note of the muezzin is a constant feature, the sound of scooters is always audible throughout the town, together with the strains of the latest pop song.

Kairouan the Holy, "Mother of Cities"

Founded in AD 666 by the Arab conqueror Uqba Ibn Nafi, Kairouan was at first a rear base, a resting post for soldiers and their exhausted animals – hence its name of Kairouan, *karwan*, which in Arab means "staging post". But the town's new masters saw several advantages in settling in this dry plain, located at a satisfactory distance from a sea full of threatening Christian flotillas, and from mountains full of rebellious Berbers.

Kairouan was quick to appreciate the simple delights of regular and abundant harvests, the result of irrigation and the fertile soil of neighbouring wadis. Construction started on a great fortress-like Mosque, several Moslem colleges, a medina built of earth and brick, and a more substantial surrounding wall. The town became an important market for olive oil, fruit, camels and horses, as well as for wool, pottery and, later on, carpets. The first city built in the Maghreb by the Moslem conquerors, it soon benefited from the idea that a Moslem who made the pilgrimage to Kairouan seven times could dispense with the journey to Mecca: Kairouan thus established itself as the capital of several Arab dynasties, from the Aglabids to the Zirids. It was the demands and acts of barbarity committed by the Hilalians that eventually brought about its ruin. As Ibn

Khaldoun wrote, "In this great catastrophe, everything in the town was carried away or destroyed, the inhabitants scattered far and wide". The holy city was never to regain its past influence, and it was in this dark period that a fierce spirit of distrust and an attitude of withdrawal were born in Kairouan, or in what remained of it. Until the 19C the town was known to be intolerant, refusing to accept Christians or Jews, but this was gradually reversed during the French Protectorate, and above all under the presidency of Habib Bourguiba. At this time, the Kairouan mosques were the only ones in the country to open their doors to non-Moslem foreigners; this practice was maintained over the years, and extended to most of the holy sites in Tunisia. In this way Kairouan acquired its modern appearance of a "town of shrines" open to influences from abroad. Habib Bourguiba, known for his own pure and unflinching agnosticism, was supposed to have deliberately exposed Kairouan to the "religion" of tourism, in order to bring down the holy city and make it a town like any other. In this, apparently, he was successful.

In the steps of the pilgrims
Allow half a day for a very quick visit,
or a day to absorb the atmosphere and bargain for a rug.

It is best to apply direct to the tourist office – in front of the Aghlabid basin, facing the Continental hotel (7.30am-6pm in summer; 8.30am-6.30pm in winter) – which sells a combined ticket for visiting all the monuments. Avoid Mondays, when most of Tunisia's museums are closed: tour operators along the coast choose Mondays for their organised trips to Kairouan. There are official guides in the tourist office, who charge TD10 for a tour lasting about 90min. Be wary of the unofficial guides, touts on scooters or on foot who, on the pretext of showing you the Great Mosque, will lead you straight to a rug merchant with whom they have a financial arrangement.

Kairouan cemetery, a place for the living

J.-P. Garcin/DIAF

Kairouan has around a hundred mosques and several dozen *zawiyas* (tombs of saints and benefactors). It is therefore worth being selective to make the most of the town's particular atmosphere, which consists of far more than just its religious sites. Below, however, are some essential places to visit.

Visitors need only climb the stairs of the tourist office to admire the **Aghlabid Basin**

(9C), a vast 64-sided polygon, 5m deep. Built to maintain the town's water supplies, this reservoir of 55 000cu m was fed by a 36km aqueduct which brought water from the mountains. There were fourteen reservoirs of this type, for the city had between 250 000 and 300 000 inhabitants (compared to 140 000 today). The great basins were each matched by a smaller one which was used as a settling tank.

A second set of reservoirs has just been renovated, some fifty metres to the north-east of the tourist office.

Barbier Mausoleum*** – *Can be reached by car, when leaving the tourist office turn right and follow av Ibn Aghlab for around 2km.* Improperly named the Barbier Mosque, it is in fact a *zaouïa* in which is located the tomb of Abou Dhama, a companion of Mohomet, nicknamed Sidi Sahab, which means "carrier of three hairs" of the Prophet's sublime beard. Erected in the 7C, extended in the 17C, it was restored in the 18 and 19C.

This group of several rooms displays magnificent ceramics from Nabeul and Hispano-Moorish plaster-work panels reminiscent of the Alhambra in Granada. The *zawiya* includes **dormitories** which are available free to visiting pilgrims. These are vast rooms where believers can lodge their whole family: they are supplied with rush-matting and rugs. The pilgrims traditionally present offerings to the holy place: ex-votos – you will undoubtedly see some in the room containing the mausoleum – candles, rugs, and so on. According to one custom, young girls present the first rug that they make themselves to the *zawiya*, and for this reason the great number of rugs held there is hardly surprising – there are more than 800. Not all, of course, are on display. The **medersa**, or Koranic school, no longer operates and is now a prayer room.

The Great Mosque*** – *(8am-3pm, 8am-12.30pm Fridays). Go back along the ave Ibn Aghlab and turn right beside the tourist office. Next, turn left, and then right beside a tiny cemetery at the foot of the ramparts. Following the inconsiderate behaviour of some western visitors, neither the inside of the prayer room nor the stairs up to the top of the minaret are now open to visitors.* Founded by Sidi Udqba in the 7C, enlarged in the 9C under the brilliant Aghlabid dynasty and continually restored since then, this impressive mosque is the oldest Moslem place of prayer in the Maghreb. As with European cathedrals, houses huddled close under the protective wing of the Great Mosque which had stood at the centre of the city ever since its foundation. Following the destruction of much of Kairouan by the Beni Hilal, the city's centre of gravity shifted, and the mosque now stands right at the edge of the old town, close to the ramparts.

The sheer size of the **courtyard** is almost overwhelming. Its slope enables it to retain rainwater in a central **pool**. Elegantly sculpted traps filter impurities from the water. It is difficult to imagine that this enormous paved area is supported on 7m tall columns and covers a vast space with huge cisterns. However several wellheads, their edges deeply notched by the grooves of the rope, are evidence of this feat of architecture.

The 35m high **minaret**, solid and square, consists of three storeys crowned with parapets which give it a thoroughly military appearance. It has 128 steps, which are supposed to consist of paving stones recovered from former churches, and gravestones taken from Christian cemeteries.

There is no access into the **prayer hall***** , even if the heavy doors made of cedar of Lebanon (held by joinery without bolts) are open. The visitor must be content to stop at the doorway, astonished at the forest of columns which

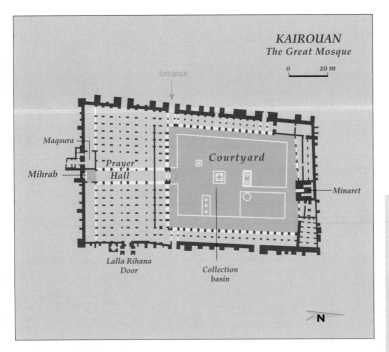

KAIROUAN
The Great Mosque

0   20 m

Entrance

Maqsura

"Prayer"
Hall

Mihrab

Courtyard

Minaret

Lalla Rihana
Door

Collection
basin

N

create a magical maze of white marble, blue granite and pink porphyry. According to legend, no one knows the exact number – although their origin is known: they come from Carthage, Sbeïtla and Hadrumetus (Sousse). The **mihrab**** at the end of the central aisle has always been famous for its elegance: the alcove, covered with pierced and carved marble panels, is surrounded by ceramics with metallic reflections, brought from Baghdad in the 9C. The **minbar**, the Imam's pulpit, made of carved teak and also dating from the 9C, is the oldest in the Arab world. The **maqsura** is a later addition (11C). This wooden screen, pierced and carved, screened off the imams from the other faithful.

From the Great Mosque you can return to the centre of the medina by exploring the streets, but it is better to leave from Bab ech Chouhada (southern rampart). Go through the gate, and then continue straight down the main street.

The **Bir Barouta** (17C) is a well where the camel-operated mechanism to haul up the bucket is set in the first floor of a private house. If legend is to be believed, this well is linked with the Zemzem well, at Mecca. It is a bit of a tourist trap however, and both visitors and guides seem to prefer the cold drinks on sale to the supposed benefits of water drawn from the well.

At the exit from the souk is the **mosquée Khâyrun** (Mosque of the three doors), one of Kairouan's oldest monuments (AD 866). It has been much altered since, but the façade retains some of the features of 9C mosques, such as the three doors under arches, with the centre one higher than the others, very much as in a church.

267

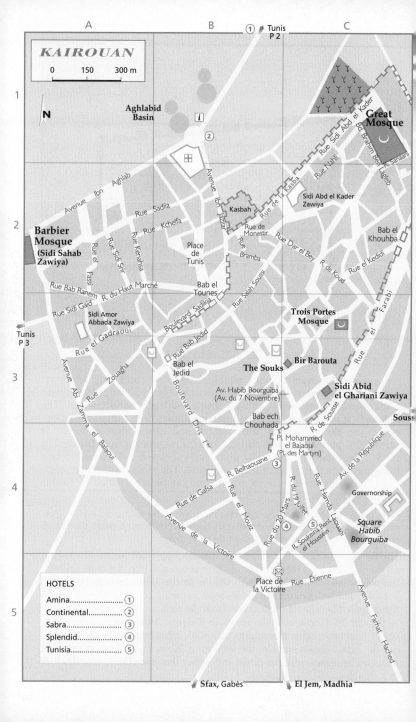

The **Sidi Abid el Ghariani zawiya** *(second street on the right after Bab ech Chouchada)*, which dates from the 14C, is remarkable above all for the **timber** of its ceiling and its finely carved plaster-work.

Although very old, the **souks** have no great architectural merit, for they have all been much rebuilt. They should be visited for their lively atmosphere, and above all for Kairouan's speciality: rugs and carpets.

In Kairouan, **wool rugs** are a family matter. There are in fact no factories, or industrial workshops. The women pass on their skills and the art of the designs (often geometrical) from mother to daughter, so that no rug can ever be the exact replica of another. Nowadays the women still draw their inspiration from the ceramic tiles in the Barbier mosque, or from the decorations in the Great Mosque. Some 6 000 families live off this activity. Kairouan has three types of rug: the *alloucha*, made of long undyed sheep's wool, uses the wool's natural colours (black, brown, beige), the *zerbia*, also long, dyed with vegetable colours (blue, red), and the *Mergoum*, woven and embroidered using a different technique based on Berber motifs *(for further information, see under "Shopping", page 108, and "Crafts", page 75).*

Making the most of Kairouan

Kairouan street names can be a problem for the visitor. Some streets seem to have no name at all, other names are shown only in Arabic and name-changes are frequent. There are even streets with several names!

GETTING THERE

By car – The most direct road from Tunis is the P 3 (154km). An alternative is to take the motorway from Sousse to Enfida and then continue on the P 2 for the remaining 62km.

By bus – The bus station is outside the city centre 300m west of the Barbier Mausoleum (not on the town plan). **SNTRI** has buses departing from Kairouan for several other cities: Tozeur (4hr), Jerba (via Zarzis: 6hr30min / via Guellala: 5hr), Tunis (2hr30min), Gafsa (3hr30min) and Bizerte (4hr).
SORETRAK (Kairouan Regional Transport Co.), ☎ (07) 300 011 / 303 772. These buses do not have air-conditioning. The following destinations are served: Nabeul (135min), Sousse (75min), Monastir and Sfax (2hr 30min).

For Le Kef, there is the choice of either **Société Régional du Kef** (Le Kef Regional Co.) or **Société Régional du Sahel** (Sahel Regional Co.).
By shared taxi – The station is located near the bus station. There is never a long wait since Kairouan is a popular stop (porte des Martyrs).
Car hire – **Hertz**, ave Ibn el Jazzar, ☎ (07) 234 529.

GETTING AROUND

By car – The tiny city centre can be easily visited on foot. A car is useful only if you plan to go to the beach, approximately 60km away or to visit El Jem.
Taxis – There are two taxi stations: Place Bab Tounes (at Porte de Tunis) and Place du Commandant Bejaoui.
Car hire – **Hertz**, ave Ibn el Jazzar, ☎ (07) 224 529.

ADDRESS BOOK

Emergency – Police Station, ☎ (07) 220 577.
Ibn el Jazzar Hospital, ☎ (07) 226 300.
Moncef Guider Night Pharmacy, Place Gargabia, ☎ (07) 220 069.

Tourist Information – ONTT, ave Ibn Aghlab, near the Aghlabides pool, ☎ (07) 221 797. Open in winter from 8.30am-1pm and 3-5.45pm Mondays to Thursdays, 8.30am-1pm on Fridays and 8.30am-1.30pm on Saturdays. Open in summer from 7.30am-6pm Mondays to Thursdays and 7.30am-1pm on Fridays. Closed Sunday throughout the year.

Regional Tourist Office, ANEP (National Heritage Agency), Located in the same building as the ONTT, ☎ (07) 220 452. Open 8am-6pm and 8am-1pm on Fridays. This office sells admission tickets to the city's various sites and attractions, and has qualified official guides who work at government-regulated rates (TD10 for up to 9 people).

Banks / Currency Exchange – BIAT, ave de la République.

BNA, 1 rue Hamda Laouani and ave de la République.

CFCT, ave du 20 Mars.

STB, ave Habib Bourguiba and rue Hamda Laouani. Cash dispenser outside this branch.

UBCI, rue Taïeb Méhiri.

UIB, Commercial Centre.

Cash Dispenser – Banque STB, ave Habib Bourguiba.

Post office – on the corner of ave Farhat Hached and rue Etienne. Open 8am-6pm Monday to Saturday. In summer, open 7.30am-1pm and 5-7pm Monday to Friday; 7.30am-1pm on Saturday. Open Sundays from 9-11am throughout the year. Money exchange and fax facilities.

Internet – Publinet, ave Abi Zamma el Balaoui (opposite the Ajil petrol station), ☎ (07) 231 041. 8.30am-12midnight, 10am-12midnight Sundays. TD2.500 an hour.

WHERE TO STAY

From US$18-42

Hôtel Sabra, rue Ali Belhaouane (opposite Martyrs' gate), ☎ (07) 230 263 – 30rm ✕ Modest, but clean establishment with a view of the medina. Only two rooms have a private bathroom, otherwise showers and toilets in the hall. Fans are available.

Tunisia Hôtel, ave Farhat Hached, ☎ (07) 231 855 / 231 775, Fax (07) 231 597 – 38rm ⌐| 🗐 This centrally-located hotel has a basic level of comfort, but staff are very welcoming.

🏠 **Hôtel Splendid**, rue du 9 Avril, ☎ (07) 230 522 / 041, Fax (07) 230 829 – 48rm ⌐| 🗐 TV ✕ CC This hotel brags about being the cleanest hotel in town but it's certainly the oldest, dating back to 1903. Ask to see the rooms so you can choose the largest one that overlooks the square. Noisy air-conditioning. Minibar optional.

More than US$42

Hôtel Continental, on the road from Tunis, across from the Aglabides basin and the ONTT, ☎ (07) 231 135, Fax (07) 229 900 – 176rm ⌐| 🗐 🖉 TV ⣒ ✕ ⌂ CC This hotel is in a good location and is quiet. Some rooms are very large and the best rooms overlook the swimming pool, but the cleanliness of the establishment is questionable. Discount for children. Friendly reception.

Hôtel Amina, on the P 2 road to Tunis when you leave the city, ☎ (07) 226 555, Fax (07) 225 411 – 62rm ⌐| 🗐 🖉 TV ⣒ ✕ ⌂ CC This hotel opened in 1994. The rooms are spacious and breakfast is served at the poolside. Unfortunately, it is out of the city centre and the view of the surrounding steppe-like landscape is not very attractive.

EATING OUT

Those who are used to Michelin-starred restaurants may find the food rather basic, and even the restaurants in Kairouan's large hotels leave much to be desired. The establishments listed below serve simple and inexpensive food. Lamb is the local speciality, most often served in a stew. Many restaurants do not serve alcohol.

Less than US$10

La Tabouna (C4), ave Hamda Laouani (30m from place des Martyrs). This family-run eating-house serves classic Tunisian specialities. The owners don't think twice about showing a video of their youngest son's circumcision ceremony during meals!

Karawan (C4), rue Soukeina Bent el Houssein, ☎ (07) 222 556. This small and basic restaurant usually offers a single meal of family-style food costing less than US$8. Try the "koucha", "kamounia", or grilled lamb. Upon request, the owner will prepare a camel "mloukhia", a stew brewed with an aromatic herb. Alcohol is not served.

Le Roi du Couscous (B5) (also known as the Restaurant des Sportifs), rue du 20 Mars, opposite the post office, ☎ (07) 231 337. Simple food served at long wooden tables. Popular with local people, the set menu (which costs less than US$5) consists of "brik" or salad, lamb or couscous, mint tea and two "makhrouds", the local speciality. Alcohol is not served.

Sabra (C4), ave de la République (to the right of Tunisia Hôtel), ☎ (07) 235 095. Family cooking on Formica tables with four set-menus under US$8. The proprietor is a mine of information about the city.

WHERE TO GO FOR A DRINK

Cafés – Most tourists get off the coaches and head straight to the open-air cafés located in the shade of the city's ramparts. A better choice might be:

Le Café (C4), Place Habib Bourguiba. A welcoming oasis where patrons are serenaded by songbirds.

Café Sabra (C4), Place des Martyrs. This is the place to come for a drink in the evening.

Café Hazouzi (named after the owner) (C4), next to La Tabouna restaurant on the ave Hamda Laouani. This typically Moorish café under stone arches is rarely frequented by tourists.

LEISURE

Hammam – **Sabra**, Place des Martyrs.

SHOPPING

Weekly souk on Mondays.

Bakeries – **Kairouan** is the capital of "makhroud", a semolina cake stuffed with dates and dipped in honey. They are stacked up like pyramids on every street corner.

Segni, ave du 7 Novembre, ☎ (07) 220 023. On the main street in the medina, this is the best-known pastry shop in Kairouan. Cellophane packets are ready prepared. On some days the famous "makhrouds" are made on the premises, however most of the time they are made in a factory.

Bookshops – **Agence Jeune Afrique**, rue Amilcar (a small street opposite the Sabra restaurant), ☎ (07) 221 438.

Antiques and Handicrafts – The city has a number of tourist-orientated sales outlets.

SOCOPA, rue Ali Zouaoui, ☎ (07) 220 047.

Okba Carpet Factory, next to the Great Mosque, ☎ (07) 221 129. Besides its large selection of carpets, there is also a lovely view of the Great Mosque from the rooftop terrace.

SBEÏTLA★★

Not to be missed
The forum and the three temples of the capitol.

And remember...
Apart from the archeological site itself, the towns of Sbeïtla
and Kasserine close by do not merit much attention.
Very hot indeed in summer.

Coming from Sousse or Kairouan, you may like to make a détour via Makthar rather than going direct to Sbeïtla on the P 3. In this case, take the P 12 (to the right, about 20km beyond Kairouan), then the P 4 and the C 71. This takes you through beautiful scenery. Between Ouesslatia and Makthar the road winds through the rocky hillsides covered with Aleppo pines, part of the forest of Kesra.

The remains are substantial, but arouse little emotion despite the lovely golden colour of the stonework. There is none of the charm here of Dougga, nor the mystery of Bulla Regia. The immediate surroundings are largely the reason for this: Sbeïtla lacks the rustic appearance of the other archeological excavation sites. The site lies at the edge of the town, and the impression it leaves can hardly be described as unforgettable. It has a dual carriageway running beside it and the few modern buildings round it, like the Suffetula Hotel are having a disastrous effect on its appearance.

Here, as everywhere in Tunisia, efforts have been made to embellish the ruins with flowers and shrubs. The effect is less successful here than elsewhere, however, no doubt because of the dry climate and the large area of the site. Only the entrance to the archeological site and the edges of the path leading down to the Arch of Diocletian are well-planted and the arch itself is surrounded with a superb green lawn. Otherwise, with its blocks of stone and broken columns emerging from sparse scorched grass, the site looks like an abandoned cemetery with toppling tombstones. Sbeïtla burns in the sun, and in the distant dust of this arid plateau one half expects to see Abdullah Ibn Saad's armies come surging in.

Sufetula, capital for a year

So far no remains have been discovered that pre-date the 1C AD, and everything indicates that Sufetula, the ancient Sbeïtla, was created out of nothing at this time by a colony of Roman veterans. With its imposing central forum, its streets set at right-angles, and its rectangular plots, Sufetula appears to reflect a pre-established plan: an ideal Roman city which did not have to compromise with the lay of the land or some older urban pattern (although the area had been occupied by the Numidians).

Like all the cities of Roman Africa, Sufetula enjoyed great prosperity in the 2C with the rise to power of the African emperor: Septimus Severus. Under the Vandals, Sufetula suffered little from Genseric and his soldiery, perhaps because of being well off the beaten track. With the 5C Byzantine reconquest, it was its outlying location which gave the city its strategic significance. Sufetula was fortified and a garrison was established here to contain the Arabs who were harassing the frontiers of Byzacena. In 646 the privincial governor Gregory, no

Sbeïtla

doubt feeling threatened by the Arab advance and perhaps forgotten by remote Byzantium, seceded from the eastern throne. Abandoning Carthage, he settled in Sufetula with all his staff. The little provincial town became the capital of an empire, but this honour came too late. The Arab armies from Tripolitania were already advancing, with Abdullah Ibn Saad as their leader. According to Arab chronicles, Gregory promised his daughter to whoever brought him the head of Abdullah. The latter made a matching promise to his troops. At the battle of Sbeïtla, Gregory and his army were wiped out and the governor's daughter was given to one of Abdullah's lieutenants. According to another legend, the princess committed suicide by the hitherto unknown method of throwing herself off her dromedary. Although the accounts of the girl's fate differ, it seems certain that Gregory was slain and the city sacked. The Arabs, dazzled by Sufetula's splendour, returned twenty years later for the final conquest.

The Archeological Park
Allow 1hr. Tickets on sale at the Capitole, to the left of the museum.
7am-7pm in summer, 8.30am-5.30pm in winter.
Entrance charge.

The entrance is guarded by several small **forts** dating from the Byzantine era. The **first**, on the left, is probably a Roman house, subsequently fortified in the 7C. It is massive in construction, measuring 20m x 24m with walls 2m thick. Continuing down the road, you will pass a similar **second fort** on your right, a two-storey house with a well, cistern and latrines.

The modest group of buildings standing back a little from this second fort are **private baths** from a later era. On the other side of the road, another private bathing establishment has kept its small pool decorated with mosaics of fish and crustaceans.

Beyond the remains of the small **church of Saints Gervais, Protais and Tryphon** (early 7C) turn right, northwards. This leads to an enormous **cistern**, with steps leading down into it. A little way ahead on the left, four great piers built of large dressed blocks of stone indicate the **church of Servus**, which was inserted into the courtyard of a pagan temple. The unevenly balanced piers correspond to the corners of the **cella**, transformed into a baptistery.

The **Great Baths** (*on your right*) occupy a substantial space, some 100m x 50m. This 3C thermal establishment was altered several times and follows no classical plan (*see the architectural plans, page 43*). The group includes some fine rooms, however, including the **frigidarium** and its basins and the **caldarium**, where the floor is supported on little pillars of tiles around which warm air circulated. The **palaestra**, surrounded by a double colonnade, still has its mosaic paving.

Continue to the right along the road running beside the baths to the **theatre** at the edge of the Sbeïtla wadi. The stage still has a few of its columns, and the stepped seating has been partly restored.

Turn back and rejoin the main street, with the imposing forum and the capitol at the end. This grand architectural ensemble is reached through the **Arch of Antonius Pius**★ (arc d Antonin le Pieux), a monumental gate with three arches which were closed by folding doors. This gate is an integral part of a surrounding wall, 4m high, which has been altered on several occasions: the gates were blocked up in Byzantine times, no doubt for defensive reasons. The 2C **forum**★, a vast paved quadrilateral of 70m x 60m, has a portico running round three of

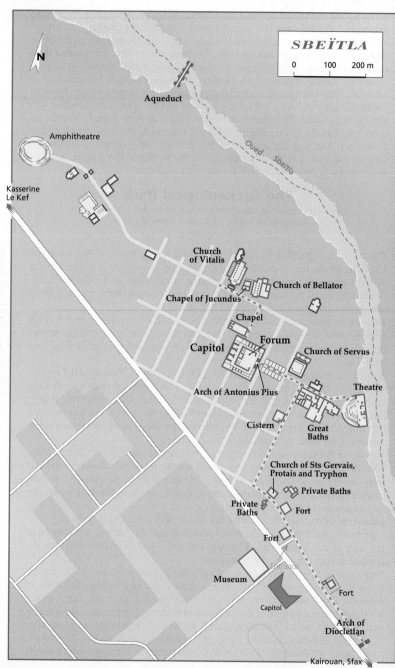

SBEÏTLA

0   100   200 m

Aqueduct

Oued Sbeïtla

Amphitheatre

Kasserine
Le Kef

Church of Vitalis

Church of Bellator

Chapel of Jucundus

Chapel

Capitol   **Forum**

Church of Servus

Arch of Antonius Pius

Cistern

Theatre

Great
Baths

Church of Sts Gervais,
Protais and Tryphon

Private Baths

Private
Baths   Fort

Fort

Entrance

Capitol

Museum

Fort

Arch of
Diocletian

Kairouan, Sfax

274

its sides. Plinths for statues have been found between the columns, with honorific inscriptions. The portico opened on to a variety of stalls, thus serving as a shopping gallery. A fairly unusual feature, the capitoline triad is not grouped together here in a single sanctuary, but is represented by **three temples*****, dedicated to Jupiter, Juno and Minerva respectively. Jupiter's temple, at the centre, has no stairs, the podium acting as tribune. It was reached by gangways linking it to the other two temples. The construction of this enormous complex probably dates back to the early 2C, but the dressing of the half-columns and the pilasters behind the temples was never finished.

Turn right to the remains near the northwest corner of the forum.

These mark a **church** of which little survives, although the nave and the two aisles can be identified. Other ruins, substantial but somewhat confusing, stretch out at the end of the street on the left. It is not easy to find a way through this tangle of churches: the first one to be come across is the **church of Bellator**, named after a bishop mentioned in an inscription. This building, which still has a stretch of wall in position, has a nave closed off by a pair of apses and two aisles separated by a double row of columns. Probably dating from the 4C, the church has been altered several times, which considerably complicates the amateur visitor's understanding of the site, a veritable accumulation of archeological layers. A baptistery was installed at the side in a room with a peristyle dating from pagan times – a few of its columns have been removed. Later this became a **chapel dedicated to Jucundus**, a bishop and apparently a martyr – and the base of a column was set up in the middle of the baptismal font as a shrine. In the 5C or 6C a new chapel known as the **church of Vitalis** was built close at hand, on the other side of the chapel, a vast sanctuary for the ever-increasing numbers of the faithful; 50m long by 25m wide, it had a nave and four aisles separated by a double colonnade. The aisle has an apse at either end, the one on the northeast having a funerary purpose: the grave of a decapitated man has been found here, no doubt a martyr. The outstanding feature of the church is undoubtedly the **baptistery*** *(to the southwest).* In an excellent state of preservation, this oblong basin covered with mosaic bears the name of its generous and blessed donors, Vitalis and Cardela.

That part of the site to the northwest of the church is really only of interest to archeology enthusiasts. It consists largely of underground features, and is still being excavated. Beyond the perimeter of the site is the **aqueduct**. It has been heavily altered down the centuries, particularly in the early 20C, to bring water to the city of Sfax.

Back at the site entrance, follow the path beside the road from Sbeïtla to Kasserine, to the southeast, ending at the **Arch of Diocletian**, or the **Arch of the Tetrarchs*** (late 3C), which marks the city's southern entrance. In ancient times the track extended towards Sfax across the plain covered with olive trees, from which the town drew most of its wealth.

The little **museum** *(opposite the entrance, on the other side of the road, 6am-1pm / 3pm-6pm in summer, 8.30am-1pm / 2.30pm-5.30pm in winter; closed on Mondays)* has a number of finds, but its most fascinating feature is the display of a series of photographs of the site under snow – a difficult condition to imagine.

EL JEM★★
63km from Sousse, 64km from Sfax
Pop c 10 000

Not to be missed
Symphony concerts.

And remember...
The little town at the foot of the
amphitheatre does not deserve a lengthy visit.

Access is only practical on the P 1, from Tunis, Sousse or Sfax.

No matter from which direction it is approached, the amphitheatre at El Jem
stands out like a colossus of ochre stone barring the horizon, or an enormous
ship unaccountably washed ashore in the midst of these arid plains. The absence
of any accompanying ruins which might have explained its presence here only
adds to the enigma. It is as if the ancient city of Thysdrus, of which this was
the jewel, had vanished into the sands like a mirage.

A fortress of rebellion

This arid plateau, with its sandy soil and lack of water, was hardly the place for
a city. But it was here that a number of roads met (to Sufetula (Sbeïtla), Taparura
(Sfax), and Hadrumetus (Sousse)). In addition, under the encouragement of the
Emperor Hadrian (AD 117-138) the plain was planted with olive trees. In the
3C Thysdrus was the second city of Byzacena, covering an area of 200ha with
a population of nearly 40 000. It was a rich town, with an impressive circus,
three amphitheatres and large public baths and its prosperity aroused the envy
of Maximinus, a greedy and uncouth emperor who forced all the cities of the
Empire to meet his demands. Around the year 238 Maximinus sent a procu-
rator to Thysdrus to raise taxes in what amounted to extortion. The inhabitants
rose in revolt, assassinated the imperial emissary and proclaimed as emperor the
venerable senator Gordian, who was serving as proconsul of the province of
Africa. But the rebels, led by Gordian's son, were defeated in battle by a legion
loyal to Maximinus, and Thysdrus was partly destroyed in reprisal. However,
by the end of the 3C it had recovered, and enjoyed a second period of prosperity lasting several hundred years.

Al Kahina

This Berber princess, a great figure in
Tunisian nationalism, gathered the tribes
of her people together to resist the
Moslem invasion. It is claimed that she
managed to recapture Ifriqiya from Uqba
Ibn Nafi, the first Arab conqueror; it was
a brief victory which forced Al Kahina
into flight. Tracked down, she took
refuge with her followers in the El Jem
amphitheatre, where they resisted enemy
attacks for nearly four years. The
princess met an end that matched her
proud history: according to legend she
was betrayed by her young lover, who
stabbed her and sent her embalmed head
to the leader of the Arab armies.

For a time in the 7C the Berbers of El
Kahina delayed the advance of the Arab
armies, turning the amphitheatre into a
rear camp. But the decline of Thysdrus
was inevitable: the olive plantations
were burned down by the invading
Moslems (olive growing would not return until the days of the French Protectorate) and the foundation of
Kairouan pushed the old city into the
background. Gradually it declined until it was no more than a little rural
township. According to the geographer
El Bekri, the amphitheatre was still virtually intact in the 11C and no doubt

remained in this condition until a new generation of rebels chose it as a refuge. In 1695 the tribes which had risen against Mohammed Bey shut themselves into the monument. The Bey decided on dramatic methods and opened a breach in the walls with cannon fire – the first onslaught on what Arab writers considered as one of the marvels of the world.

Visit
Allow 1-2hr

The Amphitheatre★★★ (L'Amphithéâtre)
7am-7pm in summer, 8am-5pm winter, entrance charge. Under the combined effects of the attacks of time and vandalism, the ampitheatre had deteriorated to such an extent that an explorer wrote: "The archways groan and appear ready to collapse under our weight; cracks and holes open in front of us, blocks of stone tremble under our feet." The amphitheatre, the largest Roman monument in Africa, has been restored since then, thanks to action by the Tunisian government and financial support from the Gulbenkian foundation.
Built in the reign of Gordian around 230-238 in the form of an ellipse, 148m long and 122m wide, the structure could seat between 30 000 and 45 000 people. Rising on three rows of semi-circular arches to a height of 36m, this made it the third-largest amphitheatre in the Roman Empire, after the colosseums in Rome and Capua. Two galleries cut across beneath the arena and led to the exterior, the larger one giving access to 16 vaulted chambers which held wild beasts.
Although the original function of the building was festive – gladiatorial combats, wild animal chases and other entertainment – the Romans also had the imagination and the skill to use this vast stone vessel for their water supply. The building contains a highly elaborate system gathering and storing rainwater and water stored in cisterns.

Archeological Museum★ (Musée archéologique)
On the edge of the town, on the Sfax road. 7am-7pm in summer, 8am-5.30pm in winter, closed on Mondays. Entrance charge. The museum contains a collection of mosaics discovered in the houses of Thysdrus, including a very fine scene of Orpheus charming the animals. Other fascinating scenes feature animals: they include a tiger attacking two asses, a lion devouring a wild boar, and two cherubs with a peacock.

Making the most of El Jem

GETTING THERE
By train – The railway station is in the city centre, not far from the amphitheatre. There are several trains connecting with Tunis, Sousse (7 trains per day) and Sfax (5 trains per day).

By bus – The bus station is located near the museum. Buses depart frequently for Gabès, Sfax, Sousse and Tunis.

By shared taxi – The station is next to the railway station. Taxis run to all the neighbouring cities.

EATING OUT
Less than US$10
Restaurant at the Hôtel Julius, not far from the train station. This restaurant offers the best value for money in a town that otherwise lacks in restaurants.

LEISURE
Festivals – *International Music Festival*, in June-July.

SFAX ★

Centre of Governorship
Pop 232 000
Pleasant climate, but some air pollution

Not to be missed
Dar Jallouli.
Fish prepared in the local style, "à la Sfaxienne".

And remember...
Try to book your accommodation in a resort hotel.

Sfax, the "capital of the South", is a lively and industrious city and the country's most important port. All kinds of goods are exported from here: phosphates, dates, building materials and esparto grass, not to mention sponges, cuttle-fish bones, and above all, olive oil. It would be possible to find one's way round Sfax blindfold, just by smell: the sickening effluvia from phosphates mixed with fresh sea breezes nearer the harbour; the scent of olive oil and muggy air away from the sea. Sfax is the second largest city in Tunisia, a feverish place in perpetual motion. Its intense commercial activity is clearly visible, and even the medina and its souks lack the usual casual atmosphere.

The people of Sfax are famous all over the world for their trading and negotiating skills and are proud of their city's dynamism. Some would say they are just plain proud. The true natives of Sfax claim direct descent from Mohammed. For this reason they used to wear a green turban and were the most fiercely opposed to the French occupation. However, even more than Tunis, Sfax now appears resolutely modern; traditional clothing has been put aside in favour of tight jeans and mini-skirts, and even thoroughly up-to-date haircuts. Sfax is not concerned to please and, like Tunis, it lacks a sea-front and fine beaches. But it is perhaps the best place to take the throbbing pulse of modern Tunisia.

The town
Allow 2hr

The modern city

The European city lies between the ramparts of the medina and the harbour. Largely destroyed during the Second World War, it was rebuilt in a not particularly stylish way. Nevertheless, it is very enjoyable to explore its broad arcaded avenues and the squares planted with palm trees, or to idle in an open air café. Some handsome neo-Moorish buildings like the town hall, the Hotel les Oliviers and the French consulate add character to this somewhat anonymous setting.

The **archeological museum** (mus e arch ologique) (*under renovation, 8.30am-1pm; 3pm-6pm, except Sundays, entrance charge*) has taken refuge in the town hall. Like all Tunisian museums, it has many **mosaics** – but sadly these are badly damaged. Most were discovered in the region's numerous archeological sites like Thina, Acholla, the Kerkennah Isles, and in Roman villas excavated in Sfax. Dining-room floors showing sea scenes, Daniel in the lions' den, hunting scenes and a bull-fight are the museum's chief attractions.

Sfax

Sfax town hall, a fine example of neo-Moorish architecture

The medina*

The **Aghlabid ramparts** (9C) extend for 2km and, in their design and layout and the sheer thickness of their walls, represent a defensive construction that is almost unique in the Arab world. Frequently restored, they have remained intact to this day. Originally built of unbaked brick, now they consist of local stone blocks and dressed limestone from neighbouring Mahdia. Denticulations, cornices, pointed revetments, oblong towers – all this elaboration makes for a convincingly majestic style.

Access to the medina is through **Bab Diwan**, a monumental triple-arched gate. Continue straight ahead (*along the rue de la Grande Mosquée*) to the **Great Mosque** (849), the true heart of the city. Its three-storey minaret is similar to the one in Kairouan. Built in the same era as the ramparts, the mosque is remarkable for its indented blind arcades and the epigraphs that decorate one of its façades.

Go back down the rue de la Grande Mosquée, and take the first turning to the left. Cross the rue Mongi Slim and continue along the rue de la Driba. At 43 rue de la Driba, the **heritage cultural centre** has been located in the **Dar Sellami** since 1998. On the programme are a wide variety of cultural events, workshops, musical evenings, all of which take place in this very pleasant Sfaxian residence (*see Making the most of Sfax*).

In the same block of houses on rue Sidi Ali Ennouri, the **Museum of Traditional Arts and Customs** (*9.30am-4.30pm, closed Mondays, entrance charge*) is housed in the **Dar Jallouli****, named after the prestigious family that built the house in the

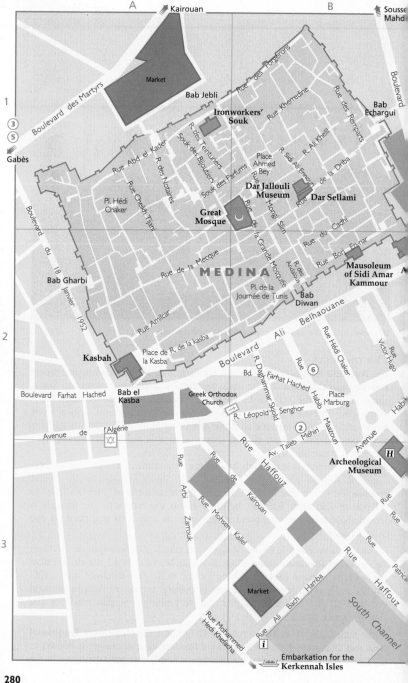

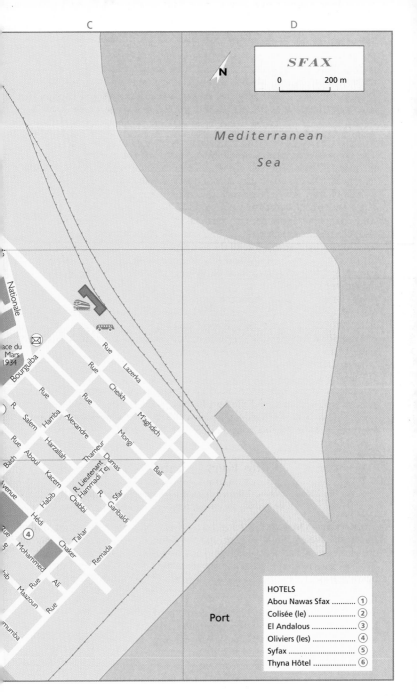

C   D

N

SFAX

0   200 m

Mediterranean

Sea

Nationale

ace du
Mars
1934

Bourguiba

Rue
Lazerka

Rue
Cheikh

M'aghdich

R.
Salem

Rue
Hamba

Rue
Alexandre

Thameur

Mongi

Rue
Aboul

Rue
Harzallah

Dumas

Bach

Kacem

R. Lieutenant
Hammadi Tej

Bali

R.
Sfar

lvenue

Habib

Chabbi

Garibaldi

④

Hédi

Tahar

Chaker

Remada

Mohammed

Rue

Ali

hib

Maazoun

Rue

umba

Port

HOTELS	
Abou Nawas Sfax	①
Colisée (le)	②
El Andalous	③
Oliviers (les)	④
Syfax	⑤
Thyna Hôtel	⑥

17C. This dynasty of governors made their fortune by fitting out pirate ships (*see page 209*). Their house is truly a little Andalusian palace, decorated with pierced plaster-work, painted panelling, stone sculpture and ceramics. There is an array of traditional objects, jewels, clothing and paintings on glass. Dar Jallouli, with its furnished rooms, its well-stocked shelves and its equipped kitchen, its full store-room, has the intimate feel of a house which is still lived in and loved.

Return to the rue Mongi Slim and turn right.

The souks have adapted successfully to the demands of modern life. They lack the picturesque atmosphere of the souks in Tunis or Sousse, but are perhaps more authentic. In effect they form a vast shopping centre where the young women of Sfax, despite being very westernised, are happy to do their shopping. There are certainly spices and *chéchias* to be found here, but jeans and jackets hang alongside *burnous,* and the shoe-maker, who still makes Turkish slippers, also sells the latest trainers.

The **ironworkers' souk**, close to the northern outer wall, is tucked away down the street at the end of a square courtyard. Anyone penetrating this lair will discover a truly Dickensian scene of sweat and grime as the blacksmiths beat out the red-hot metal.

At the far southwestern tip of the ramparts, the **Kasbah** (*9.30am-4.30pm, closed Mondays, entrance charge*) is a wonderful fortress marked by the successive invasions of Aghlabids, Zirids, Hafsids and Ottomans. Today it houses the **Museum of Traditional Architecture** (La Musée de l'architecture traditionelle). A small tree-shaded semi-circular open space has been laid out at the entrance, a good place to linger and watch the children playing football.

On the other side, to the right as you enter by the Bab Diwan gate, is the **Mausoleum of Sidi Amar Kammour** (17C), identifiable by its massive minaret pierced with windows, and the **borj En-Nar**, with its vast courtyard and two towers. This beautiful building (today the seat of the **Association for the Protection of the Medina**) was the "fire fortress", used for communicating by lighted beacon.

The Kerkennah Isles

1hr from Sfax by boat
The islands lie about 20km offshore. A ferry runs regularly from Sfax
(see Making the most of the Kerkennah Isles)

The **Kerkennah Isles** are low-lying, barely rising about the waters of the Gulf of Gabes: the average altitude is 5m, and the palms look as if they grow straight out of the sea, almost as in a mirage. The Chergui and Gharbi islands consist of two big bands of sand covered in many places by a crust of limestone and linked by a single road.

A place apart

The fate of this desolate archipelago down the centuries appears to have been to serve as a land of exile and transportation. Hannibal came here in 195 AD to meditate on his defeat at Sama. In the 6C Saint Fulgentius appears to have founded a monastery here so that he too could devote himself to meditation. Later, the Beys of Tunis deported courtesans here when they wearied of them, and Bourguiba found sanctuary here before fleeing to Libya.

Helped by their isolation, the people living in this harsh environment have a wholly distinct character. Having exhausted themselves for centuries by seeking to fertilise the sterile soil – a few olive and fig trees and a few vines still grow there – the Kerkennians turned to the sea. They undertake a very original method of fishing which is similar to a hunt: the **sautade**. They strike the water with palm branches to frighten the mullet which jump out of the water and land on hurdles arranged on the surface. The other great speciality of the Kerkennians is **octopus fishing**, trapping the octopus in the big pottery vessels known as amphorae (*see page 298*). Apart from these two fascinating activities, it must be acknowledged that distractions are rare. Even sea-bathing is difficult here because of the shallow water: a kilometre off the coast the water is barely knee-high.

The islands are not a place to do anything in particular. People come here to rest and relax, to get away from it all and enjoy the company of the local people, whose kindness and hospitality is legendary.

GETTING THERE

By air – Sfax Thyna Airport (7km), route d'Agareb, ☎ (04) 241 700. The airport bus to Sfax (no 14) leaves from the terminal exit. 18 departures per day from 4.50am to 9.35pm (25min).

By boat – A CTN ship links Marseille, France and Sfax 3 to 4 times a year.

By train – SNCFT, ave Habib Bourguiba, ☎ (04) 225 999.

By bus – SNTRI, rue Lazerka (on the corner of ave Habib Bourguiba opposite the railway station), ☎ (04) 222 355. This company runs buses to Tunis, Tataouine, Matmata and Douz. There are 3 departures daily to Jerba (4hr for TD9.330 or 6hr for TD12.760 via Zarzis). One bus leaves to Tripoli on Monday, Tuesday and Friday at 8.30pm (theoretically an 8 hour trip, not including the customs stop which can take a long time, TD17.4).

Soretras (Sfax Regional Transport Co.), ave du Commandant Bajaoui, ☎ (04) 229 522. One departure per day to Gafsa (3hr30min), Jerba (5hr), Le Kef (5hr), Sbeitla (3hr30min), Kairouan (2hr30min) and Gabès (3hr). There are three departures daily to Mahdia (2hr) and 10 to Chebba (1hr30min).

By car – Sfax is 64km from El Jem.

By shared taxi – The station is on ave de l'Armée, ☎ (04) 220 071. Departures for destinations throughout Tunisia.

Ferry for Kerkennah – See "Making the most of the Kerkennah Isles".

GETTING AROUND

By car – Driving in the city centre is not recommended because of the heavy traffic. A car is useful, however, for visiting the surrounding areas, particularly the Kerkennah Isles.

By bus – Sorestras, ave de Kairouan in front of the church.

By taxi – Allô taxi, ☎ (04) 299 900.

By tourist train – The last stop is on the Corniche near the ferry that goes to the Kerkennah Isles. Trains operate from 7am to 12am every 30min (15min, TD1).

Car hire – Avis, rue Tahar Sfar, ☎ (04) 224 605.
Hertz, ave Habib Bourguiba, ☎ (04) 228 626.
Europcar, 40 rue Mohamed Ali, ☎ (04) 226 680.
Mattei (Ada), ave Patrice Lumumba, ☎ (04) 296 404.

ADDRESS BOOK

Emergency – Police Station, rue Victor Hugo, ☎ (04) 229 700.

National Guard, rue Victor Hugo, ☎ (04) 227 688.

Hôpital Hedi Chaker, route El Aïn, 5km outside town, ☎ (04) 244 511 / 241 511.

Ambulance, route El Aïn, 5km outside town, ☎ (04) 190, 244 894.

Night doctors – ☎ (04) 221 618.

Tourist Information – ONTT, located in a little boutique on the cornice, overlooking the sea, on the corner of rue Ali Bach Hamba and rue Mohamed Hedi Khefacha, ☎ and Fax (04) 211 040. Out of season 8.30am-1pm / 3pm-5.45pm, closed Sundays. Summer, 7.30am-1.30pm; open 4pm-7pm during the week and 9am-12noon Sundays.

The **tourist office** is located in a building on ave Habib Bourguiba, in the square opposite hôtel Abou Nawas. The somewhat irregular opening hours make it more practical to contact the ONTT.

Customs – rue Mongi Bali.

Embassies and Consulates – There is no diplomatic representation for the UK, USA, Canada, or Australia in Sfax. There is a **French Consulate**, 13 ave Habib Bourguiba, ☎ (04) 220 788.

Cultural centres – Dar Sellami Heritage Cultural Centre, 43 rue de la Driba, ☎ (04) 222 972. 9am-5pm, closed Sundays. Varied programme of cultural events and guided tours of the medina.

French Cultural Centre, ave Taïeb Méhiri and ave Kairouan, ☎ (04) 221 553 / 210 880. 8.30am-12.30pm / 2.30pm-6pm. In the summer, only from 8am.

Banks / Currency Exchange – Every Tunisian bank has a branch in Sfax. Open 8am-4pm off season and 7.20am-12.20pm in July-August.

Cash dispenser outside the **STB**, on the corner of ave Hédi Chaker and Marburg square.

Post office – 4 ave Habib Bourguiba, ☎ (04) 224 722. Winter hours: open 8am-6pm. Summer hours: open 7.30am-1pm and 5-7pm. Open 9am-11am on Sundays. Express mail and money exchange services. The building is decorated with murals by famous Tunisian painters from the 1960's.

Telephone – There are numerous telephone boxes throughout the city. The public telephone service near the railway station is open from 6am-2am. Unfortunately, only dial phones are available which limits access to certain services, for example consulting your answering machine for messages. The post office also has telephone boxes, the first in Tunisia to take telephone cards.

Airline and Shipping Companies – Tunis Air, ☎ (04) 228 028, Fax (04) 299 573. Located at 4 ave de l'Armée.

Freight, Place du 2 Mars, ☎ (04) 278 017, Fax (04) 299 573.

Air France, rue Taïeb Méhiri, ☎ (04) 224 847.

Tuninter, Abou Nawas Sfax Centre, contact Tunis Air.

CTN, 7 ave Habib Maazoum, ☎ (04) 228 020 / 228 022, Fax (04) 220 822. Open 8am-12noon and 2pm-5.30pm. In summer open 7.30am-1pm.

WHERE TO STAY

Most hotels are in the city centre. The most charming of these is Les Oliviers, unfortunately closed for renovation. Less appealing accommodation is available until it reopens.

From US$18-42

Thyna Hôtel, rue Habib Maâzoun (on the corner of Place Marburg), ☎ (04) 225 266 / 225 317, Fax (04) 225 773 – 27rm 🛏 🞂 ✕ This hotel is centrally-located and inexpensive. Unfortunately, maintenance leaves much to be desired. Televisions are optional.

Hôtel Le Colisée, ave Taïeb Méhiri, ☎ (04) 227 800 / 227 806, Fax (04) 299 350 – 63rm 🛏 🞂 ✕ Also located in the city centre, this hotel has a 1950's charm in a basic sort of way with wooden furniture and olive-green paint. Air-conditioning available in certain rooms.

From US$42-75

Hôtel Syfax, in the public garden, on the road to Soukra (take the ave des Martyrs in the medina, then the road from Gabès, turn right onto the road to Soukra), ☎ (04) 243 333, Fax 245 226 – 127rm 🛏 🍽 🞂 📺 ✕ 🛝 CC This Tunisian hotel belongs to the French

hotel chain, Novotel and caters essentially to businessmen. Although it is only a short distance from the city centre, the surroundings are peaceful and there is a swimming pool set in a small garden.
Hôtel El Andalous, ave des Martyrs, ☎ (04) 299 100, Fax (04) 299 425 – 92rm 📶 📋 🔎 TV ✕ CC A little off the main route, but only 2min from the medina. This somewhat nondescript hotel is nonetheless equipped with all modern comforts.

More than US$75
Hôtel Abou Nawas Sfax, ave Habib Bourguiba, ☎ (04) 225 700 / 225 701, Fax (04) 225 521 – 130rm 📶 📋 🔎 TV ✕ 🛎 CC Located in the city centre, this 9-storey hotel is ideal for businessmen. The swimming pool is on the 2nd floor.

EATING OUT
The local speciality is fish marinated in a cumin sauce and then grilled over charcoal.

• In the modern city
Less than US$10
Le Bec fin (C2), Place du 2 Mars, ☎ (04) 221 407. This is a clean and simple place to sample Tunisian specialities. Closed Sunday lunchtime.

From US$10-20
🍴 **Le Bagdad** (B2), 63 ave Farhat Hached (near the Hôtel Thyna), ☎ (04) 223 856. 🍷 CC Local people do not eat out much, but the Bagdad is always full until late at night. And it's a mixed crowd – there are veils as well as plunging necklines. It would be unthinkable not to recommend the fish but, for a change, trade the usual "mechouia" salad for a soup prepared in true Sfaxian manner. Closed on Fridays.
Le Printemps (B3), 57 ave Habib Bourguiba, ☎ (04) 226 973. Although the menu lists numerous dishes, they are not always available. You can always settle for the wide choice of fish and also enjoy some Franco-Tunisian specialities. Closed Sundays.

More than US$20
Le Corail (B3), 39 rue Habib Maazoun, ☎ (04) 227 301 🍷 CC The city's most prestigious restaurant. Its international decor, cooking and service are all in keeping with its reputation.

• Médina
Less than US$10
Restaurant du 7 novembre Kimo (A2), 127 rue de la Mecque, ☎ (04) 228 719. Closed Mondays. In the winter, the lady cook rustles up a rare speciality: couscous au "besbes" (fennel). A very friendly, family-run eating house.

WHERE TO GO FOR A DRINK
Cafés – Contrary to those of the more touristy towns, Sfax cafés are almost exclusively frequented by men.

• In the modern city
Grand Café de la Paix (B2), 13 ave Farhat Hached. This is a good central place for people-watching.
Café des Palmiers (B2), Place du 2 Mars 1934. Here you will find a shaded terrace.

• In the medina
🍵 **Le Diwan** (B2), at the medina's ramparts. Take Bab Diwan and turn left. The tea here is rather expensive but there is a good atmosphere and a fine view of the old town.

LEISURE
Sports – *Municipal swimming pool*, on the road to the airport (0.5km), ☎ (04) 240 372.

FESTIVALS
• Sfax
Music Festival, in July-August. Variety shows and musical performances are not very popular with the Sfaxians, despite the organisers' desire to place this event on the same level as the Carthage or El Jem Festivals.

• In the surrounding area
Art Festival in Mahrès in July. Exhibits by little-known artists.
Fantasia Festival in Agareb in July.

Hammams – **Hammam Essalem**, rue des Aqueducs (on the corner of ave Farhat Hached, near the Masmoudi bakery). Open 11am-4pm for women and 6-10am / 5-10pm for men. (Entrance: TD1.250, Massages: TD1.5).

SHOPPING

Souks – Open daily (except Mondays) from 8.30am-7pm. The jewellery souk is open 8.30am-12noon and 2-5pm (approximately), but only in the mornings during summer months.

Bakeries – *Masmoudi*, on a small street across from 6 ave Farhat Hached, near the roundabout on the way to Gabès. Open 8am-1pm and 2-6pm, except Sundays.

Siella, across from 171 rue Mongi Slim in the medina. Specialises in doughnuts that many Sfaxians enjoy for breakfast while they are still warm, accompanied by a glass of "lagmi" (milk wine). Open 6-11am only.

Bookshops – *Librairie-papeterie el Mouna*, 9 ave Farhat Hached, ☎ (04) 210 133. As well as books, this establishment has a selection of international (mainly French) newspapers and periodicals. Open off-season from 8am-12noon and 2.30-6.30pm. In summer, open 7.30am-12noon and 4-7pm. Closed Sunday afternoons and Mondays.

Antiques and Handicrafts – - SOCOPA, rue Hamadi Tej (near the Libyan Consulate), ☎ (04) 296 826. Winter, open 9am-12noon and 3-7pm. In summer, open 9am-7pm. Closed Sundays.

Carpets – *Zribi Ahmen Ben Taher*, 30 souk des étoffes (the fabric souk), ☎ (04) 222 224.

Sponges – *Neptune de Abdelkader el Maghrebi*. Open 7.30am-12noon except Sundays.

Mohammed M'Barek – This wholeseller has sponges that vary in size from 8 to 24cm and in price from TD1 to TD10. Open 9am-1pm and 4-6pm, except Sundays.

Making the most of the Kerkennah Isles

GETTING THERE

By ferry – SONOTRAK, landing stage in Sfax, ave Mohammed Hédi Khefacha (the entrance is difficult to find for cars; you'll need to zigzag your way left of the building), ☎ (04) 222 216 / 222 615 / 226 316, Fax (04) 298 496. Rates: for cars: TD4, for passengers: 570 millimes. There are 4 crossings per day during the winter, from 6am-8pm. In summer, there are 10 departures daily from 4am-8pm. The crossing lasts 75min.

GETTING AROUND

By bus – There is a bus station at the ferry's landing stage.

By taxi – Taxis are waiting when the ferry arrives. There is a stand next to the Remla mosque. You can also hire the services of **KEFI minibus**, Aouled Kacem, ☎ (04) 481 234.

Bicycle hire – At the Hôtel Cercina.

ADDRESS BOOK

Emergency – *Police Station*, Remla, ☎ (04) 481 053.

Border Police, ☎ (04) 481 328.

Hospital, Remla, ☎ (04) 481 052 / 481 119.

Tourist Office – Since there is no office on the island, obtain information at the tourist office in Sfax.

Banks / Currency Exchange – UIB, ave Farhat Hached.

Post office – Remla, ☎ (04) 481 000.

WHERE TO STAY

From US$18-42

Hôtel Cercina, route de Sidi Fredj, ☎ (04) 489 953 / 600, Fax (04) 489 878 – 32rm 🛏 ✗ 🐾 CC This is a back-to-basics hotel, with a level of comfort approximating to that of a beach hut. Potential guests should not be put off, however, even if the solar panels frequently fail to provide hot water; the proprietor has a heart of gold and is always willing to help you organise a fishing trip on one of his felouques.

Aziz, on the road from Sidi Fredj, ☎ (04) 489 932 – 22rm 🛏 ✗ 🔧 While this hotel lacks charm, it is clean and modern. Each room is equipped with a kitchenette. The beach is 200m away on the far side of the road.

Grand Hôtel, on the tourist road, ☎ (04) 489 861 / 866, Fax (04) 481 485 – 108rm ⁌ ℰ ⏉ 🛁 **cc** The largest hotel in Kerkennah is a favourite with the older generation of British package tourists. The decor is faded 1960s and the rooms rather barrack-like. The foods tends to be insipid with yoghurt served regularly for dessert. You would be better off eating in the snack bar in the garden near the beach. On the other hand, the Grand Hôtel can boast the only swimming pool on the island and the only beach more or less worthy of its name.

Hôtel Cercina (see above). 16 new rooms, with air-conditioning, telephone and television, all of which are attractively decorated with wrought-iron furniture, and as always, Chokri's inimitable welcome. The only thing missing is a view of the sea.

EATING OUT

Fish is king in the Kerkennah Isles, caught in the hoop nets that can be seen all over the island. During the season, try the freshly-caught mullet.

Less than US$10
Restaurant at the Hôtel Cercina, on the road from Sidi Fredj, ☎ (04) 481 228 / 259 453, Fax (04) 481 262 ♱ 🛖 This restaurant is considered to be one of the best on the island. Try the fish "melthouth", the barley couscous and anything that is made with octopus and cuttlefish. The terrace is a good place to watch the sun go down.

From US$10-20
🍴 **Restaurant la Sirène**, at Remla beach past the ave Farhad Hached, ☎ (04) 481 118 🛖 This establishment specialises in cuttlefish eggs and octopus salad which are served overlooking the sea. The lamb is delicious too. This is the connoisseurs' choice.

WHERE TO GO FOR A DRINK

Cafés – At the bars in the **Hôtel Cercina** and the **Grand Hôtel**.

LEISURE

Boat trips – The hotels in Kerkennah organise sea outings. Yasser Achour, ☎ (04) 484 035, arranges day trips fishing and idling aboard his felouque.

Festivals – **Mermaid Festival** in July-August. Boat trips and folklore.

J.-F. Galmiche

The port of Sfax

The Sahara near Douz

THE SOUTH

The road to the South from Sfax follows the curve of the Gulf of Gabès. This deep indentation marks the threshold of another Tunisia: a land of great arid spaces, of an implacable sun where life is concentrated in luxuriant oases, with their tall palms, orchards and vegetable gardens. Each of these Gardens of Eden has its own personality: Gabès, bathed by the Mediterranean; Gafsa, modest and withdrawn; Nefta, with its crater-like "Corbeille"; Tozeur, emerging like a mirage from a beautiful fertile plain. These are the great oases but there are others, like Douz, the "gate to the Sahara" struggling endlessly against the inexorable advance of the sands. The advancing dunes make an adventure playground for off-road adventures and camel races. More intimate, the oases of Chebika, Midès and Tamerza seem to be asleep in the folds of the mountains along the Algerian frontier. To the south of Gabès, the eroded folds of the Jebel Dahar protect a string of traditional villages, many of them abandoned. Between Medenine and Tataouine the *ksour* (fortified villages), consisting of hundreds of grain-stores, create veritable fortresses, often clinging to dizzy rocky peaks. At Matmata, the soft yellow rock has enabled the establishment of astounding villages consisting of underground or pit dwellings. These fantastical troglodytic living quarters have even influenced major film directors – George Lucas came here to film several scenes of his *Star Wars*. But for many the first contact with the Tunisian south, or even with Tunisia itself, begins at Jerba, the island of ten thousand palm trees, a temperate climate in all seasons, vast beaches of fine sand and warm shallow seas.

Exploring the South

A land of tradition and trade

Less won over to progress than the North of the country, this part of Tunisia remains attached to traditional ways of life. This is a place to linger, to admire the costumes, to breathe in the atmosphere, to appreciate the pace of life, to seek out the most beautiful items produced by the local craftsmen, to bargain over jewellery, leather, fabrics, esparto ware and pottery, before allowing yourself to be persuaded over a glass of mint tea that you have chosen the best. Contact with local people is easy, for although reserved they are friendly and approachable, particularly if you speak a little French. A transitional land between Africa, the East and the Mediterranean, the Tunisian South, despite its lack of outstanding monuments, is none the less the proud possessor of a rich history illustrated by the diversity of its people. The population includes the last Berber-speaking people of Dahar, the Jews of Jerba, semi-nomad but now settled shepherds, descendants of black slaves – together with the Arabs, they make up a dazzling range of faces and costumes.

More than in other regions of Tunisia, the French Protectorate's creation of modern frontiers disturbed trading patterns which dated back to classical times. The slow caravans of slaves and gold from black Africa no longer arrive in Gabès; from Morocco and Algeria, Moslem pilgrims travel to Mecca by charter flight, abandoning the route through the Tunisian south which reached Arabia by way of Libya and Egypt. After years of economic difficulty which saw many of its people emigrate, the region is now concentrating on its oases, its phosphates and above all on the tourism which makes significant contributions to income and employment.

En route...

The Tunisian south often forms a destination in itself. Within three hours' flight-time from London, lovers of the desert and its oases can be in Tozeur; those who are simply looking for complete relaxation will land at Jerba. The larger towns on the mainland are all accessible by bus or by inexpensive shared taxis, while the towns and villages on the island of Jerba are linked by a network of public transport and taxis.

On the other hand, routes through Dahar and the mountain oases (west of Gafsa), which in parts are simply tracks, require a private vehicle. Even if you are told otherwise ordinary hire cars, like Renault Clios or Peugeot 106s, for example are adequate to cover these two routes outside the periods of heavy rainfall. Highway maintenance departments look after the tracks, and every year, many kilometres of previously unsurfaced roads are covered with asphalt. Off-road vehicles are not essential to venture into the Sahara, although visitors unfamiliar with the terrain should always be accompanied by a guide.

To link the two tours suggested here, and to visit the larger oases, rent a vehicle for a week and allow some extra days to make the most of a well-deserved rest in Jerba. If you only have a week, allow three days of excursions in the Dahar and visit Gabès on the way back.

The ksar of Medenine

JERBA★★
The large island in the Gulf of Gabès
Pop 120 000; 514sqkm

Not to be missed
The daily market and narrow pedestrian streets of Houmt Souk.
The traditional villages and beaches.
And remember ...
Visit Houmt Souk in the evening when the tourists have gone.
Sleep in one of the charming Arab inns in Houmt Souk.
The island is best visited on two-wheels.

The Lotus-eaters' magic

Jerba invites rest, relaxation and physical pleasures. Everything here is designed to relieve care: endless beaches, calm seas, dramatically blue skies, cooling sea breezes and hotels to satisfy the most demanding holiday-makers. It is not surprising, then, that this is claimed to be the legendary land of the Lotus Eaters, whose temptation almost caused Ulysses and his companions to abandon their voyage. Once settled in the vast "tourist zone" on the east coast many visitors ignore the rest of the island. This is a great shame, for Jerba is far more than a vast seaside resort. Its island nature has shaped its landscape and its population. Scarcely more than 35km at its widest, it is nowhere higher than 55m. The villages of widely scattered, low-lying houses are barely visible. Strange buildings stand amidst the olive trees, figs and palms; they include the fortified farms known as *menzel*, mosques with thick-set shapes, and weaving workshops with triangular pediments and half-buried potters' studios. The brilliant white limewash of all these buildings, glittering in the sun, makes a dazzling contrast with the azure sky.

A coveted island

Despite the flood of tourists the people of the island guard their identity jealously, as they have always done, for this land without natural defences has seen far less peaceful invasions. The original Berber population had to come to terms with the Greeks, Phoenicians and Romans, who all established trading posts at Jerba. The original settlements were called Meninx, Tipasa and Girba, the latter giving its name to the island in the 3C at a time when Christianity was expanding. The murex, an abundant form of shell-fish along these coasts, was used at this time for the purple dye that coloured the robes of high dignitaries. Jerba was a flourishing link connecting Africa and the West, invaded by the Vandals and Byzantines before its conquest by the Arab horsemen in 667. It accepted the version of Islam advocated by the Kharidjite sect (though not without a struggle), faced the Hilal in the 9C, and later had to deal with Fatimid, Bedouin, Norman, Aragonese and Spanish invasions. In the 16C, the island was a haunt of pirates; in 1560 a European expedition attempted to dislodge them, a venture which proved a disaster for the attackers. The coasts of Jerba remained infested by these sea-rovers until the 18C. These various periods of insecurity have formed the character of the island, for the ancient coastal towns have been abandoned in favour of villages in the interior, made up of *menzel*, while the coast is studded with watch-towers and fortresses (*borj*).

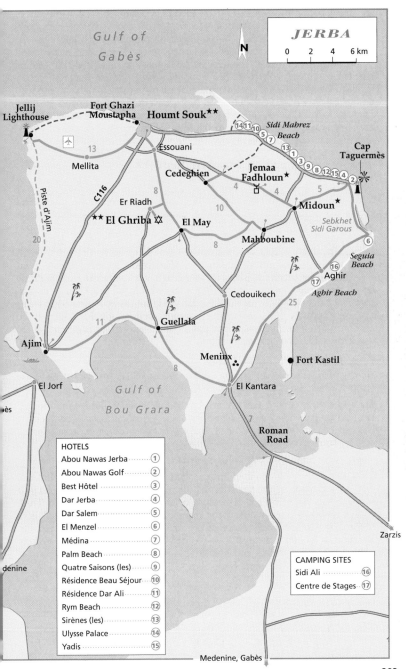

JERBA

0   2   4   6 km

Gulf of Gabès

N

Jellij Lighthouse
Fort Ghazi Moustapha
Houmt Souk ★★
Sidi Mahrez Beach
Cap Taguermès
Essouani
Mellita
Cedeghien
Jemaa Fadhloun ★
Piste d'Ajim
C116
Er Riadh
★★ El Ghriba
El May
Midoun ★
Mahboubine
Sebkhet Sidi Garous
Seguia Beach
Aghir
Aghir Beach
Cedouikech
Guellala
Meninx
Fort Kastil
Ajim
El Jorf
Gulf of Bou Grara
El Kantara
Roman Road
Zarzis
Medenine

13
8
10
4
4
5
8
20
11
8
25
7
8

14 11 10
5 7
13
1
3 9 8 12 15 4 2
6
16
17

Medenine, Gabès

As a result of this turbulent history, the island's population is remarkably mixed, and includes Malekite and Ibadite Moslems, Arabic and Berber-speakers, Jews in Er Riadh and Hara Kébira, black Africans in Midoun. For a long time the absence of running water limited expansion on the island, and often forced young people to emigrate. The Jerbians are famous travellers, and their trading talents have spread far beyond their frontiers – many of them run local grocery shops in Paris. The island's economy is increasingly turning to tourism, and with a hotel capacity of more than 10 000 beds, Jerba has become a holidaymakers' paradise as Italian, German and above all French visitors flock to its magnificent beaches. On the mainland to the south is the recently developed tourist area of Zarzis, an extension of Jerba.

■ Houmt Souk★★
Allow half a day

Jerba's only real town, Houmt Souk, invites leisurely exploration. The island capital has a delightfully old-fashioned atmosphere, with its beautiful houses from the early 20C and *fondouks* (inns), elegant lanes, souks and squares draped with bougainvillea shading restaurants and cafés.

Despite the influx of tourists, the town still draws in villagers from all over the island to do business or visit the market. Many of the local women still wear the costume for which the island is famous; it is made of white cloth perfectly set off by orange trimmings, topped by a broad-brimmed straw hat. In its harmonious framework of white buildings bathed in sunshine, Houmt Souk seems to expect no more of its visitors than a gentle stroll, an idle hour spent in an open-air café or restaurant, and perhaps some not-too-serious bargaining at the jeweller's stall or the craftsman's shop.

A walk around Houmt Souk
Starting from the taxi rank this route will take around half an hour for anyone able to resist the temptation of the souks.

The taxi rank is flanked to the north by the **Sidi Ibrahim and Hemni mosque** founded in 1674 *(the Houmt Souk mosques are not open to visitors)*. This building was part of a complex that included a bakery, a mausoleum, a médersa (Moslem college) and a domed hammam *(still in operation to the left of the mosque)*.

Take the lane between the café with a covered terrace and the Turkish bath.

The peace of the pedestrianised town centre is only disturbed by the splutter of scooters and mopeds. The first street on the right leads to the Youth Hostel next to the Hôtel Marhala. Each is housed in an enchanting old **fondouk.** These ancient travellers' rests, known in the Orient as "khans" or "caravanserais", have in this case retained their function of providing accommodation. The fondouks are laid out around a courtyard with a well. The ground floor, once used for stables and storage, has been converted into modest bedrooms.

Go under the arches across the rue Moncef Bey, then turn left towards the Place d'Algerie.

One of the town's busiest cafés is the popular establishment with tables set out beneath the shadow of a number of leafy trees. As in all the Jerba *moka* (cafés), only tea, coffee or soft drinks are available. On some days a small pottery market takes place here. The **Turkish Mosque** (Mosquée des Turcs) close by is topped by a lantern in Wahhabite style.

Go to the right from the café.

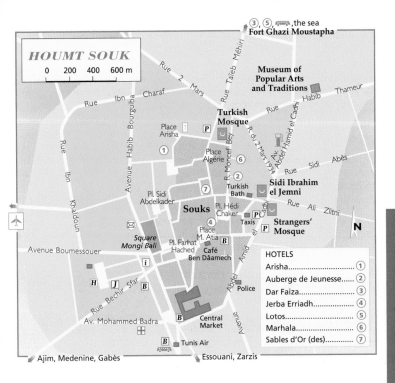

The little street leads to the Place Arisha, which used to be the forecourt of the town's Christian **church.** With its two great bell-towers the church is used as a sports hall, though one chapel is reserved for Catholic worship (*Mass on Sundays at 10am*).

The street goes past the Hôtel Arisca (another pretty *fondouk*), plunges into quiet lanes where beautiful red fabrics are woven on looms, then reaches the **covered souks.** This is the jewellers' quarter, traditionally a Jewish trade. Further on are weavers, leather-workers and craftsmen in wickerwork, selling some of the best of Jerbian and Tunisian craftsmanship. At the far end of the souk, the lane opens out into a large slightly raised square with an open-air café.

Go down to the left of the café.

Beyond the café, the square flanked by the ave Bourguiba has a splendid display of colourful ceramics for sale, with the **market** facing it. In the stalls, long strings of peppers spice the atmosphere. One of the market's most striking sites is the morning fish auction. Presiding from a chair set on a table, the auctioneer, red chéchia clamped firmly on his head, calls up bids for the fish displayed in little festoons.

Retrace your steps as far as the excellent Ben Yedder pâtisserie, then turn right.

This brings you to the handsome rectangular square and the tables of the **Ben Dâamech café,** the most popular café in the town, and a good place to pause for a glass of tea while shopping. A passage-way leads to the smaller

Place Hédi Chaker, full of bougainvillea, and the most handsome hotel in the town centre is only a step away; this is the Erriadh, which is also located in a small *fondouk.*

From the Place d'Algérie go past the Turkish Mosque then, on the right, continue past the pretty little Moorish-style building housing the local tax office. The museum is 300m along on the left, among a number of travel agencies.

Museum of Popular Arts and Traditions**
(La Musée des Arts et Traditions populaires)

(9.30am-4.30pm in summer; 8am-12noon, 3pm-7pm out of season, closed on Friday; entrance charge.) The museum occupies an elegant *zawiya*, built in the late 18C to house the tombs of two *marabouts* (Moslem holy men), Sidi Zitouni and Sidi Ameur.

Opposite the ticket desk is the small square **prayer room** that was used by pilgrims. On display are collections of traditional Jerbian costumes, while to the right of the entrance, a tiny **domed room** is the setting for three manuscripts as well as a number of *calames* (reed pens used for calligraphy) and an ink-well. Facing the entrance, a chamber with a ceiling of painted wood panels leads to the **koubba** (monument set over the grave of a marabout) – this was the chosen location for the two saints. The splendid vault of the dome consists of ceramic tiles set in rows, alternately glazed and unglazed. It is supported on a drum with plaster work representing *mihrabs* (niches indicating the direction of Mecca) framing cypress trees. On display is an outstanding collection of traditional jewellery to admire.

Two successive courtyards lead to the **pilgrims' hall** beneath a large dome. According to popular belief, after a night devoted to meditation and prayer, certain men who were in communication with the after-life married invisible women and fathered children who were equally incorporeal. More prosaically, the visitor's eye is drawn by three tombs discovered in the courtyard of the *zawiya*, and the chests and shelves of painted wood.

There is a fine array of amphorae in a **building** in the first courtyard, together with a set of ten oil lamps above two ritual pots.

The Ghazi Moustapha fort

8am-6pm, closed on Fridays, entrance charge. This fort, also known as the El Kébir *borj*, overlooks the sea at the far end of the rue Taïeb Méhiri which runs from the Place d'Algérie *(700m from the town centre).* This *borj*, which was built of beautiful ochre stone in the 15C by the Sultan Abou Farès, has recovered its former glory after substantial restoration work. In 1560, the Spanish who had taken refuge here were besieged by the pirate Dragut. After two months the fortress fell, and the 6 000 besieged were slaughtered. A walk around the outside reveals two outer walls (the inner, older, wall dates back to the work of Roger de Loria in the late 13C). The view from the top of these ramparts looks over the harbour close at hand. At the centre, an *impluvium* (open-air basin to collect rain water) stands in front of a building with two domes. Stone balls, bases of columns and Roman remains discovered in the fort are visible, no doubt from Girba, the ancient city which gave the island its name.

■ A tour of the island
Allow a day. 116km of roads and good tracks

This tour shows how surprisingly widely the houses are scattered; many of the villages consist of a few public buildings (post office) or a religious establishment (mosque) beside the main road, a few shops under arcading and the inevitable café where the men meet around a game of cards or dominoes. Life continues peacefully at the *menzel* (fortified farms) surrounded by their gardens (sadly, the farms are not open to visitors).

The tour is in short stages of 10km and there is no risk of getting lost. The network of roads suitable for cars is limited, so you will need to use by-ways and tracks as well. The harmonious interior of the island is a world away from the gargantuan developments of the coast. Here the people have kept their traditions of hospitality, and visitors should not be surprised to be invited into a family home.

■ From Houmt Souk to Jellij Lighthouse – *Take the airport road from the town centre.* The road takes you through ancient olive groves before passing the **Jemaa el Kébir** on the left *(after 5km)*. Also known as the great mosque of Mellita, dating from the 10C, stands at the centre of a courtyard with an *impluvium* feeding underground cisterns. Its corner minaret is squat and topped with a masonry cone. The little village of Mellita (a name of Phoenician origin) lies 2km further on.

Continue past the entrance to the airport.

Water coolers in the port of Houmt Souk

S Viron/DIAF

Mellita airport has scheduled and charter flights from several European cities. Since the air embargo was imposed on Libya (1992) it has become the nearest airport to Tripoli, and naturally benefits from passengers en route to the Libyan capital. Libyan-registered taxis make the 4 hour trip to Tripoli.

The road runs along the airport fence to the junction with the side-road to Ajim (*turn right along it*). **Jellij Lighthouse** (*2km further on*) stands on the site of a former *borj* founded in the 18C. To the right of the lighthouse, behind the *impluvium*, can be seen the fish traps made using palm fronds.

■ **The west coast** – *Go south along the minor road towards Ajim, The road is in a reasonably good state despite a few sandy stretches.* The shoreline to the west of the island is in complete contrast to the tourist zone. No main road and no hotels – only a few villas and unspoilt inlets of turquoise water with perhaps a dozen fishing boats at their moorings. No lovely beaches of fine sand, but the rocks do not prevent swimming. The road runs beside the most substantial stand of palm-trees on the island, which produce dates of modest quality, before rejoining the road leading to the centre of Ajim.

Zriba, amphorae and nets

Three traditional methods of fishing are still in use on Jerba. The "zriba" (a fixed fish trap) operates by encouraging fish to swim into nets beside rows of palms planted in the mud, in line with the direction of the current. For fishing with amphorae, lines of jars are strung together and submerged, then taken up again when octopus have settled in them. Net fishing uses double funnels made from date-palm branches: the fish go through the first funnel and are trapped in the second.

■ **Ajim** – The area around Ajim split off from the red cliffs of El Jorf, less than 2.5km away on the mainland, around a million years ago. People and animals used to be taken across by telucca, but with its ferry (*for details of crossing, see page 303*), Ajim is now the island's main port. Sponges hang in the breeze outside the shops, for this is also a sponge-fishing centre; Tunisia supplies most of Europe with sponges via the markets of Sfax and Gabès. Before leaving the village, be sure to have a drink in the Oasis café in the town centre.

At the main roundabout, identifiable by its clock, turn right on the road to Guellala which runs along the coastline of the Gulf of Bou Grara.

■ **Guellala** – A sign indicating *"Atelier de poterie d'art"* (pottery) welcomes you on the way into the small town. A little further on, the road passes a derelict kiln on the left before reaching the town centre, with its displays of amphorae, coloured dishes, vases and ceramic tiles. There can be no doubt that this is indeed Guellala, the island's pottery capital.

Undecorated jars and amphorae are local specialities: essential pottery for the housewife and fisherman, but no particular draw for tourist eyes – pottery glazed in tempting colours, imported from the mainland, is more immediately attractive. If jars and dishes seem too cumbersome, you may be tempted by the famous magic camel, a small and ingeniously designed piece of local pottery; you will be shown how one side pours out milk and the other coffee. After a shake, the animal's mouth delivers café au lait!

A visit should be made to at least one of these dark workshops, half underground, with stone arches supporting ceilings covered with split palm-tree trunks. In the cool shadows the potter's skilful hands continue their traditional craft, shaping the plain pottery which will be fired after drying.

In the town centre, take the road for El Kantara, situated 8km away.

JF Galmiche

Oil-press, Guellala

■ **Roman causeway** – This ancient routeway, 7km long, is the island's umbilical cord, linking El Kantara with the mainland. The Romans called the causeway the Pons Zita, and used it to link their trading posts at Meninx and at Zita near Zarzis, but it was abandoned and gradually disappeared, leaving only a ford used by camel-drivers and called the *"Trik el Jemel"* (the Camels' Way). The current road was built in 1951 with a bridge half way across to allow small boats to reach the Gulf of Bou Grara. The enormous and unattractive pipe on the right of the road brings drinking water from the mainland to the island.

■ **Excursion to Zarzis** – *(66km round trip)*. The road which continues the Roman road and leads to **Zarzis** on the mainland has little interest. The magnificent beaches and their attendant hotels in this tourist zone are merely an extension of Jerba. Further to the south *(12km away)*, the town of Zarzis is still looking for an identity. It has none of the charm of Houmt Souk; only the museum of **Popular Arts and Customs**, installed in a vast underground oil store, is worth a brief visit *(8.30am-12.30pm; 2.30pm-6.30pm (5.30pm in winter), closed on Sundays; entrance charge, 2km from the centre along the bvd de l'Environnement)*.

■ **Jerba's tourist zone** – *At El Kantara, take the Midoun road after the police station.* A signboard indicates the site of ancient **Meninx**, probably founded by the Phoenicians – a trading post with substantial warehouses, a *columbarium* and a large basilica. The site has been cleared and the ruins scattered, and there is now little of interest.

3km from El Kantara, the **fort of Kastil** can be seen on the right at the end of a peninsula. Built in 1285 by Roger de Loria, admiral of Aragon and Sicily, it was overwhelmed in 1334 by the Jerbians who wanted to be free of Spanish domination. They reduced the fort's garrison to slavery. A little further on, the hotels which mark the beginning of the tourist zone appear to be reflected in the water, but this is only a mirage, an optical illusion which vanishes as you approach Aghir.

The **public beach at Aghir** lies at the southern end of the great Seguia beach. The road runs past the hotels set round the *sebkhet*, or salt marsh, of Sidi Garous, before reaching the red and white lighthouse at **Cap Taguermès** ("Taguemess" on some maps), at the extreme northeast tip of the island. The **Houmt Souk public beach** with its beautiful fine white sand is reached at the northern end of the tourist zone by the Hôtel Ulysse Palace.

To get to Midoun, turn left by the lighthouse at Taguermès.

■ **Midoun★** – The town of Midoun makes much of its livelihood from tourism, and its narrow streets have little of the charm of Houmt Souk. It is a place to stock up with souvenirs or enjoy a drink of tea on the shady terrace of the café facing the ONAT shop.

From Midoun, take the main highway towards Houmt Souk.

On the left of the road after 4km, a white mosque *(not signposted)* is well worth a visit. This is the **Jemaa Fadhloun★**, a very interesting example of a Wahhabite religious complex. The mosque is approached through several rooms, including a mausoleum at the left corner of the complex, which is immediately followed by a room designed for ritual washing. The water gathered in the big *impluvium* opposite was fed into cisterns. A little further on, an opening in the wall leads to the courtyard of the dazzling white mosque. The square prayer room has four pillars and on the right, stairs lead up to the minaret.

A further 4km beyond the mosque, turn left on the road to the village of Cedeghien.

■ **Cedeghien** – Once past the tiny centre of this Berber-speaking village, the by-road runs between the gardens of Cedeghien, among the most flourishing and densely planted in the island. The garden plots are bound by earth banks *(tabias)*, up to 2m high and planted with Barbary figs and aloes. Behind them, pomegranates and orange trees grow in the shade of palm trees. Several *menzel*, some in ruins, shelter beneath the trees, their size demonstrating the wealth of the area.

■ **Mahboubine** – The by-road ends at the junction with the highway between Mahboubine and El May. A detour via Mahboubine *(1km away, turn left at the fork)* leads to the **El Kateb mosque** with its Turkish-style domes. The mosque is just beyond the fork to Cedouikech, among pretty gardens.

■ **El May** – *Continue to El May (8km from Mahboubine). In the centre, turn right on the road to Houmt Souk.* The **El May mosque** stands a little to the right of the road, immediately beyond the fork. It has the typically solid appearance of a Jerbian mosque, a style which, as with the *menzel*, enabled it to play a defensive role. Its courtyard forms a vast *impluvium*.

Continue towards Houmt Souk. 2km futher on, turn left towards Er Riadh; after another 1.5km, turn left again for the synagogue at El Ghriba. Park in the open space in front of the religious buildings.

■ **El Ghriba★★** – *Closed on Saturdays, entrance free but donations appreciated.* The synagogue, a modest building with steely blue reflections, was rebuilt in 1920. This sanctuary is one of the key points of North African Judaïsm *(see -*

under the heading "Religions", page 58).
An annual pilgrimage (on the 33rd day of the Jewish feast of Passover) brings the Jews of North Africa together. El Ghriba (the "Wonderful") consists of two halls. The vast pillared aisle which greets the visitor is decorated in oriental style with coloured ceramics and windows, and on the benches ageless attendants cool themselves with fans that originate in the Tunisian south. Visitors must remove their shoes and cover their heads. In this place of prayer, a religious atmosphere is created by the light from oil lamps and by the intonations of the *batlanim* who

The menzel

With its windowless walls and corner towers, the menzel looks like a small fortress but it is in reality simply a large farm designed for a completely self-sufficient life in times of trouble. Each menzel, for example, has an impluvium to collect the vital rain-water. The rooms are arranged round an inner courtyard. The alcove used for sleeping in winter is covered by a dome, while the store-rooms, like ghorfas, are covered with barrel vaulting. The menzel, a type of structure found only in Jerba, is being increasingly abandoned in favour of modern buildings.

recite for payment from believers. Passing pilgrims give them small notes, seeking a cure or a success. Beneath fine carved panelling on the wall, ex-voto offerings in metal depict houses, vases or Stars of David. The place is particularly venerated, and the synagogue, probably founded in the 6C BC, prides itself in possessing a Torah which is one of the oldest known. The neighbouring village of Er Riadh (formerly Hara Sghrira) has a Jewish community several hundred strong.

Return to the El May – Houmt Souk road and turn left along it to return to the island capital.

On the left, shortly before reaching Houmt Souk, is Hara Kebira (Essouani), the island's other Jewish village.

Mosque at Houmt Souk

JF Galmiche

Making the most of Jerba

GETTING THERE

By air – Jerba-Zarzis Airport, ☎ (05) 650 233. The airport is in Mellita, 8km from Houmt Souk and has most of the usual facilities, including taxis to Houmt Souk (TD4), car rental agencies (Hertz, Avis and Europcar), money exchange and telephones.

By bus – Bus Station, ☎ (05) 650 076. Used by the national company, SNTRI and regional companies such as SRTG Gabès, SRTG Medenine and SORETRAS. There are 2 departures daily to Tunis (8hr), 1 to Bizerta, 1 to Sousse, 3 to Sfax (4hr), 3 to Medenine and Tataouine, 3 to Gabès and 9 to Zarzis (of which 2 go via Zarzis' tourist area – 75min).

By car – Ferry, ☎ (05) 655 015 / 655 011. The ferry is the best way to get to the island for drivers coming from Kairouan, Sfax, Gabès or Medenine. The boat departs from El Jorf on the mainland and arrives in Ajim after a 15min crossing (although you normally have to queue for at least half an hour). Operates 24 hours a day every 10min during the day, every hour after 8pm and every 2hr from midnight to 6am. Rates: TD0.6 for cars, free for passengers).

From Zarzis, it is better to take the 7km long causeway that connects the island to the mainland. The crossing can be unnerving when the weather is bad. The road emerges at El Kantara (the Bridge) where there is a police check-point.

By shared taxi – Station, near the train station, ☎ (05) 650 475. Some taxis can only operate in certain parts of the island, others can go anywhere, including the tourist area.

GETTING AROUND

By bus – Bus station, Houmt Souk, ☎ (05) 650 076. SRTM has a bus service serving the hotels as well as the following destinations: 3 to Mellita (20min), 5 to El Ghriba (20min) and 5 to Guellala (45min). Approximately every hour, a shuttle goes between Houmt Souk and Midoun.

By taxi – Small taxis, Place Sidi Brahim and ave Habib Bourguiba, ☎ (05) 650 205.

Large taxis, near the post office in Houmt Souk. They are licensed for full day excursions to Zarzis, Tataouine and even Tozeur.

By car – A car will allow you to visit the tourist sites on the island as well as the ksour and the various oases. In view of the growing mileage of paved roads, a 4-wheel drive is not essential on the mainland (see the section "Exploring the South", page 290). 4-wheel drives can nevertheless be hired for the day at travel agencies (from TD100 to TD140 per day). The price includes the services of a driver who will also act as a guide. These drivers tend to stick to the classic tourist trail.

Car hire – Avis, ave Mohammed Badra, ☎ (05) 650 151.

Budget, Houmt Souk, ☎ (05) 653 444, Fax (05) 653 438.

Europcar, ave Abdelhamid El Cadhi, ☎ and Fax (05) 650 357.

Express Euro Rent, Hôtel Dar Jerba, ☎ (05) 657 569.

Hertz, Place Mongi Bali, ☎ (05) 650 196 / 650 039 and Hôtel Dar Jerba, ☎ (05) 657 158. Rental agencies at the airport, ☎ (05) 650 233.

Mattei (Ada), ave Habib Bourguiba, ☎ (05) 651 367.

Intercar, rue Abdel Hamid el Cadhi, ☎ (05) 651 155.

Moped hire – Numerous hotels rent mopeds or bicycles, as do the following agencies:

Holiday Bikes, at Moncef Bourguiba in the tourist area 14km, ☎ and Fax (05) 657 169. Credit cards accepted.

Abdellaziz Raïs, ave Abdel Hamid el Cadhi (opposite the Ettebsi Restaurant), ☎ (05) 650 301.

Hôtel Dar Jerba, ☎ (05) 657 191. Tandems are available to rent.

G. Degeorges

The El Ghriba synagogue

Address book

Tourist information

• Houmt Souk

Regional Tourism Board, road to Sidi Mahrez, ☎ (05) 650 016 / 650 544, Fax (05) 650 581. Open 8.30am-1pm and 3-5.45pm Mondays to Thursdays, 8.30am-1.30pm Fridays and Saturdays. In summer, open daily from 7.30am-1.30pm; 10am-12pm and 3pm-5pm on Sundays and bank holidays. **Airport Tourist Information point**, ☎ (05) 650 233.
Tourist Information Office, Place des Martyrs, ☎ (05) 650 915.
Federation of Tour Guides, ☎ (05) 651 755 / 651 557.

• Midoun

Tourist Information Office, on the pedestrian street opposite the café de la Jeunesse, ☎ (05) 658 116 / 657 413. Open 9am-1pm and 3-6pm. Occasionally open Sundays.

Banks / Currency Exchange

• Houmt Souk

BNT, Place Ben Daamech.
BT, rue du 20 Mars.
CFCT, Place Farhat Hached.
STB, Place Farhat Hached.
Visa, several cash dispensers are available in the town centre.
American Express, ave Habib Bourguiba.

• Midoun

There are several banks in the town centre

• In the tourist area

Emergency – Police, Houmt Souk, ☎ (05) 650 015.
Police, Midoun, ☎ (05) 657 311.
Road Assistance, ☎ (05) 657 311.
Visa, cash dispensers at STB, Hôtel Dar Jerba.

Post office – PTT, ave Habib Bourguiba, Houmt Souk.
PTT, Midoun, ☎ (05) 657 339, 657 240.

Telephones – There are several public phones in the centre of Houmt Souk, including one opposite the Erriadh Restaurant and another at the bus station, ave Abi Zamma el Balaoui (opposite the Ajil fuel station), ☎ (07) 231 041. 8.30am-12midnight, 10am-12midnight Sundays. TD2.500 per hour.

Internet – Jerba Cyber Espace, rue Mohammed el Ferjani, to the right of hôtel Jerba Erriadh, ☎ (05) 621 666. everyday from 8am-1pm / 3pm-6pm.

Health

• Houmt Souk – Hospital, ave Habib Bourguiba, ☎ (05) 650 018.
Echifa Clinic, ☎ (05) 650 441.
Yasmine Private Hospital, ☎ (05) 652 054.
Dialysis Centre, route Sidi Zayed, ☎ (05) 650 269 / 657 280.
Hospital, Midoun, ☎ (05) 657 280.
Airline Companies – Tunisair, ave Habib Bourguiba, Houmt Souk, ☎ (05) 650 159 / 650 410, Fax (05) 653 104. Airport, ☎ (05) 650 233.
Tuninter, airport, ☎ (05) 650 233, extension 5235.

Where to stay

There are no business hotels in Jerba. The choice is between tourist hotels by the sea and small typical hotels in Houmt Souk.

• Houmt Souk

Because this is Jerba, even the most basic hotels are expensive. However, prices are considerably lower in winter. Some inexpensive hotels are located in the former fondouks.

Less than US$18

Youth Hostel, rue Moncef Bey, ☎ (05) 650 629 – 100 beds ⚛ ✗ Situated in a former fondouk, the hostel provides basic comfort at reasonable prices. The showers are on the landing. Open to everyone.

Hôtel Marhala (Touring Club of Tunisia), rue Moncef Bey, ☎ (05) 650 146, Fax (05) 653 317 – 38rm ✗ The rooms, on two floors of a former fondouk, are organised around a pretty courtyard scented with jasmine and bougainvillea. Only the ground floor rooms have a private shower. Spartan but clean.

Hôtel Arisha, place de l'Église, ☎ (05) 650 384 – 25rm ✗ ⌇ A relatively-basic hotel located in a former fondouk. Although the rooms (with or without shower) could do with a coat of paint, they do have a certain charm.

Excellent Tunisian restaurant. Don't be put off by the pool's green water, it comes from a thermal spring.

From US$18-42

Hôtel Jerba Erriadh, 10 rue Mohammed El Ferjani, ☎ (05) 650 756, Fax (05) 650 487 – 39rm ⚊ ⚊ This peaceful little haven is located in the heart of Houmt Souk. The rooms are decorated with typically Tunisian furniture and are arranged around a patio full of chirpy birds. The hotel doesn't serve meals but there are a number of restaurants less than a 5min walk away.

Hôtel des Sables d'Or, rue Mohammed Ferjani, ☎ (05) 650 423 – 12rm ⚊ The courtyard here is not as attractive as the patio of the Jerba Erriadh, but this is still one of the better hotels in the inexpensive category. The price does not include breakfast.

Hôtel du Lotos, rue du Port, ☎ (05) 650 026 / 651 828, Fax (05) 651 127 – 17rm ⚊ ✕ ⚊ A small seaside establishment with a welcoming, well-worn feel to it. Some of the rooms have a terrace overlooking what will be the future marina.

Hôtel Dar Faiza, rue d'Ulysse, ☎ (05) 650 083, Fax (05) 651 763 – 25rm ⚊ ✕ ⚊ ⚊ ⚊ A hotel that combines charm, typical furniture and irreproachable cleanliness. The owners decided to preserve the villa as it was when a French count resided there up until the mid-1950s. Home to Jerba's first tennis court and swimming pool, it is set within a delightful garden. A warm, peaceful aura emanates from this hotel just a few minutes from the town centre.

• **In the tourist area**

From US$18-40

Résidence Dar Ali, Sidi Mahrez beach (opposite Ulysse Palace), ☎ (05) 758 671, Fax (05) 758 045 – 15rm ⚊ ⚊ ⚊ ✕ ⚊ ⚊ The modest size of these premises contributes to its friendly atmosphere. In the summer, guests can relax around the pool or take a dip in the sea from the hotel's private beach, a few hundred metres away. In the winter, a fire is lit in the living-room. The hotel also has an à la carte restaurant (music in the evenings) and a pizza-grill.

Résidence Le Beau Séjour, Sidi Mahrez tourist zone (opposite the Ulysse Palace), ☎ (05) 757 287 / 368, Fax (05) 757 367 – 14rm ⚊ ⚊ ✕ ⚊ ⚊ A small hotel with a very friendly atmosphere. The rooms open either onto a tiny garden or a balcony. Air-conditioning and fans are available. Guests are also welcome to use the neighbouring Hôtel Ulysse Palace's leisure facilities, for a charge.

Hôtel Dar Salem, Sidi Mahrez beach, (between hôtel Télémaque and Ulysse Palace) ☎ (05) 757 667 / 668, Fax (05) 757 677 – 22rm ⚊ ⚊ ⚊ ✕ ⚊ ⚊ ⚊ Giving into his clients, the owner of the Dar Faïza agreed to build this hotel in the heart of the tourist zone. It combines the feel of a family-run establishment with three-star comfort.

From US$75-100

Hôtel Les Sirènes, on the northeast tourist road, ☎ (05) 657 266 / 657 317, Fax (05) 657 267 – 120rm ⚊ ⚊ ✕ ⚊ ⚊ ⚊ Since its opening in 1969, this tourist hotel has managed to maintain loyal customers of a respectable age that ensures a certain tranquillity in the establishment. The staff are competent and attentive and will not hesitate to serve breakfast at 11am, even if service is officially over at 9.30. In addition to the swimming pool, hotel amenities include a thermal bath with waters rich in sulphur and iron.

Hôtel Abou Nawas Jerba, on the northeast tourist road, ☎ (05) 757 022, Fax (05) 757 700 – 251rm ⚊ ⚊ ⚊ ⚊ ✕ ⚊ ⚊ ⚊ This tourist hotel is noticeable for its discrete elegance. An orchestra plays next to the pool in the evening. The pool is covered during the winter.

Hôtel Les Quatre Saisons, on the northeast tourist road, ☎ (05) 658 582 / 659 013, Fax (05) 658 590 – 285rm ⚊ ⚊ ⚊ ✕ ⚊ ⚊ ⚊ Amenities include a heated pool in winter and a thermal bath. Televisions are available in the room for a supplement.

Hôtel Médina, tourist route, ☎ (05) 657 171, Fax (05) 657 385 – 330rm ⚊ ⚊ ⚊ ✕ ⚊ ⚊ ⚊ ⚊ ⚊ ⚊ The complex, located at the back of Hotel Télémaque if you're coming from Houmt Souk, is hidden behind a large, white gate. The hotel's appeal lies in its design based on the principle of a

Moorish village, with a central square and little cafés. The UCPA sports centre organises activities from December to May.

More than US$115

Hôtel Ulysse Palace, on the northeast tourist road, ☎ (05) 757 422, Fax (05) 757 850 – 300rm ⌇ ▤ ▣ ♪ ✗ ⌅ ⌖ **cc** This hotel is one of the oldest on the island and has become one of the best since its renovation. The pool is covered in the winter.

Hôtel Abou Nawas Golf, on the northeast tourist road, ☎ (05) 746 910, Fax (05) 746 918 – 251rm ⌇ ▤ ▣ ♪ ✗ ⌅ ⌖ **cc** This is the deluxe version of the other establishment belonging to the same chain, and is built in the low-roofed style of the island's menzel. There is an impressive black marble entrance.

Hôtel Yadis, on the northeast tourist road, ☎ (05) 747 235 / 236, Fax (05) 747 223 – 287rm ⌇ ▤ ▣ ♪ ✗ ⌅ ⌖ **cc** This hotel specialises in groups and provides a very efficient service.

Hôtel Palm Beach, on the northeast tourist road, ☎ (05) 657 350, Fax (05) 657 580 –287rm ⌇ ▤ ♪ ✗ ⌅ ⌖ **cc** A stylish hotel, distinguished by its excellent service. The pool is heated in winter.

• **Abhor Beach**

Two camp sites are available within a short distance of Abhor beach, some 30km from Houmt Souk, on the east of the island.

Below US$10

Camping Sidi Ali, hôtel Sidi Slim, ☎ (05) 657 021, Fax (05) 657 001.

Centre de Stages, ☎ (05) 657 366, Fax (05) 642 435.

EATING OUT

Jerba has the best fish in Tunisia, particularly when it arrives freshly-caught from the Bibane lagoon, a hundred or so kilometres away in the direction of Libya. In the autumn months, request "sberres" couscous (sparre or sparlote in Greek) or fish roe. The adventurous might like to try the camel, or "ghroud", young camel that is less than 6 months old.

• **In Houmt Souk**

Less than US$10

Les Palmiers, rue Mohammed El Ferjani. ⌖ This simple restaurant is favoured by locals. The house speciality is couscous made with squid. The seafood salad is pleasantly surprising with cumin sauce. Try the dried octopus spaghetti when it is offered. Alcohol is not served.

Restaurant Berbère, Place Farhat Hached, ☎ (05) 650 884. ⌖ **cc** The atmosphere is clean and simple and the menu includes the classics of Tunisian cuisine. Closed Fridays. Alcohol is not served.

From US$10-20

Jerbanova, Place Sidi Brahim, ☎ (05) 650 226. ♥ ⌖ **cc** The owner of Les Palmiers recently opened this restaurant which caters more to an international clientele. The Jerbian couscous (steamed) is particularly recommended. Alcohol is served.

Baccar, 16 Place Hédi Chaker, ☎ (05) 650 708. ⌖ **cc** One of the oldest restaurants on the island, now run by the owner's son, and still a good establishment.

Ettebsi, rue Abdelhamid El Cadhi, ☎ (05) 651 399. ♥ It's difficult to resist the freshly-caught fish that is served here. A spick and span establishment.

La Colombe Blanche, rue Ibn Khaldoun, ☎ (05) 622 808, Fax (05) 622 809. ♥ This restaurant serves Jewish-Tunisian cuisine which shows the impact of the Jewish community on the island. House specialities include "banatage" (doughnut), "akoud" (tripe stew) and "bkaila" (a dish with a spinach sauce). When the atmosphere is animated, the owner sometimes plays the "oud" (lute). Closed Friday evenings and Saturday lunchtime.

More than US$20

😀 **Haroun**, Port de Jerba, ☎ (05) 650 488 / 658 307, Fax (05) 650 815. ♥ ⌖ **cc** This harbour restaurant is Jerba's most upmarket establishment. There are belly dance performances in the evenings. The owner also organises lunch excursions to Pink Flamingo Island and co-organises the Jerba Film Festival. During this event, films are shown on the terrace starting at 10pm. The fixed menu costs less than US$10.

- **Midoun**

Less than US$10

Zitouna, 4 rue Sidi Cherif, to the left of the café de la Jeunesse, ☎ (05) 658 126. ☕ This is a worthwhile stop to sample Tunisian salad, a pizza, grilled fish or a chorba (soup). The vegetable keftas are extremely fresh as is every dish on the menu. Portions are copious and the welcome is warm.

From US$10-20

Le Khalife, on the road to the lighthouse, ☎ (05) 657 860. ♟ ☕ CC There is a pleasant terrace on the 2nd floor where you can sample grilled fish and, upon request, lamb cooked in an earthenware pot.

- **Essouani**

Cheap restaurants in this Jewish village, serve delicious Jewish briks and lamb kebabs. The grill is open every afternoon from 7pm except Fridays and Saturdays.

WHERE TO GO FOR A DRINK

- **Houmt Souk**

Mid-morning around 11am is the time when Jerba's domino fanatics come out into the street to indulge in the island's favourite pastime. A sight not to be missed.

Café Ben Daâmach, Place Mokhtar Attia, in the heart of the souk. This modest café is the oldest in the city and has the best reputation. Tunisians come here in droves to watch the sun go down.

Café Pingwin, Place Hédi Chaker. This is the café where the sailors come during the afternoon to sip a coffee before resuming their work in the evening.

Café Hadji, Place Farhat Hached. The enormous terrace of this café, set right in the centre of the square, is a favourite among the locals, who come here to listen to concerts of traditional music in the evenings.

- **Midoun**

Café de la Jeunesse, (on the pedestrianised street to the right of the post office) has a good reputation for its location and its large terrace under the shade of a tall tree.

Mhirsi Café-Bakery, on the road to the lighthouse. An establishment with an open-air section on either side located at the end of ave Mohammed Badra, next to the Khalife Restaurant.

- **In the tourist area**

Café-Bakery, public phones available, across from the Palm Beach Hotel.

- **Ajim**

Café-Restaurant in a large garden surrounded by palm trees.

LEISURE

Sports – Jerba Golf Club, Midoun's tourist area, ☎ (05) 745 055, Fax (05) 745 051.

Micro-light centre, on the road from El Kantara, ☎ (05) 606 996. Open 8.30am-12.30pm and 2.30pm-5.30pm. Land yachts and micro-lights available. The base can also offer a tour around the island by hydroplane for a set price of approximately US$50.

Centre de plongée Merryland, hôtel Golf Beach Aghir, ☎ (05) 600 250, Fax (05) 600 244.

Holidays and Festivals – El Ghriba Pilgrimage, at the island's synagogue in late April/early May. The date coincides with the 33rd day of Passover.

Ulysses Festival – Open-air screenings of mythological and historical films, in front of the restaurant Haroun and at the harbour. In July-August.

Pottery Festival – in August in Guellala.

Jerbian Traditions – at the theatre in Midoun every Tuesday at 3pm. Folklore groups, horse races, enactments of traditional weddings, wizards who walk on nails, swallow sabres or tow 4-wheel drives with their teeth! Don't be surprised if you recognise the local head of tourism. **Puppet Festival** in November.

Excursions

Excursions to Matmata, Ksar Ghilane or Chenini on the mainland. You can also explore the island with its underground oil mills and its menzels, or take walks by the sea with a picnic.

Boat trips to Flamingo Island with lunch on site. These are organised by the owner of the Haroun Restaurant.

Nightclubs – in all the hotels in the tourist area.

SHOPPING

Markets – Houmt Souk – Mondays and Thursdays.

Midoun – Fridays
Guellala – Wednesdays
Mellita – Fridays
Ajim – Sundays
Cedouikech – on Tuesday mornings the market specialises in basketwork.

Bakeries – Ben Yedder, Place Farhat Hached, Houmt Souk. This café-bakery is reputed to be the best establishment in the chain, its cakes and lemonade much appreciated by local people. It is also a favourite target for jasmine vendors.
Fatou's, Houmt Souk near the Sidi Brahim Hammam. Café-bakery.

Antiques and Handicrafts – SOCOPA, ave Habib Bourguiba, Houmt Souk, ☎ (05) 650 040. Place Habib Bourguiba, Midoun, ☎ (05) 657 556. Jerba-Zarzis Airport, ☎ (05) 650 233.
Ben Mahmoud Pottery, Guellala, ☎ (05) 656 021. On-site demonstrations. Pottery from Guellala is virtually unfinished or at best very lightly glazed in shades of green, yellow or brown. The more sophisticated pottery with glistening colours comes from Nabeul.

Jewellery souk, Houmt Souk. The jewellery industry is one of Jerba's most characteristic activities and is primarily controlled by the island's Jewish inhabitants. Most of their workshops are in the centre of Houmt Souk. Traditional jewellery is in silver, filigree, or inlaid with coral from Tabarka.
Ben Ghorbal Fabrics, 10 Place Mohammed Ali, ☎ (05) 651 985. This is the place to purchase the traditional veils worn by Jerbian women. Open until 7.30pm.
Sponge Market in Ajim during the summer fishing season.
Souks in Houmt Souk and Midoun are the places to buy woven carpets (kilims) and blankets. The blankets can be woven upon request, providing you are staying in Jerba long enough for them to be completed.

Bookshops – Newspaper stands, ave Habib Bourguiba across from the tourist information office. International newspapers and periodicals, mostly in French.
Librairie Saber, rue Habib Bourguiba, ☎ (05) 650 921. Open daily until 8pm.

Making the most of Zarzis

GETTING THERE

By air – Jerba-Zarzis Airport, Mellita, ☎ (05) 650 233. The airport is approximately 60km from Zarzis, slightly less from the hotels in the tourist area.
By bus – Bus Station, ave Farhat Hached, ☎ (05) 680 372.
SRT Médenine, on the road to Medenine, ☎ (05) 682 078.

By shared taxi – The station is on ave Farhat Hached, ☎ (05) 680 078.

GETTING AROUND

By taxi – Station, ave Mohammed V, ☎ (05) 680 063.
Car hire – Avis, on the tourist road, ☎ (05) 681 706.
Hertz, on the hotel road, ☎ and Fax (05) 650 280 / 680 989 / 680 124.

Mattei, on the hotel road, ☎ (05) 680 989.

ADDRESS BOOK

Emergency – National Guard, ave Habib Bourguiba, ☎ (05) 680 245.
Police, ave du 20 Mars, ☎ (05) 680 063.
Hospital, ave du 20 Mars, ☎ (05) 680 302.
Night Pharmacy, ave Farhat Hached, ☎ (05) 681 124.

Tourist information – ONTT, on the hotel road, Souihel, ☎ (05) 680 445.

Banks / Currency Exchange – BNT, rue de Palestine.
BT, rue d'Algérie.
Banque du Sud.
CFCT, ave Mohammed V.
STB.

Post office – ave Habib Bourguiba, ☎ (05) 680 125.

Zarzis is attempting to emulate Jerba's tourist boom. All activity is concentrated around the hotels built along the fine beaches of fine sand. The city itself has almost nothing of interest to tourists.

From US$18-42
Hôtel Ziha, ☎ (05) 684 304, Fax (05) 683 380 – 31rm 🏠🗏✗⌑🍴 This is the least expensive place to stay in Zarzis. The beach is nearby but the swimming pool is pocket-sized. There are local guests during mid-season.
Hôtel Nozha Beach, route de la Corniche, ☎ (05) 690 888 / 694 593, Fax (05) 694 335 – 25rm 🏠🗏🅿✗ 🍴 CC Although not exceptional, this hotel is extremely well-situated, opposite the beach and near to the town centre. The rooms with a sea view and en suite bath are more expensive.

From US$42-75
Hôtel Giktis, ☎ (05) 705 800, Fax (05) 705 002 – 191rm 🏠🗏🅿✗ ⌑🍴CC Boasts an indoor heated pool.
Hôtel-Club Oamarit, ☎ (05) 705 770, Fax (05) 705 685 – 375rm 🏠🗏🅿✗ ⌑🍴✂CC Conceived in the style of a Moorish village, this establishment has accommodation in its main building or in chalets. It caters mainly for package holiday-makers.

More than US$75
Sangho Club, ☎ (05) 705 124 / 705 715 – 370rm 🏠🗏🅿✗⌑🍴♨✂🐎 CC Accommodation is in little white buildings scattered around a palm grove.

Constant background music and constant attention from costumed staff. Full board only in this package-tour paradise.

There are no interesting restaurants in the town. It is better to eat in the hotels or in one of the numerous establishments found along the tourist road.

• **In the tourist area**
The restaurants are rather less attractive in the off-season, when those that serve alcohol become a rendezvous for bar flies.

From US$10-20
Abou Nawas, on the tourist road heading towards the Hotel Zarzis, ☎ (05) 680 583. 🍷🍴 CC The best restaurant in the area with a very good seafood salad.
Le Pirate, on the tourist road, ☎ (05) 683 252. 🍷🍴 This restaurant specialises in Franco-Tunisian cuisine. The terrace is unfortunately rather noisy because it is next to the road.

Sports – **Tennis Club**, Club Sangho, ☎ (05) 705 124.
Fishing School, ave de l'UMA, ☎ (05) 705 259.
Equestrian Centre, Club Sangho, ☎ (05) 705 124, Fax (05) 705 715.

Markets – Mondays and Fridays.

Antiques and Handicrafts – **SOCOPA**, 1 ave Farhat Hached, ☎ (05) 680 699.

Making the most of Zarzis

KSOUR AND CAVE DWELLINGS**

Two or three day tour starting from Houmt Souk – About 450km
Staying in Medenine, Tataouine or Matmata
Map page 313

Not to be missed
The villages of Douiret and Chenini.
The trip between Toujane and Matmata.

And remember...
Sleep in a cave hotel in Matmata.
The countryside is quite magnificent in February and March.

Strange landscapes

To the south of Gabès, the long escarpment of the **Jebel Dahar** reaches heights of between 200 and 600m. In many places, the rugged outline of the crest resembles a series of fortifications dominating the broad wadis far below. Thin tufts of grass, the only vegetation, give the landscape its uniformly dappled appearance. Local people have long been resigned to a semi-nomadic life on this harsh soil; they have managed to settle on the flanks of the massif, but only through patient efforts to retain the rare rainfall. The villagers make a meagre livelihood from the olives, figs and cereal crops grown on the terraces laid out in the wadi beds (*jessour*), as well as from small numbers of livestock. For visitors, the chief attraction of this harsh landscape is its traditional buildings: cave villages in the Matmata region and fortified granaries (*ksour; singular: Ksar*) in the south.

An insubordinate area

Climate and natural forces have formed the character of the people of the Dahar. Proud and rebellious, the inhabitants have always been attached to their distinctive way of life, and when Rome adopted Christianity this Berber stronghold opposed its new master with violence. Once converted to Christianity, it rejected the triumph of Islam – but when finally converted to Islam, it turned to Kharidjism, a particularly strict form of Moslem belief. Although the Berbers gradually became more Arabian, to the extent that the Berber-speaking villages can now be counted on the fingers of one hand, the Arabs who settled in the plains copied the Berbers' fortified granaries and joined with them in large confederations. The powerful league of the Ouerghamma, which brought together semi-nomadic tribes and village residents, supported the Husseinite Beys before opposing the French occupation.

The people of the Dahar are poorer than the inhabitants of northern Tunisia. Visitors are likely to be approached openly by beggars and should be cautious. If you use your own vehicle for this tour, follow the advice in the introduction to the Tunisian South (*see page 290*).

■ **Houmt Souk**★★ – (*See Jerba, page 294*). *For the centre of Houmt Souk, take the road for Ajim Bac.* The road soon leaves the town and runs through villages scattered among the olive groves. The village of Ajim (*22km*) lies hidden behind a screen of palm trees.

■ **Ajim** – (*see Jerba, page 298*). *In the village, head for the ferry, 1km away.* The ferry runs to the mainland every 10-20mins in the daytime (*see Making the most of Jerba*). There is a police check before travellers embark on the

"Al-Jazira" or one of the three other ferries which run on this crossing. The mainland, with its low ochre-coloured cliffs, is reached at El Jorf. The little timber shacks serving drinks by the quayside might tempt you to linger but the Roman remains at Gightis are only 20km away along the ruler-straight highway, just beyond the little village of Bou Grara. *Take the Medenine road, 400m after leaving El Jorf.*

■ **Gightis** – *8am-noon; 3pm-7pm in summer, 8.30am-5.30pm out of season, closed on Friday, entrance charge. Allow 30min.* The modest Roman remains at Gightis lie between the Medenine road and the sea, bordered on the east by a broad sand-bank. The main interest of this ancient site is that it is the only one in the Tunisian South not to be buried beneath a modern town. Discovered in 1860 by the French explorer Victor Guérin, Gightis is on the Gulf of Bou Grara – a veritable small inland sea, of 500sqkm, almost completely enclosed at the north by the island of Jerba. This well protected sea outlet to the Mediterranean made Gightis prosperous. Gold, ivory, slaves and wild animals were shipped here to the great cities of the Mediterranean basin. A Phoenician trading centre and then a Roman port, the town reached its peak in the 2C and 3C AD. Its last true overlords, the Byzantines, built a fort here.

A tour of the site begins with the **baths,** which were flanked by a palæstra, or sports arena. Water-channels fed basins which have been partially restored. From the far side of the wadi *(cross the waste ground towards the sea)*, it is possible to make out a platform which ends in a semi-circle: the stalls which occupied it formed the town's **market**. The **Temple of Jupiter Serapis***, the most sub-stantial remaining element of the site, looks towards the sea. The podium, which still has the bases of the six columns of its façade, was faced with white marble. The top of its two stairways dominate the **forum**, a large paved area surrounded on three sides by a broad portico. Next to the forum, on the right, the remains of mosaics belonged to another **baths complex** built among dwelling-houses. Past the remains of the portico is a building on the left with handsome marble tiling in opus sectile (a formal design of squares and circles). Continue towards the **east door** of the forum with its two ribbed pilasters. The street beyond led to the jetty of the harbour.

Continue along the main road to the centre of Medenine, and park in front of the ksar (28km from Gightis).

■ **Medenine** – The *ghorfas* (store-rooms) of the **ksar*** of Medenine, laid out around a square, are constructed on two storeys. Craftsmen's shops have taken over the ground floor of the disused grain stores; fabrics with dominant shades of red are draped over the façades, while the classic coloured pottery of Nabeul is piled up at the door. The centre of the *ksar* is occupied by a traditional well, together with a basin to hold the water that is drawn up.

The little town of **Metameur**, 6km to the west of Medenine *(turning off the road to Gabès)*, also has a small *ksar* in the same style, built on three levels.

From the ksar, continue along the road from Gightis and take the road to Tatouine.

The route approaches the Dahar range, with its indented and sometimes pyramid-shaped peaks, across the plain studded with tufted grasses and marked by broad and dusty wadis. At 41km, handsome modern buildings in traditional style housing the post office and the national guard mark the entrance to the town of Tataouine. The town centre itself lies 10km away at the foot of the impressive rock face crowned with a tall radio mast.

■ Tataouine

For some, the name evokes the end of the world. For the French convicts who were part of the African light infantry battalions who made up the garrison at Tataouine, it was indeed the end of the world: here, in addition to a pitiless sun, these soldiers suffered the weight of a double hierarchy – the army, and the officious attention of the Caïds. Tataouine was founded under the Protectorate to oversee and manage the pacification of the Tunisian South, and the disciplinary battalions were assigned to control tribes who were always ready to make trouble. To the south of Tataouine the Algerian and Libyan frontiers mark the edge of the desert which covers nearly one-third of Tunisian territory. Only the markets on Mondays and Thursdays stir Tataouine out of its lethargy. This is the best place to stay when visiting the *ksour*.

■ Excursion to Ksar Ouled Soltane★★ – *47km round trip from Tataouine.*

Leave Tataouine on the main road to Remada; 1.5km from the centre, turn left on the road signposted to Maztouria. The road runs along a fold in the Jebel Dahar, and follows the Zandag wadi; on the heights, some ruins of *ksour* are visible. Beyond Tamelest with its mosque, turn left towards Ksar Ouled Soltane. The grain store soon appears with its minaret. *Park opposite the mosque.*

Ksar, ghorfa and kalaat

"Ksour" (the plural form of *ksar*) are the fortified villages which occur in northern Africa from Morocco to Libya. In the Tunisian South they indicate a group of communal grain-stores consisting of chambers called "ghorfa", extended rooms covered with barrel vaulting, with a door and tiny ventilation windows. They were grouped round a vast square, and sometimes reached a height of up to five storeys. Set for preference on rocky promontories, the *ksour* turned their backs on attackers in order to protect the property of semi-nomadic peoples. They were used for storing provisions for both humans (cereals, fruit, oil) and animals (fodder). The *ksour* on the plain are larger than those in the mountains, which are often referred to as "kalaat" (fortified castle). The village was located near the *ksar*, never in the hinterland.

The *ksar*, with its grain stores built on four levels, is laid out around two very photogenic courtyards. The stone façades are hidden under rendering – which makes the *ksar* look as if it is built of modelling clay. Gravity-defying stairways run across the façades, and the tiny entrances are on the scale of the grain-stores. The little café at the entrance serves a very bitter tea flavoured with *chirh*, a kind of artemisia widely found in the area.

On leaving Tataouine, take the Remada road again. Keep left at the turnings for Chenini and Douiret (after 8.5km). 500m beyond this second fork, go left at a single white house towards ksar Ouled Debbab, passing round it to the south.

■ Ksar Ouled Debbab★ – This *ksar* is one of the largest in the region. Its manifold *ghorfa*, built of small stone blocks, are set on a mountain spur. The ceilings of the granaries retain the marks of the planks which were used for coffering for the vaulting; you can make out hands and triangles, and a design in large dots which imitates the motifs of tattoos. The lime-washed constructions *(on the left of the entrance)* were used as a hotel for a time, but then abandoned.

Take the Douiret road, at the foot of the ksar.

The road crosses the hilliest part of the Dahar: a harsh landscape with a succession of distinctive high peaks topped by great slabs of rock. Only the *jessour*, the little walls marking out fields which cross the wadis *(see page 15)* indicate

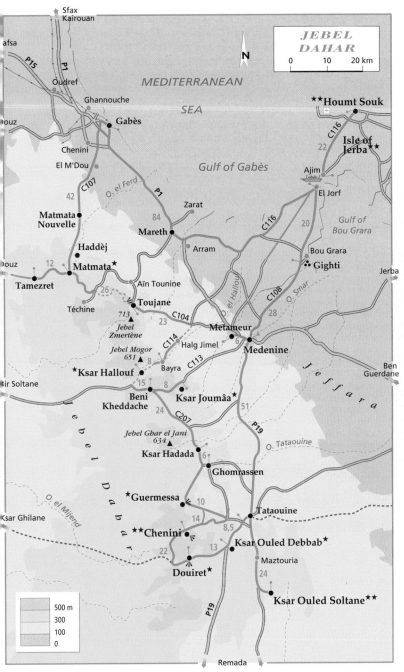

some sort of human presence. The road goes through the modern village of Douiret (*11 km from the fork on the Tataouine road*) before reaching the old abandoned village on the mountainside. *Park near the holiday centre.*

■ **Douiret**★ – This remote Dahar village stands in a magnificent setting of sharply delineated peaks. Its buildings hang half-way up a steep mountainside, and a white mosque is prominent, crowned by a stone *kalaat*.

A steep pathway leads to the main "street" through the abandoned houses. In the middle of the 19C, when it was a caravan relay post, the village had a population of 3 500. The path leads past a stone grain-store to a courtyard and a series of rooms literally cut into the hillside. The rooms formed the main living area, alternatively there were two interconnecting rooms with the second known as "the bride's room". These cave "houses" are less affected by changes in temperature; in this way, local people enjoyed relatively cool conditions in summer, and a few extra degrees of warmth in winter. There is a fine example of this type of dwelling just before the white mosque. A track along a ledge leads to a mountain cirque with the only **underground mosque**★ in Tunisia (*visitors permitted*); the roots of the splendid fig-tree in front of it reach down into the cisterns under the courtyard. The courtyard is used as a prayer room in summer. On the right, a black stain marks the outlet of an **underground oil-press**.

The traditional oil-press
In a dark cellar cut out from the rock, a millstone is operated by a camel plodding around on a large circular stone platform. This crushes the little black olives, whose flesh is then shovelled into esparto grass baskets. These are placed under the press and the precious liquid extracted by a skilful arrangement of weights and counterweights. Oil and water separate naturally because of their differing densities. Traditional oil-presses are still in use at Douiret and Ksar Hallouf but no-one knows for how long.

The **kalaat** provides a magnificent **view**★ over the region. The child-guides who like to accompany visitors on the steep but short climb to the top enjoy explaining the signs on the vaults of the buildings: they include Hands of Fatima, triangles and signatures.

Go through the modern Berber-speaking village of Douiret, round the side of the mosque, and head towards a clump of giant olive trees.

Chenini is 20km away; the road there takes you through what at first appears to be a totally-deserted region. However, each oued is cleverly put to good use through the system of *jessour*. Continue on, passing the track that forks left to Ksar Ghilane (*see the "Douz and the Sahara" chapter, page 352*). The route passes through a gorge and the white exterior of the Chenini mosque, hidden beyond a palm grove (*car park at relais Chenini*).

■ Chenini★★

Perched on top of a dizzy ridge, this is one of the few Berber-speaking villages that is still inhabited. The *ksar* lying along the long northern spur was probably founded in the 12C. The village has expanded along several levels of the mountainside and a path along a sharp edge, favoured by children, runs between the two ridges separated by the mosque. To the right it leads to the inhabited part of the village. Low walls outline barns and stables, while the houses are dug into the hillsides, as in Douiret. The **view**★ over the other slope, where the mosque clings to the hillside, looks over cultivation terraces stretching along the wadis.

To the left, narrow paved streets run past abandoned buildings before reaching the top with the ruins of the *ksar*. The children who accompany visitors for a small fee will point out the bakery and the oil-press, which are entered through tiny palm-shaped doors made of olive wood and heavily studded.

The same children will no doubt suggest a visit to the **mosque** (*20min on foot from the village*), which they will describe as "underground" because it houses a grotto. It stands beneath another grotto which is said locally to be the **tomb of the Seven Sleepers of Ephesus.**

The sura (chapters of the Koran) of the cave

On his way to Ephesus in 250, the Roman emperor Decius commanded that seven young Christians should be walled up in a cave. Plunged into a deep sleep, they woke again two hundred years later … only to die immediately. Belief in the Seven Sleepers was widespread, both in the west (particularly in the caves of Noirmoutier, in western France) and in the Islamic countries. According to the Koran, the Sleepers will announce the Day of Judgement.

Take the Tataouine road which goes round the ksar. It runs along a superb arid mountain cirque and passes the track to Guermessa (not recommended) before reaching a fork, 14km from Chenini. Turn left here for Guermessa.

As the mountain comes nearer, the straggling old village of Guermessa comes slowly into view, its dwellings blending in to the steep sides of the jebel.

Follow the road until you reach the entrance to Ghomrassen, turn left (a signpost indicates that the town is 2km away). Go through this administrative centre, linked to Tataouine by a direct road.

■ **Guermessa★** – Guermessa does not open up easily to the visitor, but the very extensive **view★★** from the old village is a rich reward for the painful climb (30min). As at Chenini, the village divides in two beside the dazzling white mosque. On the right is the *kalaat*, on the left a village partly built of stone which extends over several levels, making full use of the different strata of the soft local rock.

Take the road to Ghomrassen.

Ghomrassen is an administrative centre linked directly by road to Tataouine. The town, which has a few troglodyte dwellings and *ghorfa* of no great interest, has made a speciality for itself in the delicious **cornes de gazelle**, a crescent-shaped patisserie stuffed with almonds and sesame. The skills of the Ghomrassen inhabitants have crossed frontiers, and this is the home town of the proprietors of many a Tunisian patisserie in France. The large white house on the heights is evidence that at least one family did well during their time abroad.

Continue to Ksar Hadada. At the foot of the village, turn right to the main square.

■ **Ksar Hadada** – Since 1968 part of the *ksar* has housed a hotel of the most spartan kind – the *ghorfa* are undoubtedly better adapted to storing provisions than to welcoming visitors. Although formerly abandoned, the establishment is expected to open again after lengthy renovation work. In the meantime, walk around the narrow streets of the *ksar*, overrun by weeds and lined with walls into which are set tiny doors that communicate with one another via minute staircases without a handrail.

An excellent 24km stretch of tarmacked road runs from Ksar Hadada to Beni Kheddache. Starting on the left of the former hôtel Ksar Hadada, it comprises a number of superb **viewpoints★★**. On leaving Ksar Hadada, follow a deeply

Chenini

hollowed-out **gorge***. After 5km, the road to Oued el Khil branches off on the right and the scale of the landscape increases, with strata coloured yellow, pink and red, before another valley. The view is dominated by peaks that have fallen in on themselves and by elongated table-top mountains, their superimposed strata picked out by tufts of grass. After 13km, a cluster of barrel-vaulted houses indicates the beginning of the village of Oued el Khil. The road runs along terraces planted with trees, the source of the village's wealth. The track continues across a plateau before reaching the outskirts of Beni Kheddache. The Café Tunis marks the junction of the road from Medenine (*33km to the right*) to Ksar Hallouf (*to the left*).

■ **Beni Kheddache** – The village has little of interest; the old *ksar* was demolished in 1958, during a period of misguided modernisation. This was the time when the Tunisian president encouraged the state to "move on from the mud huts which mar the landscape and release the local population and tourists from this degrading spectacle" – a policy which accelerated the loss of many of the southern *ksour*. At Beni Kheddache the shops established in some of the few surviving *ghorfa* form a little market, on the left of the telecommunications tower.

■ **Excursion to Ksar Joumâa** – *16km round trip from Beni Kheddache. 7km from Beni Kheddache on the road from Medenine and 500m from the village of Ksar Joumâa, a 700m dirt track, inaccessible in a regular car, leads to this eagle's nest (the ksar is signposted for drivers arriving from Medenine).*

The *ksar*, although abandoned, has escaped the classic pattern of destruction. Perched on a peak, it provides an impressive view over 3-sheer slopes. The visit begins with the three-bayed **mosque** at the top of a flight of concrete steps. The building is approached past the **cisterns** for storing the rainwater ingeniously funnelled into them by low walls built along the hillside. The water was led into the little building , next to the mosque which was used for ritual ablutions. From the far end of the *ksar* – now alas gutted – there is a fine view over the cultivation terraces stepping down the slopes below.

Return to Beni Kheddache, then take the Matmata road up the mountainside between low stone walls. Turn left 2.5km from Beni Kheddache; this takes you through a wild valley with a few troglodyte farms among beautiful olive plantations. In a village 10.5km from Beni Kheddache, turn right towards the village of Ksar Hallouf which is a further 4km along a track.

■ **Ksar Hallouf*** – Dominating a little oasis stretching out along a wadi, Ksar Hallouf with its pretty façades of brown stone is one of the most peaceful places in Tunisia. The six *ghorfa* open to travellers are too small to take in groups, and visitors are likely to have them to themselves. The climb up is very steep, but the final stretch of track is surfaced. The *ghorfa* round the main square are set out on two levels, with a traditional oil-press inside one of them. From the top of the hillside which dominates the *ksar*'s little mosque, now disused, there is an irresistible view of the sun setting over the palm-trees and the neighbouring peaks.

N Thibaud/HOA QUI

Chenini, one of the rare villages to retain its Berber-speaking population

Leave Ksar Hallouf along the track which bears right at the foot of the ksar. The road which continues it follows the bed of a wadi. In the village of Bayra, turn left towards the wadi of El Hallouf (no signpost). Continue straight on for 8km to the junction, heading for Halg Jimel. Cross through Halg Jimel and 2km further take a slightly difficult track (for 3km), that you follow, using the white mosque as your reference point.

This track returns to the narrow winding road between Medenine and Toujane. The road soon climbs offering magnificent **viewpoints★★** over the Jeffara, the vast bare plain that stretches to the sea. The hillsides are full of sagebrush and thyme growing in thick clumps. The road finally descends to Toujane.

■ **Toujane** – The big stone-built village of Toujane, only partially inhabited, is spread out along the slopes of a mountain cirque. Women in colourful garb disappear from time to time into an enclosure with their flock of goats. They can also be seen on the roads, weighed down with great bundles of firewood, followed by their children carrying water; the heavy container is supported on the back by a strap round the forehead.

The road follows the cirque to the fork for Mareth and Matmata *(turn left)*. It then climbs to offer you a last fine **viewpoint★** over the village. *Three kilometres further on, take the track on the right to Matmata (follow the signs for El Abdech).* This route keeps to the hill-crest, a superb drive between the occasional isolated house, cultivation terraces, narrow wadis, and views over the Jeffara plain below. Large concrete markers indicate directions which it would be unwise to follow. The track ends 15km further on, at the end of a eucalyptus plantation. One road goes left for Téchine *(cave village, 5km from the fork)*, while the route continuing to Matmata goes through another buried village. It runs past large numbers of Barbary fig trees, and passes the foot of a large radio mast before descending once more into Matmata *(after 10km)*.

Ksar Hallouf

J.-F. Galmiche

■ Matmata★

At first, nothing remarkable stands out in this village lying in a hollow surrounded by hilltops. The low houses, modest but clean and neat, are surrounded by walls. You need to gain height (above the main square near the tourist office, for example) to discover a lunar landscape pocked with craters. Each depression forms the courtyard of one of the famous underground dwellings.

If you are not invited – often with insistence and always in the hope of shifting a craft product or receiving a tip – into one of these underground houses, go to the museum behind the Sidi Idress hotel (*access by the road opposite the tourist office*). The **Matmata Museum** (*variable hours, entrance charge*) is installed in a troglodyte house. It uses a few rooms spread round a courtyard with well and cistern to reconstruct the traditional life of Matmata. There is a handsome bed, its uprights covered with whitened clay and looking like genuine lace. This type of fixed "furniture", which also includes shelving, is still common in the houses of Téchine.

■ Excursion to Tamezret – *24km round trip from Matmata*. Only 12km west
of Matmata along a twisting road, the village of Tamezret is a complete contrast to Matmata: cave dwellings give way to stone houses and the streets are lined with high walls that echo with Berber voices. To gain a full view of the village, cross to the other side of the hill to leave the unappealing telecommunications relay station behind. Beside the track to Douz (*a shortcut of 100km to reach Le Nefzaoua*), it is possible to climb to the mosque on foot and enjoy a stop in the little café nearby.

Return to Matmata

■ On the road to Gabès – From the little col on the way out of Matmata
there are extraordinary **views★★** over the Jeffara. The road then carves its way between the ravines which mark the northern point of the Dahar. 3.5km from Matmata a family has turned its house, on the right, into a living museum. Few groups can resist the pleasure of being photographed with the housewife who pretends to grind grain with an old mill-stone. **Haddej**, 2km further on (*to the right of the main road*), is another underground village, better preserved than Matmata. Visitors may be invited to visit one of the houses. The road then crosses through **Matmata Nouvelle**, built to rehouse the residents of Matmata, without great success. A broad boulevard, its central reservation planted with lamp-standards, runs through this soulless town. The road then continues directly to Gabès.

Underground dwellings

The troglodyte houses of Matmata and Téchine, are laid out round an open-air courtyard some 5-10m deep, and reached down stairs carved out of the hillside. The courtyard is about 9m across. Around it are five or six ground-floor rooms serving as kitchen, bedrooms and living-room. Provisions are stored on the upper floor, reached by stairs cut into the clay. This somewhat unusual type of house is a response to the demands of construction rather than to defence: the soft earth made it possible to provide accommodation at little expense in a region which lacks timber suitable for construction, and to benefit from excellent insulation. This type of underground housing was used in Roman times by the Numidian overlords at Bulla Regia.

Matmata

■ **Gabès★** – *(page 326)*. From Gabès, the road leads to the ferry at Ajim for the island of Jerba *(106km further on)*. Shortly beyond Mareth it leaves the Medenine road, the site of severe fighting during the Second World War. In 1943, it took the troops of Generals Montgomery and Leclerc 40 days to dislodge Rommel from here. A **military museum** tells the story of the Mareth line and Tunisia's role in the Second World War *(8am-12noon in summer; 8.30am-5.30pm out of season, entrance charge)*.

The village of Tamezret

J.-F. Galmiche

Making the most of Medenine

GETTING THERE

By bus – SNTRI, ave Habib Bourguiba, ☎ (05) 640 427.
SRTGM, ☎ (05) 640 005 / 640 007.
Car hire – Mattei, rue du 18 Janvier, ☎ (05) 643 540.

ADDRESS BOOK

Emergency – National Guard, ☎ (05) 640 062 / 640 086.
Police, ☎ (05) 640 033 / 640 201.
Regional Hospital, on the road to Tataouine, ☎ (05) 643 735.
Red Cross, 23 rue Taïeb Méhiri, ☎ (05) 640 786.

Tourist information – Tourist Office, ave Hédi Chaker, not far from hôtel La Gazelle, ☎ (05) 850 850, Fax (05) 850 999. In addition to informing the public, this branch also supplies visitor's permits for the out-of-bounds zones of the Great Southern Erg. Summer, 8am-1.30pm, out of season, 8.30am-1pm / 3pm-6pm. 8am-1.30pm Fridays and Saturdays, closed Sundays.

Banks / Currency Exchange – BNA, ave Habib Bourguiba.
Banque du Sud, ave Habib Bourguiba, on the road from Gabès.
CFCT.
STB, ave Habib Bourguiba.
UIB, ave Habib Bourguiba.

Post office – Place des Martyrs.

Telephones – There are public phones opposite the post office.

Airline Companies – Tunisair, rue du 18 Janvier 1952, ☎ (05) 640 817, Fax (05) 642 490.

WHERE TO STAY

Medenine lacks tourist attractions and is not an interesting place to stay in. It is better to continue to Tataouine, Matmata or Jerba. However, it does have one reasonable hotel:

Around US$40
Hotel Ibis, place du 7 Novembre, ☎ (05) 643 878, Fax (05) 640 550 – 44rm 🛏 🖉 ✖ CC This is the only hotel in Tunisia belonging to this French hotel chain. It is also the best hotel in a town that has very few. In keeping with its reputation, the establishment is impersonal but comfortable and functional and is located in the city centre.

EATING OUT

• **In the modern city**
Less than US$10
Restaurant de la Liberté, behind the place du 7 Novembre near the Hotel Ibis, ☎ (05) 642 350. 🍴 It's difficult to resist the smell of a "mechoui" when the barbecue is lit at the beginning of the afternoon. This is a good place for grilled lamb, liver or merguez sausage. There are also grilled half-heads of lamb – a particularly popular dish in the area. Alcohol is not served.

From US$10-20
Restaurant at the Hotel Ibis, place du 7 Novembre, ☎ (05) 643 878, Fax (05) 640 550. CC The restaurant has the same image as the hotel, nothing special but adequate and clean. House specialties are lamb "coucha" and "skouffa" (stews).

Shopping

Ksar in Medenine, in the city centre. Numerous handicraft shops are located in the ghorfas.

Ksour and Cave Dwellings

GETTING THERE

By bus – *SNTRI*, 71 ave Habib Bourguiba, ☎ (05) 862 138. Connections with Ksar Hadada and Ghomrassen.

By shared taxi – The station is on rue du 1ᵉʳ Juin, near ave Habib Bourguiba.

Covered Peugeot lorries for Chenini and Ksar Ouled Soltane leave from near the Hôtel de la Gazelle.

ADDRESS BOOK

Emergency – *National Guard*, ave Habib Bourguiba, ☎ (05) 860 350 / 860 354.

Police, cité du 7 Novembre, ☎ (05) 860 500.

Regional Hospital, cité du 7 Novembre, ☎ (05) 860 114; Emergency Service, ☎ (05) 860 902.

Tourist Office – *Tourist Information Office*, ave Habib Bourguiba, ☎ (05) 862 002. Unfortunately there is little information here with the exception of a few brochures in Italian on underwater fishing and a list of hotels in Jerba. A sign indicates the telephone numbers for the hotels. During our last visit, the information officer didn't speak any English or even French.

Banks / Currency Exchange – *BH*, rue Farhat Hached.
BNA.
Banque du Sud, ave Farhat Hached.
CFCT, rue Farhat Hached.
STB, ave Habib Bourguiba.

Post office – ave Hédi Chaker, on the corner of ave Habib Bourguiba.

WHERE TO STAY

The hotels in Tataouine are mostly used as a stopover on the way to Chenini.

• In the city centre
From US$18-42

Hôtel La Gazelle, ave Hédi Chaker, ☎ (05) 860 009, Fax (05) 862 860 – 23rm ⁿ 🖥 🛁 ✗ cc This hotel has all the allure of an army barracks, but the rooms are relatively clean and comfortable.

• In the tourist area
From US$42-75

Hôtel Dakyanus, El Ferch, route de Chenini, ☎ (05) 832 199, Fax (05) 832 198 – 46rm ⁿ 🖥 🛁 ✗ 🛁 This recently-built hotel provides a comfortable stop-over for travellers en route to Chenini, 5km after leaving Tataouine.

Hôtel Mabrouk, tourist zone, route de Chenini, ☎ (05) 862 805, Fax (05) 850 100 – 30rm ⁿ 🖥 🛁 ✗ This hotel opened in August 1999. Designed in the style of the traditional habitat of the region, it combines excellent facilities, attractive decoration and the appeal of novelty. A swimming-pool should soon be available.

Hôtel Sangho, in the tourist area, route de Chenini, ☎ (05) 860 102 / 860 124, Fax (05) 862 177 – 66rm ⁿ 🖥 🛁 ✗ 🛁 cc This hotel has elegant architecture with chalets scattered around a beautiful garden. On the other hand, its construction is not without flaws – the plumbing is particularly deficient which serves as a reminder that, despite appearances, this is a fairly modest establishment.

• New Tataouine
From US$18-42

Hôtel Relais du Sahara, cité du 7 Novembre, ☎ (05) 870 201, Fax (05) 870 288 – 20rm ⁿ ✗ On the road from Medenine, 8km before you enter the old town. A modern building that may well age prematurely if it isn't better looked after. It nonetheless provides decent accommodation given the price range.

EATING OUT

Hardly any of the eating places in Tataouine can be recommended. For a light snack, try a Tunisian sandwich or a fricassé (fried dough stuffed with tuna, olives and Tunisian salad). For dessert, try a "gazelle horn" (corne de gazelle). This is a speciality of the region, the best coming from Ghomrassen.

● **In the modern town**

Less than US$10

Restaurant Carthage Tataouine, 63 rue du 20 Mars (red and orange sign). This is practically the only establishment in the city that resembles a restaurant. House specialities include mutton stew with beans. Alcohol is not served.

Mabrouk Station, on the Chenini road, ☎ (05) 862 805. The large impersonal dining room feels like a cafeteria and serves only one menu – chorba, mechoui or couscous. At least the food is reasonably good and a meal costs less than US$8.

Restaurant at Hôtel La Gazelle, ave Hédi Chaker, ☎ (05) 860 009, Fax (05) 862 860. There is little choice here and the dishes are rather poor. You can eat for less than US$8.

LEISURE

Festivals – Festival of the Ksour, in April. Demonstration of local handicrafts and folklore events: dances, fantasias and song.

SHOPPING

Weekly Souk – Tuesdays.

Antiques and Handicrafts – Chez Moktar el Megbli, 68 ave Habib Bourguiba. Carpets, kilims, veils and jewellery.

Making the most of Ghomrassen

Ibn Arafa Bakery, ave Habib Bourguiba. The best "cornes de gazelle" in Tunisia as well as delicious fricassé (fried dough stuffed with tuna, hard-boiled eggs, black olives and harissa) can be found here.

Bakery, ave Habib Bourguiba, next to the tobacco store. Another excellent bakery to buy "cornes de gazelle" and mrharek (round doughnuts filled with honey).

Making the most of Ksar Hallouf

WHERE TO STAY

Less than US$18

Hotel Ksar Hallouf, ☎ (05) 647 037 – 6rm ✗ The owner is proud of his hotel-restaurant-bar, though you can barely stand up in the six rooms, the WC is outside and taking a shower is unlikely. The owner himself lives in a modern house a little further away.

WHERE TO GO FOR A DRINK

At the bar belonging to the same owner.

GETTING THERE

By bus – SRTG Gabès, one bus daily to Matmata Nouvelle (the new village) and Jerba.

ADDRESS BOOK

Tourist information – Tourist Information Office, in the town centre, ☎ (05) 230 114. The guides working from here stick to the beaten track and are only prepared to take visitors to the most-visited ksour.

Bank / Currency Exchange – There are no banks in town.

Post office – In the middle of the town.

WHERE TO STAY

• Underground dwellings

There are three hotels located in underground dwellings. You have to pay for the exotic atmosphere by sharing bathrooms, sleeping an average of 6 to a room and putting up with poorly fitted doors without locks. The mosquitoes can be a nuisance too.

Less than US$18

Hôtel Sidi Driss, ☎ (05) 230 005 / 230 015 – 20rm ✗ There are 20 rooms with a total of 130 beds in this underground hotel. The bar was used as a setting in the film "Star Wars". This is the most charming of the 3 underground hotels.

Les Berbères, ☎ (05) 230 129 / 230 024, Fax (05) 230 097 – 11rm ✗ Similar to the Sidi Driss, this hotel has 120 beds in 11 rooms. Book ahead if you want the only room with 2 beds. The restaurant caters particularly to groups.

Hôtel Marhala Matmata (a member of Tunisia's Touring Club), ☎ (05) 230 015, Fax (05) 230 109 – 36rm ✗ This is the most basic of the 3 underground hotels but the one with the warmest welcome.

• Regular hotels

From US$18-42

Matmata Hôtel, ☎ (05) 230 066, Fax (05) 230 177 – 32rm ✗ 🍴 📺 ✗ 🛏 This establishment has been supplanted by the area's newer hotels, unsurprisingly, since the service is lamentable, the air-conditioning and the heating are incredibly noisy, the showers often don't have hot water and the swimming pool is emptied as soon as summer is over.

From US$42-75

Hôtel Kousseila, ☎ (05) 230 303 / 230 355, Fax (05) 230 265 – 35rm 🍴 📺 🛎 ✗ A good conventional hotel among the underground dwellings. Recently built by the owner of the Hôtel Sidi Driss. Clean and spacious rooms.

Hôtel Ksar Amazigh (formerly the Hôtel Troglodytes), ☎ (05) 230 088 / 062, Fax (05) 230 173 – 50rm 🍴 📺 🛎 ✗ 🛏 A new establishment with all the necessary comforts for a pleasant stay.

WHERE TO EAT

OR GO FOR A DRINK

Good cuisine is not a priority in the area.

Less than US$10

Restaurant Aouled Azaiz "Chez Abdoul", opposite the tourist information office, ☎ (05) 230 189. 🍴 This restaurant serves mediocre couscous and a rather greasy mechouia but is fine if you are hungry. Managed by a former guide, it is open on Sunday and serves late into the evening. It is also the café where the local Tunisians gather.

LEISURE

Matmata Festival, folklore shows, cultural activities and variety shows. End of August.

B. Juge

A cave dwelling in Matmata

GABÈS
Centre of Governorship
Pop 90 000
136km from Sfax, c 100km from Jerba

Not to be missed
A horse and carriage ride to an oasis.
And remember...
Try to book into a hotel by the sea.

An oasis by the sea

The oasis of Gabès is an introduction to the Tunisian south. Uniquely in North Africa, its palm trees stretch as far as the shore of the Mediterranean. They were acclaimed by the Roman writer Pliny, as well as being fondly evoked by the contemporary Tunisian poet Tahar Bekri, who wrote "And then the palm trees appear: an offering at the gates of the desert ... The scent of plants and the seaside blended together". Whether your destination is Jerba, Tozeur, Matmata or Tunis, this is an essential stopping-place, and a visit to its oasis is not be missed.

Historically, Gabès was a transshipment point where the cargoes from trans-Saharan caravans were loaded on to the coasters trading along the shores of Northern Africa. When this profitable trade was abandoned, the area took a long time to recover. The discovery of oil under the sea in the Gulf of Gabès has led to the construction of a modern port, as well as an industrial complex, although both are overshadowed by the much more extensive facilities at Sfax.

The modern, rather quiet town developed around a number of large villages (Chenini, Menzel, Jara and Petite Jara) sited on the edge of a broad wadi, and now extends all the way from the oasis in the south to the harbour. Here, opposite the town's two large hotels, is the beginning of a long **beach**, which is very attractive as long as the *bahri*, the off-shore wind, is not blowing.

From the palm grove to the town
Allow half a day

Exploration of the town is often limited to visiting the **oasis***, taking one of the carriages that wait in front of the coach station *(TD12 for a 1hr visit)*. Comfortably settled in leather seats, gently rocked by the horse's trot, you can see over the palm hedges and take in the diversity of crops growing on three levels. The 300 000 date palms in the oasis supply dates of modest quality but, above all, they provide shelter for beautiful orchards; which include pomegranates with their magnificent red flowers in spring, lemon, orange and apricot trees. Under their foliage little banks of earth mark out the plots where every imaginable vegetable seems to be grown, as well as tobacco, and above all the henna for which the town is famous.

Henna
Henna is a shrub which grows to about a metre in height. Its green leaves are gathered in the autumn, then dried and crushed. They provide a powerful colorant used by women to dye their hair, and for the hand tattoos done during marriage ceremonies.

On the way is the little **Chenini Zoo** *(7-30am-7pm in summer, 7.30am-5pm in winter; closed on Mondays, entrance charge)*, which proudly shows off its Nile crocodiles. The low wall opposite the entrance to the zoo which is known, rather pompously, as the **Roman barrage**, is a later reconstruction.

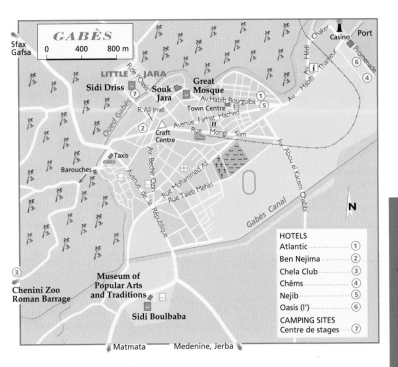

From the coach station, head for the town centre.

Opposite the imposing modern mosque, the entrance to the **Jara market** is enlivened with a mass of baskets, the speciality of the Gabès region. Under the arcading of this former slave market with its squat pillars, precious spices are displayed next to pyramids of henna which vary in price according to quality. The **Sidi Driss mosque** in the neighbouring district of Little Jara (*discreet visits possible at prayer times*) dates back to the 11C. The columns in the court and prayer hall will have an impressive array of capitals.

The **Museum of Popular Arts and Traditions** (*8am-1pm, 4pm-7pm in summer; 9.30am-1pm, 4pm-6.30pm in winter; closed on Mondays; entrance charge*), 2.5km south of the town (*easy access by taxi*), is housed in a former 17C medersa, which has been thoroughly restored. The cells of this Koranic college, laid out round a courtyard, display superb traditional woven fabrics, jewels and tools of daily life in the Tunisian south. The prayer room has a representation of a traditional marriage. To the left of the museum the **Sidi Boulbaba mosque** (*open to Moslems only*) contains the tomb of a companion of Mohammed. This significant pilgrimage site has contributed to the town's prosperity.

Making the most of Gabès

GETTING THERE

By car – The most direct road from Tunis is the P 2 via Kairouan, then the P 1 from Skhira. The whole journey is 406km. From Jerba, take the ferry at Ajim (see Making the most of Jerba).

By boat – Harbour, ☎ (05) 270 367.

By train – SNCFT, rue Mongi Slim, ☎ (05) 270 944 / 270 744. There are 3 trains daily to Tunis (7hr) stopping in Mahrès, Sfax, Sousse and Bir Bou Rekba.

By bus – SRTG, ☎ (05) 270 323. The bus stations are on ave Farhat Hached and on the road to Sfax. There are several buses a day to Matmata, Kébili, Douz, Jerba and Tunis.

By shared taxi – There are 2 stations. The one for local taxis is on ave Farhat Hached, 700m from the bus station. The other, for vehicles licensed to travel outside the governorship, is at the Chmama roundabout, on the road to Sfax: Jerba (75min), Tunis (4hr), Sfax (1hr 45min), Gafsa (2hr), Tozeur (90min) and Tataouine (90min).

GETTING AROUND

By bus – Inside the souk at Jara.

By barouche – Opposite the bus station (TD12 for a 1hr excursion). This is the starting point for the walks to the Chenini palm grove.

Car hire – Avis, rue du 9 Avril, ☎ (05) 270 210.
Hertz, 29 rue Ibn el Jazzar, ☎ and Fax (05) 270 525.

ADDRESS BOOK

Emergency – Bon Secours Private Hospital, rue Mongi Slim, ☎ (05) 271 400.

Police Station, on the road to Medenine, ☎ (05) 270 390.

Tourist information – ONTT, on the square on the corners of ave Habib Thameur and Hédi Chaker, ☎ (05) 270 254, open 8.30am-1pm / 3pm-5.45pm; Fridays and Saturdays, 8.30am-1pm. Closed Sundays.

Cultural Committee, rue Mohammed Ali, ☎ (05) 270 321.

Tourist Information Office, across from the Hôtel Nejib. Always closed.

Banks / Currency Exchange – BCT, rue Mohammed Ali.
BIAT, ave Farhat Hached.
BNA, ave Habib Bourguiba.
Banque du Sud, 131 ave Bourguiba.
UIB, ave Habib Bourguiba.

Post office – ave Habib Bourguiba

Telephones – Public phone offices are to be found throughout the town.

Internet – Publinet, Gabès Center, ave Habib Bourguiba.

Emergency – Bon Secours Private Hospital, rue Mongi Slim, ☎ (05) 271 400.

Police Station, on the road to Medenine, ☎ (05) 270 390.

Airline – Tunis Air, ave Habib Bourguiba, ☎ (05) 270 697 / 271 250, Fax (05) 277 606.

WHERE TO STAY

As well as some very old hotels in the town, there are 2 picturesque establishments on the beach.

• **In the town**

From US$10-18
Camping Centre de Stages, rue de l'Oasis, quartier de la Petite Jara, ☎ (05) 270 271.
Small camping site and dormitories located on the edge of the palm grove, near Sidi Driss mosque. Dubious showers and toilets.

Hôtel Ben Nejim, 66 rue Ali Jmel, ☎ (05) 271 591 – 15rm This is the best of the inexpensive hotels. The rooms are reasonable but the showers are on the landing.

From US$18-42
Hôtel Nejib, ave Farhat Hached, ☎ (05) 271 686, Fax (05) 271 587 – 64rm ⌂ 📺 ✑ ✘ This is a clean but somewhat noisy hotel. Some of the rooms have television.

Hôtel Atlantic, 4 ave Habib Bourguiba, ☎ (05) 220 034, Fax (05) 221 358 – 64rm ⌂ ✘ This hotel with antiquated charm has a very attractive colonial-style façade. On the other hand, the interior is deceptive: the rooms are decrepit and poorly maintained.

• On the beach

From US$18-42

Hôtel Chêms, route de la Plage, ☎ (05) 270 547 / 270 549, Fax (05) 270 485 – 154rm ⌁ 🗏 📺 ✐ ✗ 🐾 ⚒ CC The best hotel in Gabès is close to the beach. Spacious, tastefully decorated, spotless rooms.

L'Oasis, on the beach road, ☎ (05) 270 381 / 270 884, Fax (05) 271 749 – 112rm ⌁ 🗏 📺 🐾 ✗ ⚒ CC A charming, rather quaint hotel, with corridors like a ship's gangway.

• In the oasis

From US$18-42

Chela Club, 6.2km from Gabès on the road to Sfax. After 1.5km, follow the sign towards Kébili, then after 1.9km, go towards Chenini. A further 5km brings you to a sign where you turn right, then right again in 400m on the road heading towards the oasis. ☎ (05) 227 442 / 227 446, Fax (05) 227 446 – 50rm ⌁ 🗏 ✗ ⚒ Basic level of comfort in stone bungalows with "natural" heating and air-conditioning: in the summer, the palm trees guarantee a relatively cool atmosphere; as soon as the nights become cold, blankets become necessary.

EATING OUT

Gabès has a number of pleasant places to eat.

• In the city

Less than US$10

Pacha (towards the Hôtel Atlantic), ave Farhat Hached, ☎ (05) 272 418. A large square dining room with traditional "oja", "mechouia", or couscous.

Restaurant at the Hôtel Atlantic, 4 ave Habib Bourguiba, ☎ (05) 229 034 / 221 358. This restaurant specialises in grilled meats seasoned with the intensely aromatic rosemary, typical of the Tunisian South.

Boukachouka (heading towards the Hotel Ben Nejima), rue Ali Jmel. 🍴 Fish in sauce and grilled liver in this very simple restaurant much frequented by local people.

From US$10-20

Restaurant de l'Oasis (opposite the Hotel Atlantic), ave Farhat Hached, ☎ (05) 270 098. ♀ CC This simple restaurant, with its curtained windows and wooden chairs, serves good dishes in a quiet atmosphere. Try the octopus risotto, the "malsouka" tajine (wrapped in a brik leaf, this dish needs to be ordered 2 hours in advance) and the fresh fish.

El Mazar (towards the Hôtel Nejib), 39 ave Farhat Hached, ☎ (05) 272 065. ♀ 🍴 CC Eclectic menu here with rabbit and tajine cooked in Tunisian-style as well as roast with a Lyonnaise sauce and escalope Milanaise. The restaurant caters primarily to tourists. Shady terrace on the second floor. There is also a menu for under US$10.

• In the oasis

Less than US$10

Restaurant at the Chela Club, Chenini, ☎ (05) 227 442, Fax (05) 227 446. The best place to enjoy a meal in the oasis. The food is simple, served beneath a thatched canopy among the palm trees.

WHERE TO GO FOR A DRINK

Café La Chicha, at the Hôtel Atlantic. This café is composed of various rooms, each catering for different people: families, parties and or groups of friends. No alcohol.

LEISURE

Festivals – Regional Music and Popular Arts Festival, in June.
International Festival of Gabès, in July-August. Variety shows and theatre performances, mostly in Arabic.
Festival of the Spring, in September.
Sidi Boulbaba Religious Festival, at the end of Ramadan.

Nightclubs – Hôtel Chems, ☎ (05) 270 547, Fax (05) 274 485.
Hôtel Oasis, ☎ (05) 270 728, Fax (05) 271 749.

SHOPPING

Souk de Jara – closed Mondays.

Antiques and Handicrafts – SOCOPA, ave Farhat Hached, ☎ (05) 271 260 / 270 775.

Bookshops – Nefoussi, in the centre of Gabès.

GAFSA

Centre of Governorship
Pop 60 000
146km west of Gabès; alt 313m

Not to be missed
The Roman pools.
And remember...
Try to find accommodation in Tamerza.

One day caravans reached Gafsa and did not leave again. After that the town languished at the foot of the jagged mountains which rise to 1 100m. The discovery of phosphates in the area in the 19C made no difference. Gafsa is one of the poorest towns in the country, the children beg and their elders complain of the high cost of living – yet traffic flows along broad, modern-looking boulevards. They outline the modest medina, its lanes sloping gently down to the kasbah and the vast palm-grove. The town probably lies on the site of Numidian, later Roman, Capsa, the only remains of which are the unexpected pools.

A walk in old Gafsa

Allow about 1hr

From the Hotel Maamoun at the entrance to the town, go past the coach station and turn left into the rue Ali Belhaouane.

A modest open-air market is held along this road, which has arcading along one side. It leads to the **Dar Loungo**, a fine town house restored in 1997 *(signposted in an adjacent street, 300m on the right)* with, beyond, a lane that descends to a peaceful square. The two open-air basins at its centre are the famous **Roman pools***, 5m deep, with Latin inscriptions legible round the border of one of them. The water from the hot water sources (30°C) was the delight of the children who used to play there. Unfortunately, due to the damaging effects of irrigation, the superficial layer of the pools began to dry out. However, restoration has started to bring the source back to life and the swimming pools should soon be restored to their former glory.

Next to the tourist office in the same square, the **archeological museum** *(7.30am-noon / 3pm-7pm in summer; 9.30am-4.30pm out of season; closed on Mondays; entrance charge)* has a **Capsian figurine** that is evidence of occupation of the site since Neolithic times (8000 BC). The masterpiece of the museum is a superb mosaic representing **Athletic games and a boxing match**** (4C AD).

Go along the covered passage under the old official **residence of the Dey of Gafsa**, which leads to the road overlooking the palm grove *(100m away)*. The **oasis*** owes its existence to the abundant springs which are now supplemented by artesian wells. Paths dive into the abundant vegetation: there are few palm trees, but figs, pistachio trees and olive trees, giving shade to crops of barley and wheat.

Leave the kasbah on your right and go in the opposite direction, to the nearby mosque.

The **Great Mosque**★ has benefited from recent restoration *(the courtyard is open to visitors during prayer hours)*. No fewer than 120 capitals and ancient columns have been used for the portico of the courtyard and the prayer room. *(Return towards the kasbah)*. An attractive walk takes you between the high crenellated walls of the **kasbah** and the oasis; this is a make-believe scene, for nothing remains of the interior of the citadel since it was gutted by an ammunition explosion. *(Go round the kasbah to the ave Bourguiba)*. From here the rue Metoui crosses the **medina** and brings you back to your starting point.

Making the most of Gafsa

GETTING THERE

By plane – *Gafsa Ksar Airport*, 6km from the town on the route de Tunis, ☎ (06) 272 710 / 720 / 730. At present, there are only 2 flights to Tunis per week, but international flights are planned in the not too distant future.

By train – *SNCFT Station*, is actually in El Ksar, 3km from Gafsa on the P 15 heading towards Gabès, ☎ (06) 270 666. This station is only used for a night train that connects to Tunis via Sfax and Sousse. It is better to take a bus or a shared taxi.

By bus – *Bus Station*, ave du 2 Mars 1934, opposite the public garden, ☎ (06) 220 335 140.
SNTRI ☎ (06) 221 587. 8 departures daily to Tunis (5hr30min), 5 departures to Tozeur (2hr), 1 departure to Kebili and Douz.

Les Caravanes (Gafsa Regional Transport Co.), ☎ (06) 220 335. 8 departures to Tozuer and Nefta (2hr), 3 departures per day to Redeyef with a connection to Tameghza (2hr), 2 departures to Le Kef, 6 departures to Sbeïtla and Sfax and 11 departures to Kairouan.

By shared taxi – The station is on ave Taïeb Méhiri, behind the Hôtel Maamoun.

By car – The P 3 connects Gafsa directly with Tunis, passing close to Kairouan (360km). You can enjoy the magnificent countryside of jebel Bou Hedma by taking the P 15 from Gabès (149km). Gafsa is 93km from Tozeur.

ADDRESS BOOK

Emergencies – *Police*, ave Mohamed Khadouma, ☎ (06) 225 012.
National Guard, ☎ (06) 221 522.
Regional hospital, rue Avicenne, ☎ (06) 225 055 / 177.
Night chemist, ave Amor ben Slimane (opposite the National Guard), ☎ (06) 222 843.

Tourist Information – *ONTT*, in the square with the Roman pool at the end of ave Habib Bourguiba, ☎ (06) 221 664 / 221 644. Open 8.30am-1pm and 3-5.45pm Mondays to Thursdays, 8.30am-1.30pm Fridays and Saturdays. In summer, open daily from 7.30am-1.30pm, with someone on duty from 4-7pm. Closed Sundays. An information brochure aimed at tourists is currently under preparation.

Banks / Currency Exchange – There is someone on duty on Saturdays, Sundays and holidays from 9am-12pm. You can also change money at the Hôtel Maamoun.

Post office – ave Habib Bourguiba, on the corner with the road to Tozeur.

Internet – *Publinet*, ave Mohamed Khadouma, opposite the police station, ☎ (06) 227 830. TD2.400 per hour of connection, everyday 10am-11pm.

WHERE TO STAY

Under US$10
<u>❀ *Camping La Galia*</u>, Sidi Saleb (in the oasis 3km from the centre of Gafsa, well-signposted from ave Habib

Bourguiba), ☎ (06) 229 135 / 165 ✗ ⚓ An array of pretty stone buildings set right in the heart of an enormous garden in the oasis house a restaurant, Moorish café, pizzeria and shower and toilet facilities (hot-water showers extra). The ideal spot to put up a tent, park a caravan or just spend a day around the pool.

Between US$10 and US$18

Hôtel Khalfallah, rue Lazhar Fouli (to the left of the police station), ☎ (06) 225 624 – 11rm ✗ This is a simple and moderately attractive hotel. The showers are en-suite, but the outside toilet needs some attention.

From US$18-42

Lune Hôtel, ave Jamel Abdenaceur (route de Tunis), ☎ (06) 220 218, Fax (06) 220 980 – 18rm ⚑ 🖃 ✗ A modest, decent little hotel, despite somewhat dubious showers and toilets. Still under construction in 1999, it should comprise 40 rooms when finished.

Gafsa Hôtel, rue Ahmed Snoussi, ☎ (06) 224 000 / 225 000, Fax (06) 224 747 – 48rm ⚑ 🖃 ✗ CC This clean and functional hotel is located in the centre of Gafsa.

Hotel Maamoun, ave Taïeb Méhiri, on the corner of the old road leading to the railway station, ☎ (06) 224 441 / 226 701, Fax (06) 226 440 – 68rm ⚑ 🖃 TV ✗ ⚓ Although the decor is a bit old and shabby, this is the only hotel in the city centre with a swimming pool.

EATING OUT

Less than US$10

Sémiramis, rue Ahmed Snoussi, ☎ (06) 221 009. ♆ The wine menu is particularly impressive with a good selection of Tunisian wines.

Restaurant at the Gafsa Hôtel, rue Ahmed Snoussi, ☎ (06) 224 000 / 225 000, Fax (06) 224 747. ♆ CC There are in fact 2 restaurants here – one in the basement adjoining the hotel and the other on the first floor across the street. In the first, the menu lists elaborate dishes like "chakchouka" or steamed lamb. The second specialises in grilled meats.

Restaurant Errachid (at the Hôtel Maamoun), ave Taïeb Méhiri, ☎ (06) 224 441 / 222 433, Fax (06) 226 440. ♆ This pleasant restaurant has picture windows that look out over the patio and the swimming pool.

SHOPPING

Weekly Souk, Wednesdays.

Crafts – ONAT, rue Mohamed Glanza, near route de Tozeur, ☎ (06) 220 152. 8.30am-1pm / 3pm-5.45pm, 8.30am-1.30pm Fridays and Saturdays, closed Sundays. The official craft store houses a gallery of old and modern weaving carried out in the region. The workshops can be visited in the morning.

F. Dyan

EL JERID
TOZEUR★★★ – NEFTA★
Two beautiful oases, 23km apart

Not to be missed
A walk through the palm groves,
the Dar Cheraït Museum in Tozeur in the evening
and the old Ouled el Hadef quarter.

And remember...
Allow a full day for each oasis.
Explore the oasis in the morning or evening,
but watch out for the mosquitos in August and September.

Like Nefta, Tozeur emerges slowly from the immense flat cracked land of the chotts, crushed beneath the light and heat. Just when you think you are still looking at a mirage, the reality convinces you. These long green views with the extraordinary clumps of palm trees standing out are entirely genuine. The water which flows from basins along irrigation channels winds between luxuriant plots, havens of peace and freshness, and spreads life. You have to explore on foot, by scooter or in a carriage through these gardens of Paradise which seem to bring together all the species of creation. A visit to these two oases of Le Bled el Jerid (land of palm trees) – surely among the most beautiful in the world – constitutes one of the greatest moments of travel in the Tunisian south.

The oasis economy
As staging posts and trading centres for thousands of years, the oases saw slaves, gold and dates passing through. Multi-layered cultivation, with fruit bushes and market-garden produce growing under the palm trees and irrigated from abundant springs, dates back to Classical times. The "khammès" is a kind of sharecropper who maintains the oasis and is responsible for the harvest. The name, which means "fifth", is linked to the way in which he is paid: his entire salary consists of one-fifth of the harvest. At the end of the 19C, the introduction of modern frontiers and the abandonment of the date as a winter fruit sent the caravan trade into decline, and profoundly disturbed the oasis economy. Today, tourism is seen as a way of stemming the outflow of the population which has gone on throughout the 20C.

■ Tozeur★★★
Allow half a day

The oasis of Tozeur and its ever-abundant springs have long attracted people to settle here. As the Libyan Thuzuros it was incorporated into the boundaries of Roman Tripolitania, the more or less continuous fortified area which linked Gabès with Biskra in Algeria. Tozeur probably reached its peak under the Aghlabids, in the 9C; chronicles speak of the 1 000 dromedaries laden with dates that departed daily. Nowadays, its international airport has made it the gateway to Saharan Tunisia. The tourist zone to the west of the town is expanding steadily.

The oasis★★
Tozeur's main attraction, the oasis, waits to be discovered in its own way, and visitors should take time to explore the pathways on foot, the only way to appreciate the atmosphere of the gardens. Some of the *khammes* are pleased

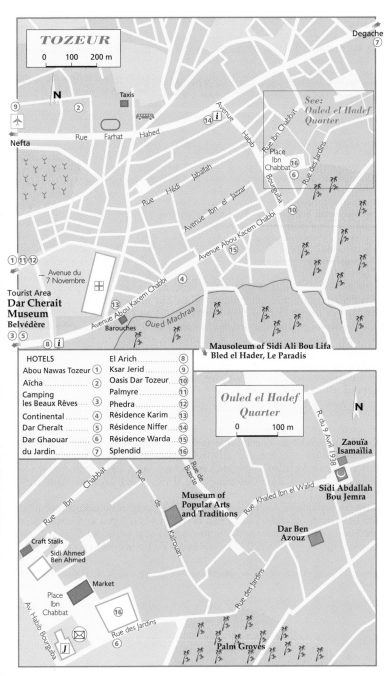

TOZEUR

0   100   200 m

N

Degache ⑦

Taxis

⑨ ✈
Nefta

② Rue Farhat Hahed

⑭ ℹ Avenue Habib

See:
Ouled el Hadef
Quarter

Rue Hédi Jaballah

Avenue Ibn el Jazzar

Rue Ibn Chabbat

Place Ibn Chabbat ⑯ ⑥

Rue des Jardins

Bourguiba ⑩

Avenue Abou Kacem Chabbi ⑮

① ⑪ ⑫

Avenue du 7 Novembre

Tourist Area
Dar Cheraït Museum
Belvédère

⑬ Avenue Abou Kacem Chabbi ④

Barouches Oued Machraa

③ ⑤

⑧ ℹ

Mausoleum of Sidi Ali Bou Lifa
Bled el Hader, Le Paradis

HOTELS			
Abou Nawas Tozeur	①	El Arich	⑧
Aïcha	②	Ksar Jerid	⑨
Camping les Beaux Rêves	③	Oasis Dar Tozeur	⑩
Continental	④	Palmyre	⑪
Dar Cheraït	⑤	Phedra	⑫
Dar Ghaouar	⑥	Résidence Karim	⑬
du Jardin	⑦	Résidence Niffer	⑭
		Résidence Warda	⑮
		Splendid	⑯

Ouled el Hadef Quarter

0   100 m

N

R. du 9 Avril 1938

Rue Ibn Chabbat

Rue de Bizerte

Rue de Kairouan

Museum of Popular Arts and Traditions

Rue Khaled Ibn el Walid

Zaouïa Isamaïlia

Sidi Abdallah Bou Jemra

Dar Ben Azouz

Craft Stalls

Sidi Ahmed Ben Ahmed

Market

Rue des Jardins

Place Ibn Chabbat

Av. Habib Bourguiba

⑯

J ✉

Rue des Jardins ⑥

Palm Groves

335

Dates

The order of palms covers 3 000 species, including the date-palm of African origin. Botanists classify the date-palm not as a tree but as a type of giant grass which reaches a height of up to 20m, and may live for a hundred years. The name of the "deglet nour", the most succulent of all dates, means "finger of light" and evokes its translucent appearance and long shape. Everything contributes to make the date a winter fruit: its fruit is harvested late in the autumn, it is easily preserved, and its sweet pulp is highly nutritious. The female flowers are fertilised artificially in the spring – a male shoot is slipped into a female cluster, and the wind does the rest. Nothing is wasted; the trunk of the palm tree is used for building, for furniture and for heating, the fronds are used for roofing, the fibre is woven, the fruit stalks make stout brooms. Finally, the juice is fermented immediately after harvesting and makes "laghmi", the intoxicating drink of the oasis dweller.

to show off their crops, proffer tea and dates, and explain how to distinguish between the different species of palm. Their agility as they climb up the palm trunk to pick the famous *deglet nour* dates is something to be seen (Jerid produces the best in the country).

At the bottom of the ave Habib Bourguiba, turn into the first road to the right of the Hotel Oasis and go past the Petit Prince restaurant.

The road crosses the **Machraa wadi**, the main water course in the oasis which branches out beside the pleasant El Berka café. There is a fine view from here of the oasis in all its profusion, with banana palms, pomegranates and fig-trees sheltering under the tall palms. The main road leads to **Paradis***, 3km from the town centre (*6.30am-7pm summer, 7.30am-7pm winter, entrance charge*). This **botanical garden,** founded in 1936 also doubles as the **zoo of the Sahara** devoted to desert fauna (hyenas, lions, leopards, etc). The attendants delight in treating tour groups to such edifying spectacles as a Coca-Cola loving camel, a scorpion living in a cigarette box and reptiles crying out in fright at the approach of human beings (*groups of 6 people minimum*). At a lower level there is a richly-planted but ill-maintained garden.

In the hamlet of Abbès near by, it is said that the impressive jujube tree on the left of the road has roots which grow as far as Mecca. The dome of the **Mausoleum of Sidi Ali Bou Lifa** is visible behind the tree.

On the way back to Tozeur, the road goes through the village of **Bled el Hader**. The main square, probably laid out on the site of ancient Thuzuros, has a mosque (founded in the 11C) and a minaret on what may be a base of Roman stone-work. The road crosses the Machraa wadi once more and ends near the Hotel Continental.

Turn left towards the tourist zone then take the sandy track leading away from the front of the splendid Dar Cherait hotel. This brings you to the springs of the Machraa wadi, known as **Ras el Aïn**, on the edge of the palm grove. Since the springs have been replaced by artesian wells, the water emerges through a large pipe and feeds a small basin at the foot of a hillside (*to the left of the path, 200m before the belvedere*). The city's youth often congregates here during the hottest parts of the day. When temperatures cool down, they cross over to the other side of the track (*the belvedere on your left*) and walk down to a little river lined with palm trees. Here a crystal-clear source meets the boiling water that bursts forth some 100m further up. Despite the litter on the river banks, it's a delightful spot and the water temperature (30°C) is ideal.

At the summit of the **belvedere's** enormous rocks is a pleasant view over the oasis, bordered by hotels. Sunsets are always popular among tourists.

From the craggy outcrop, you can see the little camp fires which periodically cough their bitter smoke upwards. Don't miss the **brick factory***, where the few families who work there will show you how the famous stone of Tozeur is manufactured. Kneading the clay, casting and drying, right up to the ingenious layers of bricks inside the oven, fired with palm wood.

The Ouled el Hadef quarter★★

Allow 45min. The town centre of Tozeur is laid out along ave Bourguiba. On both sides there are souks, cafés and shops selling wicker-work, woven fabrics and souvenirs. *(From the town centre, turn into the shop-lined passageway on the left of the STB bank. Cross the road at the end of the passage and turn right, following the "musée" signs).* This leads abruptly into an area marked by great unity of appearance. The Ouled el Hadef quarter is built entirely of brick, its façades covered with geometrical motifs resembling the designs of tattoos and fabrics. The narrow alleys, the massive doorways and the pillared porches lend this old quarter of Tozeur a medieval air.

The **Museum of Popular Arts and Traditions*** (Le musée des Arts et Traditions populaires) *(8am-1pm, 4pm-6pm in summer, 3pm-6pm out of season, closed on Mondays, entrance charge)*, is housed in a former Koranic school founded by Sidi Aïssa in 1357, and illustrates daily life in the oases in past centuries. The former schoolroom *(on the right of the entrance)* reproduces a marriage chamber with its beautiful wedding dresses. Strange wooden African masks belonging to the black slaves who worked in the oasis are shown on the walls of the prayer room round the little courtyard of the *koubba*. The room next to this was used as a mausoleum. It now contains a collection of manuscripts, including a document setting out the rules for distributing precious irrigation water throughout the oasis. The system was originally devised in the 13C by the Moslem mathematician Ibn Chabbat, whose grave is in Tozeur, but had to await the arrival of the French before being printed. The friendly guide here is happy to show the brick minaret which backs on to the outer wall, together with the thousand and one objects held in this little museum.

You need to plunge further into this pedestrian quarter with its narrow lanes to fully appreciate its character. Turn left beyond the museum, and go under the vaulting into a magnificent square to reach the **Sidi Abdallah Bou Jemra mosque** and the neighbouring **Ismaïlia zawiya** *(no visiting)*. Turn right, then right again and go past the front of a fine town house, the **Dar Ben Azouz**, which has been under restoration for years, before reaching the Hotel Splendid behind the town centre.

The Dar Cherait Museum★★★ (Le musée Dar Cherait)

This museum *(8am-midnight, entrance charge)* at the entrance to the tourist area is the most outstanding establishment of its kind in the South. Tunisia's first private museum, it was intended by its proprietor to be both Saharan and urban. Behind the plain light-coloured brick walls is the replica of a small middle-class house from the north of the country. It contains a collection of art objects from the 17-20C, from the main regions of the Ottoman empire such as Turkey and Syria, as well as from Tunisia. The main courtyard, a pleasant place to stop for a drink, is to the left of the museum entrance.

Opposite the ticket desk, there are monumental stairs typical of the entrance *(skifa)* of any traditional house, lined with wooden panelling and braziers. The plaster figures in the vestibule below illustrate a procession in honour of a

337

marabout, or holy man *(kharja)*. Beyond another figure, of a scholar (a lawyer), is the **second courtyard***. Adorned with a fountain, it has a patio with four covered galleries (a luxury reserved for sovereigns' houses) decorated with sumptuous ceramics, fine marble colonnettes and plaster-work with delicate tracery. The private apartments open off the courtyard. Each room evokes the luxury in which the beys lived: the rich costumes in the reception room reflect those depicted in the engravings and canvases in the first hall. In times gone by an elaborate meal would be simmering in the kitchens with their dazzling copper equipment. Further on, two rooms are arranged as a wedding chamber, displaying a splendid collection of **traditional jewellery*****. A master of the Koranic school *(el kouttab)* is shown on esparto-grass matting, surrounded by his pupils. A series of small interconnecting rooms makes up a hammam, or Turkish bath, of the type found in private houses. Before reaching the gallery of paintings hung on two levels, do not miss the room devoted to glass, with lamps, soup dishes, great vases grouped together according to their colouring and even items of blown glass made in Venice and exported to the East. The painting section begins with a tribute to the poet **Abou Kacem Chabbi**, a native of Tozeur who died in 1934 at the age of 25, and continues with a collection of 20C canvases, some inspired by streetlife, some by calligraphy. On the upper floor, the last room is devoted to a fine collection of **painted glass****. This technique, which was fashionable in the 19C, was used to illustrate popular tales, but as a figurative and naïve form of painting it was scorned by Islam.

Every evening, the palace gardens echo with mysterious rumbles of thunder, waterfalls and voices from the grave, during two nightly **son et lumière*** shows *(allow 45min for each)*. These attractions, more than worthy of an Eastern Disneyland, evoke some of the episodes from the famous *Arabian Nights* in **La Médina** show *(6pm-11pm, entrance charge)*. On the same principle, **Dar Zemen** *(6pm-11pm, entrance charge)* illustrates Tunisia's history from prehistoric times to the present day.

■ Nefta*

With its superb crater-like depression known as the Corbeille and the white domes of its *zaouïas*, the oasis of Nefta, smaller and more isolated than Tozeur, 23km away, has the peaceful atmosphere of a small remote town. It is recovering gradually from the great floods of the winter of 1989-90. This is the last great oasis before El Oued in Algeria *(the border is 36km away)*. On the way out of Nefta, a stretch of dunes, best admired at sunset, give a foretaste of the Sahara.

Tour

The Corbeille of Nefta* – The great bowl of the Corbeille is not particularly striking at first glance. To the right of the tourist office the road runs in a loop past the Bel Horizon and Sahara Palace hotels and goes round the impressive 30m-deep basin which is best viewed from the Corbeille café. The Corbeille's many springs are used to irrigate the palm groves, most of which lie to the south of the Tozeur – El Oued road. The steep earth slopes are crowned with the white domes of *zaouïas*. The town has no less than 100 priests; Nefta is the country's second holy city after Kairouan, and the centre of Tunisian Sufism.

Façades in old Tozeur

Old Nefta is centred on the Place de la Liberation, the site of the El Habib hotel. An enormous café offers some escape from the torpor which settles on the town in the heat of the day. The medina, less restored and perhaps more authentic than that of Tozeur, retains a few ancient lanes with façades with geometric designs, reminiscent of similar features in Ouled el Hadef (*see Tozeur*). Vaulted passageways, dark and cool, lead to dead-ends. The palm tree doors of the houses have three knockers, the metal rings each producing a different sound. The head of the household uses the one on the left panel of the door while children operate the smaller one beneath the women's knocker on the right. In this traditional area, as in Tozeur, the women still wear long black clothes trimmed with white or blue.

To explore the **oasis★★** at Nefta, go past the Hotel Caravanserai on the left on the way in from Tozeur. Continue along the asphalt road, which leads you round the oasis, a distance of 3.5km (*don't miss the Firdaous restaurant, see under Making the Most of Nefta*). It is wiser not to venture by car along the side tracks, which are very sandy; go on foot, and bear in mind that the network of tracks is very complex and that it is easy to get lost. The vegetation is as luxuriant as at Tozeur and leaves little space for vegetables, which are mostly grown in greenhouses. Raised cement channels, an ineffective attempt at modernisation, have been abandoned in favour of traditional irrigation methods. En route you will pass the **shrine of Sidi Ali Ben Moussaili** (Le marabout de Sidi Ali Ben Moussaili) (*not open to visitors*). This saint, who died at Nefta in the 13C, is still deeply venerated.

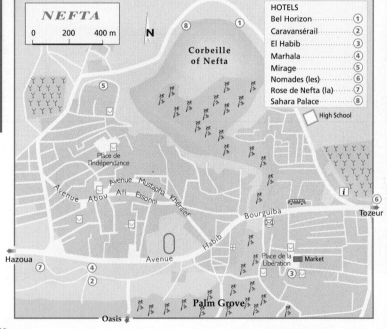

The dunes

To experience something of the sand dunes of the Sahara, leave Nefta and take the Hazoua road for 10km. When you reach the desert rose market, turn right towards the Dunes Café. After 1.5km along the sandy track *(avoid sandbanks and abrupt braking)* you will come to the starting point for camel trips. For a few dinars the camel drivers take visitors to the highest dune in the area *(45min round trip)*. Despite its great popularity, there is nothing very remarkable in the landscape, however – only the wrinkled white sand, emphasised by the shadows thrown by the setting sun. But the camel ride can be great fun.

■ Chott El Jerid

The largest chott in Tunisia runs between Tozeur and Kébili. Across this vast flat surface dominated by distant mountains, what seems to be water is usually no more than a mirage, for the bottom of the vast depression is in fact a **sebkha**, a salty and frequently dry marsh. Strictly speaking, the term **"chott"** refers to the fringes with a cover of salt-tolerant plant-life. Resembling the *playas* of the western United States and the *salares* of the South American deserts, the centre of the area is covered with soluble salts, chlorides and sulphides where no vegetation at all can grow. Its appearance varies with place and season: a veritable inland sea during the winter rains, for most of the time it consists of a translucent crust and hardened clay where the reflected light creates mirages. It is a dangerous place. In some parts, the saline crust forms an unstable surface covering a brackish mud fed by a shallow water-table. Fortunately, a straight road *(80km long)* makes it possible to cross the chott without risk, one of the country's most unusual experiences. The chott has been the subject of some extraordinary projects: at the end of the 19C, for example, there was a proposal for a canal between the Chott El Jerid and the Mediterranean.

Chott El Jerid

GETTING THERE

By air – *Tozeur-Nefta Airport*, on the road to Nefta, 3km from the centre of Tozeur, ☎ (06) 453 388. There is no airport bus and the only way of getting into town is by taxi.

By bus – The bus station is in rue Farhat Hached (route de Nefta) near the stadium, 100m from the Mobil fuel station. **SNTRI**, ☎ (06) 453 557. 5 buses to Kairouan (4hr), 5 to Gafsa (1hr30), 2 to Nefta (30min), 1 to Sousse (6hr30) and 5 to Tunis (8hr). The buses to Tunis make a halt 6km from Hammamet – where a local bus can be caught to the town centre. **SRTG**, ☎ (06) 452 086 / 136. 1 bus to Sfax (5hr), 5 to Gafsa, 1 to Sousse (via Kairouan), 1 to Douz (1hr30), 1 to Gabès (4hr30, connections for Jerba and Matmata), 4 to Nefta (30min).

By shared taxi – The station is next to the bus station behind the stadium (see above).

GETTING AROUND

The size of the town means it is best explored on foot.

Taxis – The station is near the stadium and the bus station. For a fixed price of TD1, you can get a trip round town.

Camels and calèches – depart from near the Hôtel Continental.

Car hire – *Avis*, ave Farhat Hached, ☎ (06) 453 547.

Beya Rent-a-car, ave Abou Kacem Chebbi, ☎ (06) 462 211, Fax (06) 463 211.

Europcar, ave Farhat Hached, ☎ (06) 460 119.

Hertz, ave Farhat Hached, ☎ (06) 460 214, Fax (06) 454 468.

Bicycle and motor scooter hire, ☎ (06) 460 622, near the La Palmeraie Hôtel and the Dar Cheraït Museum. It is best to book in advance.

ADDRESS BOOK

Emergency – *Police Station*, ave Farhat Hached (1km on the road to Gafsa), ☎ (06) 452 129.

National Guard, ave Farhat Hached (1km on the road to Nefta), ☎ (06) 454 295.

Tourist Police, ☎ (06) 452 194,
Regional Hospital, cité de l'hôpital, ☎ (06) 453 400.
Night chemist, ave Farhat Hached, ☎ (06) 463 066.

Tourist information – *Regional Tourist Office*, ave Abou Kacem Chabbi, ☎ (06) 454 503 / 088, Fax (06) 452 051. Brochures and detailed information on Tozeur and the region. 8.30am-1pm / 3pm-5.45pm, 8.30am-1.30pm Fridays and Saturdays, closed Sundays. The local **tourist office**, ☎ (06) 462 034, organises excursions but can provide almost no information.

Banks / Currency Exchange – *STB*, ave Habib Bourguiba. Cash machine accepting Visa cards.

Banque du Sud, ave Habib Bourguiba.
BNA, ave Farhat Hached.
Banque de l'Habitat, ave Farhat Hached.
BIAT, ave Farhat Hached.
Banque de Tunisie, ave Habib Bourguiba. Automatic cash-dispenser for Visa cards.

Post office – Place Ibn Chabbat (at the market square), ☎ (06) 460 130.

Rapid Poste, route de Gafsa, ☎ (06) 453 865.

Telephones – Public phones are available on ave Abou Kacem Chabbi across from the Warda residence and at 60 rue Farhat Hached.

Internet – *Publinet*, 11 ave du 7 Novembre, 100m from the CRT, ☎ (06) 463 357. Open everyday, 8am-8pm.

Airlines – *Tunisair*, ave Farhat Hached (route de Nefta), ☎ (06) 452 127, Fax (06) 452 033.

WHERE TO STAY

Plan to book in advance as the hotels are often full, particularly during the Festival.

• In the centre

Below US$10

🏠 **Résidence Warda**, 28 ave Abou Kacem Chabbi, ☎ (06) 452 597 / 460 000, Fax (06) 452 744 – 35rm

✍ This modest establishment right in the town centre is excellent value-for-money. Pleasant ambience and spotless rooms (air-conditioning extra). Bookings advisable.

Hôtel Aïcha, route de Nefta, ☎ (06) 452 788, Fax (06) 452 873 – 34rm ⌂ ✗ A clean, inexpensive hotel but whose shower and toilet facilities are not all they could be. Air-conditioning extra.

Résidence Karim, 89 ave Abou Kacem Chabbi, ☎ (06) 454 574 – 19rm ⌂ The austere façade of this inexpensive hotel, half-way between the town centre and the tourist zone, hides a pleasant surprise. Clean rooms (heating and air-conditioning extra) are set in a pretty building covered in ceramic tiles. No restaurant facilities for individual visitors.

Résidence Niffer, Bab el Hawa, ☎ (06) 460 610 / 555, Fax (06) 461 900 – 25rm ⌂ A brand-new establishment right in the heart of Tozeur (behind the tourist office). Reasonable prices for practical, modern rooms. When finished, the hotel should have 60 rooms. Air-conditioning extra.

From US$10-42

Hôtel El Arich, ave Abou Kacem Chabbi (next door to the CRT) – 21rm ⌂ ✍ This establishment, which is set to open at the end of 1999, looks promising. With 15 rooms and 6 one-room flats plus kitchenettes it's aimed primarily at families. The garden side, with a view over the palm grove, is delightful. TV and air-conditioning extra but the telephones had not yet been installed when we visited.

Hôtel Continental, ave Abou Kacem Chabbi, ☎ (06) 461 411, Fax (06) 452 109 – 180rm ⌂ ▤ ✗ ⌁ This is a very clean and centrally-located hotel. Unfortunately, the walls are particularly thin and you can hear everything in your neighbour's room.

From US$42-75

Oasis Dar Tozeur, Place des Martyrs, ☎ (06) 461 522, Fax (06) 452 153 – 124rm ⌂ ▤ ✍ TV ✗ ⌁ CC This old hotel has a lovely traditional brick facade. The inside is laid out around two courtyards. This is an exceptional establishment in the heart of Tozeur.

Hôtel Dar Ghaouar, ave de Kairouan, ☎ and Fax (06) 452 666 – 51rm ⌂ ▤ ✗ ⌁ This modern and comfortable hotel is near the market square.

Hôtel du Jardin, route de Degache, ☎ (06) 454 196, Fax (06) 454 199 – 40rm ⌂ ▤ ✍ ✗ A new establishment that shares its premises with Les Andalous restaurant. Its position, on the outskirts of the town in a pretty garden, is a guarantee of peace and quiet. The rooms, while very comfortable, lack charm. TV extra.

Hôtel Ksar Jerid, on the road to Nefta, ☎ (06) 454 356 / 454 357 / 454 516, Fax (06) 454 515 / 454 519 – 70rm ⌂ ▤ ✗ ⌁ This modest property just outside the city and the tourist area is used primarily by groups. There are telephones in the rooms but all calls go through the hotel operator. Television is optional.

• **In the tourist area**

Less than US$18

Camping les Beaux Rêves, on the tourist road, at the end of ave Abou Kacem Chabbi, ☎ (06) 454 208. In a beautiful garden are to be found "bungalows" built out of palm trees, similar to the huts found in the desert. You can also pitch your tent in the gardens.

More than US$75

Dar Cheraït, on the tourist road, ☎ (06) 454 888, Fax (06) 454 472 – 85rm ⌂ ▤ ✍ TV ⌁ CC One of the most striking hotels in Tozeur in a garden with palm trees and a lake. It adjoins the Dar Cheraït museum. Decor reminiscent of "A Thousand and One Nights". The pool is heated in the off-season. Some of the suites cost as much as US$400 per night.

Palmyre, on the tourist road, ☎ (06) 452 041, Fax (06) 453 470 – 105rm ⌂ ▤ ✍ TV ✗ CC There is a very pretty reception area in traditional brick and the rooms are comfortable.

Abou Nawas Tozeur, on the tourist road, ☎ (06) 453 500 / 452 700, Fax (06) 452 686 – 92rm ⌂ ▤ TV ✍ ✗ ⌁ CC This hotel has a pleasantly human dimension and simple decor. The pool is heated in the winter.

Hôtel Phedra, on the tourist road, ☎ (06) 452 185 / 452 697, Fax (06) 452 799. ⌖▤ TV ✕ ⌇ CC This hotel caters primarily to tour groups. Television is optional.

EATING OUT

There are attractive and inexpensive restaurants in Tozeur. Unfortunately, the local specialities do not feature prominently. On the other hand, restaurant owners will sometimes agree to prepare them if asked in advance.

Less than US$10

☺ **Le Paradis**, 75 rue de Tunis (narrow street parallel to ave Habib Bourguiba opposite the STB Bank). A rather inauspicious-looking eating-house which nonetheless serves the best couscous in Tozeur at unbeatable prices. Very popular among locals.

Restaurant du Sud, ave Farhat Hached, ☎ (06) 463 826. Since it's so difficult to find desert specialities, why not try specialities from Sfax? There is a choice of "osbanne" couscous (with tripe), stuffed fish, barley baked in the oven and Sfaxian "kefta". This is a modest restaurant with an attentive owner. Closed Sunday evenings.

La Médina, in the street at right angles to ave Habib Bourguiba (near the Court House). A modest little café with a Berber menu consisting mostly of couscous. This is the place to try "mettabga" (Berber pizza) or "mloukhia", beef stew flavoured with powdered coret leaves.

Le Diamanta, 94 ave Abou Kacem Chabbi, ☎ (06) 450 321. A tastefully-decorated establishment that serves excellent cuisine, providing the owner's doing the cooking.

Restaurant de la République, 99 ave Habib Bourguiba, near the Mosque, ☎ (06) 452 354 ⌂ Unpretentious eating-house in a courtyard serving dishes in the Franco-Tunisian style.

Le Soleil, ave Abou Kacem Chabbi, opposite Résidence Warda. ⌂ The Tunisian clientele is a sure sign of dependable cooking. Serves good, simple dishes, including meat or vegetarian couscous, mechouia and chorba.

From US$10-20

☺ **Le Petit Prince**, El Berka, ☎ (06) 452 518 / 450 097, Fax (06) 454 105. ❢ ⌂ As far as the food is concerned, there is some effort to offer local specialities, for example a leg of lamb served Berber-style, a bit overcooked. As for the ambience, there are some pleasant tables under the trees.

Les Andalous, road to Degache, ☎ (06) 454 196, Fax (06) 454 199. ❢ At last, an establishment with typical desert dishes (a la carte). Try the "mettabga" (Berber pizza), the "barkoukech" (a semolina soup with pieces of octopus and meat), the "m'faouer" (steamed meat) and the vegetable "chakchouka". Reserve 24hr in advance.

More than US$20

☺ **Restaurant at the Hôtel Dar Cherait**, ☎ (06) 454 888, Fax (06) 453 271. CC This restaurant serves very good meals in a grandiose setting (see below in the section, "Where to Stay").

WHERE TO GO FOR A DRINK

Cafés – Several outdoor cafés along the ave Bourguiba where a drink can be enjoyed in the company of carpet vendors.
El Berka, beyond the Le Petit Prince restaurant, on the edge of a palm grove. The tables are set out on the banks of the wadi, and patrons can enjoy a breath of cool air – until midnight.
Café of the Dar Cherait Museum, a truly lavish setting.
El Arich, enormous café on the ground floor of the hotel with the same name (see above). It is very popular to smoke chichi here in the shade of the palm trees.
Camping Niffer (despite its name, it's only a café), in the oasis. Go along avenue Abou Kacem Chabbi until you reach Hotel Oasis, continue straight on along rue des Jardins. When you reach the last houses of the old town, turn right. About 500m further on (next to a sort of fortress), turn left for 300m. The café is right in the heart of the palm grove and is an extremely welcome spot to get out of Tozeur's stifling heat. Serves cold drinks and pancakes around a

magnificent swimming pool (TD3). Unfortunately, the music can sometimes prove deafening.

LEISURE

Sports – Aeroasis, excursions in hot air balloons, ☎ (06) 452 361.

Festivals – Sahara Festival, on 12 November. Preview of the various events that take place at the oasis festival the following month.

Festival of the Oases, in December. Traditional wedding celebrations and camel races.

SHOPPING

Tozeur's souk, on Sundays in the stadium

Bookshops – International, mostly French, newspapers can be found in the kiosks at the foot of ave Habib Bourguiba.

Making the most of Degache

WHERE TO STAY

From US$18-42

Bedouina Club, is well marked by signs on the right when coming from Tozeur, ☎ (06) 420 209, Fax (06) 452 220 – 30rm 🎣 📇 The campsite has several permanent bungalows but the adventurous can always stay in tents in the desert like the Bedouins. However, be aware that the cleanliness of the toilet facilities leaves a lot to be desired. The management organises parties for groups larger than 35 people.

Making the most of Nefta

GETTING THERE

By air – Tozeur-Nefta Airport, on the road to Nefta, ☎ (06) 453 388. 26km from the centre of Nefta. No airport bus.

By bus – Bus Terminal, ave Habib Bourguiba, ☎ (06) 457 002.

By shared taxi – The station is near the bus terminal.

GETTING AROUND

By car – The town itself is quite small but it is useful to have a car to visit the surrounding area.

Camels and barouches – Opposite the tourist information office.

ADDRESS BOOK

Emergency – Police, ave Habib Bourguiba, ☎ (06) 457 134.
National Guard, road to Hazoua, ☎ (06) 430 081.

Tourist police, ☎ (06) 432 099.
Local hospital, rue des Martyrs, ☎ (06) 457 193.

Tourist information – Tourist Information Office, ave Habib Bourguiba, ☎ (06) 430 236. Functions mostly as a hiring point for official guides. On the other hand, the rates are not official; it's better to negotiate these beforehand. Avoid hiring an unofficial guide. It takes approximately 2hr to do a tour of the old city, to see the gypsum flower market and the first sand dune (an ordinary car is sufficient).

Banks / Currency Exchange – Banque du Sud, ave Habib Bourguiba, ☎ (06) 457 066.
UIB, ave Habib Bourguiba, ☎ (06) 457 153.

WHERE TO STAY

Most of the pleasant hotels are to be found in the tourist zone.

• In the town
Under US$10
Hôtel Habib, Place de la Libération, ☎ (06) 430 497 – 16rm This very modest establishment is right in the heart of Nefta's oldest district. Cleanliness is not high on the list of priorities but it's the cheapest place to stay in town.

• Tourist zone
From US$10-30
Hôtel Mirage, ☎ (06) 430 622, Fax (06) 430 644 – 54rm ⁄🍴 ▤ ✗ ⚊ A totally-characterless establishment that could do with a lot more upkeep. A pity, it could easily be the best value-for-money accommodation in town.

From US$30-75
Hôtel Marhala (Touring Club de Tunisie), ☎ (06) 430 027, Fax (06) 430 511 – 36rm ⁄🍴 ▤ ✗ ⚊ The new building is next door to the old relais and even if the new one doesn't have all the charm of its predecessor, it's without doubt much more comfortable. Excellent welcome.

Hôtel Bel Horizon, ☎ (06) 430 328, Fax (06) 430 500 – 90rm ⁄🍴 ▤ ✗ ⚊ Reasonable rates for a superb view of the Corbeille de Nefta.

More than US$75
Hôtel Caravansérail, ☎ (06) 430 355 / 430 416, Fax (06) 430 322 – 150rm ⁄🍴 ▤ 📺 ✗ ⚊ 🆑 This beautiful hotel was built in traditional style. The establishment has two types of rooms; the more expensive have bathtubs and satellite television.

Hôtel La Rose de Nefta, ☎ (06) 430 696 / 430 697, Fax (06) 430 385 – 100rm ⁄🍴 ▤ ✗ ⚊ Caters for tour groups.

Hôtel Sahara Palace, ☎ (06) 432 005 / 195, fax(06) 431 444 – 108rm ⁄🍴 ▤ 📺 ✗ ⚊ 🆑 Nefta's most luxurious establishment features five-star comfort and a marvellous view of the Corbeille.

EATING OUT
Most of Nefta's restaurants are in the hotels.

Less than US$10
Ferdaous (Le Paradis). ♈ Take the road to the oasis from ave Habib Bourguiba. A sign shows "départ des caravanes" (caravan departure) almost directly opposite the tourist information office. Go straight on until the edge of the oasis, then turn right onto the road that runs alongside the palm grove. Go left at the first small bridge and the restaurant is immediately on the right. This small eatery hidden away in the oasis merits its name "ferdaous" which means "paradise" in Arabic. Tourists and local people go out of their way to stop here for a beer or a glass of rosé wine or to sample the delicious grilled lamb....even if the few tables are not much to look at.

WHERE TO GO FOR A DRINK
Café-Restaurant Ferdaous, in the palm grove (see above).

Café de la Corbeille, this is the most romantic spot to watch the sun set, but is, of course, a real tourist trap.

LEISURE
Sahara Festival, takes place simultaneously on the 12 November in Tozeur, Douz and in the mountain oasis (see Making the most of Tozeur).

Shopping
Weekly souk, on Thursdays.

Dates – Date season is in November when there is almost too much choice as the whole of Nefta swarms with date merchants.

Bookshops – located in the hotels.

A MOUNTAIN OASIS★★
192km circuit on good roads – 1 to 2 days

Not to be missed
A trip through the Selja gorges aboard the Red Lizard.
The village of Tamerza.

And remember...
To make the most of natural lighting,
do the tour in the direction described.
Stay at the delightful Tamerza Palace hotel.

The Jebel En Negueb, close to the Algerian frontier, reaches a height of 900m. Thirty years ago there were still three villages here, living in harmony with their oasis, as they had done for two thousand years, but the torrential storms of 1969 led to their abandonment. These ghost villages are now visited only by tourists interested in traditional forms of building. Access used to be by mule along mule tracks and paths but a network of roads now makes it possible to make a day tour from Tozeur. However, it is much more pleasant to spend a night at Tamerza to fully experience the unique peace of this tiny lost corner of the world. Another attraction is the Red Lizard, the picturesque narrow-gauge train which runs through the Selja gorges.

Leave Tozeur on the Gafsa road.

▪ The Selja gorges★★

The **Lézard rouge** (Red Lizard) is a little tourist train which is very popular with tour groups. Every day *(except Mondays and Wednesdays)* it makes a round trip along the picturesque gorges of the Selja wadi, taking just under 2 hours *(see Making the most of Selja)*. The train is an attraction in itself: the meticulously restored carriages were used by the Bey of Tunis to move round the country. The deep seats help create an atmosphere of Oriental luxury, though the ambience in the bar is something else again! The background music, however, is more likely to evoke Western films and it is true that the landscapes are more like the American West than the Orient. The track goes through several tunnels and wild canyons up to 200m deep with a mysterious dark stream flowing at the bottom. The meagre thread of water washes away the residues from the phosphate mines which the train passes before arriving in Metlaoui. The deposits were discovered in 1885, and a railway to link the extraction sites with the port of Sfax was built in 1899. Eighteen phosphate trains run on the Red Lizard line every day, and a freight train also takes travellers as far as Redeyef, the end of the line.

From the station at Metlaoui, go back through the town and head for Moularès and Redeyef.

Moularès and Redeyef are two small mining towns planted in a rather desolate landscape. The road climbs gently up to them, but it is only as you approach Tamerza (Tameghza on some maps) that it becomes spectacular. Vegetation dwindles and the surroundings become increasingly bare and rocky, until a rounded jebel appears on the right, its outline reminiscent of that of Ayers Rock.

Fork right 72km from Metlaoui. Midès is 5km further on, across a broad sandy wadi.

■ Midès★

A little palm grove hides the **old village★★** of Midès, abandoned after the disastrous rains of 1969. The road arrives at the foot of the village which is built on a rocky spur above vertical gorges. Follow the narrow lane *(to the left of the café)*, which takes you through the village's tightly clustered buildings. The pleasantly cool alleyway is lined with stone buildings whose upper floor was used as a granary. Tiny openings in the façade provided ventilation. Ceilings made of split palm-trunks supported the roof covering of stone slabs. The roofs have mostly fallen in, unable to withstand the torrential rains. The last house in the village, on the right of the main road, offers a magnificent **view★★** over the gorges; high up, to the west, is the national guard post overlooking the Algerian border. 300m along the side of the palm grove is the rocky spur with the *kalaat* on top. From this viewpoint, which looks like the prow of a ship, there is another unforgettable **view**.

Return to the fork with the Metlaoui road and head for Tamerza.

■ Tamerza★★

The green splash of the Tamerza palm grove *(Tameghza, on some maps)* stands out against the rocky face of the jebel looming over it. The ruined buildings of the extraordinary ghost **village★★** are spread out on the far side of the El Horchane wadi, the river bed scoured clean by the region's violent rain. Under the name of Ad Turres, the site belonged to the military administrative region responsible

The oasis of Midès

C Vaisse/HOA QUI

for the defence of the Roman Empire's frontiers before becoming the seat of a bishopric in Byzantine times. Here and there it is still possible to make out surviving features from this era in some of the houses in the village. From the Tamerza Palace hotel there is a **magnificent view** at sunset over the silent village, with its abandoned ochre houses, shrine and mosque. As in Midès, a street crosses the village as far as the *kalaat* which dominates the village to the north. A touching detail dating from the most recent deluge of rain is the jars still protruding from the ground.

2km from the Tamerza Palace hotel on the Chebika side, a road to the left leads to the **waterfall***, with easy access past Les Cascades hotel. The sight of a 4m high waterfall would pass without notice in many areas, but here, in this arid world, it seems miraculous. From the foot of the waterfall, the water pours into a broad canyon carved into the cliffs. Close by, open-air stalls specialise in the sale of fossils and minerals.

Leave Tamerza on the road to Chebika.

The road passes a handsome oasis before entering a very uneven landscape. On the right after 2km, there is a second **waterfall**, higher than the one of Tamerza. Then, after 3km, a splendid **panorama**** opens out: the gorge cut into the mountain gives way to a uniformly flat and bare plain, the mountain recedes into the background. Descent through hair-pin bends is rapid, and in 2km the deserted floor of the El Gharsa chott, by the El Khango oasis, is reached.

5km further on, turn left towards the village next to Chebika.

■ Chebika*

Chebika enjoys the doubtful privilege of being the most visited of the three mountain oases, and also the best developed, although it has no hotel. On some mornings up to 50 off-road vehicles may be visible (although there is no real reason for the use of this type of vehicle). The influx of tourists is all the more distressing because the old village, built on a narrow promontory, is tiny. There are plenty of signs to help visitors find their way around. Beyond the shops and bars, a few steps lead downwards, then a path follows the little canalised stream to its source. On the way, steps to the left lead up the hillside to a cleft in the rock. On the other slope there is a beautiful **view*** over the old village and the desert beyond the modern village of Chebika built beside the road. This site, whose recent claim to fame is to have been the setting of *The English Patient*, was the subject of an exciting anthropological study carried out between 1960 and 1966 *(see page 114)*, a short time before the village disappeared following torrential rainfall in 1969.

The road back to Tozeur *(56km)* runs past the jebel looming menacingly over the plain, then crosses the Chott Er Rahim, the eastern section of the Chott El Gharsa which lies below sea level. Its smooth and ash grey surface, the presence of salt crusts and pools of brackish water are reminiscent of the great Chott El Jerid.

Making the most of Selja

By train – Departure on the Red Lizard at 10.30am (11am Sundays) from Met-laoui station, towards Redeyef. Doesn't operate on Wednesdays or Saturdays. The return trip takes approximately 2hr, with 2 or 3 stops in the canyon, and costs roughly TD2 per person. The company Hermès Travel, that operates this train in partnership with the SNCFT, also offers private charters with enactments of train attacks taken after Lawrence of Arabia. It is wise to reserve in advance for groups. Information and reservations in Metlaoui, ☎ (06) 241 469, Fax (06) 241 604.

Making the most of Tamerza

GETTING THERE

By car – A good tarmacked road provides access from Metlaoui or Tozeur.

WHERE TO STAY

From US$18-30
Hôtel Les Cascades, ☎ and Fax (06) 485 332 – 59rm ✗ ⌁ Set in the heart of the oasis, two minutes from the waterfall. The bungalows are made out of dried earth and covered in palm leaves, the most comfortable also have inner concrete walls. Unfortunately the place seems to be abandoned; the swimming pool is empty and there doesn't appear to be a reception.

More than US$75
Tamerza Palace, at the entrance to the village, ☎ and Fax (06) 485 322 / 344 345. Information / reservations, ☎ (06) 891 564 / 799 634, Fax (06) 799 810 – 65rm ⌁ 🗐 ✎ TV ✗ ⌁ CC The magnificent architecture of this hotel is well integrated with the grandiose setting opposite old Tamerza.

EATING OUT

The small local restaurants here suffer from a lack of custom, particularly out of season, and cannot be recommended.

From US$18-42
Restaurant at the Tamerza Palace, ☎ (06) 453 722. ⌁ ⌁ CC A superb view from the terrace but the cooking is poor and the staff are not particularly competent!

WHERE TO GO FOR A DRINK

Café des Palmiers, near the waterfall. A pleasant place for a drink.

LEISURE

Sahara Festival (see Making the most of Tozeur).

SHOPPING

Weekly souk, on Fridays.

DOUZ★ AND THE SAHARA

Half-way between Tozeur and Gabès
28km from Kébili

Not to be missed
The cattle market at Douz.
A night in the desert.

And remember...
For desert excursions,
contact a specialised agency in order to avoid problems.

Far from the well-looked after oases of Gabès, Nefta and Tozeur, the little town of Douz struggles against the sand invading its streets. In this unequal contest with a Sahara which pushes its dunes forward to the gates of the town, some neighbouring villages have already been submerged. Here the oases lack the luxuriance of their larger sisters, the fruit trees grow with difficulty, and alfalfa is often the only crop.

You arrive in Douz to find the Sahara and its population of nomads who have recently settled in the villages of the Nefzaoua. Despite their settled existence the locally-born people – mostly belonging to the Merzouguis tribe – still retain a strong identity. The Douz weekly market, a rendezvous for all the peoples of the South, is particularly colourful. But all visitors should be aware that this is only the edge of the Great Eastern Erg: in just a day or two no-one can expect to discover the spectacular dunes of the great Algerian or Libyan south, and even the high dune of Ofra is really only impressive at sunset.

Douz market★★ is held every Thursday. The first traders set up in the great square, the site of the market, the previous evening. There is nothing very spectacular to be seen here (spices, tools, clothing) apart from the tourist stalls set under the arcades and which are open all week. On market day, the most picturesque activity takes place nearby, in an enclosure in the shade of the palm trees (*should soon be located near the rental station*). From the first moment of the day, livestock farmers bring their animals to the market, which by 9am is going at full stretch, goats, sheep, lambs, horses and even camels are passing from hand to hand after discreet haggling. The Thursday market also has date seedlings, palm hearts and medicinal herbs.

The Nefzaoua oases

From Douz a road slips away to the south to El Faouar, providing access to a string of oases. It runs alongside a recently planted belt of palm trees which stretches to **Zaafrane** (*after 13km*), where the old village (*on the left of the road*) has been completely covered with sand. It has been replaced by a settlement built in red brick. The women of Nefzaoua, with their tattooed faces and brightly coloured clothes, undertake their share of the farm work, setting out for the fields in carts accompanied by their young children. Camel rides are organised at the edge of the village to the nearest dunes of white sand (*worth exploring at sunset*). Further on, on the way out of Ghidma, a stretch of water surrounded by espartograss makes a dazzling contrast in white, green and blue. The road is lined with veritable walls of sand, several metres high, planted with palms for stability. A 2km-detour leads to **Es Sabria**, another oasis, then along the main road to **El**

Faouar, which has a hotel and a large square used as a market place. Coaches and communal taxis *(near the pretty cemetery in Douz town centre)* provide a shuttle service between Douz and El Faouar.

Exploring the Sahara

Douz is now the main starting point for excursions into the Sahara, and suggestions as numerous as they are varied will probably be put to you as soon as you arrive. Before deciding what to do, bear the following in mind...

A camel ride – Getting an introductory ride on a camel is no problem. In front of the great dunes of Ofra, south of Douz, and Zaafrane, the camels await the customers *(from TD10)*. All the novice needs to know is to hold on tight and remember that as the camel gets up he leans a long way forward, and then back. The rest of the trip is completely peaceful and keeps to the pace of the camel-driver who walks alongside and guides your steed.

A night in the desert – From Douz, a rather uncomfortable *kirita* (horse-drawn cart) heads off for the desert. After a ride *(it is up to you to decide how long)* through the not very dramatic dunes, the guide will select a site for the night. While you search for dead branches of thorny bushes for the fire, the guide suddenly turns into a cook and gets busy with the couscous. A thick rug cushions some of the hardness of the desert sand, and the starry sky compensates for any discomfort. At first light there is the delicious "sand bread", a thick pancake cooked in the embers of the fire *(allow TD25 per head)*.

All-purpose vehicles – The classic desert trip involves travelling to **Ksar Ghilane***, a journey that cannot be done in an ordinary car. When booking, insist on crossing the dunes, otherwise the drive will probably follow the track, which is much less spectacular *(allow 5hr travelling)*. **Ksar Ghilane** is the most typically Saharan of the oases. The citadel, set apart from the palm grove *(60min on foot)* was part of the defences of the Roman empire. The ultimate delight is the spring in which you can swim. The camp-site, which provides bedouin tents, even has showers – but on some evenings there are so many people that it barely feels like the desert. From Ksar Ghilane it is possible to reach Tataouine *(3hr)*, visiting Chenini on the way; this transfer must be arranged before leaving Douz because there is no public transport beyond Ksar Ghilane. No visitor should explore the desert in an all-purpose vehicle without a guide, and it is best to make use of a reputable agency *(allow TD150 for a day's round trip for the all-purpose vehicle and driver, with a night in Ksar Ghilane about TD250 extra)*.

The Sahara

Douz is a gateway to the largest desert in the world. The Sahara (from an Arab word which means quite simply "desert") covers more than 8million sqkm, stretching from the Atlantic to the Red Sea. It marks the transition between the Africa of the Mediterranean north, from Morocco to Egypt, and Black Africa. With less than 100mm of rain each year, no form of cultivation is possible outside the oases. The imagination links the landscapes of the north more easily with this desert – the dunes of the Great Erg which form the greater part of the Tunisian Sahara. But the Sahara also has volcanic landscape (Hoggar, Tibesti) and vast expanses of stone. Nomadism has declined everywhere, and despite its vast expanse, the Sahara has only 1.5m inhabitants. It was not always a desert; there is considerable evidence (fossils, graffiti, tools) showing that life flourished here well into Neolithic times and that the horse was not replaced by the more sober dromedary until the 2C BC.

The méharée – A ride on a pack-camel – wrongly known as a "méharée", an expression that should be used only for saddle-camels – is the most authentic way to discover the Sahara. You should not be in a hurry. To reach the heart of the grandest landscapes, travel agents take their clients into the desert in all-purpose vehicles where their mounts await them. The crossing of the eastern Great Erg is fascinating, and each night will be a delight despite the discomfort. *(from US$160 per person for five days, full board and access from Tozeur or Jerba airport. See Making the most of Douz)*.

Making the most of Douz

GETTING THERE

By bus – **Bus Terminal**, Place de la République. 3 buses daily to Kebili, 1 to Tozeur and 1 to Tunis.

By shared taxi – The station is near the bus terminal opposite the cemetery. Taxis for Kebili, where you can find connections for Gabès, Gafsa, Tunis and Tozeur. Departures are however very rare in the afternoon.

ADDRESS BOOK

Emergency – *Police*, ☎ (05) 472 301. **National Guard**, ☎ (05) 470 510 / 554.
Pharmacie Belhadj, 31 ave Habib Bourguiba, ☎ (05) 470 220.

Tourist information – The inhabitants will be of more help than the **tourist office**, ave des Martyrs (towards the tourist zone, 200m behind the statue of the gazelle), ☎ (05) 470 351. Everyday 8.30am-1pm / 3pm-5.45pm, or the **syndicat d'initiative**, ☎ (05) 470 341, on the right of the tourist office.

Banks / Currency Exchange – Located primarily in the hotels in the tourist area.
Banque du Sud, ave Habib Bourguiba.

Post office – ave des Martyrs, ☎ (05) 490 940.

Telephones – Public phones can be found on place de la République near the bus terminal.

Internet – **Publinet**, corner of rue El Hanine and rue du 20 mars 1956 (50m from hôtel du 20 mars). TD6 per hour of connection.

WHERE TO STAY

The hotels cater almost exclusively for people staying overnight while visiting the Tunisian South, and are deserted during the day.

• **In the town centre**
Less than US$18
Hôtel du 20 Mars, between the market square and the station, ☎ and Fax (05) 470 269 – 10rm ✗ Plain simple rooms and bathrooms on the landing, but this is the cleanest and most welcoming hotel in the centre.
Hôtel Essaada, rue du 1ᵉʳ Juin in the heart of Douz, ☎ (05) 470 824, Fax (05) 470 348 – 14rm The corridors may not be very enticing, but the rooms are clean and attractively decorated. Camping is possible... with a tent pitched in one of the ground-floor rooms.
Hôtel La Tente, rue El Hanine, ☎ (05) 470 468 – 13rm 🍴 Basic, clean and welcoming. The rooms on the first floor which open onto a communal terrace are the most pleasant.
Hôtel Bel Habib, Place du Souk, ☎ and Fax (05) 471 115 / 470 309 – 10rm ✗ This hotel has a basic level of comfort and questionable cleanliness. The bathrooms are on the landing. The hotel's atmosphere retains the personality of its owner, who likes to demonstrate traditional desert hospitality by offering his guests a glass of tea on arrival. In the long term he hopes to enhance the desert experience by setting up Bedouin tents on the roof. In the meantime, breakfast is not included in the room rate.

Y Traynard

The cattle-market in Douz

355

• In the tourist area

From US$18-42

Hôtel de la Rose des Sables, ☎ (05) 470 597 / 475 484, Fax (05) 470 682 – 90rm 🛎 📧 ✗ ⚖ The reception area has recently been refurbished but not the bungalows. Even though the rooms are very clean, the state of the bathrooms leaves much to be desired.

From US$42-75

Hôtel El Mouradi, ☎ (05) 470 303, Fax (05) 470 9(05) – 180rm 🛎 📧 🆃🆅 ✗ ℘ ⚖ 🆒 This is the best value for money in the tourist area. The hotel has two swimming pools, one of which is inside and is heated (maybe a bit too much for serious swimmers) and a mixed sex hammam – an indication that the guests are mostly foreigners.

Hôtel Sahara Douz, ☎ (05) 495 246 / 470 865, Fax (05) 470 566 – 152rm 🛎 📧 ℘ ✗ ⚖ 🆒 This lovely establishment is equipped with a superb pool decorated in the style of a hammam and fed by hot springs. Television is optional.

Iberotel Mehari, ☎ (05) 470 481, Fax (05) 471 088 – 120rm 🛎 📧 ℘ ✗ 🆒 This hotel belongs to a chain that built its reputation with its buffet restaurant. Remarkable architecture resembling a desert fortress.

Hôtel Touareg, ☎ (05) 470 057 / 470 245, Fax (05) 470 313 – 134rm 🛎 📧 ℘ ✗ ⚖ 🆒 Standard tourist hotel. The pool is partly under cover and heated in winter.

• In the oasis

Less than US$10

Camping Désert Club – After the Hôtel Le Saharien, continue for 400m into the palm grove. Take the path to the right and follow it for 500m, ☎ and Fax (05) 470 575. A pleasant place to pitch your tent.

From US$18-42

Hôtel Le Saharien, at the end of the tourist road, ☎ (05) 471 337 / 737, Fax (05) 470 339 – 125rm 🛎 📧 ℘ ✗ Located in the heart of the palm grove, this hotel has typical "Tunisian" decor. The restaurant only offers one menu but it is possible to order grilled meats.

There are no restaurants catering for tourists in the Douz. Most visitors are hustled through the South at a hellish pace and barely leave their hotel. This makes it particularly pleasurable to discover the local restaurants. They are frugal, but the hospitality of desert people is not a myth. It's a shame that, here too, it's so difficult to find specialities from the Sahara.

• In the modern town

Less than US$10

La Rosa, ave du 7 Novembre, ☎ (05) 470 688. This eatery deserves credit for serving the freshest mechouia with the most tender lamb. This is the place where local travel professionals come when they are travelling on their own account.

Restaurant at the Hôtel 20 Mars, between the market square and the long-distance taxi station, ☎ (05) 470 269. 🆒 Simple food, but the owners could not be more friendly.

Les Palmiers, ave Taïeb Méhiri, ☎ (05) 472 176. Same owners and menu as La Rosa. Just a change of scenery.

Ali Baba, ave Habib Bourguiba, ☎ (05) 472 498. A pleasant welcome with decent, if somewhat ordinary, cooking. The Berber tent in the courtyard is ideal to drink tea after the meal.

Bel Habib, place du Souk, ☎ (05) 495 115. A simple and clean restaurant, much in favour with the local clientele.

WHERE TO EAT AND DRINK

Café La Rosa, opposite the restaurant with the same name. You can drink your tea (and eat) indoors, on the terrace or in a tent.

Café Le Rendez-vous, right of Grand Sud Agency. An exceptionally, well-located terrace to stop for a cold drink when returning from a bicycle ride.

LEISURE

Desert excursions – While it's quite easy to organise a day long trip, camel excursions should be booked several weeks in advance. **Douz Voyages**, Place

Douz and the Sahara

de l'Indépendance (in the town centre). ☎ (05) 470 178, Fax (05) 470 315. An experienced agency operated by Mr. Abdelmajid Letaief. Specialises in week-long trips by camel or jeep.

Horizons Déserts, rue El Hanine, ☎ (05) 470 088 / 471 688, Fax (05) 470 088, h.deserts@planet.tn. This new agency is run by a Franco-Tunisian couple who organise meharees, 4WD excursions or walks in the desert away from the more touristy areas. Trips can be organised with a theme or made-to-measure.

Sports – Pégase, on the tourist road (near the Hôtel Festival), ☎ (05) 470 793, Fax (05) 470 835. You can go carting (TD15 for 15min), have a trip aboard a hovercraft (TD15) or fly a microlight plane (TD30). For sand surfing in the Chott El Jerid, reserve in advance.

Grand Sud, ave Taïeb Méhiri, ☎ (05) 471 777, Fax (05) 470 269, saharaking@voila.fr. Tahar Barka rents mountain bikes by the hour (TD2) and also organises week-long trips in the desert, oases and the Dahar. New equipment and pleasant staff.

Festivals – International Sahara Festival, in December (or November if Ramadan falls in December). Spectacular events with camel races.

Sahara Festival, on 12 November (see Making the Most of Tozeur).

Events – La Compagnie des Sables, in the tourist area. Take the first bend on the left after the Hôtel Mehari. Organises evening activities and lunches in tents.

Nightclubs – In the hotels in the tourist area.

Weekly souk, Thursdays.

Antiques and Handicrafts – The local craft is the "chausson saharien" (Sahara slipper), a very comfortable leather shoe available in practically every store in the town (TD12-18 according to the size).

Antique jewellery, Ben Nasr Monji's house, rue du 1ᵉʳ Juin.

Making the most of El Faouar

From US$42-75
Hôtel El Faouar, on the way into town on the Douz road, ☎ (05) 491 531 / 491 887, Fax (05) 491 576 – 150rm 🎐📧 ✐ ✖ 🛏 The hotel has brand new bungalows where each room is decorated with a different fresco painted by the owner himself. This artist and former student at a German hotel school, organises folklore evenings in tents.

Making the most of Zaafrane

From US$18-42
Hôtel Zaafrane, outside the town along the road to El Faouar, ☎ and Fax (05) 491 720 – 40rm 🎐📧 ✖ 🛏 Clean chalets with superannuated plumbing. The hotel also organises nights in the desert with tents, 9km from there.

NOTES

NOTES

NOTES

INDEX

Dougga: place or attraction described in the text
Ibn Nafi (Uqba): individual
Aghlabides: term explained in the text
Glossary: practical information

Garage on the outskirts of Sousse

MAPS AND PLANS

Manufacture Française des Pneumatiques Michelin
Société en commandite par actions au capital de 2 000 000 000 de francs
Place des Carmes-Déchaux – 63000 Clermont-Ferrand (France)
R.C.S. Clermont-Fd B 855 200 507

© Michelin et Cie, Propriétaires-éditeurs, 2000
Dépôt légal avril 2000 – ISBN 2-06-855501-8 – ISSN 0763-1383
No part of this publication may be reproduced in any form without
the prior permission of the publisher.

Printed in the EU 04-00/1
Compograveur : Nord Compo – Villeneuve d'Ascq
Imprimeur : IME – Baume-les-Dames

Cover Illustrations :
Tamerza – S. Viron/DIAF
Traditional head-dress, Southern Tunisia – N. Thibaut/HOA QUI
Mosaic – G. Degeorge

Your opinion matters!

In order to make sure that this collection satisfies the needs of our readers, please help us by completing the following questionnaire with your comments and suggestions and return to:

Michelin Travel Publications   or   **Michelin Travel Publications**
The Edward Hyde Building   P.O. Box 19008
38 Clarendon Road   Greenville, SC 29602-9008
Watford, UK   USA

▪ YOUR HOLIDAYS/VACATIONS:

1. In general, when you go on holiday or vacation, do you tend to travel... (Choose one)

☐ Independently, on your own   ☐ With your family
☐ Independently, as a couple   ☐ With a group of friends
☐ With 1 or 2 friends   ☐ On organised trips

2. How many international holidays or vacations of 1 week or more have you taken in the last 3 years? _____

Last 3 destinations: Month/Year:
_____   _____
_____   _____
_____   _____

3. What do you look for most when planning a holiday or vacation?

	Not at all	Sometimes	Essential
Somewhere new and exotic	☐	☐	☐
Real experience/meeting people	☐	☐	☐
Experiencing the wildlife/scenery	☐	☐	☐
Cultural insight	☐	☐	☐
Rest & relaxation	☐	☐	☐
Comfort & well-being	☐	☐	☐
Adventure & the unexpected	☐	☐	☐

4. When travelling, do you take a travel guide with you?

☐ Always   ☐ Usually   ☐ Sometimes   ☐ Never

▪ You and the Michelin NEOS guides

5. About your purchase of a NEOS Guide
How long was your holiday where you used the NEOS guide?
How many days? _____
For which country or countries? _____
How long before your departure did you buy it? How many days? _____

6. What made you choose a NEOS Guide?
Highlight everything that applies.

☐ Something new and interesting   ☐ Quality of the text
☐ The layout   ☐ Quality of the mapping
☐ Easy to read format   ☐ Practical Information
☐ Cultural details   ☐ Michelin quality

7. Which sections did you use most during your holiday or vacation?

Score 1-4   *(1 = least used)*   *(4 = most used)*

	1	2	3	4
"Setting the Scene"	☐ 1	☐ 2	☐ 3	☐ 4
"Meeting the People"	☐ 1	☐ 2	☐ 3	☐ 4
"Practical Information"	☐ 1	☐ 2	☐ 3	☐ 4
"Exploring ..."	☐ 1	☐ 2	☐ 3	☐ 4

8. How would you rate the following aspects of your NEOS guide?

Score 1-4   *(1 = Poor)*   *(4 = Excellent)*

	1	2	3	4
Cover design	☐ 1	☐ 2	☐ 3	☐ 4
Chapter Order	☐ 1	☐ 2	☐ 3	☐ 4
Layout (photos, diagrams)	☐ 1	☐ 2	☐ 3	☐ 4
Ease of reading (typeface)	☐ 1	☐ 2	☐ 3	☐ 4
Style of writing	☐ 1	☐ 2	☐ 3	☐ 4
Text boxes and stories	☐ 1	☐ 2	☐ 3	☐ 4
Plans & Maps	☐ 1	☐ 2	☐ 3	☐ 4
Star ratings system	☐ 1	☐ 2	☐ 3	☐ 4
Format	☐ 1	☐ 2	☐ 3	☐ 4
Weight	☐ 1	☐ 2	☐ 3	☐ 4
Durability	☐ 1	☐ 2	☐ 3	☐ 4
Price	☐ 1	☐ 2	☐ 3	☐ 4

9. Did you use other travel guides during your trip?   ☐ Yes   ☐ No

If yes, which ones? _____

10. Please give your NEOS guide a rating out of 20: ____/20 (with 20 as top rating)

Would you use a NEOS guide for your next trip?   ☐ Yes   ☐ No

If no, why not? _____

Which other destinations would you like NEOS to cover? _____

11. Any other comments or suggestions: _____

_____

_____

_____

_____

_____

_____

Surname/Last Name: _____ First Name: _____

Address: _____

Age: _____ Sex: ☐ M ☐ F

Profession: _____

Where did you purchase your NEOS Guide: What type of store?
Which country?
